OUTDOOR RECREATION
AND THE URBAN ENVIRONMENT

By the same author :

Building Quantities Explained
Civil Engineering Quantities
Civil Engineering Specification
Municipal Engineering Practice
Building Economics
Planned Expansion of Country Towns

OUTDOOR RECREATION AND THE URBAN ENVIRONMENT

by

IVOR H. SEELEY

B.Sc., M.A., Ph.D., F.R.I.C.S., C.Eng., F.I.Mun.E.

Head of Department of Surveying
Trent Polytechnic, Nottingham

MACMILLAN

First published 1973

Published by
THE MACMILLAN PRESS LTD
London and Basingstoke
Associated companies in New York
Melbourne Dublin Johannesburg and Madras

SBN 333 14621 2

Typeset by
LIBRA PRESS LIMITED
Hong Kong

Printed in Great Britain by
Whitstable Litho, Whitstable, Kent

This book is dedicated to my youngest daughter

BARBARA

*for her help with recreational surveys and
data processing and because of her great love
of the outdoors*

PREFACE

THE HAPHAZARD PROVISION of outdoor recreational facilities in the past coupled with the changing recreational needs of a population which is increasing in number, prosperity, mobility and the amount of leisure time available to it, calls for a thorough investigation of the present methods and scale of provision of the various facilities and patterns of use and a complete re-appraisal of requirements and the means of satisfying them.

I have—as part of a case study—undertaken extensive user surveys of outdoor recreational facilities in Greater Nottingham, involving many thousands of participants, to secure an adequate and useful body of information on user patterns, catchment areas, socio-economic characteristics of participants and their main needs.

The main aims of the book are to examine the general philosophy and current policies in the provision of outdoor recreational facilities, together with the problems and needs of the users of a variety of recreational resources. Current research methods and economic considerations are reviewed and applied to practical situations in a city region. Finally, an attempt is made to determine past and future trends relating to a wide range of recreational activities and to establish objectives for securing the better provision and use of recreational resources.

I. H. SEELEY

Nottingham
Autumn 1972

ACKNOWLEDGEMENTS

THE AUTHOR EXPRESSES his sincere appreciation to the University of Nottingham for kind permission to reproduce some of the material used in his PH.D. thesis.

The author is indebted to the Centre for Environmental Studies for the award of a grant, which enabled him to undertake more detailed investigations than would otherwise have been possible; to the Trent Polytechnic for assistance with the duplication of thousands of questionnaire forms and in many other ways; and to Ronald Sears for preparing the final drawings.

The author acknowledges with gratitude the willing cooperation and assistance received from many organisations and individuals too numerous to mention individually. The following do, however, deserve special mention:

Professor R. H. Osborne, B.SC., PH.D., *Department of Geography, University of Nottingham*

R. Hedley, M.A., *Director of the Trent Polytechnic and formerly Deputy Director of Education, Nottingham Corporation*

W. G. Lawson, B.A., *formerly Director of Education, Nottinghamshire County Council*

R. O. Stanion, N.D.H., F.I.P.A., *Director of Parks, Nottingham Corporation*

F. Taylor, B.E.M., *Deputy Director of Parks, Nottingham Corporation*

H. Francis, F.I.B.M., *formerly General Manager and Engineer, Baths Department, Nottingham Corporation*

E. S. P. Evans, F.R.T.P.I., *City Planning Officer, Nottingham Corporation*

A. W. Becker, B.SC., F.R.I.C.S., M.R.T.P.I., *City Estates Officer, Nottingham Corporation*

H. J. Lowe, F.R.T.P.I., F.R.I.C.S., F.I.L.A., *Director of Planning, Nottinghamshire County Council*

R. Logan, *Secretary, East Midland Sports Council*

Central Council of Physical Recreation

National Playing Fields Association

Countryside Commission

British Waterways Board

Trent River Authority

National Allotments and Gardens Society Ltd.

Department of the Environment

Arnold Urban District Council

Beeston and Stapleford Urban District Council

Carlton Urban District Council

West Bridgford Urban District Council

Hoveringham Gravels Ltd.

Trent Gravels Ltd.

Grateful thanks are also due to the publishers for abundant help and consideration during the production of the book.

CONTENTS

FIGURES

TABLES

APPENDICES

1 OUTDOOR RECREATION ACTIVITIES AND NEEDS

OUTDOOR RECREATION ACTIVITIES are extremely diverse in their nature and scope and generally involve the use of large areas of land or water which are often in short supply. Furthermore, leisure is becoming an increasingly important part of people's lives, and more free time and greater prosperity enable people to extend their free time activities. An increasing population which is better educated, more prosperous and more mobile will in the next few years place a very heavy demand on many outdoor recreational facilities.

Nevertheless, the demand for various types of recreational facility is not increasing uniformly. The demand for some activities, such as water sports and golf, is increasing at a rapid rate whilst participation in others, such as cycling and tennis, may be declining. National recreational surveys have indicated that the demand for different activities can fluctuate widely between different parts of the country, and it seems evident that people's habits and attitudes are as important as physical characteristics and climatic conditions.

Hence there is a pressing need to make realistic assessments of probable demand for the whole range of recreational resources taking into account past trends, future population structure and the various factors influencing demand. This demand has to be converted into areas of resource in suitable locations, with full regard to desirable capacity standards and multiple use arrangements. These resources have to be planned and properly interrelated because the fortuitous provision of facilities, as past experience has shown, is rarely entirely satisfactory. In addition, it is necessary to cost alternative proposals to determine which will give the greatest social benefit, and this involves the difficult problem of quantifying and evaluating a host of direct and indirect costs and benefits.

Outdoor recreation in all its aspects has an important rôle to play in counteracting the monotonous and boring characteristics of many jobs. In the absence of such an outlet, many employees could break down under the strain and tension of work. Business executives and professional persons are also being subjected to increasingly heavy pressures and need opportunities for relaxation and revitalisation in an outdoor environment. This book is mainly concerned with the provision of outdoor recreational facilities in towns and cities. Over eighty per cent of the population of England and Wales is urban in character and despite its increased mobility and the existence of national and country parks, there is still a pressing need for a satisfactory level of provision of outdoor recreational resources in urban areas.

PHILOSOPHY OF RECREATION

Before considering recreation demand factors, methods of classifying resources and identifying recreational agencies and similar matters, it seems advisable to define some of the more widely used recreational terms, and to consider their essential characteristics and people's attitudes towards recreation.

Nature of Recreation

Recreation is basically a renewal or preparation for routine and necessary work or a means of escape from it. Kaplan[1] clearly sees recreation's main purpose as one of re-creating or revitalising people so that they may efficiently return to activities which are not recreational but economically gainful work. Recreation constitutes activity (or planned inactivity) undertaken because one wants to do it without economic incentive as a motivating force, emphasising a fundamental prerequisite of willingness on the part of the participant. Clawson and Knetsch[2] have shown how recreation contrasts with work, which is done primarily to provide the 'necessities' of life such as eating, sleeping, housekeeping and personal care. While Phillips[76] has defined recreation as any pursuit undertaken during leisure

1

time (that is time available to individuals when the disciplines of work, sleep and other basic needs have been met), other than those to which people are normally highly committed.

Outdoor recreation is simply recreation that is typically performed outdoors although there are a few activities, like swimming, that can take place either outdoors or indoors. Outdoor recreation is of particular significance geographically as it often requires the use of extensive areas of land or water, involving the possibility of land use conflict through competing claims. Locational aspects of recreational resources are also important from the point of view of accessibility to users of the resources. The resources range along a continuum from undeveloped wilderness areas to the highly artificial environments of urbanised resorts or landscaped parks.[78]

Butler[3] has attempted to produce a more comprehensive definition of recreation. In his opinion:

it may be considered as any activity which is not consciously performed for the sake of any reward beyond itself, which is usually engaged in during leisure, which offers man an outlet for his physical, mental and creative powers, and in which he engages because of inner desire and not because of outer compulsion. The activity becomes recreation for the individual because it elicits from him a pleasurable and satisfying response.

Recreation is any form of experience or activity in which an individual engages from choice because of the personal enjoyment and satisfaction which he receives. This concept emphasises the personal nature of recreation and indicates why recreational activities are as diversified as the interests of man. This view of recreation is also supported by Meyer and Brightbill[4] who define recreation as 'activity voluntarily engaged in during one's leisure time and primarily motivated by the satisfaction of pleasure derived from it'. Sapora and Mitchell[5] have attempted to distinguish 'play' and 'recreation'. They trace the development of play from a curious and seemingly unimportant feature of child life to its modern concept as an important factor in education.

Recreation and Leisure

Confusion often arises from the indiscriminate use of the terms 'leisure' and 'recreation'. Brightbill[6] points out that many regard leisure as freedom from work whilst others view it as an instrument of social control; a status symbol; an organic necessity; a state of calm, quiet, contemplative dignity; or a spiritual, aesthetic, cultural condition. Leisure is accordingly a block of unoccupied time—often referred to as spare time or free time—when a person is free to rest or do whatever he chooses. Leisure occupies the time available beyond that needed for existence (eating and sleeping, for instance) and subsistence (making a living). It is discretionary time to be used according to one's own judgement or choice.

Leisure can be classified under two main heads—true leisure and enforced leisure. True leisure is the kind of leisure which is not imposed upon the individual, giving him complete choice as to what he does even though he may have bad leisure habits. In contrast, enforced leisure is not the leisure which people seek or want—it is the time which a person has on his hands when he is sick, unemployed or compelled to retire from work when he would prefer to continue.

Domenach[7] observed that work and leisure in our society reflect and supplement each other, and that man works that he might have leisure and enjoy leisure as a diversion from work. There is a weakness in this approach as it seems likely that leisure is rather more an unprepared-for by-product of work.[8] Some hold the view, and not unjustifiably, that unless a man has worked he cannot really enjoy leisure. Dumazedier[9] aptly defined leisure as: 'activity to which an individual may freely devote himself outside the needs and obligations of his occupation, his family and society, for his relaxation, diversion and personal development'.

Mead[10] is of the opinion that the Puritan ideology of leisure still lingers in America. The dominant theme being that free time should be used for recreation, enabling the individual to be more fit for work or for good works. Recreation takes place during leisure but not all leisure is given over to recreation. Hence leisure and recreation are highly correlated. Leisure is time of a special kind, whilst recreation is activity (or inactivity) of special kinds. Whether or not the activity undertaken during leisure is recreation depends largely upon the motive or incentive of the doer. Basically, if the motive is enjoyment and personal satisfaction and the performance of the activity has its own appeal, then it is recreation.

Sport

Sport is essentially recreation involving physical effort. Sport has been defined as 'a physical activity in the form of structured games or play taken for the purpose of recreation or amusement in leisure time and containing an element of competition or challenge against self, opponents or the elements'.[79] An increasing demand for sport arises from man's changing way of life. There has been a diminishing requirement for physical effort, both in his occupation and his daily life, as a direct result of scientific and technological progress. McDonald[11] has described how the change from muscular work to sedentary work has led to overload becoming largely psycho-nervous in origin, manifesting itself in tension syndromes exhibiting more harmful and longer lasting effects than those associated with purely muscular fatigue. The low level of activity also has degenerative physiological effects.

It is generally believed that the most satisfactory types of exercise are 'natural' ones involving the whole body such as walking, running, cycling and swimming. There seems little doubt that leisure time sport and physical activity have a vital rôle to play in modern life, since exercise is a major factor in the maintenance of health. Various viewpoints on sport have been expounded by McIntosh.[12] At best, sport may be an instrument of education for the training of character; it may provide harmless outlets for aggressive and socially harmful impulses; or it may be a therapeutic agent in the maintenance of physical health and fitness.

The Wolfenden report[13] in its general introduction, examines some of the main attributes which are claimed to be gained from participation in sport. These attributes include reduction in development of criminal habits by young people; satisfaction of man's need for play; maintenance of good health; development of beneficial qualities such as courage, endurance, self-discipline, determination and self-reliance; character building; acquisition of sportsmanship and code of ethics; aesthetic value; general enjoyment and satisfaction; and participation in a broader range of activities.

Nevertheless, as shown in the Government's social survey, *Planning for Leisure*,[14] the Pilot National Recreation Survey[15] and the British Broadcasting Corporation's survey of people's activities,[16] except among the very young active participation in sports and games seldom occupies more than a small proportion of people's leisure time.

Characteristics of Recreation

Meyer and Brightbill[4] have endeavoured to identify the basic characteristics of recreation and it would be fruitful to consider them at this stage.

Basically, recreation involves activity—be it physical, mental or emotional—and it has no single form, as the range of activities which people enjoy during leisure is almost limitless. Recreation is determined by motivation, is fundamentally an attitude of mind and occurs in 'unobligated' time. Engagement in recreational pursuits is entirely voluntary as the moment participation becomes compulsory the activity ceases to be recreation. Recreation is universally practised and sought and can take place in a variety of settings, can be organised or unorganised and can be enjoyed alone or in groups. Recreationalists are often quite serious when absorbed in activities from which they secure satisfaction and pleasure. Finally it has by-products in that recreation can reward the participant in terms of intellectual, physical and social growth; better health; improved citizenship; and in other qualities of personal development.

Recreation can be classified as active or passive. In active recreation people participate directly in the activity—be it soccer, golf, swimming or rowing. Spectators at a county cricket match would be engaging in passive recreation as they would be onlookers and are not themselves playing cricket. This book is primarily concerned with active recreation, although in the case of team sports some importance has been attached to the ratio of participants to spectators.

Phases of Outdoor Recreation Experience

It is evident that the total recreational experience is not limited to the actual outdoor recreation activity on the site. Clawson and Knetsch[2, 17] have identified five distinctly different phases.

(1) *Planning and anticipation.* The time involved may be quite brief as when a small boy is invited by his friends to play ball on a nearby playground. A day's outing by a family to a country park may involve lengthy

3

preparations and provide considerable enjoyment in the process. It has been suggested that a fisherman may get more enjoyment from tying his own dry flies through the winter than he will later obtain from the actual fishing.

(2) *Travel to the recreation site.* The amount of travel and its cost may vary greatly. The satisfactions and dissatisfactions of travel to the site vary considerably between individuals, between routes and between sites visited. At best some persons or groups may enjoy the travel itself and some visitors to recreation areas give sightseeing as their major objective. Others regard the trip itself as a necessary nuisance.

(3) *On-site experiences and activities.* These include swimming, hiking, camping, picnicking, fishing, playing games and all the other activities pursued in outdoor recreation areas, and the satisfaction secured from them. This phase may be less than half the total, whether measured by time spent, expense incurred or total satisfaction gained. It will probably be the basic reason for the whole outdoor recreation experience, and the remaining parts of the total experience may be built around it. But it is only a part.

(4) *Travel back or return journey.* This is unlikely to be a duplicate of the travel to the site. Even when the route is the same, the recreationalists view it differently. If it has been an all-day outing they are now tired, whereas they were fresh on the outward journey. Memories of the site experience and anticipation of tasks at home are certainly different from the thoughts on the outward trip.

(5) *Recollection.* After the experience is over, the person or persons involved recollect or reminisce on one or more aspects of the total experience. These recollections may be shared with friends, relatives and associates. When the total recreation experience makes a major impression, as for example the first visit to a national park, the recollection will be strong and lasting. Recollection of one outdoor experience often provides the starting point for anticipation of another.

In many ways the whole outdoor recreation experience is a package deal; all parts are necessary, and the sum of satisfactions and dissatisfactions from the whole must be balanced against total costs. Pleasurable parts of the experience must more than balance the unpleasant parts.

Clawson and Knetsch[17] believe that this idea is basic to research on outdoor recreation, and that statistical demand analysis, for instance, can proceed with the total experience as the unit of measurement, but not on the basis of one phase alone. They believe that measurement of user satisfactions and dissatisfactions and all the financial problems of economic impact, pricing and sources of funds must be considered in the light of the total outdoor recreation experience, not merely for one or a few parts of it. This view is not, however, universally held.

Problems of Leisure

Soule[18] drew attention to the rapidly changing leisure characteristics of our age when he wrote: 'For the first-time in the history of mankind there is well on the way not a civilisation topped by a leisure class, but a civilisation characterised by unusual leisure'.

Brightbill[6] attributes the problem of coping with increased leisure in some measure to footloose young people, bored adults, discouraged old folk, highway accidents, delinquency and crime, emotional instability and poor physical fitness. It seems that a civilisation which has achieved high standards of living and less work is now faced with the problem of learning to live.

Davidson[19] continues this theme—

Time once saved in the name of Christian virtue has come to be saved in the name of simple efficiency, but the urgency to save it has hardly diminished. That efficiency, in turn, has piled up more leisure for more people than has ever been known elsewhere in history. It happened quickly, within a few short generations, and to a nation (America) with a recent pioneer tradition of unmitigated hard work—a nation trained to believe that killing time was a crime. What to do with leisure now that we had it became a major problem of our civilisation.

The British experience cannot be very different.

Martin[20] feels that people need help in learning to use leisure, when he describes the American situation—

Mental health services now (1957) cost 1½ billions yearly and the costs are rising by 100 million annually; there are 700 000 patients in mental hospitals and outpatient clinics having 3 to 6 months waiting lists. Sleeplessness, inability to relax, and fear of leisure are the first signs of mental illness. Millions of dollars are spent on sleeping pills.

It is suspected that much of this illness stems from excessive pressures and strains of modern working conditions. There is need for balance as described by Gutkind,[21] which is realised only when recreation has its proper place among other basic life interests. One is led to question whether industrial urban man in the future will find the kind of rationale of experience that will enable him to enjoy interests in his leisure while shielding him from the excessive demands of work.

Television viewing has had a very marked effect on other leisure time activities and this is clearly demonstrated in the Pilot National Recreation Survey[15] and the British Broadcasting Corporation survey.[16] Houseman[22] illustrated the situation in America in 1950 when he described how over a period of 2 years after 400 families had purchased television sets, cinema visits by them dropped by forty-six per cent, football and baseball attendance reduced by thirty per cent and book reading declined by thirty-three per cent. He claimed that high school students in Stamford, Connecticut spent more hours before television sets than before their teachers.

A rather dramatic account of the effect of the television set in an American Christian Science magazine is worthy of note.

Television has had its effect on the innermost core of personal habit. The presence of a piece of electronic furniture in the living room has changed how much people eat (more) and how much they sleep (less). It has transformed the pattern of day-by-day living more than any invention since the automobile. It has fascinated people, exasperated people and bored people; but it has reached them and, on the whole, held them. Few people who now have a television set will ever be without one again.[23]

In Great Britain, of the 14 million television sets seventy-five per cent are now used on average for over an hour each evening, with profound effect on people's use of leisure.[77]

Ernst[24] showed how leisure time is an opportunity for cultural development:

We have 8 million bird watchers, 16 per cent of all the vegetables eaten in our country are grown by the house-owners themselves. There is an entire new industry for making 'do-it-yourself' clothes. 200 000 people tonight (1956) in our Republic (America) are building boats in their cellars and garages. 20 per cent of all the homes in our country (10 million homes) have power tools, a saw and a lathe. All this shows in a sketchy way what we are doing with our leisure time.

The prospect is more leisure and less work in the future. Productive processes and consumer behaviour will change and this will result in continued social change. Leisure is a phenomenon of abundance and material wealth, and its greater abundance requires a re-appraisal of the problems that accompany it.[1]

The problem of leisure is a far more critical one for handicapped than for healthy people. Recreation assists in the treatment or adjustment of such persons and Chapman[25] has described ten possible programme areas, ranging from arts and crafts to nature and outing activities.

Leisure problems will also arise as the ratio of workers to non-workers continues to diminish in an ageing population, with earlier retirements and longer life spans. Kleemeier[26] has described how older people on retirement miss the sense of purpose given by a job, and also the personal bonds that the job set up in daily life. He suggests the need for the establishment of a minor network of social life, to ensure some meaningful activity. An American survey conducted in 1957 showed that the main leisure activities of the over 60's were watching television, visiting friends and relatives, working in the garden and reading magazines and books.[27]

The need for recreational activities to cope effectively with increased leisure is very well expressed in the Wolfenden report:[13]

Man, since Adam, must work. But man also, since society began, has played. His play may show itself in any product of his imagination, in any art or craft pursued for recreation rather than for purposes of technology, or, simply, in sport. And in so far as any of these activities is distinct from what a man regards as his work, a society which has the prospect of considerably increased leisure, needs to examine the contribution which play can make to full living, for the individual and for the society. As more and more people live urban lives, play takes its place—for one man as affording an opportunity for social activities with other town-dwellers, for another as affording an opportunity for introducing into his own life a balancing element of the countryside and the open air.

Man, in short, needs play. In the form of a game, a sport, or an outdoor activity of some kind it is desirable in itself, for its own sake, as a valuable element in a full and rounded life.

Outdoor recreation is one outlet for the available leisure time. Nevertheless, it is necessary to keep the rôle of outdoor recreation in proper perspective. Clawson[28] estimated that in the United States in 1963, only about three or four per cent of all leisure time was used for outdoor recreation. This superficially very low figure results in part because about forty per cent of all leisure time is daily leisure—after work or after school—during which it is often difficult for many people to get to an outdoor recreation area; and much leisure is at a time of year when outdoor recreation is not attractive to the average person. Roberts[80] has rightly demonstrated the need to apply sociological techniques to help fill the gap in our existing knowledge about the public's tastes and preferences as they relate to recreation.

Advantages of Recreation

Brightbill[29] has classified the advantages of recreation into four main categories:

(1) To aid body development, movement and coordination through physical activities such as football, tennis and climbing.
(2) To contribute to safety and survival, as in swimming.
(3) To foster and extend an appreciation of the outdoors, through activities like hiking and camping.
(4) To promote mental stability and to provide a change in setting and pace from the highly competitive world of work. It constitutes a form of relaxation that is an aid to emotional stability.

Meyer and Brightbill[4] in their study of recreation as a social force established many direct links between recreation and personality. They asserted that participation in recreation produced greater happiness and satisfaction, balanced human growth, creativeness, competition, character, improved mental capacity and learning, freedom, better physical condition, improved social relationships, better attitude to life and greater emotional stability. There is little doubt that outdoor recreation has many beneficial effects.

CHANGING DEMAND FOR RECREATION

Dower made a great impact with his Civic Trust sponsored survey entitled *Fourth Wave*.[30] He described how three great waves had broken across the face of Britain since 1800. First, the sudden growth of dark industrial towns. Second, the thrusting movement along far flung railways. Third the sprawl of the car based suburbs. He asserted that the fourth wave of leisure could be more powerful than all the others.

Leisure is a compound of six decisive factors—population, income, mobility, education, retirement and the free time of adults. Each of these has grown significantly in the last decade and will continue to grow in the years ahead. Table 1.1 extracted from *Fourth Wave* shows trends and predictions relating to Britain.

TABLE 1.1

BASIC TRENDS AND PREDICTIONS

	1955	1965	2000 (predicted)
Population (million)	49	52	70
Income (£ per head at 1955 values)	250	325	1000
Cars (million)	3½	7	30
People over 15 at school and university (thousand)	429	930	2000
People beyond retirement age (million)	7	8	12
Basic industrial working week (hrs.)	45	42	30

The conclusions contained in the report *Outdoor Recreation for America*,[31] published in early 1962, must give some indication of probable future trends in Great Britain, although they need adjusting to take account of British habits, climate and other factors. This report indicated that active use of leisure rises with income; that growing mobility is putting heavy pressures on recreation resources never used before; that widespread education not only releases more young people on holiday but changes their attitudes towards leisure, the better educated being the more active; and that older people are remarkably keen on the less vigorous leisure activities, such as walking, driving, sightseeing and fishing.

The broad conclusion of the American report was that their population would double, but the demand for outdoor recreation would treble, by the year 2000. It is anticipated that the population of England and Wales could increase by forty per cent by the end of the present century and that the surge of leisure could be much greater than in the States in proportion to population. Indeed, Dower has suggested that the demand for active leisure in Britain could well treble by the end of the century.

Population

The population of England and Wales is expected to increase to 54 million by 1980 and could reach 70 million by 2000. The active age group aged 15–25 years accounts for about 7 million at present, but by 1980 there will, on present projections, be nearly 8 million within this age group and by the end of the century nearly 10 million.[32] This large increase in population must generate a higher demand for outdoor recreation.

Income

Both the American[31] and the British Travel Association/Keele University[15] studies found that participation in active recreation tended to rise with the level of personal income. This would appear to apply particularly to activities which require specialised and relatively expensive equipment, like golf, riding and most of the water sports. Hence as real income rises we can expect the pressures on, for example, our inland waters for recreational pursuits, to grow.

Mobility

The rapid increase in the number of private cars in Great Britain makes possible a large expansion in the uses of leisure, particularly as regards visits to national and country parks and the coast. Since the post-war motoring boom began in 1952, the number of cars has increased at a rate of nearly ten per cent per annum.[33] Table 1.2 shows the growth of motor vehicle ownership in Great Britain since 1939.

TABLE 1.2

MOTOR VEHICLE OWNERSHIP IN GREAT BRITAIN

Year	Total vehicles	Cars
1939	3 148 600	2 034 400
1949	4 107 652	2 130 793
1959	8 661 980	4 965 774
1963	11 446 200	7 375 000
1967	14 097 000	10 303 000

Source: British Road Federation, basic road statistics, 1968.

In 1966 about forty-five per cent of British households owned one or more cars, which they used to enhance their leisure. A survey made in 1963 by the British Travel Association (now the British Tourist Authority) showed that over forty per cent of car owning households took a day or overnight trip away from home over the Whitsun weekend. Only twenty per cent of households without cars took such trips, moreover the car owners travelled farther than did other families.

Table 1.3 shows official vehicle forecasts up to the year 2010, and the prospect is rather frightening from the viewpoint of traffic congestion as well as possible saturation of recreational areas at peak periods.

TABLE 1.3

NUMBER OF CARS IN GREAT BRITAIN

Year	Number
1970	12 900 000
1980	21 200 000
1990	26 800 000
2000	31 000 000
2010	35 000 000

Source: revised forecasts of vehicles and traffic in Great Britain, Road Research Laboratory, 1967

By 1975 there will statistically be nearly one car per British household and this position could be reached in the Midlands and southern England even earlier. Mogridge[34] has estimated that car saturation level will be reached by the year 2020 with 0.66 cars per person.

Education

Both American and British studies found there was a general tendency for adult participation in active recreation to rise with length of full time education. This is probably partly a reflection of the influence that education has on occupation and income. But more important is the interest in recreational activities which is fostered in schools and other educational establishments, and which is carried on into later life. Throughout the whole field of teenage education there has been a growing appreciation of the value of outdoor recreation in its widest sense. Many local education authorities have established outdoor pursuit centres and youth clubs, while the coaching programmes of the Central Council of Physical Recreation have, in particular, assisted in widening the interest in outdoor recreation.[35]

These developments have assisted in the growth of traditional activities such as swimming, rambling and camping. But its more dramatic influence has been on those water based activities requiring costly equipment. Increasing numbers of schools are taking up sailing and canoeing, while there has been a rapid growth in water sports clubs associated with training colleges, youth clubs and local education authorities. The provision of new facilities often seems to create the appropriate demand.

Leisure Time

More leisure time will be available in the future to the average person and some of this time will inevitably be devoted to outdoor recreation. This extension of leisure time will stem from reductions in working hours and longer holiday periods. In addition, medical advances will extend life spans, thereby increasing the number of elderly people in retirement who will require increased leisure time facilities. Moreover, there will be a higher proportion of elderly people in the population because of longer life expectations due to improved health and medical care, coupled with a probable fall in the birth rate.

Changing Leisure Habits

Another important factor in the development of outdoor recreational facilities is the changing leisure habits of the population. Burton and Wibberley[36] have traced the growth of recreation in Britain from the mid-nineteenth century and have sub-divided the period into four distinct phases.

(1) Mid-nineteenth century to 1914—mass recreation was largely confined to excursions and day outings on Sundays and other occasional holidays.

(2) 1919–39 saw the sustained growth of urban recreation and the expansion in the number of people receiving annual holidays with pay—estimated at 8 million in 1937.

8

(3) 1945–55—annual holiday arrangements were extended to almost all workers, resulting in rapid extension of holidays away from home. This decade was largely the age of the spectator, with attendances at association football matches on Saturdays reaching a peak of about a million in 1948–49, and large followings at rugby, cricket, horse racing and greyhound racing. Cinema attendances reached their peak at the end of the period, when television rapidly became a 'necessity' in the homes of all sections of the population.

(4) 1955 onwards saw the rise of the active recreationalist. Sailing, golf, climbing, pony-trekking, the caravan and camping holiday and, above all, motoring for pleasure, are all activities which have shown rapid growth rates in recent years.

This last stage in the development of mass recreation has been the product of the influences previously described —paid holidays, reduced working hours, rise in real incomes and rapid growth in numbers of private cars. For the first time in British history, a large proportion of the population has not only the time to spend on outdoor recreation activities, but also the means to do so satisfactorily. The car brings to its owner the advantages of increased mobility and greater flexibility in the use of his leisure time.

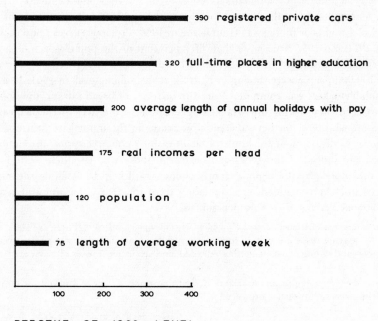

PERCENT OF 1960 LEVEL

SOURCES :

Private cars :	J.C. Tanner, Road Research Laboratory
Higher education :	Robbins report (Report of the Committee on Higher Education 1963, Cmnd. 2154).
Population :	Registrar General, 21 December, 1963.

Figure 1.1   Factors Affecting Growth of Outdoor Recreation 1960–1985

Trends in Outdoor Recreation

Figure 1.1 shows the probable position relating to the factors affecting the growth of outdoor recreation up to 1985 and was prepared by the Bow Group.[37] This indicates a rapid rate of growth in outdoor recreation in the next 15 years. The task of catering satisfactorily for the increasing numbers of recreationalists in a densely populated, highly industrialised country like Britain will not be easy.

As observed by Hookway[38] few people in 1949 visualised the way in which almost all recreation activities in the countryside would experience increased demands. Motoring for pleasure—with all its demands for parking and picnicking facilities, particularly at viewing points, and for service facilities like petrol filling stations, lavatories and cafés—has increased dramatically. On fine weekends throughout the year any area within about 50 km of an urban centre may experience the traffic of passive recreation.

Similarly, demands for active recreation have grown rapidly, and nearly every resource available for fishing, sailing and climbing is heavily used. Already demand has approached—and in some areas exceeded—the capacity of facilities and organisation to meet it. Recent authoritative studies[15, 31, 39] indicate that many present demands will double, or in some cases treble, in the next 20 years and in particular areas the changes may be even more dramatic.

At the same time significant changes have been taking place in the holiday habits of British people and to meet the new demands equally significant developments have taken place in the holiday industry. According to the British Travel and Holidays Association (now the British Tourist Authority), fifty-eight per cent of the population had at least one main holiday of 4 nights or more away from home in 1960. Previous surveys undertaken by the Association showed that between 1951 and 1955 little more than fifty per cent of the population took a holiday.

Norfolk County Council[40] estimated that the Norfolk holiday season comprised approximately 850 000 person/ weeks and that up to 100 000 people were staying in Norfolk at the holiday peak in 1961. It is interesting to observe that the number of holidaymakers was computed from the quantity of bread sales in the holiday areas.

Burton[41] had also traced the growing importance of recreation in the lives of the majority of Britons over the last 20 years, and the probability of further substantial increases in the immediate future. He makes the sobering point that little is known in detail about the kinds of facilities for public recreation throughout the country or the uses made of facilities, and indeed of the needs and desires of those who use them. The initial surveys of major recreational facilities undertaken by the regional sports councils will help in detailing the supply position.

This section can usefully be concluded by a quotation from the Duke of Edinburgh's address to the Annual Conference of the National Playing Fields Association in 1963:

We are on the threshold of the age of leisure, and the problem is no longer academic. There are stark and immediate problems facing us. The queues for playing fields are getting longer; the pressure on general sports and recreation clubs of all sorts is increasing. Swimming pools and sailing clubs are getting crowded, and recreational users of water are beginning to run into each other.

It is no longer a question of encouraging people to take part; from now on we have to concentrate on providing facilities of the right sort and in the right place, and properly organised.

CLASSIFICATION OF FACILITIES

The many types of outdoor recreation areas and the numerous kinds of activities performed on them require some form of classification for meaningful analysis. The general relationships are better understood if some grouping of areas and activities is adopted.

Classification of different recreation resources may assist with the prediction of future demands for various kinds of facilities. Burton and Noad[42] have shown that if participation in a particular pursuit can be linked by correlation and other methods to participation in other pursuits, and to certain socio-economic characteristics, then—as the socio-economic characteristics of a given population change—it should become possible to predict, at least in general terms, how participation in given pursuits and groups of pursuits will change. The reason for employing groups of pursuits rather than individual activities is based on the hypothesis that correlations between the former and socio-economic variables will be more accurate and more stable over a period of time than correlations for the latter.

Furthermore, as Cullingworth[43] has noted: 'the usefulness of any particular classification will depend upon the purpose for which it is required . . . no one classification will suffice for all purposes . . . and classifications are not mutually exclusive'.

Indeed, no study to date has produced a classification of general or universal application.

Many classification systems are possible and the methods that have been currently employed are now examined.

Locational Classification

One popular method was that introduced by Clawson, Held and Stoddard[44] based on three locational groupings of facilities, and this is illustrated in table 1.4.

TABLE 1.4

CLASSIFICATION OF RECREATION AREAS

Type of Recreation Area

Item	User orientated	Resource based	Intermediate
1. General location	Close to users; on whatever resources are available	Where outstanding resources can be found; may be distant from most users	Must not be too remote from users; on best resources available within distance limitation
2. Major types of activity	Games—such as golf, tennis, swimming, picnicking, walks and horse riding; zoos, etc.; children's games	Major sightseeing—scientific and historical interest; hiking and mountain climbing; camping, fishing and hunting	Camping, picnicking, hiking, swimming, hunting and fishing
3. When major use occurs	After hours (school or work)	Vacation	Day outings and weekends
4. Typical sizes of areas	1–100 hectares	Usually some thousands of hectares	50–1000 or more hectares
5. Common types of agency responsibility	City, county or other local government; private	National parks and national forests primarily; state parks in some cases; private—especially for seashore and major lakes	Federal reservoirs; state parks; private

User orientated areas are at one extreme of the classification and are of special concern in studies of urban recreational facilities as they include most city facilities from parks to children's playgrounds. Their most important characteristic is ready accessibility to users. Their chief time of use is after school for children, after work for adults and during the day for mothers and small children. Such areas are often individually small and their physical characteristics are not too demanding.

Resource based areas are at the other extreme. Their dominant characteristics are their outstanding physical resources such as mountains, forests, coastline and lake shores, and they usually lie at considerable distances from concentrations of population. For most people, a visit to a resource based outdoor recreation area involves considerable travel and hence such visits are usually confined to vacations. Resource based areas are generally very large units sometimes occupying several thousand hectares, and this particular classification is far more relevant in the United States than in Great Britain.

Intermediate areas lie between these extremes, both geographically and in terms of use. They must be well located to users and preferably be sited within an hour's driving time of the users' homes. Such areas are typically used for all-day outings and at weekends. Visits to them normally involve less travel time and expense than visits to resource based areas; country parks and reservoirs would fall into this category.

Not all facilities fall neatly into these groupings—Wollaton Park in Nottingham, for example, is a city park which also incorporates most of the features of a country park. Some people may be located so close to a national park that they can pay a visit to it after work. In many other ways, some usage or characteristic outside the main pattern is possible. Nevertheless, outdoor recreation areas of various sizes, locations and characteristics form an interrelated system.[2]

The pattern of use of these various areas is directly influenced by the amount and timing of available leisure. A shortened workday enables the workers to spend more time in the park or lido or on the golf course, or in some other user orientated outdoor recreation. A shortening of the working week could result in much more extensive use of resource based and intermediate outdoor recreation areas. Higher real incomes and greater mobility will also have a direct bearing on the use of the latter areas.

Wolfe[45] observes that in the United States the spatial imbalance is greatest for resource based facilities: the bulk of the American population lives in the north-east, whereas the majority of the resource based facilities are in the great national parks and forests of the west. In consequence of this Perloff and Wingo[46] assert that there has been excessive emphasis on resource based activities and that from now onwards a dominant rôle must be given to user orientated forms of recreation.

In Britain there is also considerable spatial imbalance with resource based facilities and in the least endowed areas of the country it would seem advisable to concentrate on the provision of intermediate and user orientated facilities.

Another locational basis for classification would be merely to group facilities as local, regional or national.

Use Intensity and Other Special Characteristics

The American report on outdoor recreation[31] listed six types of recreation area classified as to intensity of use and other special characteristics.

(1) *Higher density recreation areas*—these are intensively developed and used. Typical examples are popular bathing beaches and town parks.

(2) *General outdoor recreation areas*—these are substantially developed for a wide variety of specific recreational uses.

(3) *Natural environment areas*—these are suitable for recreation in a natural environment and usually in combination with other uses.

(4) *Unique natural areas*—areas of outstanding scenic splendour or scientific importance.

(5) *Primitive areas*—undisturbed roadless areas of a wild character, termed 'wilderness areas' by the Americans.

(6) *Historic and cultural sites*—sites which have strong associations with history, tradition or cultural heritage of the United States and may be relatively uninteresting visually. The National Parks Service has developed techniques to interpret the significance and to evoke the atmosphere of the association. Visitor centres incorporate audio-visual reconstructions, exhibitions and documentary evidence.

Clawson, Held and Stoddard[44] introduced an extremely useful classification of outdoor recreational areas in four groupings based on intensity of use:

(1) *Very heavy,* with perhaps 4000 or more total uses or visits per hectare per year. A large proportion of municipal parks would fall into this classification, in whole or in part, and perhaps some highly popular areas within national or regional parks.

(2) *Heavy,* with typically 100–250 uses or visits per hectare per year. Camps and picnic areas, popular lakes and river banks would fall into this use class.

(3) *Moderate,* with typically two to eight uses or visits per hectare per year. Many fishing, hiking and riding areas could fall into this class.

(4) *Light,* with typically 0.33 use or visit per hectare per year. This class could include the 'back country' of national parks.

Following the American studies, a study group of the 'Countryside in 1970' Conference in Britain suggested four classifications for recreational resources.[39]

(1) *Intensive areas*—areas where the development of facilities, not the nature of the site, is dominant. Such areas will cater primarily for the local needs of a built-up area and should be within about 15 km of it, but less if possible. Large scale proposals of this kind include the Lea Valley and the Chasewater project in Staffordshire. Smaller scale schemes would include playing fields, golf courses, youth camping grounds, sailing,

boating and fishing.

(2) *General recreation areas*—such areas would, while in general use for agriculture, forestry or water conservation, provide one or more of the following:

(a) Linear routes—particularly footpaths, bridlepaths, waterways or scenic roads. Jubilee Drive on the Malverns is a good example of a scenic drive and a convenient access to footpaths over the hills.

(b) The use of a particular site for one or a combination of activities, such as camping sites and water based recreation.

(c) General access to woods, commons, and areas of 'open country'.

The Conference suggested that 'general outdoor recreation areas are essentially well-developed natural resources, such as the New Forest, Cannock Chase, Windermere and the Solent. Due regard should be paid to existing land and water uses and the ecological balance must also be safeguarded'.

(3) *High quality environment areas*—areas in which the conservation of the landscape and natural features will be paramount. The natural resources of these areas are frequently very fragile and should not be subjected to avoidable pressures. Facilities for recreation should be limited to the enjoyment of nature, and no recreational uses should be permitted which are unrelated or clash with the unique character of the areas. Some of these areas will fall within national parks and 'areas of outstanding natural beauty', but will also include smaller areas such as Upper Teesdale and parts of the Norfolk Broads.

(4) *Buildings and sites of historic and special interest*—some of these sites have great potential and could be developed on the lines of the American pattern of 'interpretive' centres for national and state monuments. In Gloucestershire the suggestion has been made that the Battle of Tewkesbury might be more graphically illustrated on the site where it took place. Certain of the fortifications could possibly be exposed and simply presented maps could illustrate the strategy of the battle.[47] The Wildfowl Trust at Slimbridge is a good example of the use of a site of special natural interest to explain wild life to visitors.

Other Methods of Classification

Coppock[48] has classified recreational use in rural Britain into five groupings on the basis of their demands on land and other resources, and this approach must be of special interest to the geographer.

(1) The passive enjoyment of rural beauty, which requires little direct access to land.

(2) Informal activities like walking, which need access to the countryside at large.

(3) Traditional rural sports, like grouse shooting and foxhunting, which generally involve either game or land management.

(4) Sports such as cricket or motor racing, for which a pitch or other specially constructed facilities are required.

(5) Aquatic sports, like fishing and canoeing, which are practised in both coastal and inland waters and make only limited (though very localised) demands on land.

Coppock shows that for most of these recreational uses two aspects of the land are important: the quality of its landscapes or 'visual amenity', and its accessibility—in the sense both of availability for public use and of nearness to the main centres of population or to holiday resorts. They are closely linked although their relative importance varies with the kind of recreation.

Those seeking visual enjoyment of the countryside are primarily concerned with the quality of its scenery: many are motorists who (provided they can find somewhere to park and picnic, preferably at good view points) are not greatly interested in access to the land itself, although its accessibility by road is of great importance. The walker on the other hand is concerned equally with access (in both forms) and with amenity, and desires the freedom to wander in attractive country.

Some American approaches to the classification of recreational resources have had regard to the physical characteristics of the resources. Thus the Wisconsin study[49] identifies the recreational resources in the state as water, wetland and significant topography. Water is considered the major recreational resource. This view was also held by Fischer[50] when he stated that the prime resource requirement of areas for people-intensive recreation is 'an

13

attraction'. The attraction could take many forms but water was one of the most important in that most recreation is water orientated. Brockman[51] listed recreational resources as favourable climate, scenically interesting topography, water resources and interesting associations of plants and animals.

Taylor[52] also emphasises that if a site is to be of value for people-intensive forms of recreation it must be an attraction. Furthermore, he also sees the need for suitable vegetation cover, a suitable terrain or slope, an area of sufficient size for development and protective purposes, and an available source of drinking water. Accessibility is considered to be of minor importance.

These studies show just how widely the North American approach to outdoor recreation differs from that adopted in Great Britain. The wide differences in physical characteristics and climate have generated quite different needs in terms of recreational resources. Nevertheless, the emphasis on the place of water in recreation is probably significant.

Other methods of classification which might be considered include the time of the year during which the activity is undertaken; whether it can be undertaken singly or in small groups or whether it needs teams of persons; organised or un-organised; active or passive; land or water based; and single or multiple use. In this book, activities with some like characteristics have been grouped together in the same chapter, for example, sporting activities in chapter 7 and water based recreation in chapter 8.

The difficulty of classifying outdoor recreational facilities is recognised in the Outdoor Recreation Resources Review Commission report[31] which states:

It would be satisfying to be able to judge all recreation areas by a single measuring rod. No such measure is at present available, however, because different areas are managed for different purposes. For each purpose, or set of purposes, specific standards must be met.

RECREATIONAL AGENCIES

Recreational facilities are provided by three main types of agency:

(1) *Private facilities* owned and administered by private clubs and including clubs linked to industrial or business concerns.

(2) *Commercial facilities* operated by individuals and organisations with the express purpose of making a profit.

(3) *Public facilities* which may either be provided by a public authority for public use or provided out of public funds with a more restricted use.[53]

The main features of these arrangements and their shortcomings will now be considered.

Private Facilities

Most of the private recreational facilities are limited to sports grounds, especially for games such as cricket, rugby and association football, lawn tennis and golf, although some make provision for indoor sport. Most local voluntary clubs provide facilities for only one or two activities, while the industrial recreational clubs tend to cater for a wider range of activities, but in all cases they operate for the benefit of their members.

Local voluntary clubs do not always own the sports grounds on which their members play. Many association football clubs, in particular, hire playing fields from the local authority and difficulties arise when the demand for playing pitches on Saturdays exceeds the supply. Private golf clubs often have waiting lists for membership and provide good social facilities in their clubhouses, including very profitable bars.

Clubs linked to industrial and commercial concerns also play an important part in recreational provision. In 1966 it was estimated by Cullen[54] that there were approximately 1300 industrial clubs in the United Kingdom. Most of these clubs operated a limited number of activities although a few of the larger ones had about twenty different sports sections with varying amounts of activity at local league, inter-departmental and recreational levels. The facilities of these clubs are usually available to an employee's wife or family but relatively few companies extend their use to the general public, despite pressure to do so.

Cullen's enquiries show a diminishing interest in the clubs on the part of both management and employees. Management is not quite so sure now about the place of sport and welfare in industry, while in the clubs apathy is

14

often prevalent among the membership and rarely is there more than ten per cent of employees using club facilities. Indeed, some smaller companies—unable to sustain an acceptable level of interest in their sports facilities—have abandoned their clubs and sold or used the land for building development.

Commercial Facilities

Commercially operated facilities are those provided by individuals and organisations with the express purpose of making a profit. They include restaurants and concert halls, cinemas and theatres, riding stables and boatyards, dance halls, stately homes, camping sites, skating rinks and bowling alleys, marinas and golf driving ranges. They show a wide range of activities but, as indicated by Molyneux,[55] the commercial development is likely to be more limited than was anticipated a decade ago. On the other hand there are other opportunities, so far unexploited, to bring the capital and expertise of private enterprise into urban recreation—for instance, the provision of multi-purpose sports centres.

Public Facilities

Public facilities are of two main categories. First, those provided by a public authority for general use, such as town parks and swimming pools. Secondly those provided out of public funds for a special purpose but for which certain restricted recreational use has been possible; this includes facilities in educational establishments and those administered by the armed services, reservoirs and forest plantations.

Public authorities cover a wide range of bodies of varying size and responsibility. First and foremost are probably the local authorities of the cities, boroughs and urban districts (district councils as from 1974), who have the legal powers to provide a wide range of recreational facilities from large town parks to allotment plots. County councils are becoming increasingly involved through the provision of country parks, water based recreation, picnic spaces and car parks at scenic view points, and the erection of multi-purpose sports centres. In rural districts, parish councils often play an important rôle in the provision of playing fields and children's playground equipment.

There are also a number of special-purpose authorities who have a valuable contribution to make to the provision of recreational facilities. These bodies include the Countryside Commission, Nature Conservancy, Forestry Commission and the British Waterways Board.

The Sports Council[53] has drawn attention to the changing rôle of the local authority in meeting the new demands for physical recreation. The increasing pressure on land and the large expense of new capital facilities such as sports halls and swimming pools, a growing awareness of the overlap in the provision or functions of neighbouring authorities or of two or more departments (for example, planning, parks and education) within the same authority and the expectation of further demands, have all contributed to the need for local authorities to give overall consideration to recreational provision, assisted and guided by regional sports councils. It may be possible for small individual authorities to meet basic sports ground requirements but such undertakings as planning for swimming pools, indoor sports centres and recreation in the countryside suggest the need for inter-authority policies and jointly financed projects, although the 1974 local government reorganisation offers some improvement. In 1966, the Ministry of Housing and Local Government issued a circular to local authorities[56] drawing attention to the savings which can be achieved by joint provision and to the need for consultation with regional sports councils on new projects.

PROBLEMS IN PROVISION

A variety of complex problems arise in the provision of outdoor recreational facilities, and these are best considered under the following subheadings.

Diversity of Activities

Outdoor recreation covers a wide range of activities—some active and some passive—undertaken by people of all age groups. A variety of tastes must be satisfied from the love of solitude and of wild and beautiful scenery to the desire to share interests, activities and facilities with others. As shown earlier in this chapter, there is also likely to be a large increase in the demand for most recreational pursuits in the next decade.

To provide sufficient facilities of the right variety and size, suitably located to meet demand without causing excessive road congestion and adverse effects on the resources themselves, is a formidable task. It calls for extensive research to understand and measure the recreational needs, followed by imaginative planning of the scale, character and location of the facilities. It also requires considerable expenditure on land acquisition, resource development and conservation, and the provision of facilities.[32] Bonsey[57] indicates the need for a national strategy where the overall threats and demands are weighed against the overall resources available to meet them.

The analysis and prediction of demand is very difficult. People's desires differ and are influenced by social attitudes, opportunity, education and habit. Furthermore, all these factors are changing rapidly. Taking an isolated example—the number of canal cruising licences issued in the west Midlands in 1961 was twenty-five per cent above that of the previous year.[58] American research shows how increased car ownership and income and better education can cause dramatic increases in recreation demand. The apparently simple task of asking people what they would like is not necessarily the solution—people can only judge by what they are familiar with. Demand can be generated by supply. If a facility is totally absent, the number of people who say they want it is likely to be far below the number it would attract after it is introduced.

Outdoor recreation poses a planning problem of great magnitude. If the consequences are not anticipated, the result could easily be chaos, frustration and conflict: congestion on roads from holiday and recreation traffic is frustrating; popular beauty spots show evidence of heavy use with erosion of dunes, grass surfaces and footpaths; trespass by motor vehicles and pedestrians, vandalism and litter are a source of great annoyance to landowners. All of these affect the quality of the environment and point to the need for suitably planned facilities to cater for mass demand.

There are similar problems of conflict between recreational users. Ramblers resent the growing penetration of the country by motorists. Noisy motor sports disturb those who would enjoy their country pleasures quietly. Fishermen and dinghy sailors are irritated by motor cruisers, and the latter both conflict with water skiing and speed boating.[38] Davidson[59] has also referred to the adverse effects on recreation in national parks through trespass, pollution of water supplies, disturbance of wild life, fires, erosion and other factors.

Demand for Land and Water

Most outdoor recreational activities are highly consumptive of land and water and it will be very difficult indeed to meet future demands of prospective recreationalists. Staffordshire County Council and Stoke-on-Trent planning departments[60] have described the varying forms of recreational resources provided by the landscape in commons, lakes, heathland, woodland, rivers, canals, flooded pits and other natural features. It will be exceedingly difficult to provide adequate facilities for activities like golf and water based sports to meet the rapid growth in demand. Both the Countryside Commission and the Sports Council are keen to get more water open to the public, particularly in the form of reservoirs and wet gravel pits. Many new golf courses will probably need to be incorporated in country parks reasonably accessible to the larger centres of population.

Already, demand has approached and even exceeded the capacity of some areas and facilities to meet it. Parts of national parks and other unique and popular areas like the New Forest, the Norfolk Broads and certain stretches of coast are very heavily used.[61] Observation and research work, as for example carried out by Buchanan[62] in south Hampshire, has shown that in these areas planners are faced with problems of traffic congestion, often causing severe conflict between users as well as physical and biological deterioration of the resources themselves.

Changing Pattern of Recreation Needs

The pattern of recreation is changing, due mainly to three factors:

(1) Greater mobility resulting from increased car ownership.

(2) Greater desire for individual participation in leisure pursuits rather than watching organised professional or amateur sports.

(3) Changes in personal choice of recreational activity stemming from increased mobility, income and leisure

16

time and better educational opportunities.

Some sporting activities are tending to decline on a national scale, and this applies particularly to attendances at racing functions and football and cricket matches. Individual sports such as archery, golf and riding are growing rapidly. In addition all types of water based recreation are becoming increasingly popular and quite a large section of the population is favouring activities in which the whole family can participate. Wibberley[63] has also traced changing leisure habits from indoor passive types of leisure activities to active outdoor types of behaviour. Willey[65] sees a steadily increasing demand for the second family car, the family boat and the country cottage for weekend leisure.

Finally, the British Travel Association/University of Keele report,[15] based on the findings of interviews with 3167 respondents, gives further evidence of the increase in the pursuit of leisure time activities. This report also forecasts greater interest in individual and family pursuits, and for the more active pursuits such as water sports, golf, swimming, riding and winter sports.

Dower[81] believes that with the growing emphasis in recreation upon family activity, social reassurance and escape from the routine of working life, it is natural that people should increasingly expect quality in their recreation facilities. The windswept playing field and tin changing room are no longer enough.

Range of Agencies

The problems of provision are also made more difficult by the multiplicity of organisations concerned with the provision and management of recreational resources. In many cases both public and private organisations are making provision for the same activity, particularly in the case of playing fields, bowling greens and tennis courts. This varied pattern of provision must make for difficulties in matching supplies and demands and may well create the need for some measure of coordination.

In the provision of parks, different bodies are responsible for meeting needs at different levels. The Countryside Commission provides national parks, the first tier local authorities will presumably provide most of the country parks and second tier local authorities supply a variety of town parks. The distinctions between the different types of parks are not always clear cut and a national park for a nearby populous centre and a large town park could possess most of the characteristics of a country park.

Apart from local provision, there would appear to be a strong case for the majority of recreational facilities being the responsibility of a regional authority. Increased mobility of the population has been an important factor in creating a need for this type of administrative arrangement, apart from the desirability of integration of recreational resources.

Economic Aspects

The economic impact of outdoor recreation is becoming a matter of increasing interest to many people, particularly as the demand for recreational facilities continues to grow. Provision of outdoor recreation costs money, and the difficulties of obtaining sufficient public funds may, and often does, limit the adequacy of the recreation resources.

Whether the recreationalist can expect central or local government to provide the facilities as a public service to the community, or whether the users of the facility should pay for the service, is a very relevant question and will be considered further in chapters 3 and 9. The benefits created by the resources to persons other than the users also need considering. Complex problems also arise in establishing an effective pricing mechanism to deal with the recreational function of land or water which is in multiple use.

SCALE AND RANGE OF RECREATIONAL ACTIVITIES

There is an extremely wide variation in the scale and range of outdoor recreational facilities and these aspects will now be considered.

Range of Recreational Activities

In his address to the National Playing Fields Conference in 1963, the Duke of Edinburgh stated: 'Recreational facilities are needed for the very young to the very old, for beginners and for experts, for teams and for individuals, for indoor and outdoor recreation'.

An investigation in the United States examined the problems arising from an increasing proportion of elderly citizens, as with retirement comes abundant leisure time, posing new and entirely different problems.[64]

The tremendous range in outdoor recreational pursuits is shown up in a report by the North West Sports Council.[66] The Council has grouped outdoor recreations in the following manner:

Use of Outdoor Turf Area
Cricket, soccer, rugby, baseball, rounders, polo, lacrosse, archery, hockey.

Motor Circuits
Motor racing, motor cycle racing, go-kart racing.

Other Circuits
Horse racing, pony racing.

Use of Coastal or Other Water Areas
Sailing, canoeing, diving, sea or river swimming, water sports, fishing, rowing, boating, pleasure craft cruising.

Use of Hills and General Rural Areas for Special Activities
Hiking, climbing, caving, camping, skiing, motor cycle scrambling, picnicking and sightseeing.

Use of General Coastal Areas
Picnicking and sightseeing, day visits.

Use of Roads
Motoring for pleasure, rallying, cycling.

Ungrouped
Tennis, golf, swimming at baths, bowls, putting, croquet, shooting, athletics, roller and ice skating, netball, basketball.

By way of contrast the California Public Outdoor Recreation Plan[67] lists the main outdoor recreational pursuits as: use of scenic roads and waterways, gliding, visits to historic sites, picnicking, camping, riding, hiking, swimming, boating, fishing, hunting, winter activities and golf. These activities must be considered against the vastly different and widely varying climate, land form and natural vegetation characteristics as compared with Great Britain.

Range of Recreational Projects

The scale of recreational facilities can vary from a single park bench located beside a walkway to a great recreational complex of the type planned for the Lea Valley. The scale of expenditure is very high indeed with the larger projects, ranging from £1 million for the Billingham Forum, built in 1962 as a multi-purpose building to house a wide range of activities,[68] to the £30 million scheme envisaged in the Civic Trust report on the Lea Valley regional park.[69]

The Lea Valley scheme covers a 32 km strip from West Ham to Ware. The southern end consists of a 6 km stretch in the heavily built-up area; further north the great chain of Metropolitan Board reservoirs extending for 10 km from Walthamstow to Enfield lock; and beyond them, the gravel digging area which runs for 16 km up to Ware. Within the total strip sixteen separate areas can be identified—each could become a park with its own distinctive character. The combined area reaches the staggering total of 2400 hectares, which is more than sixty-six per cent of the total of existing public open space in the former County of London. In time it will also be possible to create a series of water parks from the worked-out gravel pits, which could rival the Broads. Footpaths, cycleways and bridlepaths can run through the whole valley, linking the urban parks, the reservoirs and the countryside.

It is interesting to examine and compare New Town recreational proposals. The proposals for Stevenage, the first of the first generation New Towns, provided for a town park on the highest plateau within the designated area and a golf course on its outskirts. Playgrounds were planned for each neighbourhood, ranging from small enclosures for kindergarten age children to larger play areas incorporating natural hollows and small copses for the older children. In addition, the proposals included tennis courts, bowling greens and football and cricket pitches.[70] In 1961, the London County Council published its proposals for Hook.[71] These exciting plans provided for the siting of the major open spaces to form a continuous belt around the town. This green belt incorporated a chain of new lakes, the largest lake for sailing and rowing and the smaller lakes for swimming and angling. Provision was also to be made for playing fields, playgrounds and allotments.

The later New Town proposals for Milton Keynes[72] with an ultimate design population of 250,000, recognised the need for parkland 'lungs' in the city. The report proposed the creation of a linear park running through the heart of the new city, embracing the Grand Union Canal and the River Ouzel and other streams. Along the streams a number of small lakes will be formed, which can be used for boating and other forms of recreation. Thus the later New Town proposals attempt to cater for the increasing demand for water based recreation.

The published plan for the development of Greater Peterborough[73] incorporates four townships, each of about 30,000 population surrounding a 680 hectare country park situated on the banks of the River Nene. Controlled excavation of substantial gravel deposits could provide the opportunity to create a large lake for sailing, boating and fishing. The Nene Valley is immensely rich in archaeological remains and an excellent opportunity is presented for formal and informal study, including planned walks between excavated sites and easy instruction of students, sightseers and ramblers.

Some indication of the immense scale and range of outdoor recreational facilities can be obtained by examining the American outdoor recreation report[31] which took several hundred people 3 years to compile. Twenty-seven study reports were also prepared and these are listed in table 1.5.

TABLE 1.5

OUTDOOR RECREATION RESOURCES REVIEW COMMISSION STUDY REPORTS

Subject	Factual	Treatment Interpretative	Both
Demand	19. National survey	22. Trends	20. Participation
Supply	1. Public areas (areas and uses)		3. Wilderness
	2. Public areas (location)		4. Shorelines
			10. Water
	8. Potential sites		11. Private areas
Demand and supply			5. Quality
			6. Hunting
			7. Fishing
			9. Alaska
Agencies	14. State directory	24. Economic studies	18. Abroad
			12. Financing
			13. Federal agencies
			15. Open Space
			16. Land acquisition
			17. Multiple use
			25. Public expenditures
Projections			21. Metropolitan regions
			23. Economics, population, etc.
			26. Demand
Literature			27. Literature survey

Numbers of Participants

Fifty million people living on 150 800 km², owning over 7 million cars; over 30 million holidays a year involving an expenditure of £500 million; national parks covering nine per cent of the country—these are a few indications of the problems of planning for leisure in this densely populated small country.[74]

Burton[75] in 1964 produced an excellent comparative schedule showing the proportions of the total population of America, Sweden and Britain participating in selected outdoor recreational pursuits at least once a year, indicating that this country has a long way to go to approach the level of interest reached in Sweden and the United States (see table 1.6).

19

TABLE 1.6

PARTICIPATION IN OUTDOOR RECREATIONAL PURSUITS IN
UNITED STATES, SWEDEN AND BRITAIN

	U.S.A. (1959–60) %	*Sweden (1963)* %	*Britain (1964)* %
Driving for pleasure	70	79	56*
Swimming	45	65	25§
Fishing	38	41	7
Camping	15	25	6
Hiking	19	—	8
Tennis	—	6	7§

* This figure refers to Whitsun holiday period 1963

§ Estimates. A rule denotes figures not available

Sources: ORRRC, *Outdoor Recreation for America*. Commission to Review Resources for Outdoor Recreation, *Outdoor Recreation in Sweden*. British Travel Association, *A Survey of Whitsun Holiday Travel 1963*. Countryside in 1970 Second Conference, *Report of Study Group No. 6, Outdoor Recreation: Active and Passive*, Annex 1

TABLE 1.7

LEISURE AND OUTDOOR RECREATION STATISTICS 1951–66

Statistics	*1951*	*1961*	*1966*
Camping: membership of the Camping Club	13 900	61 000	101 000 (1967)
Caravanning: membership of the Caravan Club	11 000	44 000	90 000 (1967)
Fishing: membership of National Federation of Anglers	—	—	350 000 (1965)
Sailing: number of clubs affiliated to the Royal Yachting Association	300 (1952)	1 000 (1962)	1 280 (1964)
	(estimated that more than 500 000 have practical interest)		
Canoeing: membership of British Canoe Club		35 000 (1964)	50 000
Rowing: membership of Amateur Rowing Association		30 000 (1964)	(estimated 270 000 craft of all kinds in Britain in 1967, increasing by 8 per cent annually)
Underwater Swimming: membership of the British Sub Aqua Club		6 000	8 000
Water Skiing: membership of British Water Ski Federation			60 000–70 000
Riding: Membership of Pony Club		20 000 (1962)	29 000 (1964)
	(estimated that over 150 000 people ride)		
Cycling: membership of Cyclist's Touring Club	35 000 (1952)	25 000 (1962)	22 000 (1967)
National History Council for Nature: estimate of active naturalists		100 000	270 000
Wild fowling: membership of Wildfowl Trust	3 000	5 800	8 000
Birdwatching: adult membership of Royal Society for Protection of Birds	6 500	14 200	35 500

These statistics show that, with the possible exception of tennis, Britain has plenty of leeway to make up in participation in outdoor recreational activities, even allowing for the longer periods of hot, dry weather enjoyed by the other two countries.

Table 1.7 contains a summary of statistics relating to leisure and outdoor recreation (1951–66) prepared by Hookway.[38] It gives some interesting information on numbers and trends, although it must be borne in mind that these numbers refer only to members affiliated to the main clubs and there are numerous participants who are not.

REFERENCES

1. KAPLAN, M. (1960). *Leisure in America—a social inquiry,* J. Wiley, N.Y.
2. CLAWSON, M. and KNETSCH, J. L. (1966). *Economics of Outdoor Recreation,* John Hopkins Press, Baltimore
3. BUTLER, G. B. (1959). *Introduction to Community Recreation,* McGraw-Hill
4. MEYER, H. D. and BRIGHTBILL, C. K. (1956). *Community Recreation—a guide to its organisation,* Prentice-Hall, N.J.
5. SAPORA, A. V. and MITCHELL, E. D. (1961). *The Theory of Play and Recreation,* Ronald Press, N.Y.
6. BRIGHTBILL, C. K. (1960). *The Challenge of Leisure,* Prentice-Hall, N.J.
7. DOMENACH, J. M. Loisir et travail. *Esprit,* **87.274,** (1959), 1103–1110
8. ANDERSON, N. (1961). *Work and Leisure,* Routledge and Kegan Paul
9. DUMAZEDIER, J., FIEDMANN, G. and MORIN, E. Les loisirs dans la vie quotidienne. *Encyclopédie Française,* **T.XIV 56.6**
10. MEAD, M. The patterns of leisure in contemporary American society. *Annals of the American Academy of Political and Social Science,* **313,** (1957), 13
11. MCDONALD, A. *Sport, Health and Leisure. Proc. Fitness and Training Section of Ergonomics Research Society, Spring Conference, Manchester University, (April 1966)*
12. MCINTOSH, P. C. (1963). *Sport in Society,* Watts
13. WOLFENDEN COMMITTEE. (1960). *Sport and the Community,* Central Council of Physical Recreation
14. SILLITOE, K. K. (1969). *Planning for Leisure,* H.M.S.O.
15. BRITISH TRAVEL ASSOCIATION/UNIVERSITY OF KEELE. *Pilot National Recreation Survey : Report No. 1,* (1967)
16. BRITISH BROADCASTING CORPORATION. *The People's Activities,* (1965)
17. CLAWSON, M. and KNETSCH, J. L. Outdoor recreation research: Some concepts and suggested areas of study. *Natural Resources Journal,* **3.2,** (1963), 252–254
18. SOULE, G. (1955). *Time for Living,* Viking Press, N.Y.
19. DAVIDSON, M. B. (1951). P. 78 in *Life in America,* Boston
20. MARTIN, A. R. Live-in the all. *American Recreation Society Bulletin,* **9.3,** (1957), 8
21. GUTKIND, E. A., (Ed.). *Creative Demobilisation,* (1944), 66
22. HOUSEMAN, J. (1950). *Battle over Television,* Harper
23. *Christian Science Monitor,* (22 November, 1957)
24. ERNST, M. L. (1956). P. 7 in *New Sources of Energy, Leisure and World Culture. Proc. International Recreation Congress, N.Y.,* National Recreation Association
25. CHAPMAN, F. M. (1960). *Recreational Activities for the Handicapped,* Ronald Press, N.Y.
26. KLEEMEIER, R. W., (Ed.) (1961). *Aging and Leisure,* Oxford University Press, New York
27. OPINION RESEARCH CORPORATION. The public appraises movies. *A Survey for the Motion Picture Association of America,* New Jersey, (1957)
28. CLAWSON, M. (1963). *Land and Water for Recreation,* Rand McNally, Chicago
29. BRIGHTBILL, C. K. (1961). *Man and Leisure,* Prentice-Hall
30. DOWER, M. Fourth Wave. *Architects' Journal,* 20 January, 1965
31. OUTDOOR RECREATION RESOURCES REVIEW COMMISSION. *Outdoor Recreation for America.* Washington D.C., (1962)
32. TOWN AND COUNTRY PLANNING ASSOCIATION. A policy for countryside recreation in England and Wales. *Town and Country Planning,* (December, 1965), 473
33. RUBINSTEIN, D. and SPEAKMAN, C. (1969). *Leisure, Transport and the Countryside.* Fabian research series 277, (1969)
34. MOGRIDGE, J. H. The prediction of car ownership. *Journal of Transport Economics and Policy,* **1.1,** (1967), 52–74
35. COUNTRYSIDE COMMISSION. *Coastal Recreation and Holidays, Special Study Report Vol. 1,* H.M.S.O., (1969)
36. BURTON, T. L. and WIBBERLEY, G. P. (1965). *Outdoor Recreation in the British Countryside,* Wye College, University of London
37. BOW GROUP. *A Better Country.* Conservative Political Centre, (1966)
38. HOOKWAY, R. J. S. (1968). *Planning for Leisure and Recreation,* Countryside Commission
39. 'COUNTRYSIDE IN 1970' Study Group No. 6. *Outdoor Recreation : Active and Passive.* Second conference, (1965)
40. NORFOLK COUNTY COUNCIL, *Report on the Norfolk Holiday Industry,* (1964)
41. BURTON, T. L. (1967). *The Classification of Recreation Demands and Supplies : Research Memo No. 1,* University of Birmingham, Centre for Urban and Regional Studies

21

42. BURTON, T. L. and NOAD, P. A. (1968). *Recreation Research Methods,* University of Birmingham, Centre for Urban and Regional Studies

43. CULLINGWORTH, J. B. *The Classification of Recreational Activities*—private communication, (1965)

44. CLAWSON, M., HELD, R. B. and STODDARD, C. H. (1962). *Land for the Future,* John Hopkins Press, Baltimore

45. WOLFE, R. I., Perspective on outdoor recreation—a bibliographical survey. *Geographical Review,* **44.2,** (1964)

46. PERLOFF, H. S. and WINGO, L. Trends in American living and outdoor recreation. *Outdoor Recreation Resources Review Commission Study Report 22,* Washington D.C., (1962)

47. GLOUCESTERSHIRE COUNTY COUNCIL. *Outdoor Recreation and the Gloucestershire Countryside,* (1968)

48. COPPOCK, J. T. The recreational use of land and water in rural Britain. *Tijdshrift voor Economische en Sociale Geographie,* **57.3,** (1966)

49. WISCONSIN DEPARTMENT OF RESOURCE DEVELOPMENT. (1962). P. 4 in *Recreation in Wisconsin,* Madison

50. FISCHER, W. F. (1962). Methods of evaluating lands for recreation use. *Recreation in Wild Life Management.* University of California, Agricultural Experimental Station

51. BROCKMAN, C. F. *Recreational Use of Wild Lands,* Toronto, (1959)

52. TAYLOR, G. D. An approach to the inventory of recreational lands. *The Canadian Geographer,* **9.2,** (1965)

53. SPORTS COUNCIL. (1968). *Planning for Sport.* Central Council of Physical Recreation

54. CULLEN, P. Whither industrial recreation now? *Sport and Recreation,* **7.4,** (1966)

55. MOLYNEUX, D. D. Working for recreation. *Journal of Royal Town Planning Institute,* **54.4,** (1968)

56. MINISTRY OF HOUSING AND LOCAL GOVERNMENT, Public Expenditure—Miscellaneous Schemes. *Circular No. 31/66*

57. BONSEY, C. The rising tide of outdoor recreation. *County Councils Gazette,* **61.11,** (1968)

58. WEST MIDLANDS SPORTS COUNCIL, TECHNICAL PANEL. *Regional Recreation,* (1966)

59. DAVIDSON, J. M. The Countryside Commission. *Proceedings of Conference on Recreation in the Countryside, University of Loughborough,* (1969)

60. STAFFORDSHIRE COUNTY COUNCIL AND STOKE-ON-TRENT, PLANNING DEPARTMENTS. *Planning for Recreation,* (1966)

61. GREAVES, J. (1968). *National Parks and Access to the Countryside and Coast : Trends in Research.* Countryside Commission

62. BUCHANAN, C. and PARTNERS. (1966). *New Forest Survey : Supplementary Volume 2 of South Hampshire Study,* H.M.S.O.

63. WIBBERLEY, G. P. The British countryside in the year 2000. *Annual Conference of Council for the Protection of Rural Wales,* (1969)

64. WHITE HOUSE CONFERENCE ON AGING. *Aging in the States.* Washington D.C., (1961)

65. WILLEY, F. T. Leisure in the countryside. *Annual Conference of Royal Institution of Chartered Surveyors,* (1966)

66. NORTH WEST SPORTS COUNCIL. *The Case for a Leisure Activities Survey,* (1967)

67. CALIFORNIA PUBLIC OUTDOOR RECREATION PLAN COMMITTEE. *California Public Outdoor Recreation Plan,* (1960)

68. PINCHES, J. W. Recreation. *Sport and Recreation,* (January, 1969)

69. CIVIC TRUST. *A Lea Valley Regional Park,* (1964)

70. STEVENAGE DEVELOPMENT CORPORATION. *The New Town of Stevenage,* (1949)

71. LONDON COUNTY COUNCIL. *The Planning of a New Town,* (1961)

72. LLEWELLYN-DAVIES, WEEKS, FORESTIER-WALKER AND BOR. *Milton Keynes : Interim Report,* (1968)

73. PARK ADMINISTRATION, Town expansion. *Park Administration,* **33.11,** (1968), 25

74. CULLINGWORTH, J. B. Planning for leisure. *Urban Studies,* **1.1,** (1964)

75. BURTON, T. L. Outdoor recreation in America, Sweden and Britain. *Town and Country Planning,* (October, 1966), 459

76. PHILLIPS, A. A. C. (1970). *Research into Planning for Recreation,* Countryside Commission

77. DOWER, M. Leisure—its impact on man and the land. *Geography,* **55.3,** (1970)

78. MERCER, D. C. The geography of leisure—a contemporary growth-point. *Geography,* **55.3,** (1970)

79. COUNTRYSIDE RECREATION RESEARCH ADVISORY GROUP. (1970). *Countryside Recreation Glossary,* Countryside Commission

80. ROBERTS, K. Sociology and recreation planning. *Recreation News Supplement 4.* Countryside Commission, (1971)

81. DOWER, M. General Philosophy of Recreation. *Proceedings of Conference on Outdoor Recreation,* Department of Surveying, Trent Polytechnic (1972)

2 LAND USE PROBLEMS

THIS CHAPTER EXAMINES the problems encountered in using a fixed area of land for the satisfactory accommodation of a wide range of uses. Intensity of recreational use, multiple use techniques and open space standards are investigated, and consideration is given to the need for the reclamation of derelict areas and conservation of areas of special natural beauty and interest.

CHANGING LAND USE REQUIREMENTS

Land Use Patterns

Clawson, Held and Stoddard[1] have judged our present day basic concern to be the conflict between the demands of an expanding economy and a fixed area of land. Wibberley[2] has shown how Britain has a high man/land ratio and a pattern of increasing old and new uses. The area of England and Wales is approximately 15 million hectares. As against a 1971 population of 48.59 million this gives a man/land ratio of about 320 persons per km². In the year 2000 with a population probably around 66 million, this ratio will have changed to over 430 persons per km². Comparable present day man/land ratios for some other countries are 350 persons per km² for the Netherlands, 250 for Japan and twenty for the United States.

Land is unique in that each parcel or plot has a specific location with its own particular geography. Height above sea level; slope; latitude and longitude; soil and subsoil; rainfall; sunshine; temperature; wind exposure; drainage; and distance from other places—all vary from one plot of land to another. Some of these variables can be partially controlled by the use of other resources—capital and labour, but there is no homogeneity or easy interchangeability—each site has its own peculiar characteristics.[2]

Furthermore, many of the expanding uses are detrimental to the landscape. This aspect is well illustrated by Man[3]—

More vehicles use our inadequate roads to convey our increasing population, as well as foreign visitors, longer distances from home for recreation. Tourism is rightly a thriving industry, yet destinations become more and more congested. Pylons and their network of power lines increase in numbers and height too. More and varied chemicals are needed to improve land productivity with increasing threats to all kinds of wild life; the once clean rivers, seashores and air have all become increasingly polluted by effluents, oil and waste. Houses, chalets, caravans and camping sites want more and more land; too often their permitted locations have detracted from the lovely scenery which residents, old and new, wanted to enjoy.

Industrial expansion, employment outlets, additional accommodation are essential national requirements, but where should they be, in these congested Islands and in what proportion, should be included in an overall master plan.

Dower[4] has drawn attention to the gross deficiencies in urban areas and the inability of such areas to meet the basic needs of their residents:

In the older towns, few houses have adequate gardens, and those that exist are polluted by soot; parking the car gets more and more difficult; often there is no room to have pets or to mend a motor cycle. Playgrounds and playing fields are few and often terribly dull, small open spaces exist only where the Victorians chose to provide them: yet bombed sites still fester more than 25 years after the blitz, and unwanted allotments lie derelict.

In the newer suburbs, the gardens are adequate, sometimes the garages also. But where are the pubs, the clubs, the meeting rooms? Where, in the smaller towns, are the social centres that people increasingly need? Where are the sports halls, the all-weather playing surfaces, the decent changing rooms, the swimming baths? Only in the New Towns and one or two enterprising boroughs do the facilities begin to match the demand.

The changing pattern of urban growth has been well portrayed by a number of writers. Jones[5] refers to the general broad pattern of growth; decay; rebuilding; the central business and shopping core; and the outer residential suburb.

On the other hand, Chapin and Weiss[6] foresee that in a 25 to 40-year period scientific advances and technological change may profoundly affect patterns of urban development; and the shifting character of life styles and consumer tastes in large segments of an increasingly affluent society may further complicate the problem of prediction. These writers describe how land development is the consequence of many decisions and implementing actions of both a public and private nature. They illustrate by giving examples of how priming actions often trigger secondary actions which, taken together, produce the total pattern of land development. Thus, an industrial or commercial location decision may set in motion a whole chain of other decisions and actions, for example, location decision of households, firms and institutions. Alternatively, a highway location decision, a decision on an extension of water or sewerage facilities, a decision on building a new school, or a combined series of decisions of this nature can serve to prime such secondary decisions and actions. A priming action has two main characteristics—the structuring effect on the distribution of land development and the timing effect in fixing the sequence of development.

Best and Coppock[7] have traced the changing pattern of urban development in this country from the compact towns of the industrial revolution to the more open development of inter-war years assisted by the increased mobility of the urban population through improved public transport services. These developments now require extending to include the more compact and higher density residential layouts of the last decade.

Ciriacy-Wantrup[8] has investigated the changes in the competition for land arising from urbanisation and industrialisation and has shown how at the margin of urban-industrial development, agriculture is quickly priced out of the land market. He also shows how there has been a great increase in the demand for various types of outdoor recreation in California since the last war but that this demand often has complementary relations to the demand for land by agriculture, forestry and grazing. Another important implication which follows from the increasing competition for land for urban uses is the irreversibility of the results, so different from merely replacing one agricultural use by another.

Chisholm[9] asserts that the central problems in the economics of land use are those of location and of competition between alternative users and uses to command each particular site, although he omits to include the influence of legislation.

Norton[10] has attempted to sub-divide the main determinants of land use patterns into two distinct groups:

(1) Intrinsic factors in the form of physical attributes—area, position, soil, climate and so on.

(2) Cultural factors and the many ways in which man can modify the natural state.

Urban Land Use

Best[12] has shown that housing is easily the greatest urban land use, and in the New Towns of England and Wales it accounts for just over half of the total urban area. This is a higher percentage than in the older towns where the areas zoned for residential use account for forty-three to forty-five per cent. Table 2.1 shows that open space is the

TABLE 2.1

PROPORTIONATE COMPOSITION OF URBAN AREAS

	Housing %	Industry %	Open space %	Education %	Four main uses %	Residual uses %
New Towns—London region	50.5	9.3	17.4	8.9	86.1	13.9
New Towns—Provincial	50.2	7.7	25.3	7.4	90.6	9.4
New Towns—England & Wales	50.4	8.9	19.3	8.6	87.2	12.8
New Towns—Scotland	38.8	14.1	24.2	7.7	84.8	15.2
New Towns—Great Britain	48.9	9.6	19.9	8.4	86.8	13.2
County boroughs (79)	43.9	9.4	19.6	6.1	79.0	21.0
Large town map areas (186 over) (10 000 pop.)	44.7	8.9	18.8	6.5	78.9	21.1

Source :   BEST, R.H., *Land for New Towns*

second main use in urban areas, although there is a surprisingly wide variation in planned provision between the various groupings of New Towns but a very high correlation between the average New Town and old county borough.

Furthermore, following the recommendations of the Ministry of Housing and Local Government,[13] the more recent New Town proposals show a noticeable reduction in space standards. This is particularly so with housing, where the newly planned residential areas have an average net residential density of about 8 hectares per 1000 population, which is under half the provision recommended by the New Towns Committee.[14]

Best[15] has calculated the area of agricultural land in this country transferred to urban and other uses, from which the figures in table 2.2 have been computed and converted to hectares.

TABLE 2.2

ANNUAL TRANSFERS OF AGRICULTURAL LAND TO URBAN AND OTHER USES IN ENGLAND AND WALES

Transfers to : Period	Building and general constructional development ha	Sports grounds ha	Total urban area ha	Service departments and miscellaneous ha	Allotments, woodlands and forestry development ha
1927–34	15 300	3 600	18 900	500	n.a.
1934–39	20 000	4 300	24 300	6 000	n.a.
1945–50	13 200	3 600	16 800	+15 000	7 900
1950–60	13 600	1 300	14 900	+ 2 100	8 700
1960–65	14 200	1 250	15 450	+ 1 000	6 500

+ indicates net gains to agricultural area

ha = hectare

These figures show a continuous reduction in the area of land devoted to agricultural use but at a much reduced rate compared with the pre-war trend. During the wars land was acquired by service departments at a rate exceeding 40 000 hectares per annum, and in the post-war years half of this has been returned to agricultural use.

The annual figures for the post-war years produced by Best show a close association between economic trends and transfers of agricultural land to urban use. The stop-go oscillation in economic controls has been reflected by a marked fluctuation in urban demands on land from year to year.

Table 2.3 prepared by Best compares past and estimated future growth of the urban area in England and Wales and the United States, but with the unit of area changed to the hectare.

TABLE 2.3

PAST AND ESTIMATED FUTURE GROWTH OF THE URBAN AREA
IN ENGLAND AND WALES AND THE UNITED STATES

Year	England and Wales		United States*	
	million ha	%	million ha	%
1900	0.8	5.4	9.0	1.2
1910	—	—	10.7	1.4
1920	0.9	5.9	13.1	1.7
1930	1.1	7.0	14.5	1.9
1940	1.3	8.6	14.9	1.9
1950	1.5	9.7	16.8	2.2
1960	1.8	10.8	19.0	2.5
1970	1.8	11.9	—	—
1980	2.0	13.2	24.2	3.2
1990	2.1	14.3	—	—
2000	2.3	15.4	30.3	3.9

* estimate prepared by Resources for the Future

The density of urban development in the United States is much less than in Great Britain and this partially accounts for the much greater expansion of urban area per decade in the United States. The rate of growth is, however, remarkably constant in both countries. Jones[16] has pointed out that Best's estimates are based on the assumption that we will continue to build at approximately the densities of New Towns, but that this is open to question.

The figures in table 2.4, extracted from a schedule prepared by Clark,[17] indicate that the open space provision in our New Towns is quite generous by American standards and the Cumbernauld residential density is extremely high.

TABLE 2.4

URBAN LAND USE (m²/person) m² = square metres

	Whole developed area	Residential	Industry	Parks and playgrounds
Averages of US cities				
central cities over 250 000 pop.	204	82	18	17
central cities under 50 000 pop.	404	159	23	21
satellite cities over 25 000 pop.	234	94	32	8
British New Towns (Best)	222	109	22	44
Cumbernauld New Town	143	47	27	47

Impact of Changing Use Pattern on Agriculture

It has already been shown that agriculture continues to lose land in two main directions—some of its poorest land to afforestation at a rate of about 8000 hectares a year, and some of its better land to urban uses at a rate of about 14 000–16 000 hectares per year. The latter rate of transfer being directly influenced by the density of the urban development.

Wibberley[2] estimates that by the year 2000 about seventy-six per cent of the total land surface may be available for agricultural use, but British agriculture will tend to adjust itself to the area of land left for its use. Increases in population and rising real incomes create demand pressures for more land in agriculture, but improvements in the physical efficiency of food production economise on land area. Again, if imports of food products are increased, home land can be saved for other uses. If pressures lead to a decrease in food imports, more home land will be pressed into more intensive service. Edwards[18] has also referred to the possible development of synthetic foodstuffs.

Jones[16] holds the view that the present average increase in agricultural productivity of 1.3 per cent per annum will more than offset the land likely to be needed for urban uses. This view is supported by Wibberley[19] and Edwards[18] provided that the choice of new urban sites is made with sensible discrimination and, in particular, that development is not concentrated to an unnecessary extent on our most highly productive farmland. The same authors asserted in 1971 'that the overall land use position of this country should not be difficult in terms of the availability of land for all major users'.[11]

Recreational Land Use

'Pleasure and enjoyment should be regarded as a use and among the most essential uses of land', said Lord Holford in his address to the National Trust in February 1963. As human productivity increases and labour inputs decline, the advanced industrial nations seem to be moving inevitably towards societies based rather on leisure than labour. Not all leisure is spent recreationally, nor does all recreation express itself in demand for space and facilities; but the outdoor pursuits which are probably the chief growth sector are prodigal in their demand for land, and they lead also to difficult problems of management where recreation is involved in the multiple use of land.[20]

There are regional differences in recreational patterns which seem to be mainly geared to access. For example northern England has a particular interest in moorland recreation, the south and west of the country in sailing and the Midlands in fishing.

The majority of land use studies give little information on the amount of land in recreational use and there are many instances, particularly in country areas, where recreation is a supplementary use to the main activity which could be agriculture, forestry or even water supply. Burton and Wibberley[21] estimated that in 1962–63 approximately eight per cent of total rural land was in effective recreational use, although this was not equally distributed over the various regions. As one moves from the north-west to the south-east of England, the area of recreational land per head decreases. This can possibly be accounted for by the better quality of land and, to a lesser extent, the higher population of south-east England. Often the lack of facilities stems from the traditional resistance of the landowner, public or private, to recreation as a secondary activity—a problem not of shortage of land but of attitude.[22]

LAND USE PLANNING

Land Use Planning Objectives

A universal interest has developed in land use planning and the determinants of land use.[23] There is also an increasing awareness of the advisability of forward planning and of the need to overhaul and improve our predictive techniques.[24]

The author once wrote that town and country planning is necessary to ensure that all development is coordinated with an eye to the future, and carried out in such a way to assist in producing a community environment that will advance human welfare in health, well-being and safety.[25] Many defects are apt to arise from unplanned development —waste, congestion, disharmony, undesirable mixing of incompatible uses, lack of social services and unnecessary loss of good agricultural land. Chapin[26] also sees the need for the city planner to view land use in the context of 'health, safety and general welfare' and generally to ensure that development is in the public interest. Hoyes[27] expresses the view that the broad objective of planning is to ensure that land is put to the best use from the point of view of the community, and to secure a proper balance between competing demands for land. Furthermore, the regulation and control of the use—in urban areas—of land resources within proprietary land units is necessary, in order to prevent the repetition of the undesirable mixture of land uses which has emerged over time in towns and cities.[28]

The World Health Organisation[29] has shown the importance of thinking of the metropolitan area as a coherent whole and to recognise the interplay of social, political and economic factors, which must be taken into consideration. This organisation defined planning objectives as 'a model of an intended future situation' and 'a programme of action and predetermined co-ordination', illustrating the dynamic nature of the process and of the need to improve human conditions.

Arvill (Boote)[30] has established certain principles in land use planning—the unity of the environment (fusion of town and country), comprehensiveness (controlling many activities, often conflicting) and quality of the environment. He also contended that planning must accept that there is always a limit on the resources available and so must actively encourage management and development—public and private—to accept and work for strategic goals. Various writers emphasise the need for land use plans to take full account of social and economic factors, with the general objective of maximising social net benefit or public interest.[8, 31–33]

Planning the countryside of Britain is largely a matter of conservation of natural resources. The basic objective is to make full use of our minerals, soil, water and wild life, while ensuring that we do not allow exploitation to endanger their future supply. Planning our towns, on the other hand, is fundamentally concerned with the development of land resources with buildings, roads and other urban services, to accommodate changing demands.[34]

Up until the last decade it was generally considered that land use planning objectives could be achieved by a control mechanism which operated at local planning authority level, but since then it has become accepted that many of the activities we want to influence take place over an area larger than that administered by a single authority. Hence regional and sub-regional planning has been undertaken and there is a pressing need for a larger degree of national planning.[35]

Willhelm[36] has described how in land use planning we control land use and that in controlling land use we are controlling people. Hence it is vitally important that the public is permitted to participate actively in the planning process—the subject investigated by the Skeffington Committee. The use of a series of seminars in the first stages of preparation of the plan for Milton Keynes New Town is a practical illustration of its application.[37]

Finally, it is interesting to examine the geographical and historical reasons for the differences between British and American patterns of urbanisation. The town planning movement in Britain had its roots in a reaction against urban growth as represented by the nineteenth century industrial town, and it sought an orderly countryside and contained towns which could not spread across the surrounding country, engulfing land unchecked. In the United States a different attitude is adopted towards land use. The vastness of the North American continent and the tendency of its inhabitants to move on periodically from one location to the next has resulted in successive exploitation and abandonment. This has given rise to the expression 'God's own junkyard', describing many Americans' attitude to land—a resource that can be used, even squandered, with little thought for the future.[38]

Economic Aspects of Land Use Planning

The economic theory which had competitively established price as its keystone, concluded that since consumer desire and producer capacity tended towards a balance at any moment in time, the most efficient allocation of resources was ever present through market forces. In certain spheres, especially in the use of land, this conclusion is suspect. The analysis is too narrow as it ignores a whole host of side effects. Furthermore many forms of land development are relatively inflexible—for example, land developed with houses is not readily returned to agriculture—and there is no opportunity to correct the adverse effects of bad decisions.[27]

Lean and Goodall[39] postulate that, subject to certain provisos, if town planning leads to higher land values than would exist without it then a better or more efficient use of resources has been achieved, based on rent theory. This is a dubious hypothesis as the planner may artificially reduce the supply of land for a particular kind of use and thus force up its price, putting the owner in a monopolistic situation. To ensure the best use of resources the economic consequences of alternative courses of action should be considered, although non-economic implications frequently deserve attention.[40] Difficulties arise in attempting to place monetary values on non revenue-producing public sector development.

Furthermore, the fragmentation of the ownership of land may prevent land being used for the most efficient purpose. Some public urban land uses such as roads, parks, schools and sewage disposal works will be non revenue-producing, but the profitable uses often depend on the non revenue-producing uses. Urban planning can, by control and reorganisation of both types of use, lead to a more efficient use of urban resources. If urban planning increases the accessibility within an urban area, then this again is likely to increase efficiency and land values. Hence the economic approach to the study of urban land use patterns is an important one. The patterns that emerge are the sum total of a large number of individual appreciations of locational values. Successful planning must be based on an intimate knowledge of the economic forces at work within cities.

Through planning we aim to produce a new geography, a better distribution of activity and land use related to contemporary social and economic needs; yet we must remain fully aware that needs change more quickly than physical forms. Geographers, in their turn, must be concerned with the effects of planning decisions upon patterns of land use.[41]

Mention should perhaps be made of the Land Commission Act, 1967, which established a Land Commission with wide powers of acquisition, disposal and management of land and who were empowered to collect a levy on betterment (development value), although it was subsequently abolished in 1970. The main aims of the Act were stated by the Minister as:

(1) To secure that a substantial part of the development value created by the community returns to the community.

(2) To secure that the burden of the cost of land for essential purposes is reduced.

(3) To secure that the right land is available at the right time for the implementation of national, regional and local plans.

In practice, the price of building land rose appreciably and there was an acute shortage of building land in various parts of the country.[42-44] Betterment levy introduced in 1967 and abolished in 1970 was a modified successor to the 100 per cent 'development charge' introduced by the Town and Country Planning Act, 1947, and abolished in 1953.

Recreational Planning

The supply of land in Britain is fixed but the country's population is growing and the planner is continually faced with the choice between alternative land policies. The planner must accommodate five basic needs in land use planning—the need for places to work, places to live, need for food, recreation and communications.[45]

In planning for recreation, the planner must know the needs of recreationalists and the capacity of local land and water resources. He acts as an intermediary, trying to cater for the recreationalists' needs by providing the physical basis for recreation.[4] Not only is it necessary to quantify and project current levels of recreational demand into the future but also to predict what kinds of recreational activities will be popular in 10 to 20 years' time.

Planning for outdoor recreation should be an integral element in local land use planning. Through long-term planning, schedules of priorities and investment requirements can be prepared. The public must be convinced of the need for taking full advantage of existing public areas and facilities, and acquiring new ones. Areas can often serve several purposes in addition to recreation. A marsh can serve as a sponge for flood protection, a wild life sanctuary, a place for nature study and as a visual contrast to congested areas. Preservation of stream valleys can provide valuable recreation areas.[46]

The usefulness of land and water for outdoor recreation hinges on three main factors: proximity to population; physical and legal accessibility; and suitability for recreation purposes.

There is a need for recognition of the concept that recreation is a legitimate form of land use, as are the sister uses of agriculture, forestry and wild life.[47] Yet, at the same time, the increasing demand for space could damage the environment—both urban and rural—unless we plan well with taste, efficiency and imagination.[48] Land for recreational use must compete with the more basic economic needs.[49] Indeed, the total complex of recreational needs must be reconciled against the claims of other forms of land use, for recreation rarely has sole rights to the spaces it uses.[20]

It is likely that public opinion will stress the use of land of low productive capacity, and particularly derelict or unused land, for recreation. Unfortunately, unsuitability for other uses does not necessarily mean suitability for recreation. The land may be wrongly located; too small in extent; have bad access; be too costly to adapt; be too expensive to service and manage; or its use for recreation might introduce conflicts with other land uses.[22]

LAND VALUES

Land Value Determinants

While various users are in competition for sites, the sites vary considerably in their suitability for different purposes. The value of a site depends upon three main considerations: physical, locational and legal consents as to use. The prices of sites are very much influenced by the use to which they can be put. For example, in 1962, Peters[50] gave the average price of vacant farms as £134 per acre (£333 per hectare). At the same time, Stone[51] calculated the average price for residential sites at £5000 per acre (£12 400 per hectare). Both prices have increased considerably since 1962.

Wendt[52] has stated a general model for determination of land values: land value equals aggregate gross revenues minus total expected costs, all divided by capitalisation rate.

Revenues are influenced by the investor's expectation of the size of the market; income spent for various urban services; the competitive pull of the urban area; supply of competitive urban land; and prospective investment in public improvements. Expected costs are the sum of local property taxes; operating costs; interest on capital; and depreciation allowances. The capitalisation rate is affected by interest rates, allowances for anticipated risk and expectations concerning capital gains.

According to land economics theory, these factors are taken into account in the property market. Users of land bid for sites in accordance with what will maximise their profits and minimise their costs. Land users in retail businesses and services tend to bid for space at the highest prices, and land best suited to these activities shows the highest value.[26]

In practice, the market prices of the developed real properties determine the land values (the residual figure in the developer's budget which he can afford to pay for the site). Land values are influenced by a variety of factors, such as accessibility of the land and its complementary nature. If there is a shortage of land available for a specific use, prices will tend to rise until further land is transferred to this use, unless land use planning frustrates it.

Values are best established by reference to the price paid for comparable properties in the market.[53] In practice, there are few really comparable sites or buildings and there is often little information available on property transactions. Generally, auction prices are accepted as the truest indicators of market prices.[54]

Effect of Town Planning on Land Values

According to the Uthwatt Report[55] the effect of town planning is to shift land values but not destroy them. Planning schemes frequently cause a redistribution of values, where the permitted land uses differ from the existing patterns of land use. If, for example, a town map limited the supply of land for residential purposes, and permitted high densities on the outskirts and lower densities in inner districts, then the land on the outskirts would in all probability have a higher value than that nearer the centre—there would have been a shift of values. Where the shift in land values, caused by a redistribution of the profit uses of land, settles, will partly depend on the planned redistribution on the non-profit uses, such as open spaces.[39]

Farmland near towns often has a potential development value, described by the Uthwatt Committee as 'floating value', which increases as the likelihood of development becomes more certain.[56] This enhanced value was the 'betterment' of which the Land Commission required a forty per cent share under the Land Commission Act, 1967, and which was abolished in 1970. The aim was to collect some share of increases in value representing the community's actions while leaving some share to the benefit of the private individual, thus allowing the market to continue to operate.[57] It did however result in a reduction in the amount of land available for development.

Successful planning should seek to understand the economic and social forces which shape our environment and assist in the allocation of land uses to meet those needs in a manner beneficial to the whole community. This involves ensuring an adequate supply of land to meet various anticipated demands.[58]

Pattern of Land Values

Commercial and similar users are located in city centres as they are able to pay the high land prices and secure the benefits of maximum accessibility and convenience. Hence rents serve to act as sorters and arrangers of land use patterns; planning control alone does not decide land use. It has been suggested that the outgrowth of this market process of competitive bidding for sites among the potential users of land is an orderly pattern of land use specially organised to perform most efficiently the economic functions that characterise urban life.

TABLE 2.5

INDEX OF LAND AND RETAIL PRICES, 1913–60

| Year | 1938 = 100 | |
	Land prices	Retail prices
1913	60	64
1919	67	139
1920	69	159
1925	75	112
1930	81	101
1935	87	92
1938	100	100
1939	102	103
1946	150	154
1950	175	185
1953	238	216
1955	307	242
1958	640	272
1959	765	273
1960	875	274

Generally, commercial and industrial uses can attract land away from residential uses. Competition between firms to be in the desired positions will force the land values above those of the surrounding land used for residential purposes. If all the land in a given part of the town is used for complementary purposes this is likely to enhance the land values, whereas if they are incompatible, this may lower the land values. For example, if there is a residential district well served by schools, open spaces, transport and other amenities, persons will wish to live there and both property and land values will be higher than if it lacked these facilities.[39]

Developments in transport systems may also lead to changes in urban land values. For example, the extension of a bus route, the building of a railway station or the carrying out of major road improvements, may cause major changes in land values in the adjacent areas.

Andrews[59] compiled the figures given in table 2.5 which shows the rapid increase in land prices in a London residential suburb between 1950 and 1960, well in excess of the general inflationary trends.

Over the period 1960–62, the median price for residential sites was about £12 400 per hectare, the corresponding price for industrial sites was £20 000 per hectare and for commercial sites £62 000 per hectare. Maximum prices recorded over this period were £124 000 per hectare for residential sites, nearly £250 000 per hectare for industrial sites and almost £1.7 million per hectare for commercial sites.[51]

The greater the permitted residential density the higher the price per hectare which can be obtained. For example, an increase in permitted densities from twenty-four to thirty-six dwellings per hectare would, in 1962, tend to reduce site costs per dwelling by only £50 to £100 but would raise the price per hectare by £5000 to £7500.[54] Denman[60] has shown that a developer will pay more per hectare for the marginal piece of land needed to complete a development site than he will for the site as a whole.

Further substantial increases in residential land prices occurred between 1965 and 1969 and the trend is accelerating. Median London prices rose from £50 000 to £93 000 per hectare, while in the east Midlands the rise in prices was not quite so spectacular—£12 400–£17 500 per hectare.[61] Part of this substantial increase in land prices could conceivably have stemmed from the payment of betterment levy to the Land Commission and this could have produced distorted land values.[62] Thorncroft[53] in his survey of world property prices over the last 20 years shows that the trend in property values has been a persistent rise.

Finally the benefits of land value maps as a bridge between valuers and planners has been clearly demonstrated by Anstey.[63] The planner needs to consider present values, how they may change, and how far present values should be maintained in the interests of urban efficiency.

Value of Recreational Land

The American outdoor recreation report[46] emphasises the high user benefits to be obtained from parks in heavily populated areas, which can outweigh the much higher land costs compared with those in more remote locations. Clawson and others[1] have advised the acquisition of land for open spaces well ahead of urban expansion, while land is relatively cheap.

A Liverpool planning report[64] condemns the practice of justifying a central location for facilities simply in terms of economy or functional necessity. Social desirability or even necessity should be seen as an equally valid reason. This concept is particularly relevant to recreational facilities. Ciriacy-Wantrup[8] poses the question 'How can one measure the contribution to social welfare of outdoor recreation and compare it with that of types of housing or systems of communication?'.

There may be a case for a more explicit expression of the social value of different land uses. An example of such a divergence of private evaluation and public or social values of alternative uses of resources is Wibberley's argument for the existence of a social worth of an acre (or hectare) of agricultural land in Britain which bears little relationship to the market price.[65] A shadow price is determined, in this case, by the alternative cost of acquiring the produce from the land in question. He finds this to be much higher than the going land price.

A similar, value problem is involved in the recognition or establishment of the value of non-market uses of land, and creates the need for attaching social values on land for parks and other related publicly available open areas. The market establishes values for land used for most purposes, but while parks have significant social value, there is normally no comparable values given to them, so that such a use cannot compete with other uses in any meaningful sense. If we are to secure a better distribution of land uses in urban areas, it seems that some recognition of the value of parks must be made and allocations made accordingly.

Knetsch[66] suggests that a meaningful approach to the evaluation of the economic worth of parks and other open areas can be made by examining two sets of values. One source of values is that which is capitalised in the price or value of land surrounding a park. The other set of values is essentially user benefits of the values which people other than immediate landowners received from visits to the area. This approach will be considered in greater depth in the next chapter and the techniques expounded will be applied to two Nottingham parks.

INTENSITY OF USE

Need for Optimum Use of Resources

As Britain's land resources are limited in relation to population, it is essential that they are used as effectively as possible. Some land must be made to serve a number of purposes simultaneously where this is feasible and this aspect will be considered later in this chapter. It seems advisable to bring more marginal land under cultivation and for the timber line to extend higher up the hills and mountain slopes. Most forms of development should proceed at higher densities where this can be achieved without lowering standards intolerably. The extractive industries should work to phased programmes to avoid sterilisation of land by excessive reservations. Concerted efforts are needed to bring back existing derelict industrial land into beneficial use.[67]

Recreational Facilities

With recreational resources, there tends to be over utilisation with some facilities and under utilisation of others. Serious problems arise when outdoor recreational resources are used too intensively. Erosion of vegetation, in some cases to bare ground, is a feature of heavily used recreation areas such as cliff tops, sand dunes, woodlands, downland slopes, scenic view points and trails. On water areas, popular for power boating, the wake from craft leads to flooding of adjacent land and eroded banks. In addition to the effects of trampling, wild life—and indeed many visitors—may be disturbed by noise, dogs, children and fires.[68]

The Minister of State for Housing and Local Government said on the second reading of the Countryside Bill in 1967:

It is impossible to prevent the pressures flowing into the countryside in an affluent, motorised society. It is a tremendous undertaking to see that the reasonable demands for access and enjoyment are satisfied and that in the process those who enjoy them do not destroy the things we all love.[69]

The space hungry recreations of golf, riding, sailing and winter sports all have a potential for quick and extensive growth. Because they are at present minority sports even a slight proportionate increase in demand could saturate existing facilities; and because they are also space demanding even a modest growth in facilities might involve an impossible scale of land allocation.[20]

The use capacity of some recreational facilities such as playing fields, tennis courts and bowling greens can be estimated fairly easily although the optimum capacity is never achieved, due to climatic and other causes. In the case of most of the coastal, countryside and moorland recreations, no firm basis for a calculation of carrying capacity exists. Capacity is often determined empirically by waiting for physical destruction of the environment or uncomfortable conditions for the users. Inadequate country lanes and restricted car parks may in themselves form metering devices and so prevent over use of countryside areas.

Improved land management techniques are needed to make the most effective use of existing resources. Conflicting demands upon a scarce recreational resource can be reconciled by spatial or time separation of activities. Pursuits like traditional field sports are seasonal and other sports can be enjoyed at other times of the year. For inland water resources, there may be an inadequate area for the spatial separation of activities and a rota system will have to operate to ensure that water skiers, sailors and fishermen can all use the same stretch of water.[70] The American outdoor recreation report[46] forecasts that the already heavy pressures on American water resources will reach critical proportions, and that the problems stemming from this pressure are among the most difficult in the entire outdoor recreation field.

Assessment of Capacity

The measurement of capacity brings together two basic elements—supply and demand—and attempts to compare them in a meaningful way. The primary aim is to see how far the resources are or are not adequate to meet present demand; to determine whether there are any surpluses; to ascertain what new resources would be needed if demand increases; and to conserve scarce resources.[71] Capacity is based primarily on standards which are an expression of the balance between cost, conservation and exploitation.[72]

Capacity standards should not imply a uniform standard over time and similar terrain. Each recreation authority will have to compile its own capacity formula to take account of resources peculiar to its area.[71] Capacity standards of resources may vary through time. For example, a stretch of Forestry Commission woodland will have a different capacity to absorb recreational activities according to whether the trees are 5, 10 or 30 years old. Intensity of use may increase with the age of trees and some pursuits which were not allowed during the earlier growth phase of the woodland may be permitted later. Possibly capacity criteria can be considered under the heads of physical, sociological and ecological.

(1) *Physical constraints* on capacity are probably the easiest to assess. Sports facilities will have limits to the numbers of participants. A ski-slope, sailing reservoir and even a set of rock climbing crags all have capacity maxima. If the number of people exceeds the physical capacity, the result will be overcrowding and discomfort, and greater risk of accident in the case of some active pursuits.

(2) *Sociological constraints* on capacity are more difficult to assess but the system is partially self-regulating. In some parts of the countryside too much access will minimise enjoyment of the rural scene for everyone.[73] Although some people seem gregarious not everyone enjoys being in a crowd; nevertheless, those who like to enjoy the country-side alone or with a few companions can usually find a remoter area.[74] This constitutes a need to zone land for low and high density recreational uses and give people the choice of facility.

(3) *Ecological constraints* relate human beings to the physical environment. If the human impact on an attractive landscape is high, it is possible that in time the flora and fauna will have changed. Change is an essential part of nature but certain changes may be undesirable from an ecological viewpoint and also for recreational needs.

Nature's timescale is so long that the consequences of a bad decision may not be evident for a considerable time and it will be several more years before the mistake is rectified. In some instances it might be desirable to allow access to a limited area of land and then to close it after say 2 years to allow the vegetation to be restored.

Dower[75] devised a methodology for assessment of capacity by sub-dividing a recreational area into districts and arbitrarily determining existing capacity, for example, 1 person/km^2 of upland (all day). A study is made of visitors to identify shortfalls and surpluses and to assess the impact of an increase in visitors to the area. Dower is undertaking further investigations at the Dartington Amenity Research Trust by developing specific sites and projects, such as country parks, woodland, picnic sites and water areas and examining the physical, ecological, economic and social impacts.[76]

The ecological impact has been considered in depth by the Nature Conservancy[77] and their findings are best described by reference to specific examples. Watson[77] has described how the Cairngorm region contains an area of high-arctic terrain unique in Britain and is also one of the largest national nature reserves. Problems have been caused by the large number of tourists following the uncoordinated building of roads, ski-lifts and hotels. Damage occurred to the soils and vegetation during construction of the roads and lifts, and is still increasing due to human trampling and the passage of tractors. In addition, these developments have caused local eyesores on an attractive landscape, and some fear that the unusual arctic-alpine plant communities and animal life may suffer.[159] This damage demonstrates the need for well defined paths with concrete or tarmacadam surfaces and possibly the need for obligatory return tickets on chair lifts to prevent people coming downhill on many different routes. All roads should be properly surfaced and drained and restrictions are needed on the use of caterpillar tractors or bulldozers.

In Snowdonia, Goodier[77] found that there has been a marked deterioration in the appearance of the habitat in the immediate vicinity of public footpaths. In the case of camping it would be useful to have even a rough classification of the stages of sward deterioration under camping pressure, so that some acceptability level could be defined and related to the number of tents/nights/annum for different sward types. The same type of approach could usefully be adopted for picnic sites and car parks.

Schofield[77] investigated the effect of human impact on fauna, flora and natural features at Gibraltar Point on the Lindsey coast near Skegness, which contains a nature reserve of about 525 hectares and embraces foreshore, sand dunes and saltmarsh. The number of people visiting the reserve is very high—123 000 in 1965 and 151 000 in 1966 (based on 3.06 persons/car) and ninety per cent of the visitors remained within 180 metres of the access roads. Seven thousand and five hundred people per season walked off concrete paths on to mature saltmarsh causing complete loss of vegetation cover. A similar density of people walking over yellow dunes completely eliminates marram, sea-couch and prickly saltwort and results in considerable dune erosion (with protection, recovery takes 4 years). On a grey-dune system, approximately 3500–4500 people cause local exposure of soil and sand.

Box Hill and Newlands Corner, popular Surrey open spaces, are visited by many people for picnicking and wandering. They tend to do considerable damage, principally by wear and tear, vandalism and flower picking, together with the scattering of litter. This seems to indicate that methods of educating visitors need to be devised, as well as assessment of capacity. Munton[156] undertook transect surveys in the Scilly Isles to relate numbers of people to particulars of vegetation, such as cover, height and flowering frequency, in order to indicate the threshold values at which trampling pressures lead to changes in species composition or total loss of vegetation.

MULTIPLE USE

Application of Concept

Recreation has had a hard struggle to establish its claims on the supply of time, money and resources. Even when it has succeeded in doing so in principle the battle over priorities is by no means finished. There is constant pressure for the most efficient use of resources, and the multiple use of land and water resources can assist in satisfying both needs.[78, 80] Although, as Willey[79] has shown, it requires much careful and detailed formulation. Multiple use has been defined as 'the planned shared use of a facility or area by several different activities and interests'.[161]

American achievements have demonstrated how multiple use can be operated on a vast scale. It is estimated that 147 million visits were paid to national forests for recreational purposes in 1965, and 14 million recreational visits were made to national wild life refuges and 156 million such visits to Corps of Engineers reservoirs in 1964. The number of boats on Tennessee Valley Authority lakes rose from 9600 in 1947 to 52 700 in 1964.[81]

A World Health Organisation expert committee[29] lists the advantages of open space as relief in built-up areas, as a noise barrier and to separate and contain urban areas. In their opinion the multiple uses of open space have not yet been fully exploited. In this country there have been significant developments in the last decade in the recreational use of canals and reservoirs, the use of forestry land for recreation and the establishment of combined sports centres. As a recent annual school building programme included approximately ninety new gymnasia and fifteen new swimming pools, there is ample scope for extension of the joint use concept.

Farmland

Multiple use of rural land in Great Britain takes place in a variety of ways—by people hiking, rambling, picnicking, camping, hunting, shooting and fishing on land which is being actively farmed. Wibberley,[2] however, foresees dangers in major developments in this field, through the imposition of strains on land uses, productivity and personal loyalties and desires. A major increase in public demand for access to private rural land could lead to a sharp reduction in permitted access by private owners on the grounds of excessive numbers of visitors.

The Nature Conservancy and the Forestry Commission make agreements with private landowners to secure that land is managed in a certain way, thus ensuring that private and public interests are in harmony. The Peak Park Planning Board, in particular, uses 'access agreements' to permit rambling over moorland. Hookway[22] questions whether the use of agreements should not be extended to cover a wider range of recreational use—including farmland —to maintain footpaths, provide car parks and picnic areas, clear litter and improve visual amenity. This suggestion introduces the concept of the landowner or farmer becoming a recreational land manager. Wibberley[84] has proposed that experimental types of multiple use farming should be introduced within Milton Keynes New Town with protective agreements.

Forestry

In America the rapid increase in forest visitors is already affecting management practices and may, eventually, change the theories that guide forest policy. Only after recreation has been accepted by foresters as a respectable use of the forest—commensurate with wood, water and forage—can much progress be made. The manager of a forest recreational environment is directly subjected to the pressures of the consuming public. This can be a frustrating experience for men trained to handle the slow process of tree growth (100–150 years) and to produce primary raw materials. They will need re-training to cope with this new rôle successfully. Nevertheless, the possibilities for multiple use in forests are great, provided the mechanics of resource allocation and management can be rationalised to allow the public to enjoy recreation, while wood and other forest products are obtained from the same forest.[82]

The recreational use of forest land has been consciously and imaginatively implemented in Nunspeet Forest which has an area of 1500 hectares, is situated in the north-west part of Guelderland and is controlled by the State Forest Service of the Netherlands. The area is used for a day's recreation and for holiday recreation. By careful siting of the recreational facilities, the public is able to enjoy some attractive parts of the forest without harming the interests of sylviculture and nature conservancy. Recreational facilities include a recreation road (the Petersom Ramringweg), a playing pond (the Zandenplas), picnic areas, playgrounds, day camping sites and walking routes.[83]

Water Resources

A World Health Organisation expert committee[29] emphasised that regional planning in relation to water resources should include all potential uses of water such as municipal water supply and waste disposal, hydro-electric production, irrigation, transport and recreation. Chapter 8 investigates the conflicting requirements of the various recreational uses of water.

Playing Fields and Educational Facilities

The advisability of operating dual use or multi-use of many facilities provided by industrialists and educational authorities has long since been recognised.[85] Surveys by the National Playing Fields Association[86] show that many local education authorities permit some outside use of school playing fields. For many years individuals, groups and voluntary organisations have quite justifiably pressed for more extensive dual use. The most common plea is for dual use of school playing fields, but other facilities like gymnasia, sports halls, swimming pools, tennis courts and playgrounds may also be the subject of joint arrangements.

A joint ministry circular issued in 1964[87] emphasised the desirability of dual use and dual provision. Most of the regional sports councils have prepared reports on the extent of dual use of sports facilities in their regions and the east Midlands report also includes dual use of industrial facilities.[88–90] The dual use of both educational and industrial playing fields will be considered in more detail in chapter 7. Dual provision of facilities is of much more recent origin and yet it makes economic sense. In 1966 the Minister with special responsibility for sport pointed the way—'I have often said that school recreational sports facilities should not be built in the schools, but adjoining it, so that they may be shared by the rest of the community. The Department's cost limits for education building do not restrict this sort of arrangement if the local authority is willing to underwrite the extra cost of providing for the wider community'.[91]

In recent years some first-class joint projects have been provided in which combined sports centres have been built alongside new comprehensive schools, involving joint planning, finance and management by local authorities. Typical examples are the Madeley educational and recreational centre at Dawley New Town—involving the Salop County Council, Dawley Development Corporation and Dawley Urban District Council[92]—and the Bingham sports centre in Nottinghamshire, involving the Nottinghamshire County Council and the Bingham Rural District Council.[93] Both schemes involve the provision of a swimming pool, sports hall, social centre and floodlit all-weather playing surfaces. Both capital and running costs are apportioned between the various local authorities in a manner agreed between them. At Bingham for instance, Nottinghamshire CC agreed to pay the loan charges on the facilities required for the school (£70 000) and Bingham RDC the remainder (£130 000), with running costs apportioned on a fifty-fifty basis.

SUPPLY-DEMAND RELATIONSHIPS

It is imperative that both demand and supply factors should be taken into account in planning for recreation. An investigation of both factors shows that there are real problems in their measurement and that they must not be considered in isolation.

Assessment of Demand

The demand side of the recreation equation is extremely complex and difficult to quantify in meaningful terms that can be related to known or probable supplies of land and inland water.[94] There are difficulties even in attempting to establish the basic unit of measurement for existing participation—be it the number of separate visits to the facility, the number of hours spent on recreation or the frequency of participation. The first of these alternatives, expressed in 'visitor-days', was used in the American studies[46] and the last alternative was adopted in the Pilot National Recreation Survey.[23]

The demand for recreation facilities is frequently influenced by their location relative to the users' homes. Hence demand for a facility can be reduced by locational restraints.

Social surveys have been employed to try and determine what people want, but tend to be subjective. The Pilot National Recreation Survey[23] is the most significant of this type so far undertaken in Britain but the number of persons approached was inadequate to produce conclusive results applicable to all parts of the country. Surveys of outdoor recreation resources in relation to demand and standards provide very useful information.

Another method of approach is to examine the different characteristics influencing demand as was done in the American studies.[46] The Cheshire Countryside study[95] bases demand on past trends and the relationship of individual activities to income and car ownership.

The American outdoor recreation report[46] shows that demand for recreation in the United States is surging. Whatever the measuring rod—visits to recreation areas, number of fishing licence holders, number of outboard motors in use—it is clear the Americans are seeking outdoor recreation as never before. It is estimated that by the year 2000 the population should double and the demand for recreation treble. Both the British and American studies[23, 96] indicate that participation in outdoor recreation increases with rising income and improvements in educational and occupational status.

Changing Demand

Griffiths[97] asserts that fashions occur in what people are ready to do, and that changes in fashion are social phenomena which move through and affect groups of people. This aspect provides the rôle of the sociologist in studying leisure, as he observes people in groups and studies the way in which their behaviour is influenced by their membership of these groups. Quite often social forces will produce a gap between what people say they like or will do and what they actually do, and the sociologist is concerned with the gap between appearance and reality.

Although recreation participation entails cost which influences the number of visits to recreation areas, most areas—especially those provided publicly—are customarily available at zero or nominal charges. The millions of outdoor recreation days currently being consumed are those prevailing at near zero prices for those resources. If these prices were raised substantially by the imposition of entrance fees or by some other means, a far different quantity would be demanded or consumed.[98]

In the case of some recreational resources the demand is metered by the capacity of roads or car parks, and the flow of participants thus becomes self-regulating and self-selecting. Rodgers[20] has drawn upon examples in the Lake District and the Scottish Highlands. In these circumstances, the full demand potential is not capable of expression due to the physical restraints.

Ciriacy-Wantrup[99] asserts that existing projections of land and water use have no validity as predictions largely because they pay little regard to changing attitudes and needs. The method of prediction which was most fully developed in America[46] was one in which existing participation rates were established for defined socio-economic groups and the derived indices then applied to the projected future size of each socio-economic group. The prediction element itself requires much consideration; can it be assumed, for example, that future socio-economic groups will behave in the same way as their present day counterparts? Existing use characteristics are very closely related to the present supply and distribution of facilities—how much will demand change when not only supply and distribution are varied but new forms of recreation and of transport supplant the old?[100] The questions posed illustrate some of the difficulties in making predictions.

Supply Characteristics

In any recreational study the first step is to prepare an inventory of existing resources.[101] In the United Kingdom much valuable work has been done in this connection by the regional sports councils who have prepared surveys and appraisals of the major recreational facilities in their areas. In America public areas designated for outdoor recreation cover 12.5 per cent of the total land surface but the supply is still inadequate. The problem is not one of acres or hectares—but *effective* acres or hectares of land and water, available to the public and usable for specific types of recreation. Much of the land is poorly distributed in relation to the people.[46] Nevertheless, the effective area of land in recreational use can be raised by access agreements, multiple use projects and the dedication of new footpaths.[70]

The supply is best analysed in terms of the amount available, capacity and accessibility. It covers land and water in both public and private ownership, from vast national parks to small roadside areas, used for a wide range of different activities. New recreational developments are likely to be primarily on lands with lower amenity values and will involve some evaluation to determine suitability for recreational use. The user orientated and intermediate types of recreation facility are relatively 'footloose' in location, although they need to be reasonably accessible to centres of population.

The need to be able to evaluate a resource in terms of its capacity to serve recreational requirements is now generally recognised and tentative capacity ratings have been advanced by a number of agencies. For instance the State of California[102] suggested 1440 persons per hectare of bathing beach, twenty-five persons per kilometre of riding and hiking trail and one water skier and boat for each 0.4 hectare of water.

Consideration of accessibility immediately throws up a number of related aspects—accessible by vehicles or pedestrians, legal right of access, and psychological factor (distance and relative power of attraction).[100] Hence, the supply of land for recreation is not easily quantifiable and existing facilities need careful evaluation and definition.

Interrelationship of Supply and Demand

'It may be that to relate population to environment optimally is the greatest technical task of the end of the century', said Lord Florey in his address to the Royal Society in November 1965.

Supply and demand are important elements in themselves but they achieve greater significance when we try to establish supply/demand interrelationships. We have to consider the capacity of the landscape to absorb various recreational pursuits and the need to reconcile public access with conservation policies. There is not only the conflict between recreational and other claims on use of land but also between different recreational activities.

There have been a number of recreational studies undertaken in this country which have examined supply and demand in the context of a local area as, for example, Windsor Park,[103] Box Hill[104] and Berkhamsted Common.[105]

A statistical analysis of existing surpluses and shortfalls of recreational facilities within a study area in relation to known demands must be of value in assessing future needs, but it cannot give the complete answer. The participation rate figures observed are taken under prevailing recreation opportunity conditions. This use or attendance is determined both by demand and the availability of supply. Improper accounting of supply considerations leads, for instance, to the assumption that people demand only increasing quantities of what they now have, thereby perpetuating present imbalances.[98]

For example, if some areas of the country show far greater participation rates for swimming and no consideration was given to the relative availability of opportunities, it could lead to decisions to build even more facilities in the areas most adequately served, rather than attempting to provide opportunities in deficient areas. Building squash courts will attract people who wanted to play squash and also people who were not aware previously that they wanted to play it. But supply does not always create demand, particularly in the short term. Surveys show that half as many girls like sport as boys, but this should not result in making only half the provision for girls as for boys.[97]

The single most serious and fundamental deficiency in demand surveys and studies is that they do not provide any means of determining how recreation use will respond to changes in supply.[98]

Different forms of open space are required to satisfy the needs of persons of different ages. A very broad age classification would be

childhood 0–15 years of age
adulthood 16–60 years of age
old age from 61 years of age onwards

This broad pattern can be sub-divided into further distinct stages at which recreational needs are quite different. For instance, childhood can be sub-divided into

infants 0–4 years of age
primary school children 5–10 years of age
secondary school children 11–15 years of age

Hence the open space needs in a particular area are influenced considerably by the age structure of the population.

Open Space Recommendations in Planning Schemes

Attempts have been made from time to time to assess desirable standards of open space in relation to population, in the absence of a universally recognised and applicable standard. Some of these will now be examined.

The Greater London Plan (1944)

This advocated 10 acres (4 ha) of open space for every 1000 residents, comprising 3 acres (1.20 ha) for education and the remaining 7 acres (2.80 ha) distributed as follows: parks and parkland—1 acre (0.40 ha); public playing fields—4 acres (1.60 ha); and private sports grounds—2 acres (0.80 ha).

The County of London Plan (1943)

The total provision in this plan was 4 acres (1.60 ha) per 1000 population because of the difficulty in achieving any higher standard in such a densely built-up area.

The City of Manchester Plan (1945)

This plan allocated 4.5 acres (2.80 ha) per 1000 population for organised games. Of this land 2.5 acres (1 ha) was to be obtained by the partial use of school playing fields outside school hours.

It seems evident that open space provision in the major cities has been very much influenced by the high price of land and high density development. Post-war New Town proposals have shown a much increased open space/population allocation. For instance the Harlow Master Plan (1952) showed the following provision:

use	acre/1000 population	ha/1000 population
children's playgrounds	0.50	0.20
sports centre	0.50	0.20
public playing fields	3.00	1.20
private playing fields	2.00	0.80
allotments	1.50	0.60
parks and parkways	1.00	0.40
Total	8.50	3.40

National Playing Fields Association Standard

Soon after the Association was founded in 1925, it formulated a standard of playing space required in order to meet the physical needs of the population, namely 6 acres (2.40 ha) of playing space per 1000 of the population. This standard was based on an analysis of the age structure of the population which showed that approximately fifty per cent of the population was between the ages of 10 and 40 when active games are mostly played. Of this 500 per 1000, it was assumed that probably 150 would not wish or be able to play games and that a further 150 would be attending schools or colleges with their own recreational facilities, leaving 200 persons per 1000 for whom provision should be made.

The standard was re-examined in the light of the 1971 census and expressly revalidated in October 1971. In a statement issued in 1967[106] the Association listed the types of recreational space that can be included in the standard provision.

(1) Play space and general recreational areas provided by a local authority for public or private use, including children's playgrounds.

(2) Privately owned playing space including sports grounds of industrial and commercial firms.

(3) Such areas of school playground or playing fields that are in regular use out of school hours and during weekends and school holidays.

(4) Miniature and Par-3 golf courses and driving ranges.

(5) Small spaces for special recreational purposes, e.g. limited areas of water where there is a concentration of recreational use by local residents.

(6) Adequate car parking space for users of public and private grounds.

The Association also stressed the need for the playing space to be situated where it is most needed. The Ministry of Housing and Local Government[107] stated in 1950 that 'no better assessment of need has so far been put forward', indicating a qualified acceptance of the standard.

Educational Facilities

The Education Act, 1944, provided the first statutory requirement relating to school playing fields. The latest standards derive from The Standards for School Premises Regulations, 1959,[108] and the specified ranges are shown in table 2.6.

TABLE 2.6

SCHOOL PLAYING FIELD STANDARDS

Type of school	Lowest number of pupils	Area of playing fields		Highest number of pupils	Area of playing fields	
		ac	ha		ac	ha
Junior	80	1.0	0.4	480	3.0	1.2
Junior/infant	80	0.5	0.2	480	2.25	0.9
Mixed secondary	150	4.5	1.8	1500	19.0	7.6
Boys' secondary	150	4.5	1.8	1500	19.5	7.8
Girls' secondary	150	4.0	1.6	1500	15.5	6.2

Source: Building Bulletin 28, Department of Education and Science (1966)

American Open Space Standards

In 1938 the Natural Resources Board[109] recommended the following extremely high park provision in towns under 8000 population:

| | Park area | |
Population	Inhabitants/acre	Inhabitants/hectare
5000–8000	75	187
2500–5000	60	150
1000–2500	50	125
under 1000	40	100

The Committee on Park and Recreation Standards of the American Society of Planning Officials[110] considered that this standard would not be practical of attainment in the large cities, and suggested 1 acre per 200 people (1 hectare/ 500 people) in cities with populations between 500 000 and 1 million, and 1 acre per 300 people or more (1 hectare/750 people) in cities above 1 million.

In 1961 the tentative regional recreation standards listed in table 2.7 were suggested for Illinois.[111]

TABLE 2.7

TENTATIVE TABLE OF REGIONAL RECREATION STANDARDS

| Category | Service area | Area/1000 population | | | | | |
| | | Minimum (1960) | | Short-range (1980) | | Long-range (2000) | |
		ac	ha	ac	ha	ac	ha
Urban	walking distance	3	1.2	5	2.0	7	2.8
City wide	¼–½ hour	7	2.8	10	4.0	13	5.2
Regional							
Parks	½–1 hour	10	4.0	15	6.0	40	16.0
Reservations	½–2 hours	10	4.0	20	8.0	60	24.0
Total		30	12.0	50	20.0	120	48.0

The tentative standards for year 2000 are indeed immense and one wonders whether they are capable of achievement. At about the same time the Regional Plan Association was estimating recreation land requirements within 15–20 minutes of New York homes at 12 acres (4.8 ha) per 1000 population, which would be the 1970 requirement by Illinois standards.[112] Chapin's estimate of about 4.75 acres (1.9 ha) per 1000 population for local recreation areas also tends to support the previous figures.[26] Clawson and Stewart[113] have also emphasised the difficulties of defining recreational land where intermingled or dual use is involved.

Factors Influencing Open Space Standards

It is impracticable to lay down rigid open space standards and to try and apply them to all urban areas, as the requirements will be influenced by a variety of factors which will vary from town to town.

These factors include the following:

(1) Age structure of the population.

(2) Sex and marital status of population.

(3) Socio-economic characteristics of population.

(4) Extent of private open space.

(5) Extent to which school playing fields are available for use by the general public.

(6) Local attitudes and habits.

(7) Climatic conditions.

(8) Health characteristics of population.

(9) Size of town and proximity of countryside.

(10) Possible potential demand from school leavers.

(11) Club structure and organisation of sport.

(12) Density of residential development.

(13) Extent of car ownership.

For example, Willis considered that 1.5 acres (0.6 ha) per 1000 population would be a suitable provision for playing fields after investigating ten New Towns,[114] whereas Winterbottom considered that 2.5 acres (1 ha) per 1000 population would be the correct standard for Colchester.[115]

DERELICTION AND RECLAMATION

'Derelict land' has been defined by the Ministry of Housing and Local Government[116] as land which has been so damaged by surface or underground development that it is likely to remain out of use unless subjected to special treatment. 'Reclamation' refers to those operations which may be required to make land fit for beneficial use.

Derelict Land

Most derelict land takes the form either of heaps of waste or holes in the ground. Derelict land usually disfigures the landscape, is often a source of nuisance and is sometimes dangerous. The form reclamation can most usefully take varies from site to site. Holes may be filled with waste material—such as pulverised fly ash from power stations—and subsequently be returned to agricultural use as has happened in the Trent Valley, or be filled with water to provide recreational facilities as at Batchworth Lake near Rickmansworth and Winsford Flash in Cheshire.

Colliery spoil heaps which are too expensive to reclaim for other uses may sometimes be landscaped or planted with trees. Prominent heaps with a regular outline are not always unsightly; the groups of finely shaped conical tips near Wigan give relief and character to an otherwise flat landscape. The waste is best concealed by grass, perhaps with trees and bushes at the base to act as a foil or screen, and contribute to an ecological balance, soil stability and improved conditions of microclimate.[117]

Many writers have expressed serious doubts as to whether all the dereliction in this country will ever be cleared and the Hunt Committee recommended the setting up of a Derelict Land Reclamation Agency.[118-120]

Cost of Reclamation

There are probably about 40 000 hectares of derelict land in England and Wales (although estimates do vary appreciably) and to reclaim the hard core of about 25 000 hectares could cost £30 million, but the increased value of the reclaimed land would need to be offset against this figure.[121,124,125] This derelict land consists broadly of 16 000 ha of spoil heaps, 16 000 ha of excavations and holes in the ground and 8000 ha of other types of dereliction.[123] The largest amounts of dereliction are in Staffordshire, Lancashire, Northumberland, Durham, West Riding and Monmouthshire. In Nottinghamshire and Derbyshire alone, however, the area of derelict land is about 2300 ha and constitutes a serious problem.[122]

The Civic Trust[124] has prepared calculations showing the net cost of reclaiming derelict land for agricultural use and these figures, suitably updated to 1972 values, are:

	Cost per hectare
	£
Cost of purchase and reclamation	2400
less Current market value of reclaimed land	750
Net financial cost	1650
less Replacement cost of derelict pasture or saltings thereby saved	550
Net economic cost of benefits of reclamation	1100

In urban areas the net economic cost per hectare could be much less as the value of the reclaimed land would conceivably be much higher and there could also be increased social benefits. In some cases reclamation schemes will be eligible for government grant—for instance, about eighty-five per cent of the cost is recoverable by local authorities in 'development areas' (Industrial Development Act, 1966, and Local Government Act, 1966). A seventy-five per cent grant may also operate in national parks and 'areas of outstanding natural beauty' and less generous grants of up to fifty per cent are available to the remainder of the country.[126] Derelict land converted to recreational use may be eligible for grant under the Countryside Act, 1968.[68] The Local Employment Act, 1970, springing from the deliberations of the Hunt Committee, extended to derelict land clearance areas a seventy-five per cent grant, subject to certification by the Minister, and to certain intermediate areas specified in validating orders. Local authorities are the prime movers in the restoration of derelict land and it is they who initiate the various proposals for reclamation work; prepare plans and quantities; consider the planning applications in relation to after uses of sites; apply to the Government for grant; and negotiate with the district valuer on after values and purchase prices.[154]

Extractive Industries

Approximately 200 million tonnes (metric tons) of sand, gravel, coal and sandstone are extracted annually. The National Coal Board used 51 000 hectares of land for open cast working between 1942 and 1966, under agreements whereby the land is restored to its original condition after a 5-year period of agricultural treatment.

In some cases the National Coal Board has combined restoration with the creation of new amenities. At Bogside in Fife, where about 30 million tonnes of coal were extracted from a low lying, waterlogged site, 50 million tonnes of soil are being imported to convert 140 hectares of peat bog into farmland and a new lock will be formed and stocked with fish. In Staffordshire, which contains areas of extensive dereliction, the National Coal Board—in consultation with the County Planning Department—is planning a large recreational complex on 2500 hectares of worked land. The facilities are to include fishing, walking, golf, sailing, riding, skiing and motor cycle scrambling.[121]

Deep coal mining has, however, left many problems of dereliction. The majority of the dying coal mining areas have large areas of abandoned pits and spoil heaps. In the east Midlands, the increase in mechanisation and the exhaustion of the thicker, higher quality seams have resulted in an alarming increase in the quantity of colliery waste, which is now running out at 12 million tonnes per year in Nottinghamshire alone and probably about 250 million tonnes a year in the United Kingdom as a whole.[154] The National Coal Board has stated that underground stowage is financially impossible and the Nottinghamshire County Planning Department has suggested transport of the waste to the brick clay excavations in Bedfordshire and Cambridgeshire or to sand and gravel excavations in the region. Lowe[126] estimates that at present rates of working a further 5000 hectares (50 km^2) will be needed in Nottinghamshire by the end of the century to accommodate the colliery waste.

New Life for Dead Lands[123] contains descriptions of a number of successful schemes for the reclamation of derelict colliery land—a housing estate at Wallbrook, Staffordshire; playing fields and housing at Ince-in-Makerfield, Lancashire; playing fields at Hoyland, Yorkshire; and agricultural use at Bickershaw, Lancashire. Furthermore, experiments by the Lancashire County Council at Bickerstaffe and Bickershaw showed that grass could be sown direct onto colliery shale, and Graham and Butler[127] produced a playsward on colliery shale at Hindley, Lancashire, without using soil but applying the grass seed at six times the normal agricultural rate of spread. With large prominent conical mounds, reshaping into a rolling hill blending with the surrounding landscape can often produce a dramatic change.[123]

In recent years considerable emphasis has been placed on the desirability of tree planting, particularly in connection with reclamation schemes. One of the pioneering organisations was probably the Midland Reafforesting Association which was responsible for the tree planting of 40 hectares in the Black Country between 1903 and 1924 although, unfortunately, most of their plantations have since been destroyed. Wise[128] has shown how the Association contributed actively to the sum of experience in the general problem of revegetating industrial waste, in selecting suitable species and in influencing the climate of public opinion.

Some valuable research into tree planting on colliery spoil heaps has been undertaken by Wood and Thirgood.[129] Spoil heaps were classified into four groups:

(1) Low to medium mounds up to 15 m (15 metres) high including the hill-and-hollow of the older exposed coal fields and typical of south Staffordshire.

(2) High mounds and flat topped cones ranging from 15 to 16 m in height and generally single mounds with plateaux-like tops.

(3) Cones arising from mechanical tipping practices and often exceeding 60 m in height.

(4) Ridges resulting from tipping by tramway or aerial cable.

To support tree growth, the coal heap must provide a reasonably stable surface and an adequate supply of moisture and nutrients. Some degree of stability occurs within 2 years of the cessation of tipping. Weathering of the typical spoil material takes place rapidly, but unless vegetation cover is present much weathered material is lost. Spoil heaps are surprisingly moist, particularly those consisting largely of unburned shales and mud stones.

Most of our native broadleaved trees have become established naturally on old spoil heaps, and birch has been one of the most important pioneers. Many unburned heaps in favourable situations seem to proceed quite normally to oak forest, via hawthorn and ash. Of the conifers, the most successful recorded by Wood and Thirgood[129] are European and Japanese larch, and Corsican and Austrian pines. Most tree failures are due to vandalism, damage by animals or incorrect choice of species often in relation to atmospheric pollution.

In fact Wood and Thirgood's main conclusions were that spoil heaps are usually potentially fertile; difficulties due to instability and erosion are not usually excessive; toxicity is probably rare; the very high modern conical mounds may present special difficulties due to exposure on higher slopes; choice of planting species is mainly governed by local conditions; special measures such as levelling and the importing of soil are not usually warranted; and vandalism is the main cause of failure.[129] Durham County Council had by 1962 acquired twenty-eight colliery spoil heaps occupying 70 hectares and successfully planted them with thousands of Lodgepole and Corsican pine and grey alder, birch and red oak, at a spacing of 1.5 m.[130]

Sand and gravel, reckoned by bulk, is second only to coal among minerals worked in this country. Before the 1914–18 war, annual production was about 1.5 million m³ (cubic metres) from small, scattered hand worked pits. The Sand and Gravel Association of Great Britain[131] has estimated the needs in 1975 as 105 million m³. Assuming an average yield of 40 000 m³ per ha, this would mean an annual consumption of over 2600 ha of land.

The main source of sand and gravel is the irregular mantle of pleistocene drift deposits. Wooldridge and Beaver[132] in a review of gravel working from 1920 to 1950 traced the tendency of the gravel working industry to move into the valleys, largely because of the superior quality of the valley gravels and the introduction of 'wet working'.

To an ever increasing extent, engineers are demanding higher grade aggregates, rigidly controlled as to sizes, and proportions of sizes, and the result has been to increase the complexity of the washing, crushing and screening plant and to encourage the production of a great variety of sand and gravel qualities. The heavy capital expenditure on plant requires a long 'stand' on any one site. It cannot be assumed that the same plant will avail for another site, and a period of not less than 15 years' working is normally regarded as the economic desideratum. In general, sites of at least 20 hectares are required.[132]

Dry pits are best restored to agricultural use in many instances and often provide useful disposal points for house refuse and other waste material. With the increasing number of wet pits, the needs of recreation in angling, sailing, rowing, water skiing and nature reserves should not be overlooked. Although, Hartwright[133] has emphasised the need for their proper landscaping and this is becoming increasingly apparent.

If nature is left unaided to heal the scars left after excavation, lakes will result with a solid bank of willow and alder round the fringes. The natural process takes time and the eventual result presents an unkempt and uncared for appearance. If trees such as weeping willows have been planted, a few islands retained and the work of nature controlled, the effect can be improved almost beyond recognition. As to choice of trees, observation of what grows locally will give a good guide. The indigenous trees should be noted, such as willows, silver birch, poplar and the conifers, and in the early years it is advisable to concentrate on these as they are relatively cheap and will form the backbone of the planting scheme. In later years the more ornamental varieties may be added to provide colour in flower and in leaf. Rushes will appear quite naturally in time and are most useful in breaking up the sharp outline of the excavation. This process can be accelerated by scattering seed from a few bullrush heads along the margins in

February and March.[133]

It is important to obtain contrasts in both shape and colour—the many shades of green provided by willows and poplars; the silver birch with its delicate shape and silver bark; the purple leaved maple and beech; the darker foliage of the evergreens; and the varying shapes of the weeping willow, Lombardy poplar and cypressus. Among the small plants the rushes, bamboos and grasses provide new shapes and rich shades of green; and against this whole background, flowering trees can be seen to best advantage.[133]

Other Forms of Reclamation

One of the most ambitious reclamation schemes proposed in the last decade must surely be that of the Lower Swansea Valley.[134] In the preface the Duke of Edinburgh states:

The Lower Swansea Valley today is a stark monument to a thoughtless and ruthless exploitation and while it remains in its present state it is a standing reproach to each generation which shrugs its shoulders and looks the other way.

In this project the University College of Swansea, assisted by other bodies, has investigated the causes of dereliction in the Lower Swansea Valley and its social and physical consequences, and has then proceeded to formulate recommendations for bringing back nearly 500 hectares of largely derelict river valley into use. Whilst surveys were being undertaken by people from many disciplines, Royal Engineers were demolishing derelict buildings and levelling sites and the Forestry Commission was planting 100 000 trees. Problems are accentuated by the widespread disposition of industrial waste, intense air pollution and liability to flooding. Forest trees and grasses have been successfully established on relatively innocuous waste materials, although an application of fertiliser is required with the grass seed. Indeed, certain strains of grasses, notably common bent-grass and creeping bent-grass, can grow on the copper and zinc waste spoil heaps which have accumulated during two centuries of smelting.

Stabilisation of the present tidal movement in the River Tawe is recommended in the form of a movable barrage at a cost of about £120 000. Future development of the area could include 164 ha for industry and commerce, 46 ha for housing and 48 ha for amenity. The amenity proposals include two parks, a riverside walk, free ranging open space, playing fields and an indoor recreation centre for winter recreation in particular.[134]

Stoke-on-Trent, containing about 650 ha of derelict land, has more dereliction than any other town or city in England and is taking active steps to reclaim some of the land. The first phase consists of converting a coal tip into a forest park at a cost of over £20 000 (£6000 per hectare). The corporation's long-term programme includes a water park, in addition to the forest park, and a system of 'greenways' based on disused mineral railway lines. The 'greenways' are intended for use by pedestrians and cyclists, and possibly also by equestrians.[155]

There are many disused railway tracks in England and Wales with a positive recreational potential. The new uses to which the tracks, or part of them, can be put include bridleways, footpaths, nature trails, cycle tracks, picnic areas, rural car parks, camping and caravan sites. The abandoned railway buildings could be used for hostels, museums, information centres, refreshment and toilet facilities.[68] A recent example is the conversion of a 14 km length of disused railway track in County Durham into a walking and pony-trekking route, linking various recreational facilities.[135] A much earlier example is the delightfully landscaped 5 km long railway walk on the line of the former narrow-gauge railway track from St. Aubin to Corbière which was acquired by the States of Jersey and opened to the public in 1937, and is sometimes referred to as a 'trailway shrubbery walk'.

There is little doubt that reclamation of derelict land can help in meeting increased recreational needs. Oxenham[67] found that in 1952 sixty-four per cent of reclamation in the Black Country was for housing purposes, twenty per cent for industrial use, thirteen per cent for public open space and three per cent for schools and public buildings. A similar analysis in the Potteries showed forty per cent for housing, eighteen per cent for public open space, seventeen per cent for industry, fifteen per cent for schools and their playing fields and ten per cent for agriculture.

Reclamation of derelict land for recreational purposes can take many forms. From the possible establishment of linear parks in the seriously disfigured Aire and Calder valleys on the doorstep of a large industrial conurbation,[136] to the reclamation of 6 hectares of disused river bank at Newcastle-upon-Tyne for passive recreation.[137] From the transformation of 120 hectares of spoil heaps at Wigan into a multi-activity recreation area,[138] to the rehabilitation of many disused and derelict canals into navigable waterways for power cruising under the provisions of the Transport

Act, 1968. There is also the recreational potential of water conservation schemes in estuaries as, for example, Morecambe Bay and the Wash.

CONSERVATION

Nature of and Need for Conservation

Smith[139] has defined conservation as the wise use of those resources which constitute the major elements of our natural environment: air, land, water and wild life. Arvill (Boote)[125] refers to the strict management of each resource, to ensure optimum value and continuity of supply. Hookway[140] has also emphasised this concept in suggesting that conservation is 'the planning and management of resources to ensure their wise use and continuity of supply while maintaining and enhancing their quality, value and diversity'.

It is the increasing pressure on the environment of human populations and human activity that has made conservation a fundamental and an urgent problem. One of the aims of conservation is to create or retain an ecological balance in natural or humanised landscapes. Probably the most urgent need for the application of conservation techniques is in the areas classified as high quality environment areas, where the natural resources are frequently very fragile and should not be subjected to avoidable pressures.[141]

Stamp[142] has shown how a man's care for his natural environment has become recognised as an essential concern of civilised society in general and of governments in particular. Nature reserves are no longer the concern of a minority organised in a few voluntary groups, but are areas held in trust for the nation by national and local bodies, official and unofficial, professional and amateur, all working in close liaison. Coppock[157] has described how geographers have an important rôle to play in the field of conservation, particularly on the impact of outdoor recreation on the countryside.

Conservation Policies and their Implementation

In this country the work of preserving plants and animals and their natural surroundings is undertaken by a wide variety of organisations:

(1) Preservation of natural areas basically for scientific purposes, for example, the Nature Conservancy.

(2) Preservation of countryside in its natural state primarily for the benefit of visitors, such as the Countryside Commission, National Trust and the Council for the Preservation of Rural England.

(3) Protection of resources, for example, the Forestry Commission.

(4) Preservation of particular creatures for their own sake, for example, the National Society for the Protection of Birds.

(5) Work undertaken by central and local planning authorities in restoration of derelict land and preservation of amenity.

(6) Preservation activities of great estates, colleges, and other bodies.[143]

TABLE 2.8

AREA OF NATIONAL NATURE RESERVES (IN HECTARES)

	Owned	Leased	Nature Reserve Agreement	Total (woodland area in brackets)	Number of reserves
England	6075	7850	9070	22 995 (1790)	60
Scotland	20 300	2138	51 850	74 288 (2025)	37
Wales	997	2567	3564	7128 (472)	27
Total area Total woodland area	27 372	12 555	64 484	104 411 (4287)	124

Source: *Nature Conservancy Handbook 1968*

Nature reserves have as their first priority the conservation of wild life but the Nature Conservancy's expressed policy is that human access is desirable in so far as this is compatible with the primary objects of conservation.[77] The Hertfordshire Countryside Appraisal[144] submits that many wild life protection areas are too small to be viable as isolated units, and their value lies very much in their relation with the surrounding countryside.

Ratcliffe[77] claims that conservation is a means of enriching the human way of life, in an intellectual or aesthetic sense, in the satisfaction gained by those with an interest in wild life. Approximately thirty-three per cent of the national nature reserves are open to the public free from any restrictions.[145] Table 2.8 shows the area of national nature reserves in 1968.[146]

Hedgerows and Roadside Verges

In agricultural land wild life is based largely on the hedgerows. Locke[147] estimated that in 1962 there were 990 000 km of hedgerows in Great Britain. Assuming an average width of hedgerow of 2 metres, we had in 1962 198 000 hectares of this habitat, equivalent to almost twice the total area of our national nature reserves. Hedge removal is proceeding countrywide and it is particularly severe in the east Midlands. In one study area in Huntingdonshire over seventy per cent of the hedges present in 1946 had been removed by 1966.[148] Smith[139] describes how large areas of Lincolnshire are now hedgeless and treeless arable prairies. Rationalisation of farm layout and careful budgeting of farm running costs often point to hedge elimination.[162]

As hedges are removed, the species diversity of birds is reduced. In much of East Anglia and the Midlands, where there are relatively few woods, the large scale reduction of hedges would have a considerable effect on the flora and fauna.[77] From the economic point of view there is the destruction of pests by wild life in the hedges and the soil erosion resisting properties of the hedges themselves. The continued removal of hedgerows has aroused considerable public interest and in the summer of 1969 was the subject of television features and correspondence in *The Times*.

Roadside verges are becoming increasingly important in the conservation of wild life, as arable land is cultivated more intensively and the character of parts of common land, heath and moor are changed. Stamp,[45] in 1962, estimated that there were 208 000 hectares of road in England and Wales and that thirty-three per cent of this could be taken as roadside verge—a total of about 69 300 hectares. Highway authorities are often under pressure from neighbouring farmers to clean up the verges and destroy the weeds. Way, of the Monks Wood Experimental Station,[77] maintains that very few of the plants that grow on roadside verges are weeds of agricultural land, and that it is doubtful whether they are of any real significance compared to those already on the agricultural land. Chemical spraying programmes are difficult, expensive and often suppress grass growth.

Of different groups of animals—forty per cent of British land mammals, 100 per cent of reptiles, twenty per cent of birds, forty per cent of butterflies and forty-five per cent of bumblebees have been known to breed on roadside verges or in their associated hedges and ditches.[77] Lindsey and Kesteven County Council scheduling of road verge nature reserves illustrates the need for more careful consideration of the use and management of verges.[139]

Conservation and Recreation

In evaluating an environment for its recreational potential, Law[100] has listed three techniques which can usefully be applied:

(1) Identify any unique natural areas which should be preserved from over use by humans and vehicles.

(2) Assess the level of use—the environmental capacity—for the remainder of the area, sub-divided into smaller units of uniform character for recreational purposes.

(3) Use management techniques to keep actual use levels on a par with theoretical levels—in particular by the use of parking controls to restrict use of the site.

With the spectacular increase in mobility and leisure time, the pressure of recreational use on the countryside has become much more intense and this has given rise to problems in reconciling recreational needs and nature conservation. Whenever too many people visit an area, its natural interest is likely to be reduced by loss of the more sensitive species of plants and animals.[148]

Coastal sand dunes, for instance, are particularly attractive to human beings but also especially vulnerable to the pressure of their feet. Great concentrations of visitors on relatively small areas of scenic and scientific importance present both a problem and an opportunity. The problem is to ensure the conservation of the very features which make the areas attractive; the opportunity is that of having people in a situation where they are particularly receptive to information about the environment they are enjoying and its management and conservation.

The shallow lakes, rivers and waterways of the Norfolk Broads form a good example of a region of high scientific interest which is being used for recreational purposes on an ever increasing scale. To the naturalist, geographer and research worker, the region is of the greatest possible interest. This is partly because of the survival of extensive areas of unreclaimed fenland containing an abundance of plant and insect rarities, and partly because of the fascinating history of the region. The Broads originated as mediaeval pit diggings which became flooded, and almost all the surrounding fenland was in former times used as a source of reed, marsh hay or peat for fuel. Two national nature reserves have been established at Hickling Broad and Bure Marshes.[148]

The holiday industry was well established before the Second World War, when some 80 000 visitors came to the Broads annually, many of them to enjoy the peaceful unspoilt surroundings. Since the war great changes have occurred—the number of holiday visitors has increased more than threefold, and the character of their demands has changed. Most of them are no longer sailing enthusiasts, but prefer motor driven craft. They tend to be more gregarious than formerly and to enjoy crowding together at moorings and for communal entertainment. There is also heavy pressure, especially at weekends, from the rapidly increasing numbers of day visitors who use the area for dinghy sailing and racing, angling, canoeing, sightseeing and picnicking.[148] A Norfolk County Council report[149] refers to the sharp conflict between holiday interests and those associated with conservation in certain parts of the Broads.

An excellent example of the multi-purpose planning of a harbour is the scheme prepared by the Nature Conservancy for Poole Harbour.[150] The report suggests the zoning of the harbour into four distinct sectors:

(1) Wharves, jetties, piers, moorings and marinas to be confined to the already much developed shores on the Poole-Sandbanks side.

(2) Recreation to be accommodated both afloat and ashore in the central strip of the harbour.

(3) To avoid exploitation of the islands in the south-western parts of the harbour by confining recreational use to the deep water channels.

(4) To preserve the bays and creeks of the remote shores on the Purbeck approaches as wild life sanctuaries and feeding grounds.

In this way it should be possible to keep the balance between man and wild life; between artificial and natural; between noisy and peaceful.

It is interesting to read of the nature trails laid out by naturalists in the Algonquin Park conservation area, occupying 7500 km², in Northern Ontario.[151] Most are about 1.5–3 km in length and all culminate in some point of interest, possibly a lake, a beaver's dam or an elevated view point. Highland hiking trails are planned to take 1, 2 or 3 days with overnight camp sites. Guidance is given on the best places in which to see rare birds, wild flowers and unusual trees. In the evenings there are film shows and lectures by experts on country subjects.

Wider Implications of Conservation

The World Health Organisation[29] has drawn attention to the need to take immediate steps in many parts of the world to control gross pollution of the air, land and water. Water, for instance, is a resource to be shared by industry, power, transport, agriculture, and communities, as well as individuals. Far too often self-interest prevails and irreparable damage results. The expert committee expressed the view that in general pollution should be controlled at its source—prevention is very much more effective than cure. This theme is re-asserted in the government report on river pollution,[160] as a result of which the Government authorised the spending of £1300 million over a 5-year period in tackling sources of pollution.

During 1970 over twenty European countries took part in a European Conservation Year. It was organised under the guidance of the Council of Europe, and aimed to focus attention on the way people affect and change the lands they live in by their various activities, and to agree on conservation policies. Throughout Europe there is growing concern about the adverse effects on the environment—especially on air, water, coast and countryside—from increasing pressures caused by population numbers and technologies.[152]

Prince Philip in his ECY inauguration address stated:

From now on the problem will be to create the right kind of administrative organisation to cope with the conservation of our environment. The conservation of our environment includes refuse disposal, pollution, building, industrial development, transport, leisure activities, agriculture, wildlife, water resources, extraction, noise, unsightliness, smell and dirt. These are all inter-related, they all have an influence on the quality of existence for all people and they cannot be dealt with piece-meal.[153]

REFERENCES

1. CLAWSON, M., HELD, R. B. and STODDARD, C. H. (1962). P. 1 in *Land for the Future,* John Hopkins Press, Baltimore

2. WIBBERLEY, G. P. Land scarcity in Britain. *Journal of Royal Town Planning Institute,* **53.4,** (1967), 129

3. MAN, A. M. The countryside challenge. *The Young Farmer,* (March 1969), 8

4. DOWER, M. Fourth wave—the challenge of leisure. *The Architects' Journal,* (20 January, 1965), 125

5. JONES, E. (1962). P. 21 in *The City in Geography,* London School of Economics and Political Science

6. CHAPIN, F. S. and WEISS, S. F. (1962). *Factors Influencing Land Development,* Institute for Research in Social Science, University of North Carolina

7. BEST, R. H. and COPPOCK, J. T. (1962). *The Changing Use of Land in Britain,* Faber and Faber

8. CIRIACY-WANTRUP, S. V. The 'new' competition for land and some implications for public policy. *Natural Resources Journal,* **4.2,** (1964), 252–267

9. CHISHOLM, M. (1966). P. 12 in *Rural Settlement and Land Use,* Hutchinson

10. NORTON, G. A. *An Economic Analysis of Outdoor Recreation as a Rural Land-using Activity in North Wales.* Private communication, University College of North Wales, Department of Agriculture, (1968)

11. EDWARDS, A. M. and WIBBERLEY, G. P. (1971) *An Agricultural Land Budget for Britain 1965–2000,* Wye College of Rural Economics

12. BEST, R. H. (1966). *Land for New Towns,* Town and Country Planning Association

13. MINISTRY OF HOUSING AND LOCAL GOVERNMENT. *Planning Bulletin No. 2: Residential Areas—higher densities,* H.M.S.O., (1962)

14. NEW TOWNS COMMITTEE REPORTS, *Cmd. 6759, 6794 and 6876,* H.M.S.O., (1945–46)

15. BEST, R. H. Extent of urban growth and agricultural displacement in post-war Britain. *Urban Studies,* **5.1,** (1968)

16. JONES, E. Resources and environmental restraints. *Urban Studies,* **6.3,** (1969)

17. CLARK, C. (1967). P. 352 in *Population Growth and Land Use,* Macmillan

18. EDWARDS, A. Land requirements for United Kingdom agriculture by the year 2000. *Town and Country Planning,* (March 1969)

19. WIBBERLEY, G. P., Pressures on Britain's land resources. *Tenth Heath Memorial Lecture.* University of Nottingham School of Agriculture (1965)

20. RODGERS, H. B. Leisure and recreation. *Urban Studies,* **6.3,** (1969), 368–384

21. BURTON, T. L. and WIBBERLEY, G. P. (1965). *Outdoor Recreation in the British Countryside—studies in rural land-use,* Wye College

22. HOOKWAY, R. J. S. (1969). *Landowners and Land for Leisure,* Countryside Commission

23. BRITISH TRAVEL ASSOCIATION/UNIVERSITY OF KEELE. *Pilot National Recreation Survey; Report No. 1,* (1967)

24. WEBBER, M. (1968). *Beyond the Industrial Age and Permissive Planning,* Centre for Environmental Studies

25. SEELEY, I. H. (1967). P. 228 in *Municipal Engineering Practice,* Macmillan

26. CHAPIN, F. S. (1965). *Urban Land-use Planning,* University of Illinois Press

27. HOYES, T. (1968). *The Evaluation of Alternatives in Land-use Planning.* Proceedings of the Nottingham Symposium on Sub-regional Studies, Regional Studies Association

28. DENMAN, D. R. and HOYES, T. (1968). P. 11 in *Land Systems and Urban Development,* International Federation of Surveyors

29. WORLD HEALTH ORGANISATION. *Technical Report No. 297: Environmental Health Aspects of Metropolitan Planning and Development,* World Health Organisation, Geneva (1965)

30. ARVILL, R. Planning and the future. *Forward in Europe,* Strasbourg, (1968), 11–12

31. KIEFER, R. W. Land Evaluation for Land-use Planning. *Building Science 1,* Pergamon Press, (1965), 109

32. MCCULLOCH, F. J. (1965). Pp. 1–24 in *Land-use in an Urban Environment—the Social and Economic Determinants of Land Use,* Liverpool University Press

33. CLEMENS, K. (1968). *Planning Policies and Organisation,* International Federation of Surveyors

34. HOOKWAY, R. J. S. and HARTLEY, J. A. (1969). *Resource Planning,* Countryside Commission

35. THORBURN, A. (1968). *The Process of Sub-regional Planning.* Proceedings of the Nottingham Symposium on Sub-regional Studies, Regional Studies Association

36. WILLHELM, S. M. (1962). *Urban Zoning and Land-use Theory,* Free Press of Glencoe, New York

37. BELLCHAMBERS, R. G. An exercise in participation. *Town and Country Planning,* (September, 1969)

38. COWAN, P. Developing patterns of urbanisation. *Urban Studies,* **6.3,** (1969)

39. LEAN, W. and GOODALL, B. (1966) *Aspects of Land Economics.* Estates Gazette

40. LEAN, W. (1969) *Economics of Land-use Planning: Urban and Regional.* Estates Gazette

41. TOWN PLANNING INSTITUTE. Geographical factors in the location and size of settlements. *Research for Urban Planning, Report F,* (1963), 15–17

42. HEAP, D. (1967). *Introducing the Land Commission Act,* Sweet and Maxwell

43. BRACKETT, W. R. and HOYES, T. (1966). *Possible Influences of a Land Commission on the Property Market and the Availability of Land. Proceedings of the Annual Conference of the Royal Institution of Chartered Surveyors*

44. DENMAN, D. R. The implication of the Land Commission in urban renewal. *Urban Renewal,* University of Salford (1967), 1–17

45. STAMP, L. D. (1962). *The Land of Britain; Its Use and Misuse,* Longman

46. OUTDOOR RECREATION RESOURCES REVIEW COMMISSION. (1962). *Outdoor Recreation for America,* Washington D.C.

47. TURNER, D. B. *Providing an Adequate Resource Base for Public Recreation. Resources for Tomorrow Conference,* Montreal, (1961)

48. CURL, J. S. The upsurge of leisure: towards a national plan. *Official Architect and Planner,* **32.8,** (1969), 936–939

49. DARBY, H. C. British National Parks. *Advancement of Science,* **20.86,** (1963)

50. PETERS, G. H. Farm sales prices in 1962. *Estates Gazette,* **185,** (1963), 543

51. STONE, P. A. The price of sites for residential building. *The Property Developer,* (1964)

52. WENDT, P. F. Theory of urban land values. *Land Economics,* (August 1957)

53. THORNCROFT, M. E. T. (1968). *Appraisal Technique and Practice,* International Federation of Surveyors

54. STONE, P. A. (1965). The Price of Building Sites in Britain. *Land Values,* Sweet and Maxwell

55. UTHWATT COMMITTEE. *Expert Committee on Compensation and Betterment, Cmd. 6386,* (1942)

56. LICHFIELD, N. (1966) *Economics of Planned Development* Estates Gazette

57. HALL, P. (1965). The Land Values Problem and its Solution. *Land Values,* Sweet and Maxwell

58. CLARKE, P. H. (1965). Site Value Rating and the Recovery of Betterment. *Land Values,* Sweet and Maxwell

59. ANDREWS, J. S. *A Study of the Development of Land Values in a North London Dormitory Area, Relating the Changes to Demand and Supply Factors, with Particular Reference to Planning Legislation and Practice in the Post-1945 Period.* Private communication, University of London, (1961), 102

60. DENMAN, D. R. *Land in the Market. Hobart paper No. 30,* Institute of Economic Affairs, (1964)

61. MCAUSLAN, J. Price movements for residential land: 1965–1969. *Chartered Surveyor,* **102.3,** (1969), 123–127

62. BRITTON, W. *Control through Fiscal Policy. Paper 2—Public Control of Land Use,* College of Estate Management/University of Reading, (1966)

63. ANSTEY, B. (1965). A Study of Certain Changes in Land Values in the London Area in the Period 1950–64. *Land Values,* Sweet and Maxwell

64. SHANKLAND, G. *Planning Consultant's Report No. 10: City of Liverpool,* (1963), 40

65. WIBBERLEY, G. P. (1959). *Agriculture and Urban Growth,* Joseph

66. KNETSCH, J. L. Land values and parks in fringe areas. *Journal of Farm Economics,* **37.4,** (1961), 1723

67. OXENHAM, J. R. (1966). *Reclaiming Derelict Land,* Faber and Faber

68. HOOKWAY, R. J. S. (1969). *Planning of Land Resources: Recreation in the Countryside,* Countryside Commission

69. MACDERMOT, N. Second reading of Countryside Bill. *Parliamentary Debates (Hansard),* **753.9,** (1967), cols. 1427–8

70. WALTERS, I. S. *Planning for Outdoor Recreation in the British Countryside.* Private communication, University of London, (1968)

71. AN FORBAS FORBARTHA. *Planning for Amenity and Tourism,* Dublin, (1966)

72. BUCHANAN, C. D. *South Hampshire Study. Vol. 2,* H.M.S.O., (1966)

73. NATURE CONSERVANCY. *The Countryside in 1970. Proceedings of Study Conference, London,* (1964)

74. CENTRAL COUNCIL OF PHYSICAL RECREATION. *Sport and the Community,* (1960)

75. DOWER, M. and MCCARTHY, P. E. Planning for conservation and development. *Journal of Royal Town Planning Institute,* **53.3,** (1967)

76. ROYAL TOWN PLANNING INSTITUTE. *Planning for the Changing Countryside,* (1968)

77. NATURE CONSERVANCY. (1967). *The Biotic Effects of Public Pressures on the Environment. Monks Wood Experimental Station, Symposium No. 3,* Natural Environment Research Council

78. WOLFE, R. I. Perspective on outdoor recreation: a bibliographical survey. *Geographical Review,* **44.2** (1964), 203–235

79. WILLEY, F. T. *Leisure in the Countryside. Proceedings of Annual Conference of Royal Institution of Chartered Surveyors,* (1966)

80. AMERICAN ASSOCIATION FOR THE ADVANCEMENT OF SCIENCE. *Land and Water Use. Publication No. 73,* (1963)

81. CLAWSON, M. and KNETSCH, J. L. (1966). *Economics of Outdoor Recreation,* John Hopkins Press, Baltimore

82. GOULD, E. M. Forestry and recreation. *Harvard Forest Papers No. 6.* Harvard Forest, Massachusetts, (1962)

83. HEYTZE, J. C. (1969). *Recreation in the Forestry of Nunspeet,* State Forest Service of the Netherlands

84. WIBBERLEY, G. P. (1969). *The British Countryside in the Year 2000,* Council for the Protection of Rural Wales

85. SPORTS COUNCIL. (1968). *Planning for Sport,* Central Council of Physical Recreation

86. NATIONAL PLAYING FIELDS ASSOCIATION. *School Playing Fields—dual use policies in operation,* (1964)

87. MINISTRY OF HOUSING AND LOCAL GOVERNMENT. *Circular No. 49/64,* and DEPARTMENT OF EDUCATION AND SCIENCE. *Circular No. 11/64, Provision of Facilities for Sport,* H.M.S.O., (1964)

88. EAST MIDLAND SPORTS COUNCIL. *Dual use of Sports Facilities in Education and Industry,* (1968)

89. WEST MIDLANDS SPORTS COUNCIL. *Dual Use Committee Report,* (1967)

90. YORKSHIRE AND HUMBERSIDE SPORTS COUNCIL. *Report on the Dual Use of Educational Facilities,* (1968)

91. HOWELL, D., Joint Provision. *Times Educational Supplement,* (18 February, 1966)

92. DAWLEY DEVELOPMENT CORPORATION. *Dawley New Town—Madeley Educational and Recreational Centre*

93. FARRER, J. A modern approach to the provision of a sports centre: An example of co-operation between local authorities. *Report of a Conference on Planning for Management.* National Playing Fields Association, (1967)

94. LICKORISH, L. J., Planning for recreation and leisure. *Journal of the Royal Town Planning Institute,* **51.6,** (1965)

95. CHESHIRE COUNTY COUNCIL. *Cheshire Countryside—an interim report on recreation,* (1968)

96. OUTDOOR RECREATION RESOURCES REVIEW COMMISSION. *Study report 20. Participation in Outdoor Recreation: Factors Affecting Demand among American Adults,* Washington D.C., (1962)

97. GRIFFITHS, I. *Sociology of Leisure. Proceedings of Conference on Planning for Recreation of West Midlands Branch of Regional Studies Association, Birmingham,* (1969)

98. KNETSCH, J. L. Communications: Assessing the demand for outdoor recreation. *Journal of Leisure Research,* **1.1,** (1969)

99. CIRIACY-WANTRUP, S. V. Conceptual problems in projecting the demand for land and water. *Paper 3 of Land Economics Institute, Urbana,* University of Illinois, (1960)

100. LAW, S. Planning for outdoor recreation in the countryside. *Journal of Royal Town Planning Institute,* **53.9,** (1967), 383–386

101. PALMER, J. E., *Recreational Planning—a bibliographical review. Planning Outlook 2,* (1967)

102. STATE OF CALIFORNIA. *Park and Recreation Information System. Planning monograph No. 2,* (1966)

103. BURTON, T. L. (1967). *Windsor Great Park: A Recreation Study,* Wye College, University of London

104. BURTON, T. L. A day in the country. *Chartered Surveyor,* **98.7,** (1966)

105. WAGER, J. F. How common is the land? *New Society 4,* (1964)

106. NATIONAL PLAYING FIELDS ASSOCIATION. *Planning for Recreation: Application of NPFA Standard,* (1967)

107. MINISTRY OF HOUSING AND LOCAL GOVERNMENT. *Open Spaces. Technical Memorandum No. 6,* H.M.S.O., (1956)

108. DEPARTMENT OF EDUCATION AND SCIENCE. *Building Bulletin 28. Playing Fields and Hard Surface Areas,* H.M.S.O., (1966)

109. NATURAL RESOURCES BOARD. *Recreational Use of Land in the United States,* (1938)

110. BUTLER, G. D. Standards for municipal recreation areas. *Recreation,* New York, (July/August 1948)

111. LEWIS, P. H. (1961). *Recreation and Open Space in Illinois,* University of Illinois, Urbana

112. WINGO, L., (Ed.) (1967). *Cities and Space: The Future Use of Urban Land,* John Hopkins Press, Baltimore

113. CLAWSON, M. and STEWART, C. L. (1965). *Land Use Information,* John Hopkins Press, Baltimore

114. WILLIS, M. Provision of sports pitches. *Town Planning Review,* **38.4,** (1968), 293–303

115. WINTERBOTTOM, D. M. How much urban space do we need? *Journal of Royal Town Planning Institute,* **53.4,** (1967), 144–147

116. MINISTRY OF HOUSING AND LOCAL GOVERNMENT. *Derelict Land and its Reclamation. Technical Memorandum No. 7,* H.M.S.O. (1956)

117. DOWNING, M. F., *The Reclamation of Derelict Landscape. Planning Outlook 3,* (1967), 38–52

118. DAVISON, D. J. Reclamation—do we mean business? *Town and Country Planning,* (November 1969), 507–511

119. CASSON, J. Derelict land. *Chartered Surveyor,* (February 1967), 435–437

120. FORD, B. J. Industrial dereliction and Britain's beauty. *New Scientist,* (28 August 1969), 428–429

121. LORD ROBENS. *The Use and Development of the Nation's Resources. Proceedings of the Annual Conference of the Royal Institution of Chartered Surveyors,* (1966)

122. NOTTINGHAMSHIRE COUNTY COUNCIL AND OTHERS. *Nottinghamshire and Derbyshire Sub-regional Study,* (1969)

123. MINISTRY OF HOUSING AND LOCAL GOVERNMENT. (1963). *New Life for Dead Lands,* H.M.S.O.

124. CIVIC TRUST. *Derelict Land,* (1964)

125. ARVILL, R. (Boote). (1967). *Man and Environment,* Penguin

126. LOWE, H. J. Industry in the countryside. *Town and Country Planning,* (April 1968), 218–221

127. GRAHAM, M. and BUTLER, B. Play sward on colliery shale. *Town and Country Planning,* **30.2,** (1962), 70–74

128. WISE, M. J. The Midland Reafforesting Association, 1903–1924 and the reclamation of derelict land in the Black Country. *Journal of Institute of Landscape Architects,* (February 1962), 13–18

129. WOOD, R. F. and THIRGOOD, J. V. Tree planting on colliery spoil heaps. *Colliery Engineering,* (December 1955 and January 1956)

130. LAURIE, I. C. A tree planted pit heap at Littleburn, Co. Durham. *Journal of Institute of Landscape Architects,* (November 1962), 14–15

131. SAND AND GRAVEL ASSOCIATION OF GREAT BRITAIN. *SAGA,* (1967)

132. WOOLDRIDGE, S. W. and BEAVER, S. H. The working of sand and gravel in Britain: A problem in land use. *Geographical Journal,* **115,** (1950), 42–54

133. HARTWRIGHT, T. U. (1960). *Planting Trees and Shrubs in Gravel Workings,* Sand and Gravel Association

134. HILTON, K. J., (Ed.) (1967). *The Lower Swansea Valley Project,* Longmans

135. RUBINSTEIN, D. and SPEAKMAN, C. *Leisure, Transport and the Countryside.* Fabian Research Series 277, (1969)

136. CASSON, J. Reclamation and recreation. *Paper to Institute of Advanced Architectural Studies Conference on Planning for Recreation, York,* (1967)

137. DOWNING, M. F. and VYLE, C. J. Landscape reclamation research project, University of Newcastle-upon-Tyne. *Journal of Institute of Landscape Architects,* (August 1969), 6–7

138. SAYERS, P. R. New towns from old: A plea for more active use of open space. *Park Administration,* **33.11,** (1968), 30–32

139. SMITH, A. E. (1969). *Nature Conservation in Lincolnshire,* Lincolnshire Naturalists' Union

140. HOOKWAY, R. J. S. The management of Britain's rural land. *Paper to Town and Country Planning Summer School,* (1967)

141. THE COUNTRYSIDE IN 1970. Report of study group No. 6 *Outdoor Recreation: Active and Passive.* Second Conference, (1965)
142. STAMP, D. (1969). *Nature Conservation in Britain,* Collins
143. CLARK, S. B. K. Recreation and the preservation and restoration of amenity. *Chartered Surveyor,* (December 1966), 314–315
144. HERTFORDSHIRE COUNTY COUNCIL. *Hertfordshire Countryside Appraisal,* (1969), 15
145. THOMPSON, J. A. (1969). *The Right to Conserve. Proceedings of Conference on Recreation in the Countryside,* University of Loughborough
146. NATURE CONSERVANCY. (1968). *The Nature Conservancy Handbook 1968,* H.M.S.O.
147. LOCKE, G. M. A sample survey of field and other boundaries in Great Britain. *Journal of Forestry,* **56,** (1962)
148. NATURE CONSERVANCY. *The Nature Conservancy Progress 1964–1968,* (1968)
149. NORFOLK COUNTY COUNCIL. *Report on the Norfolk Holiday Industry,* (1964), 17
150. NATURE CONSERVANCY. *Poole Harbour and the Isle of Purbeck: A Conservation Study,* (1967)
151. HOLMES, A. W. Countryside conservation in Canada. *Town and Country Planning,* (April 1968), 226–230
152. EUROPEAN CONSERVATION YEAR 1970, E.C.Y. pamphlet, (1969)
153. EUROPEAN CONSERVATION YEAR 1970, E.C.Y. Newsletter, (January 1970)
154. CLARK, S. B. K. *Restoration of Derelict Land. Proceedings of Annual Conference of Royal Institution of Chartered Surveyors,* University of Warwick, (1970)
155. INSTITUTE OF LANDSCAPE ARCHITECTS. Stoke-on-Trent reclamation programme. *Journal of Institute of Landscape Architects* **90,** (1970)
156. MUNTON, R. J. C. Recreation in semi-natural environments—methods of investigation employed in the Isles of Scilly. *Recreation News,* **16,** (1970)
157. COPPOCK, J. T. Geographers and conservation. *Area 2,* Institute of British Geographers, (1970)
158. LICHFIELD, N. Evaluation methodology of urban and regional plans: A review. *Regional Studies,* **4.2,** (1970)
159. PEARS, N. V. Man in the Cairngorms: A population/resource balance problem. *Scottish Geographical Magazine,* **84.1,** (1968), 45–55
160. DEPARTMENT OF THE ENVIRONMENT. *Report of a River Pollution Survey of England and Wales, Volume 1,* H.M.S.O., (1971)
161. COUNTRYSIDE RECREATION RESEARCH ADVISORY GROUP. *Countryside Recreation Glossary,* Countryside Commission, (1970)
162. TEATHER, E. K. The hedgerow: an analysis of a changing landscape feature. *Geography,* **55.247,** (1970)

3 ECONOMICS OF OUTDOOR RECREATION

THIS CHAPTER INVESTIGATES the problems involved in the evaluation of recreational benefits and the methodology which has evolved. Cost-benefit analysis techniques and their applications are also examined and an attempt is made to produce a basis for a realistic approach which is then applied to specific facilities in Nottingham. There are indeed many problems inherent in the quantifying and evaluation of social costs and benefits. The central core of most approaches to the economics of recreation is the distance travelled concept, as the cost of travel to a non-priced facility must give some indication of the value of the use of the resource to the visitor. There is, however, an evident need to refine present techniques.

PROBLEM OF EVALUATING NON-PRICED FACILITIES

Many think of outdoor recreation as a public service aimed at improving the health, education, culture and general well-being of the population.[1] Viewed in this way it might even be argued that recreation has a special set of values and cannot be a subject for normal economic analysis.[2] On reflection, many goods have personal, spiritual and psychic values which vary from person to person and outdoor recreation is not unique in this respect. Enjoyment of outdoor recreation in public parks is often regarded as free because no charge is made for entry to the facility. In fact, the service is provided by society at a cost and the participant will probably contribute to the cost through rates and taxes.[3] Robinson[4] expresses the view that parks, as a non-chargeable facility, satisfy recreational needs when the participants cannot afford to pay for other forms of recreation. In this way parks provide a means of income redistribution through subsidies-in-kind,[5] although this is not wholly true since the rich as well as the poor visit parks.

Evaluation of recreational resources has been made difficult as many of them are not regulated by conventional market pricing and are not subject to formal prices or fees.[6] Yet some measure is often needed to establish a priority among projects or among uses of a given resource. For example, in economic terms, a public park is justified only if no alternative use of that resource yields a greater satisfaction to the community as a whole.[1] In the absence of the usual market indicators of value, the solution lies in estimating demand for the recreation from indirect evidence as to how much users would be prepared to pay if the facilities were marketed in the usual way. It may be argued that the willingness of individual users to pay a price will underestimate the social worth of recreational resources because of important external benefits.[7] Hence, it would seem opportune at this stage to examine the concept of cost-benefit analysis which aims at enumerating and evaluating all relevant costs and benefits, both direct and indirect.

COST-BENEFIT ANALYSIS

Nature of Technique

Cost-benefit analysis has its origins in a paper presented by a French economist, Dupuit, in 1884, on the utility of public works. The technique has been further developed in the United States where its sphere of operation has been extended into many aspects of society, including river and harbour projects and flood control schemes.[8] Cost-benefit analysis aims at setting out the factors which need to be taken into account in making certain economic choices. Most of the choices to which it has been applied involve investment projects and decisions—whether or not a particular project is worthwhile financially; which is the best of several alternative projects; or even when to undertake a particular project. The aim is generally to maximise the present values of all benefits less that of all costs, subject to specified restraints. Hender[20] has defined cost-benefit analysis as 'a technique of use in either investment appraisal or the review of the operation of a service for analysing and measuring the costs and benefits to the community of adopting specified courses of action and for examining the incidence of these costs and benefits between different sections of the community'.

It has the basic objective of identifying and measuring the costs and benefits which stem from either the investment of monies or the operation of a service, but in particular it is concerned with examining not only those costs and benefits which have a direct impact on the providing authority but also those which are of an external nature and accrue to other persons. Furthermore, the costs and benefits to be measured are those which accrue throughout the life of the project.

Prest and Turvey[9] considered that the principal criteria to be determined were:

(1) Which costs and benefits are to be included?

(2) How are they to be valued?

(3) At what interest rate are they to be discounted?

(4) What are the relevant constraints?

Wilson[21] has described the methods to be used in a cost-benefit study and the methodology can be usefully summarised as:

(1) Define the problems to be studied.

(2) Identify the alternative courses of action.

(3) Identify the costs and benefits
   (a) to the providing authority
   (b) to external parties.

(4) Evaluate the costs and benefits.

(5) Draw conclusions as to the alternative to be adopted.

Enumeration of Costs and Benefits

Some of the more commonly used expressions are defined and described.

Social costs may be defined as the sum total of costs involved as the result of an economic action. *Private costs* are those which affect the decisions of the performers. Hence production costs include those of labour, materials, land and capital. There may also be *external costs*—for instance damage to buildings or decline of property values through smoke emanating from a factory, the costs incurred not being met by the industrialist.

Similar effects may occur on the other side of the equation—benefits are reflected in the amount paid by consumers for goods produced; but, in addition, favourable externalities might also accrue to society. An example could be a dam which, in addition to generating electricity for sale in the market, gives flood protection to others for which they may not pay.[10]

Where there are strong relationships on either the supply or the demand side, allowance must be made for these in cost-benefit calculations. Thus where an authority responsible for a long stretch of river constructs a dam at a point upstream, this will affect the water level and hence the operation of existing or potential dams downstream. The construction of a fast motorway which in itself speeds up traffic and reduces accidents, may lead to more congestion or more accidents on feeder roads if they are left unimproved.

Externalities are the costs and benefits which accrue to bodies other than the one sponsoring a project. The promoters of public investment projects should take into account the external effects of their actions in so far as they alter the physical production possibilities of other producers or the satisfactions that consumers can obtain from given resources; they should not take side effects into account if the sole effect is through the prices of products or factors.[11]

An example of an external effect to be taken into account would be the construction of a reservoir by the upstream authority of a river basin which results in more dredging by a downstream authority. An example of a side effect is where the improvement of a road leads to a greater profitability of the garages and restaurants on that road and the employment of more labour by them, higher rent payments, and so on. Any net difference in profitability and any net rise in rents and land values is simply a reflection of the benefits of more journeys being undertaken, and it would be double counting if these were included too.[9]

Valuation of Costs and Benefits

With benefits in particular we are often concerned with streams of payments over a period of time, and it is essential that all costs and benefits shall be expressed in equivalent terms. For instance, a payment of £1 per annum for a period of 60 years is roughly equivalent to a lump sum payment of £19 today, assuming a compound rate of interest of five per cent. Nineteen pounds is the sum which would need to be invested today to provide sufficient funds from which to make the annual payments.

We may be concerned with three types of cost—present, initial or capital costs; annual costs; and periodic costs. All these require reducing to a common basis for comparison purposes by discounting future costs. There are two possible approaches:

(1) To discount all future costs at an appropriate rate of interest—often taken at five or six per cent (long-term pure interest rate with no allowance for risk premium)—and so to convert all payments to present value (PV) or present worth. (There are valuation tables available for this purpose.)

(2) To express all costs and benefits in the form of annual equivalents, taking into account the interest rate and annual sinking fund.

Interest Rates

Wilson[21] points out that there are three ways of assessing the interest rate to be used:

(1) *The social time preference rate:* this is a positive rate of interest which expresses the value persons place on having assets now, rather than at some time in the future. Adopting the kind of life tables used by insurance companies, a social time preference rate could be as low as one or two per cent.

(2) *The rate of interest at which the Government lends and borrows:* this is, roughly, the risk-free rate of interest.

(3) *The opportunity cost rate of interest:* this is the rate of return which could operate if the project being evaluated were not carried out, and so freeing the capital for an alternative opportunity.

Constraints

Projects are frequently subject to a variety of constraints or restricting factors and these have been classified by Eckstein.[12]

(1) *Physical* constraints—the most common is the production function which relates the physical inputs and outputs of a project. Where a choice is involved between different projects or concerning the size or timing of a particular project, external physical restraints may also be relevant.

(2) *Legal* constraints—restrictions such as rights of access and time needed for public inquiries may be encountered.

(3) *Administrative* constraints—possibly limiting the size of the project.

(4) *Uncertainties*—resulting from possible unreliability of estimates on future trends and other factors.

(5) *Distributional and budgetary* constraints—for instance, tolls on a motorway will affect the volume of traffic and may influence the width of the carriageways.

Applications of Cost-benefit Analysis

Cost-benefit analysis techniques are being applied to a wide range of projects.

In Great Britain one of the first cost-benefit studies was that conducted by Coburn, Beesley and Reynolds[13] on the economic assessment of the London-Birmingham motorway. This attempted to provide the economic justification for the expenditure of large sums of public money on motorway construction by showing the benefits which would flow from their development. It was restricted in as much as it was concerned with the benefits directly attributable to the construction of motorways and did not take account of the effect these new roads would have on neighbouring communities.

A further important study was undertaken by Beesley and Foster[14] on the construction of the Victoria underground line in London. This study took place after the decision to construct the line had been taken and attempted to show the benefits which would accrue to different sectors of the population when it became operational. It is a particularly useful study for the way it illustrates the difficulty of placing measurements on certain intangible items, such as time savings during leisure hours, and also for the way it emphasises the importance of exercising extreme care in deciding the 'cut-off' points in a practical exercise.

The action of public authorities often has a ripple effect—the costs and benefits spread out from the centre and get more diffuse and difficult to measure as they become more remote from the direct action taken by the authority. Hender[20] gives the example of a local authority providing a housing estate which affects the tenants and also shopkeepers and others who provide them with services. It could also affect servicing arrangements in neighbouring communities and a decision has to be taken as to the extent to which attempts are made to measure these indirect effects. Determining cut-off points is often one of the most difficult problems because if it is too tightly circumscribed then major effects will be omitted from the study.

Lichfield[15-18] has evolved a methodology known as the planning balance sheet by which he has applied cost-benefit analysis to a wide range of town and regional planning problems. A brief account of the methodology of analysis will explain its distinctive features.

An initial step is to enumerate the sectors of the community which are affected by the alternative proposals, treating them on the one hand as producers and operators of the investment to be made in the new project and on the other hand as consumers of the goods and services arising from that project. Then for each sector the question is asked: 'What would be the difference in costs and in benefits which would accrue under the respective schemes under examination?'.

The costs and benefits comprise all those which are of relevance to the planning decision. They thus include those which are direct as between the parties to the transaction and those which are indirect and come within the conventional definition of social costs and benefits; those which relate to real resources and those which are transfers; those which cannot be measured as well as those which can. Thus it is possible to evolve and summarise a set of social accounts for each sector of the community showing clearly the differences in costs and benefits which will accrue to them under the alternative plans. This final summary of social accounts does not produce the decision itself any more than any other economic calculus, but is the basis for the judgement leading to the decision. In some studies the judgement that ought to be made is apparent; in others the issues are more finely balanced.

Cost-benefit analyses carried out by or on behalf of government departments include the Cambrian coast railway (1968); congestion costs in London (1968); Thamesmead river crossing (1969); dispersal of government offices (1969); rural water supplies (1968); recreation at Grafham Water (1969); improvement areas (1969–70); development in the Clyde Estuary (1968); and the third London airport (1969). A series of cost-benefit studies prepared under the auspices of the Institute of Municipal Treasurers and Accountants[19] included alternative forms of housing (Coventry), industrial site development (Durham) and city centre redevelopment (Norwich).

Wide divergences of view have been expressed about the rôle and usefulness of cost-benefit analysis. Peston[22] and Stocks[23] both stress the perplexities stemming from uncertainties about the consequences of various courses of action and the difficulties of measuring the costs and benefits. Diverse types of benefit, avoidance of double counting, dealing with externalities and choice of discount rates pose a formidable range of problems.

On the other hand it must be considered whether or not there is a better alternative. The situation was well summed up in the Resources for Tomorrow Conference at Montreal in 1961:[24]

There was general agreement that benefit-cost analysis is a basically useful tool in project evaluation. While it has certain limitations and is sometimes difficult to apply, it is, nevertheless, an objective approach to the selection of projects. It was emphasised that benefit-cost analysis should be regarded only as a tool to be used in the decision making process but not as a substitute for that process.

An important advantage of cost-benefit study is that it compels those responsible to quantify costs and benefits as far as possible, rather than resting content with vague qualitative judgements or personal hunches. Furthermore, quantification and evaluation of benefits—however rough—does give some indication of the charges which consumers are willing to pay.[9] Its limitations are clearly shown in the Roskill Commission's report on the third London airport, where after costing all the intangibles relating to the four sites and arriving at total figures in excess of £4000 million, the cheapest site at Cublington is only five per cent less than the most expensive at Foulness. This is hardly a large enough margin to be conclusive in making a choice.

EVALUATION OF OUTDOOR RECREATION

At the commencement of this chapter some of the difficulties in evaluating a non-priced resource were described. Crutchfield[25] describes two approaches which find an economic analysis of outdoor recreation completely untenable. The first approach asserts that it is not feasible to attach values to such nebulous concepts as beauty or nature while the second maintains that it is quite wrong to attempt to value the higher aspects of man's activities. While accepting that these arguments have some validity, they do not in themselves preclude the measurement of the more basic components of the recreational experience which are related to the abstract aspects. Consideration will now be given to the various methods which have been devised for the evaluation of recreational resources.

User Days

One method which has been used extensively in the United States is to compute the number of days of use of a facility by visitors over a specified period. The main weakness of this approach is that it assumes that hours of use by different persons on different sites are identical in value. Yet the distances travelled to the sites, the activities pursued and the amounts of satisfaction obtained could vary widely. Hence the user day is not in itself a satisfactory unit of measurement of the value of the recreational experience.

Mack and Myers[26] developed a more sophisticated approach with a weighted user day. Persons from areas less well served with facilities would be allocated user days of higher value as they were assumed to receive greater satisfaction from their visits. Another approach is to regard the user day of recreation as an alternative to a user day spent at work and to value it as a day's wages. This concept is based on the false presumption that the individual has a free choice between work and leisure.

Cost of Providing Recreational Facilities

One of the earlier methods used by the United States Bureau of Reclamation in connection with multi-purpose reservoir projects was to assume that the recreational benefits were equal to the costs of the recreational developments. The reason for estimating benefits is to decide the economic feasibility of the proposals and whether the costs should be incurred at all. To assume that benefits are equal to costs in every case is to make all recreational projects feasible and to eliminate the basis for establishing priorities among projects.[27]

User Expenditures

In this approach the recreational benefit is assumed to be equal to the expenditure incurred by those persons engaging in it. For example, in 1954 American recreationalists' daily expenditure figures ranged mainly between $6 and $10.[27] In 1960 the average visitor to an American state park was estimated to have spent $4.50 per day, mainly for food, petrol and accommodation.[3] This cannot be regarded as a satisfactory method of measuring the intangible values to the person enjoying recreation. Indeed, many so-called recreational expenditures are normal daily disbursements made under slightly different circumstances. This applies particularly to payments for food. An extension of this method is to include the costs of equipment used in the recreational activity but it does not make the approach any more satisfactory.

Imputed Prices

One method is to base the value of the public recreational facility on charges made for similar facilities provided by private enterprise. This approach takes no account of the need for recreation in the area, nor for the differences in satisfaction and experience that may be provided in the private facility. Thus charges that users are willing to pay at private facilities may largely reflect payments for benefits in excess of those obtainable at publicly owned facilities—

better natural resources, improved services, better management, less crowding, and so on.[28]

Another method attempted to establish a demand curve by enquiring of the recreationalists the most they would be prepared to pay for access to the facility rather than be excluded.[2] Alternatively, they might be asked to state the minimum amount they would have to be paid (bribed) to abstain willingly from the recreation.[25] The answers to these two questions are unlikely to be equal as they measure two different forms of consumer surplus—compensating and equivalent.

The practical difficulty with these direct techniques lies in obtaining rational and consistent expressions of value from recreationalists simply by asking them direct but hypothetical questions, particularly in view of the emotional response often produced.[7] The last approach is sometimes referred to as assessment of 'accounting' or 'shadow' prices.[29]

Demand Schedules

Later approaches attempted to determine the willingness to pay for recreation through the construction of demand curves. They sought to establish the relationship of a series of prices (or costs) for outdoor recreation to a series of quantities demanded of it.[30] The proposals by Hotelling contained in the Prewitt Report[31] in 1949 are believed to represent the first attempt to use travel cost as a means of estimating the value of outdoor recreation. Hotelling suggested the defining of a series of concentric zones around a park within each of which travel costs would be reasonably constant. The number of people visiting the park from each zone would be calculated. It was assumed that all visitors would receive the same benefit and that the value of the benefit could not be less than the cost of travel. Hence those living near the park enjoy a consumer's surplus made up of the differences in transportation costs, as shown in figure 3.1. From a calculation of travel costs and numbers of visitors from each zone, it is possible to plot a demand curve from which the benefits accruing to the public from the park can be determined. The approach suggested by Hotelling was a great advance on earlier methods but it has a number of inherent weaknesses. For instance, it assumes that all visitors receive the same satisfaction and it overlooks the fact that part of the consumers' surplus derived from proximity may be taken in increased residential rent and/or rates.

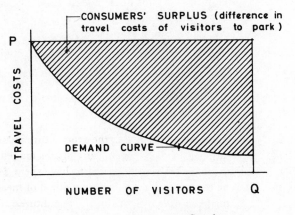

Figure 3.1 Consumers' Surplus

A number of studies have developed from this point by adapting and refining the methodology adopted by Hotelling. Trice and Wood[27] pursued this approach with their work in California, where 582 parties of visitors to three river resource areas were interviewed and information was recorded on the number of persons in each visiting party, the days spent on the sites, the total number of days spent on the entire recreational trip and the home city or county of each visitor. The distance travelled to the site can be found since the home city or county is known and—assuming a constant travel cost per mile or kilometre—the travel cost for each party can be estimated. The travel cost per visitor day was obtained by dividing the total travel costs (in both directions) by the total number of days spent on the trip and the number of persons in the party. A demand curve was produced and from this Trice and Wood attempted to give a shadow price to the recreation. The median travel cost of the majority of the visitors (cut-off at the ninetieth percentile) was found to be around $1 and, since the highest travel cost (taken at the ninetieth percentile) was about $3, they estimated that the consumers' surplus or benefit was in the order of $2. Trice and Wood asserted that the use of a fixed cost per mile or kilometre travelled had the dual advantage of removing income differences and at the same time producing per visitor day differences in cost of enjoying a recreational area.

A more refined analysis has been made by Clawson[32] who, using the results of a travel survey for Yosemite National Park, determined the numbers and origins of visitors to the park. Using the base population of each county, he was able to express consumption in terms of the number of visitors per 100 000 population. In addition, he estimated a total cost figure per visit related to each county, made up of an average expenditure of $9 per day plus 10 cents per mile (return journey) per car load of four persons. Hence Clawson was able to express demand in terms of the number of visitors per 100 000 population at various travel costs.

However, unlike Trice and Wood, Clawson distinguishes between the total outdoor recreation experience of the entire trip and the recreation activity on the specific site. From the overall demand schedule for the entire trip experience, Clawson proceeds to construct a demand schedule for the recreation site itself. First, he determines a formula for the total number of visitors as a function of the cost of the visit from a regression equation of the empirical study. By adding varying levels of shadow entrance fee to the cost of the visit, Clawson then assesses the effect of the various entrance fees on the total number of visitors and so establishes the demand schedule for the recreation site, as distinct from the recreation experience.

Clawson makes two assumptions in this type of analysis:

(1) All costs incurred in the overall recreation experience are homogeneous to the visitor; an extra dollar spent on travel is regarded in the same light as an extra dollar spent on entrance fees.

(2) The experience of visitors from one area provides a measure of what people in other areas would do if monetary and time costs of the visit were the same.

More recent studies have attempted to construct more sensitive demand indicators by the inclusion of additional factors. Knetsch[33] from his experience of empirical studies on a modest scale advocated that consideration could usefully be given to income of population groups, extent of alternative recreation possibilities and amount of congestion at the recreation site. Merewitz[34] studied a number of factors associated with water recreation and found that, by various statistical tests, three criteria were most useful in predicting the number of visitors, namely—size of population, population density and the distance of the home county from the recreational lake. Boyet and Tolley,[35] on the other hand, found that for visits to national parks in the United States, travel cost (measured by distance), size of population and income were the most important parameters in prediction of demand.

Wennergren,[36] making a boating survey, concentrated on the effect of various costs on the number of trips made. He classified the costs incurred by recreationalists into three categories: travel and on-site costs per trip; total equipment costs; and total annual costs.

He found that the travel and on-site costs were by far the most significant factors influencing the number of visits. These costs tend to constitute the marginal costs of the boating experience and thus simulate the rôle of 'price' in the consumption process.

Distances travelled from homes to recreational sites are usually measured as straight lines and not the actual road distances. This results in all distances being shortened. As demonstrated by Wood[37] travel time may be more important than distance. For instance, a party may wish to visit a park but may not want to spend more than an hour in travelling to it.

CRITICAL EXAMINATION OF DEMAND SCHEDULE APPROACH

Assessment of Price of Recreation

In the studies that have been examined, the quantity of recreation consumed is measured by number of visits or visitor days. The use of visitor days or user days is more particularly applicable to national parks and similar facilities where visits may extend over a weekend or longer period. For urban recreation sites, the number of visits or hours of visiting time would seem more appropriate, as relatively few visitors will spend a whole day at the site.

It has been customary to take as a substitute price for the outdoor recreation (or recreation experience) the cost of travel, equipment costs, entrance fees and other costs incurred in the recreation trip. It is questionable whether all of these costs give a positive indication of the value of outdoor recreation at a particular site. The cost of travel can be regarded as an essential preliminary cost to outdoor recreation. Without incurring this cost, the recreationalist cannot usually participate in the activity. Some satisfaction may be gained in travelling but this is unlikely to be of sufficient importance to merit any adjustment. The inclusion of costs of food or accommodation is inappropriate as they have no direct relevance to the value of the recreation experience, and are merely part of the necessities of life. Equipment costs need allocating according to the proportion of total use on the particular site.

Travel Cost Concept

The travel cost concept contains some inherent weaknesses. Hotelling's inclusion of the most distant traveller is unrealistic; for instance, some day visitors to Nottingham parks have come from as far distant as Manchester—solely for the purpose of visiting a park—but it would be unreasonable to credit those living within 1 km of the park with the travel cost from Manchester to Nottingham, less 1 km. Trice and Wood[27] attempted to solve this by excluding the most distant visitors (farthest ten per cent) but this is an arbitrary decision. It is also unsound to assume that all visitors to a recreational site gain the same amount of satisfaction. Length of stay and number of activities pursued must influence the satisfaction received.

Clawson estimates the travel cost per person by assuming a standard cost per mile (km) from home to recreation site and a complement of four people in each car. This approach is open to considerable error as the number of occupants per car varies appreciably and, on average, is likely to be less than four. For example, a survey of motorists to the Lake District National Park by Mansfield[38] in 1966 revealed an average of 3.1 persons per car whilst American studies showed 3.5 persons per car.[1] Furthermore, some visitors may not have travelled from their homes and the visit to the park may not be the main purpose of the journey as, for example, a commercial traveller visiting a local park to eat his lunch.

The assessment of cost of travel per mile or kilometre can be approached in a number of ways. Burton and Wibberley[39] after an examination of travel costs by private car, rail and public road transport adopted an average travel cost per person of 6d per mile ($1\frac{1}{2}$p/km) in 1964 and this seems excessively high. The Road Research Laboratory[40] estimated direct car operating costs at 4d per mile (1p per km) in 1965. Norton[41] in his survey of visitors to North Wales asked them for petrol costs or fares in travelling there. Petrol costs are increased by 66.6 per cent to cover oil, tyres, maintenance and other running costs, based on figures given by the Automobile Association.[42] Even these costs may not be entirely adequate as Riley[43] has shown that although motorists usually include petrol, oil, repairs, tax and insurance in their car running costs, they rarely include depreciation. Mansfield[72] believes that the travel cost on a journey to a recreation site should include an allowance for both time and money. Clawson's method of analysis includes the whole bundle of commodities associated with the recreational trip and, as indicated earlier, this can give unrealistic results.

It is evident that the distance which a person is prepared to travel in search of outdoor recreation is an indicator of the value which he expects to receive from that recreation, but, as pointed out by Burton and Wibberley,[39] it can be no more than this. The travel cost approach permits part of the recreational experience to be valued, but it cannot produce a total monetary valuation of a subjective, qualitative experience. Different people can obtain differing amounts of satisfaction from the same recreational experience. Furthermore, the quality of the site must influence the value of the recreational experience.[44]

Norton[41] postulates that individuals, when faced with the choice of making a recreational trip, can be assumed to act in a pattern similar to the consumption behaviour for market goods. In this way the travel cost can be taken to represent the substitution value for the trip. On interviewing 689 groups of people visiting six recreational sites in North Wales, Norton estimated their average travelling costs at 33p per person per day. By estimating the total number of visitors per annum to each site he was able to evaluate the social benefit for outdoor recreation at around £9 per hectare from which he deducted £2 per hectare for rent and management, to give a net social benefit of

£7 per hectare. This compares very favourably with its value for agricultural purposes.

Up to now we have been attempting to evaluate recreational resources for which no entrance fees were charged. Consideration will now be given to methods of charging and the problems involved.

Ability to Pay

It has often been argued that recreation benefits everyone directly or indirectly and so all should share the costs.[28] This assertion is undermined by the majority of leisure surveys which show that only a minority participate regularly in any form of outdoor recreation. Hence a much stronger case could be made for free schools and free libraries than for free parks. Moreover public parks are rarely located close to the densely populated poorer class residential areas. Seckler[45] questions the propriety of providing outdoor recreation out of general tax revenues and then allocating use by devices (prices) which exclude a substantial portion of the taxpayers (the poor).

The pertinent question is generally how much the visitors would have paid if they had been compelled to pay; and the amount of the maximum total fee revenue that could have been secured. Some, of course, would have been unwilling to pay any entrance fee, as the total costs of the whole recreation experience were already high in relation to the pleasures and satisfactions to be obtained, and any entrance fee would tip the balance. At the other extreme some visitors derive such large satisfactions from visiting the area that they would be prepared to pay large entrance fees rather than forgo the experience.[46]

As the users become accustomed to paying fees for recreation, the price may be gradually raised until the operating level (including amortisation of capital outlay) is reached or even exceeded. The users are then repaying the authority for providing the facility. If the recreation is of such a nature that it can and should be privately provided, then public authorities can be relieved of the responsibility for providing this type of recreation, although they should still operate in a regulating capacity.[47]

However, there is some danger in continually raising charges merely because they can be collected. As the price becomes higher, more and more persons from low income brackets are prevented from participating in this form of recreation.

Need for Entrance Fees

Clawson[3] showed how the provision and management of resource based and intermediate public recreation facilities in the United States were costing approximately $300–$400 million annually in 1963. In addition public authorities lost the opportunity to derive income from these areas—a loss amounting to about the same figure. Judged against a gross national product of $500 billion this might not be considered excessive, but when taking into account the rapidly increasing demand and the spiralling costs of provision then the levying of entrance charges may well be justified in the future.

The advisability of establishing rates of charges that cover collection costs is generally recognised, although nominal charges also serve administrative purposes—such as providing information on visitors; offering an opportunity of drawing users' attention to safety and protective requirements; and instilling in the user more respect for the facility.[47] In 1962 the State of Ohio, Division of Parks, made a postal survey of charges in state parks. Of the forty-five states replying to the questionnaire thirty-eight per cent reported some charge for use of parks. The charges ranged from a $10 annual entrance fee to a 25 cent daily parking fee. Three states made daily admission charges only.[48] A 1960 study by the United States National Park Service found that total expenditures on state parks had increased about five and a half times between 1946 and 1959, while revenues from entrance and parking fees increased over ten and a half times.[28] In Canada, conservation/recreation stickers have been introduced which, at a cost of £2.50 in 1966, will admit a car and its occupants to all federal recreation areas for 1 year.[49]

While the imposition of user charges for public recreation areas is far from universal in the United States and even less frequently practised in Great Britain, experience to date indicates that it is operationally practical. The trend in the future will almost surely be towards greater use of such charges, as the demand for recreation grows and as the need for funds becomes more acute.[28] Even those who have a strong conviction that recreation should be free will probably be prepared to accept the introduction of user charges when it is shown that public funds will become inadequate to meet the demands for recreation.

Peppiatt,[50] when investigating the pricing of seaside facilities, found the present system of pricing to be unsatisfactory for a number of reasons: revenue from facilities as a whole fails to cover basic costs; demand for and supply of facilities is not balanced successfully by the market; there is urgent need to extend, improve and modernise facilities but available funds are insufficient; there is serious congestion and overcrowding during peak weeks and under utilisation during the rest of the season; and failure to provide facilities required by foreign tourists. Some of these failings apply equally well to outdoor recreation resources. Peppiatt postulates that to avoid further deterioration of beach and sea facilities, it is necessary either to subsidise the facilities or to levy realistic user charges. For example, he considered that deckchairs/windbreak charges could be raised to a uniform 9d (4p) or possibly 1s (5p), with an excess charge at weekends and peak holidays. To introduce new revenue, charges could be made for access to selected beaches, as on the Continent.

Effect of Price Increases on Demand

Knetsch[33] derived an estimate of the demand relationship by postulating an imposed price for the enjoyment of a park in the form of an addition to the costs of the visit from each area or zone. The number of visits which would occur from each cost group under the higher costs is determined by examining the relationship of visit rates and total costs. An example will serve to illustrate his approach. Assume that people within 20 km of a park make 150 visits per year per 1000 base population, at an average cost of 25p. If an entrance fee of 10p per visit is imposed, the total cost per visit is now 35p. Some people will discontinue visiting the park, arguing that the cost exceeds the value. Assume further that people living 20–25 km distant incur costs of 35p per visit even when entrance fees are zero, but that only 100 visits per 1000 base population are made from this zone. Both Clawson and Knetsch[33,46] make dubious assumptions about comparability of groups and rationality of behaviour. On the basis of these assumptions, the 10p entrance fee would reduce visits from the under 20 km zone from 150 to 100 per 1000 base population, but it would also produce a fee revenue from this group of 10p.

A similar process could be carried out for each zone within the catchment area. In each case the fee would reduce usage but raise some revenue. In order to calculate total revenue consideration would also have to be given to total population within each zone. The same process could be repeated for higher entrance fees, possibly 10p, 20p, 30p and so on. Clawson[46] found that in general maximum fee revenue is obtained at volumes of visitation equal to less than half, and sometimes as little as one-quarter, of the volume of visitation when no entrance fees are imposed. In the case of day use areas in the United States this amounted to $3–$5 per visit in 1960.

Smith and Kavanagh[51] have applied Clawson's methodology to estimate the effect of increasing the cost of the daily fishing permit at Grafham Water. In 1967 the fishing charge was £1 and the number of anglers visiting the water resource was 21 143; it was estimated that at £2 the volume of visitation would drop to 6447, and if further increased to £3, then the number of visitors would fall to 2737. Rodgers[52] illustrates how pricing can be applied as a regulator of demand. For example, pricing of golf not only restrains total demand but also selectively sorts it between a number of sectors (public and club courses, 'fashionable' and 'popular' courses). Without price restraint, the demand for golf would probably far exceed the capacity of existing courses, or even any likely additions to them. A similar approach can be applied to sailing facilities where a critical mooring problem may compel the provision of costly marinas with consequently higher charges to sailors.

Administrative Problems in Fee Collection

Administrative problems often arise when user charges are levied on recreational resources. For instance, a typical city park is open all day the year round and frequently has no gate or control point. With more remotely sited parks the volume of usage may be so low that the fees would do no more than cover the cost of collection.

The Countryside Commission[53] has described and compared the various methods of charging at car parks and these methods have considerable relevance to recreational facilities. Manned methods of control include collection of a fixed or variable charge, with or without the use of a manually-operated barrier. Unmanned methods of control comprise 'trust the motorist' boxes with or without enforcement procedures and automatic barrier systems with fixed or variable charges. The Countryside Commission concludes that no system enjoys an overriding advantage. They wisely advise testing the market before investing in expensive capital equipment and emphasise the advisability of operating for one season on an experimental basis, preferably using a fixed charge, attendant-operated system for which capital costs are low. Varying the charges once or twice during the season or even introducing a variable charge for a period would help in formulating a viable long-term policy.

EFFECT OF PARKS ON LAND VALUES

Clawson and Knetsch[28] postulated that as the preference for residing close to parks increases, the value of the land near the park would be expected to increase. There could however be instances where prices of property around a park could fall if the recreational site was subject to very intensive use. Knetsch[33] argues that the additional increment to the value of land resulting from visitor preference to reside near a recreation area should be credited to the economic worth of the area. It is possible, though, that the resident may be attracted by the improved environmental conditions as much as by the ease of visiting the recreation area. If recreation benefits are also being calculated on the travel cost concept, it is important to avoid double counting of benefits in respect of visitors living close to the recreation site.

The rise in land or capital values in the area of the recreation resource represents the present value of the stream of future benefits expected to be realised by residents.[1] The main problem is to determine the consistencies or patterns of land value and how these are dependent upon proximity to park areas. Knetsch[54] sees the need to determine how the effect of parks varies with the nature of the park, including size and other characteristics; with the nature of the urban area, including size and socio-economic characteristics of residents; with the number of other park areas; and with the expected changes in demand determinants over time. The American outdoor recreation report[44] indicates that there are many examples of parks enhancing the values of surrounding properties in American cities. Minneapolis, noted for its fine park system, claims that increased values in the city due to park developments have amounted to several times the cost of the entire park system. Essex city, New Jersey, found that land adjacent to parks increased in value three times as fast as other property.

Kitchen and Hendon[55] maintain that land adjacent to an urban neighbourhood park may be of more value than land which is a greater distance from the park, because of its unique location and the secondary benefits which arise and are attributable to the social welfare of the population (health and enrichment of lives of individuals). The American National Recreation and Park Association[56] supports this view and describes how estate agents invariably draw the attention of purchasers to this locational aspect. Kitchen and Hendon tested this hypothesis by reference to residential development five parcels deep around a 4-hectare park in the city of Lubbock, Texas. They found a significant correlation between land values and distance from the park.

In a study of land values adjacent to reservoirs, Knetsch[57] recommended that increases in land values adjacent to reservoirs be considered in order to improve the economic consequences of water resource development. His observations were that increased sales prices of land established in the property market reflected values due entirely to location on or near reservoir projects. Increased prices represented capitalisation of values derived from such locational advantage. The same principle applies to public parks and a strong case can be made for capturing, by rates or taxes, the land value increments resulting from proximity to recreation facilities created by public investment.

RECREATION PLANNING AS AN ECONOMIC PROBLEM

There are a number of strong arguments in support of the public provision of outdoor recreation facilities. For instance, it is often argued that the market structure of the outdoor recreation 'market' does not favour private suppliers of recreation opportunity. It is widely argued that outdoor recreation is essential to a full and well balanced personal life and that those who participate, by becoming fitter and better socially adjusted, increase the welfare of the nation. Hence everyone should be willing to pay for its provision on account of the valuable end product.

A public authority is better able to meet the uncertainties accompanying recreation provision and to secure a better balance of facilities. As the provider of highways and other public services and regulator of development through planning control, the public authority can influence the demand for recreation at a resource and the nature of its environment. In many instances society wishes to maintain a quality or condition which the private market might destroy. The private recreation operator is often under pressure to encourage mass use in order to maximise his profits and, in so doing, could destroy the quality of the area. Some American states have acquired public easements over private land for such uses as open space, parks and fishing.[58] This procedure eliminates the costly purchase of land, permits the recreational use of the land and often allows the private land use to continue.

Meeting the rapidly increasing demand for outdoor recreation must inevitably place a heavy burden on public authorities, and it is imperative that new funds shall be allocated among alternative recreation facilities in a way leading to the highest achievable social satisfaction. There is a limit individually and collectively to how much real and personal wealth would be sacrificed to obtain any recreational experience or preserve any scenic resource. The limit is defined by the incremental social gain to be realised from a unit of expenditure on recreation and from the alternatives. It would be illogical to continue investing large sums in recreation development if the funds could produce greater satisfaction in another field.[2]

Admittedly, personal valuations of a recreational experience will display greater variance than material goods such as a pair of shoes or a loaf of bread. Nevertheless, it is not unique in this respect as other forms of consumption also have personal, spiritual and aesthetic values, which vary from person to person. What we really need to know is how much recreation adds to the real income or welfare of the nation. To make a true evaluation of recreation resources it would be necessary to carry out experiments with users of outdoor recreation areas in which a range of alternative kinds of areas and facilities is made available to the public at different prices. It is possible that sufficient experience has been accumulated in certain commercial areas of outdoor recreation to provide a rough guide as to possible price ranges.

In some recreational studies users have been questioned on their willingness to pay for certain facilities which they said an area needed, although as stated earlier in this chapter there are inherent weaknesses in this approach. The essence of the interviews was in asking people how their use of the area would be affected if their costs associated with its use were to increase by certain amounts. The cost increments were bid up until a user was excluded from the area. His willingness to pay was then taken as the mean of the excluding bid and the last including bid.[2] Willingness to pay is also affected by the quality of recreation, which in turn is influenced considerably by the number of users—among other things. Hence information is also needed on interaction among users. The operator of a recreation resource may face a choice between expanding use over an enlarged area at a constant level of quality or expanding output on the original site at diminishing levels of quality.

Nisbet[59] illustrates the need for cost planning of landscape works to take account of both quality and quantity. He advocated sub-division into major categories or elements such as ground shaping; drainage; hard surfaces; grass; planting; enclosure; site furniture; and minor categories, which for planting could be forestry; specimen trees; shrub planting; herbaceous planting; and ground cover; among others. By the use of these techniques it would be easier to ensure that the promoter secured value for money and that the funds were allocated to the various component parts in a balanced and logical way.

Wilson[60] in his investigation of marinas in the United States found yield ranges varying from minus ten per cent to plus thirty-five per cent and he emphasised the need for a high quality of management and efficiency in operation. With public recreation provision there is also the need to secure a proper balance between costs and benefits, requiring careful selection of sites, skilful planning and efficient operation.

APPLICATION OF COST-BENEFIT ANALYSIS TO RECREATIONAL FACILITIES IN NOTTINGHAM

The remainder of this chapter is concerned with the application of the economic principles discussed previously to a range of outdoor recreational facilities in Greater Nottingham. There are very real difficulties in attempting to evaluate non-priced resources such as public parks, and problems also arise in attaching a value to external costs and benefits. Some of the approaches that have been adopted in the United States such as user expenditures, imputed prices and prices which people state they are prepared to pay have been discounted, as these methods have all been shown to have serious deficiencies. The distance travelled technique, with some refinements, probably offers the most realistic method so far devised of assessing the total benefits arising from the recreational experience, although there are a number of inherent weaknesses in the approaches adopted to date. The distance which a person is prepared to travel to reach a recreational site is an indicator of its value to him but cannot produce a complete monetary evaluation of the total recreational experience. In the Nottingham studies an attempt is made to adjust the monetary value of the benefits according to the length of stay and the number of activities undertaken.

WOLLATON PARK, NOTTINGHAM

Wollaton Park is both the largest and the most popular public park in Nottingham and although sited within the city of Nottingham has nevertheless some of the more usual characteristics of a country park. It is a good example of an amenity provided and maintained by the local authority at a cost and to which the public have access without charge. The operating costs of the park are readily quantifiable and are shown in the annual reports of the Baths and Parks Committee. Furthermore, they are at the present time met out of rates. The nature and monetary value of the benefits derived by visitors to the park, neighbouring residents and even passers-by are much more difficult to determine.

Accepting the premise that the distance travelled to a park must bear some relation to the value of the park to a visitor, the first step must be to assess the number of visitors to the park over a specified period of time and to determine the distances travelled by those persons.

On the basis of site user surveys undertaken by the author the probable total number annually of visitors is around a quarter of a million. The distances travelled by visitors to the park during the survey days are broken down into nine separate ranges.

Distance range in miles (single journey)	under 1	1–2	2–4	4–6	6–10	10–15	15–20	20–26	over 26
Average distance in miles	0.5	1.5	3	5	8	12.5	17.5	23	30
Average distance in km	1	2.5	5	8	13	20	28	37	50
Percentage of visitors	13	20	18	14	5	12	4	4	10

Mean car operating costs in 1970 were assessed at 3p per km and if an average car occupancy rate of three persons is adopted, this gives a travel cost of 1p per km for each visitor and has the added advantage that it corresponds quite closely to current bus fares. The car operating costs include the cost of petrol, oil, repairs, tax, insurance and depreciation on the basis of the work done by the Automobile Association[42] and Riley at the Ministry of Transport.[43]

If the cost of travel to and from the park is accepted as a measure of the entrance fee that a visitor would be prepared to pay, then the value of the park to visitors would be:

Percentage of 250 000				
13	$\times$ 2p	(2×1)	$=$	65 000
20	$\times$ 5p	$(2 \times 2\frac{1}{2})$	$=$	250 000
18	$\times$ 10p	(2×5)	$=$	450 000
14	$\times$ 16p	(2×8)	$=$	560 000
5	$\times$ 26p	(2×13)	$=$	325 000
12	$\times$ 40p	(2×20)	$=$	1 200 000
4	$\times$ 56p	(2×28)	$=$	560 000
4	$\times$ 74p	(2×37)	$=$	740 000
10	$\times$ 100p	(2×50)	$=$	2 500 000

6 650 000p

Total travel cost   £66 500

This approach contains a fundamental weakness in that it assumes that the sole purpose of the journey is to reach the park and that all visitors use public or private transport, whereas in fact a proportion journey to the park on foot. There is the possibility that some of the visitors to the park from a distance are also visiting Nottingham for other purposes. Recreational surveys conducted in the United States[44] and in Britain[61] show that driving for pleasure is a major outdoor recreational activity and can form an important part of the total recreational experience. Hence it seems advisable to include one-half only of the cost of travelling distances in excess of 20 km (single journey) to allow for part of the journey contributing to the recreational experience. This would reduce the estimated total benefit to £47 500.

Trice and Wood[27] have applied the concept of consumers' surplus to the distance travelled approach, on the supposition that visitors residing near the park enjoy a benefit which is valued at the difference between their travelling costs and those of visitors living farthest from the park. A further refinement was to exclude the farthest ten per cent although this percentage is quite arbitrary. Applying this approach to Wollaton Park and excluding ten per cent of all visitors who incidentally travel distances in excess of 40 km (mainly from Chesterfield, Lincoln, Leicester, Matlock and Sheffield), the value of benefits to visitors is more than double that calculated on the basis of actual travel costs.

Percentage of 250 000

$$
\begin{array}{llll}
13 & \times\ 78\text{p} & (2 \times 39) & =\ 2\ 535\ 000 \\
20 & \times\ 75\text{p} & (2 \times 37\tfrac{1}{2}) & =\ 3\ 750\ 000 \\
18 & \times\ 70\text{p} & (2 \times 35) & =\ 3\ 150\ 000 \\
14 & \times\ 64\text{p} & (2 \times 32) & =\ 2\ 224\ 000 \\
5 & \times\ 54\text{p} & (2 \times 27) & =\ \ \ 675\ 000 \\
12 & \times\ 40\text{p} & (2 \times 20) & =\ 1\ 200\ 000 \\
4 & \times\ 24\text{p} & (2 \times 12) & =\ \ \ 240\ 000 \\
4 & \times\ \ 6\text{p} & (2 \times\ \ 3) & =\ \ \ \ \ 60\ 000 \\
\end{array}
$$

13 834 000p

Total   £138 340

It is evident that this technique overvalues the benefits accruing to visits to Wollaton Park, as the mean benefit to visitors—adults and children alike—is assessed at 55p each. An average entrance charge of this amount would result in a substantial reduction in the number of visitors to the park. One fundamental weakness is that it takes no account of the increased rates and property prices paid by persons living near the park who are credited with maximum benefit (78p per visit) and this can give rise to double counting where the enhanced value of properties adjoining a park is evaluated separately. Hence the validity of this approach is seriously questioned.

Neither method of evaluation makes any allowance for varying degrees of satisfaction obtained by different visitors to the site. All are assumed to derive exactly the same satisfaction from the visit. To attempt to value the recreational site experience is fraught with difficulties and yet the length of time spent on the site and the number of activities performed must influence the amount of benefit obtained by a visitor to the park. It also seems likely that the value of the recreational experience may vary with the occupational status of the visitor in that a professional man, for example, will almost certainly evaluate his leisure time more highly than a manual worker, but this will to some extent be taken care of in the distance travelled approach. 'Opportunity cost' has also been suggested as being a useful tool for the measurement of recreation benefit.[62] It is however inappropriate to use hourly income as a measure of opportunity cost for people visiting a recreational resource, since work is unlikely to be the next alternative use of their time. Furthermore, were the opportunity cost concept to be applied in evaluating urban open space it would produce far too high a value.

An analysis of the site user surveys of Wollaton Park revealed that sixty-four per cent of visitors spent up to 2 hours in the park, twenty-nine per cent stayed for half a day and a remaining seven per cent spent all day in the park. On average visitors to Wollaton Park engaged in 3.3 activities during their visit. The activities listed on the parks survey questionnaire were strolling; looking at trees and flowers (for example); exercising dog; picnicking; playing games; sitting outside; sitting inside car; visiting Wollaton Hall; playing in children's playground; and other activities. It is suggested that weightings could usefully be applied to the value obtained from the distance travelled method. It could be reasonably assumed that the majority of visitors would participate in at least two activities on visiting the park and that a weighting of 0.15 could be applied to take account of the added benefit accruing to the visitor from each additional activity. Similarly 'timesing factors' of 1.25 and 1.50 might be applied to persons staying half a day and a full day respectively, as visitors staying for longer periods must obtain greater satisfaction. It is appreciated that the 'diminishing marginal utility' concept will operate, in that a visitor will secure less satisfaction from later hours on a site than he did from earlier ones, and it is considered that the timesing factors suggested make ample allowance for this.

Benefits also accrue to nearby residents and this ought to be reflected in higher property prices and increased rateable values. Discussions with local estate agents seemed to indicate that the higher prices of properties around Wollaton Park were largely attributable to the better class of house that was built in the vicinity of the park rather than to the effects of the park itself. Even if this were correct it is evident that the higher price of land in this situation must contribute towards the higher price of properties around the park. As emphasised at a Treasury Seminar on cost-benefit studies in 1969[63] far too little is known about the factors that determine property prices. Consultations with valuers in the Nottingham Inland Revenue Office also revealed that properties backing onto the park had their rateable values increased by about four per cent whilst rateable values of properties on the other side of the road remained unaffected. It was however admitted that the small percentage increase probably did not adequately reflect the enhanced value of the property stemming from its proximity to the park, and that properties a little farther away from the park could conceivably also be enhanced in value on account of their location. Certainly the quite seemingly minimal enhancement in value of properties immediately adjoining Nottingham parks does not correspond with the significant increases extending to five parcels deep around a 4-hectare park in Lubbock, Texas.[55] Again, in Essex city, New Jersey, it was found that land adjacent to parks increased in value three times as fast as other property, and at Minneapolis it was claimed that increased values in the city due to park developments have amounted to several times the cost of the entire park system.[44]

The author is left with the view that the added increment of value of property resulting from proximity to a park is generally undervalued in Greater Nottingham. Based on the district valuer's current valuation practice the increased benefit to properties immediately adjoining Wollaton Park probably would not amount to more than £1500 per annum, although on an official's own admission the enhanced rateable income could conceivably be as much as £5000 or more per annum, and the higher values of building plots around the park need to be taken into account. A cost-benefit study of Wollaton Park is now undertaken on the basis of the data collected and suppositions already outlined.

Social Benefits

	£
Travel costs of visitors to the park based on 1p/km and taking one half only of travel costs for distances exceeding 20 km, on the assumption that this is equal to the missing entrance fee.	47 500
Add weighting of 0.20 to allow for additional benefit derived by persons undertaking more than two activities in the park (0.15 per additional activity).	9 500
Add weighting of 0.25 in respect of twenty-nine per cent of visitors who stay half a day and receive additional benefit from it. ($\frac{1}{4} \times 29/100 \times$ £47 500)	3 440
Add weighting of 0.50 in respect of seven per cent of visitors who stay a full day and receive still further increased benefit. ($\frac{1}{2} \times 7/100 \times$ £47 500)	1 660

Enhanced building site values resulting from park

250 sites @ £600: £150 000
800 sites @ £300: £240 000

700 sites @ £100:   £ 70 000

Total   £460 000

Interest at five per cent per annum on £460 000 (annual equivalent)	23 000
Enhanced rateable income from properties surrounding the park (additional potential rateable income)	5 000
Amenity value: Beneficial effects to passers-by, reduced air pollution and traffic generation, etc., say (a purely subjective evaluation)	5 000
Total annual benefits	95 100
Less Net annual expenditure by Nottingham Corporation on the park (1968–69)	21 250
Net annual social benefit	£73 850

These calculations have converted an annual deficit of over £20 000 into a net social gain in excess of £70 000, (£500 per hectare) and indicates that Wollaton Park does meet a great social need and is of considerable benefit to the community. It could perhaps be argued that the enhanced value of building sites in the vicinity of the park is a benefit accruing to individuals and not to the public at large. This adds weight to Lichfield's approach wherein he sets out to evaluate the benefits accruing to different groups of persons—local authorities; the community; and owners and occupiers of land.[15] On the other hand it must be admitted that a far higher monetary return could be obtained if the park, excluding the golf course and lake, were developed for residential purposes. At current market values the 140 ha of park would fetch about £80 000 per hectare as residential building land. This would amount to a total value of £11.2 million which would produce annual interest of £560 000 adopting a five per cent rate of interest, plus additional rateable income from the houses subsequently erected. Hence the provision of parks has to be justified on grounds other than purely economic ones and this argument could be applied with even greater force in the case of smaller central parks located on very highly priced land. It would be quite unacceptable to develop the whole of an urban area with buildings entirely devoid of open space.

VERNON PARK, NOTTINGHAM

A cost-benefit study of this small neighbourhood park, adopting the same approach as for Wollaton Park, showed an excess of annual costs over benefits of about £6000. This cannot however be held to make the provision of neighbourhood or district parks unjustifiable, but indicates that it is not possible to make a case for their provision solely on economic grounds. Consideration should be given to the provision of indoor recreational facilities in urban parks primarily for use in inclement weather, and to the siting of new neighbourhood parks in areas of high density residential development when amenity benefits to neighbouring residents will be maximised.

BULWELL FOREST GOLF COURSE, NOTTINGHAM

A municipal golf course (Bulwell Forest), as opposed to a private course, has been chosen for a cost-benefit study because details of annual income and expenditure were readily available. The approach is similar to that used for Wollaton Park but with the major exception of the omission of the weighted travel costs. The place of these costs has been taken by the fees paid by golfers which becomes the measure of the satisfaction that they derive from the game. The inability to meet demand at weekends indicates that charges could probably be increased particularly at weekends without causing a significant fall in demand.

Social Benefits (1968–69)

	£
Income from golfers (629 season tickets, 996 day tickets and 7900 round tickets)	5 500
Enhanced building site values resulting from golf course 30 ha @ £1500 = £45 000. Interest at five per cent per annum on £45 000 (annual equivalent)	2 250
Enhanced rateable income from properties in the vicinity of the golf course (600 dwellings @ £1.50)	900

Amenity value: Beneficial effects to passers-by, walkers, reduced air pollution and traffic generation, etc. (a purely subjective evaluation)   1 500

Total annual benefits   10 150

Less Net annual expenditure by Nottingham Corporation on the golf course.   7 000
(Note: in recent years the Golf Development Council[64] estimated the total annual maintenance bill for an 18-hole golf course as between £5000 and £6500, to which must be added the amortised cost of the land)

Net annual social benefit (about £100/ha)   £3 150

The net social benefit in this case is relatively small and indicates the need for more intensive use of golf courses and possibly more careful siting to increase their amenity value and the amount of satisfaction obtained by persons other than the users of the resource itself. The Golf Development Council has advocated the greater provision of driving ranges and par-3 courses both of which would permit the more intensive use of facilities. The amenity value and enhancement of the value of neighbouring properties at Bulwell Forest is nowhere near as great as it might have been, owing to the existence of railway lines on two sides of the golf course and a disused railway embankment fairly close to much of the remainder. When siting golf courses in the future the aim could usefully be to maximise benefits to persons other than the users of the resource wherever practicable by surrounding golf courses with good class residential development. As golf courses require such large areas of land this may not always be possible and new courses may often have to be sited away from residential areas on lower priced land.

On purely economic grounds the use of land as a golf course is unlikely to compare favourably with its use for residential purposes. If Bulwell Forest were to be developed as housing land it would probably fetch about £50 000 per hectare giving a total market value of £1 500 000 (30 × £50 000). The annual equivalent of this sum would be the interest accruing from the purchase price without any provision for a sinking fund as the land will exist in perpetuity. Assuming a long-term interest rate of five per cent, this gives an annual value of £75 000 to which should be added the increased rateable income flowing from the dwellings subsequently erected on the site. This is a twenty-fivefold increase in the benefits generated by the golf course but, as with parks, it is obvious that other considerations besides economic ones must be taken into account when planning urban areas. It would not be feasible to develop the whole of an urban area with roads and buildings, even though it would produce the greatest monetary return. Town planning aims at coordinating development to assist in producing a community environment that will advance human welfare in health, well-being and safety.[65] Social and aesthetic considerations are as important as economic criteria.

ALLOTMENTS

The application of cost-benefit analysis to allotment gardens is fraught with difficulties, largely because of the virtual impossibility of attaching a realistic monetary value to many of the social benefits which stem from their provision. It is advisable to consider the impact of costs and benefits under three main heads: direct income and expenditure to the local authority providing the allotments; costs and returns to the allotment holder; and costs and benefits to the community. Public allotments comprising 366 plots spread over six sites in West Bridgford Urban District, Nottinghamshire, have been selected for investigation in this study, and the costs given are those operating in 1970.

(1) *Direct Income and Expenditure to Local Authority*

Annual expenditure	*Annual income*
£1180	£350

The annual expenditure includes loan charges in connection with the original land purchases based on an 80-year loan period. The income is derived from the 304 worked plots which are each of about 450 m² and let at an annual rental of £1.25, subject also to reduced rents for old-age pensioners (senior citizens). It would seem rather absurd to let the allotment plots at very low rents which results in income from the plots amounting to barely thirty-three per cent of local authority expenditure and there are many who argue that such facilities should be self-supporting. Under the Allotments Acts local authorities are empowered to spend up to the product of a 2d rate (0.83p) in allotment provision, on the basis that this is just as much a local authority service as the provision of highways, schools and libraries. The origins of allotment provision were bound up with 'poor relief' and the object was to let land to poor persons at reasonable rates to produce food for themselves and their families. However, as shown in chapter 6, the motivating force today is likely to be recreational rather than economic. The Committee of Inquiry into Allotments[66] considered the present rent levels to be unrealistic and it seems likely that rents on many allotment sites could be increased substantially without causing undue hardship to plotholders. Indeed there are some who feel that allotment gardeners would value their plots more highly and work them in a more husband-like manner if they had to pay higher rents.

(2) *Costs and Returns to the Allotment Holder*

Annual expenditure	*Annual returns*
£9	£33
(rent, seeds, fertilisers, manures, etc.)	(estimated value of produce at shop prices)

Taking into account the un-let, uncultivated and partially cultivated plots at West Bridgford, the probable total annual costs amount to £2358 and returns to allotment holders could be valued at £8370.

Thus a comparison of allotment holders' operating costs with the probable shop prices of the garden produce show a substantial return to the plotholder. This calculation is, however, incomplete in that the value of the plotholder's time is ignored and the secondary benefits to the plotholder of relaxation, exercise, and so on, find no place in the appraisal. Operating costs will vary a little between different sites owing to differences in rents and the fact that estimated value of produce at shop prices is difficult to compute as rarely does a plotholder record details of the quantities of crops produced or attempt to evaluate them. The average annual value of produce of £33 obtained in the Nottingham area could be on the low side, as a survey conducted by the National Allotments Society in 1965 and based on the particulars contained in 1000 returns showed an average of £42.90 worth of produce from a 250 m² plot.

(3) *Costs and Benefits to the Community*

A variety of social benefits flow from the provision of allotments but most of them are not readily quantifiable. Allotment gardens can be regarded as part of the pattern of outdoor recreational facilities, catering primarily for those who have become too old to engage in organised sporting activities. The Nottingham allotment surveys have confirmed this view in that seventy per cent of the allotment holders concerned were 45 years of age and over and twenty-five per cent were over 65. Local authorities must be providing a useful service to the community through allotment provision which enables many older residents to find a relaxing, rewarding and healthy outdoor interest. Furthermore if, as is generally supposed, allotment holders enjoy better health than persons without gardens this can result in a reduction in the cost of medical services and a possible increase in work output. The families of allotment holders must also obtain some benefit from the fresh vegetables, fruit and flowers that they receive from the plot. In the Greater Nottingham survey, it was found that the majority of plotholders residing in the city of Nottingham had no back gardens at their homes, whilst the majority of those resident in the surrounding urban districts had only small back gardens (up to 80 m²). Had gardens been provided to all houses and flats in Nottingham, they would have occupied a much greater area of land than is at present allocated to allotments and would have resulted in a further extension of residential development onto neighbouring agricultural land.

On a wider scale allotment gardens can form an integral part of the open space system of a town or city and can provide additional lungs through greenery and unpolluted air space. Some improvement in the appearance of allotments will generally be necessary before they can form an effective part of the open space network. Well maintained plots containing some flowers and trees, preferably enclosed by neatly trimmed hedges, and free from ramshackle sheds, with landscaped paths winding through them as connecting links of other open spaces, could constitute a pleasant and valuable asset of town morphology. The government Committee of Inquiry into Allotments[66] also saw the need for more attractive 'leisure gardens' incorporating flowers or flowering shrubs at strategic points. More attractive allotment gardens would produce increased social benefits.

CANALS

The British Waterways Board[68] has described some of the problems peculiar to canal administration and how they spring essentially from geography and history. Every kilometre of canal represents a ribbon of property ownership—with 2 kilometres of boundary—stretching across the countryside. At the time of its construction, the route cut artificially both across such natural features as streams, ditches and roads, and through the property of other parties. The many and varied conditions upon which the canal proprietors were permitted to build their waterways and to construct works interfering with natural flows of water, were incorporated in the enabling Acts of the canals concerned. A typical 80 km length of canal was estimated to cost about £30 000–£50 000 per annum to maintain in 1964.[68]

Revenue other than from commercial traffic and associated facilities is received from three main sources: pleasure craft; water sales; and angling. The pleasure craft are primarily powered cabin cruisers most of which are kept moored on the waterways and are used for cruising at weekends and holiday times. The revenue received by the British Waterways Board from this source in 1964 amounted to over £80 000 and in the early sixties was increasing at a rate of between six and 8.5 per cent per annum.[68] More recently, powered craft licences showed an increase of 13.2 per cent between 1967 and 1968.[67] Water revenue is also an expanding source of income and the Board's total income from water sales was in excess of £760 000 in 1968 and showed an increase of 9.75 per cent over the previous year's figure.[67] Of the 3600 km of inland waterways, approximately twenty-five per cent is unsuitable for angling and the fishing rights over a further twenty-five per cent are in private ownership. Most of the remainder is let by the British Waterways Board to clubs and associations of clubs[68] and the total revenue from angling for 1968 was £22 494, showing little change from the previous year.

In deciding the future of a canal which is not scheduled as either a commercial waterway or a cruising waterway under the Transport Act, 1968, the British Waterways Board has three courses of action:

(1) To eliminate the canal by restoration to dry land.

(2) To keep the canal as a 'water channel', involving regular maintenance and weiring of locks. Revenue is obtained from water and fishing but practically all navigation revenue (except from canoes and light unpowered craft) disappears.

(3) To keep the canal open for navigation, even though the craft using it may all be pleasure boats.

Consideration is now given to the financial implications of maintaining the Erewash Canal as a cruising canal as against keeping it as a water channel, and of retaining the Grantham Canal as a water channel as against eliminating it entirely. The Erewash Canal is a broad canal, 19 km long, with fourteen locks. It connects Long Eaton and Langley Mill in Derbyshire. The Grantham Canal, also a broad canal—53 km long, with eighteen locks—connects Nottingham and Grantham. The location of these canals is shown on figure 8.1.

EREWASH CANAL

Probable annual cost of maintaining as a cruising canal £

Direct costs in dredging, maintenance and operation of canal, including
provision for major repairs to locks north of Ilkeston | 7 000

Other costs, including overhead and administrative charges | 3 000

Probable total annual costs | 10 000

Probable annual value of benefits

Water sales (based on 1964 figures) | 6 300

Craft revenue (allowing for substantial increase with improved facilities and increasing demand) | 1 200

Fishing licences	600
Probable total annual receipts to British Waterways Board	8 100

This shows an annual deficit to the British Waterways Board of about £2000 per annum and is little different from the figures published by the Board in 1965.[68] It is not however the complete picture and is not providing for use of the full recreational potential of the renovated canal. Admittedly it passes mainly through semi-industrial and relatively unattractive country, nevertheless, the use of towpaths for both long and short distance walks; organised nature study rambles; investigations of industrial archaeology in the form of bridges, locks and cottages; and improved amenity value; must have considerable social benefits even if unpriced. It is also felt that recreational use of the canal could be extended by the provision of more mooring places; some landscaping; conversion of cottages into cafés; greater use of pleasure boats—particularly converted narrow boats; establishment of camping sites beside the canal; and, possibly, siting country parks along attractive lengths of the canal or arranging for canals to form connecting links between country parks. Evaluation of these social benefits is difficult but it seems likely that they could correct the adverse balance on the Board's profit and loss account.

Probable annual cost of keeping canal as a water channel	£
Direct costs in dredging, maintenance and operation of water channel, including equivalent annual cost of weiring the locks	5 000
Other costs	2 700
Probable total annual costs	7 700
Probable annual value of benefits	
Water sales (based on 1964 figures)	6 300
Fishing licences	600
Probable total annual receipts to British Waterways Board	6 900

This shows a substantially reduced annual deficit to the British Waterways Board (£800 per annum), and some of the other unpriced activities previously described such as walking, nature study, and improved amenity value will still be enjoyed. Passage of craft would however be restricted to canoes and rowing boats and locks will be lost. Although the balance sheet is rather incomplete and inconclusive it is suspected that in the long-term the better solution would be to maintain the Erewash Canal as a cruising canal throughout its entire length, and doubtless this conclusion would have the support of the local canal preservation society who, by their own efforts, can reduce the restoration costs.

GRANTHAM CANAL

Probable annual cost of retention as a water channel	£
Direct costs in dredging, maintenance and operation of water channel, including equivalent annual cost of refilling 9 km of dry canal with water and weiring the locks (£150 each)	11 000
Other costs	4 000
Probable total annual costs	15 000
Probable annual value of benefits	
Water sales	2 000
Fishing licences	400
Probable total annual receipts to British Waterways Board	2 400

This shows an annual deficit to the British Waterways Board of between £12 000 and £13 000 per annum. Admittedly this canal passes through pleasant countryside and other recreational uses could stem from the renovation of the canal—such as walking and nature study—and there must be some social benefits resulting from improved amenity. Nevertheless, the high cost of renovation resulting from many years of very limited maintenance work since the canal was abandoned in 1936,[69] and the reinstatement of the 9 km of dry canal in the parishes of Cropwell Bishop and Cropwell Butler where the canal passes through porous gypsum beds, must make the wisdom of this course of action rather questionable.

Probable Annual Cost of Eliminating the Canal

The work of eliminating a canal to re-create the pre-canal conditions involves an extensive programme of work probably spread over a 10 year period. It includes de-watering; bulldozing banks and importing fill; restoration of hedges and fences and their extension across the site of the canal; provision of alternative water supplies; and demolition of such features as bridges and locks. The British Waterways Board[68] has estimated the probable cost at about £5600 per kilometre of canal and the total cost of eliminating the 53 km of the Grantham Canal is likely to be in the order of £300 000 (1970 prices). The annual equivalent of this sum is calculated assuming a 10 year programme of work, six per cent rate of interest and three per cent sinking fund spread over a 60 year period.

Present value of £1 per annum for 10 years @ six per cent =	£7.3602
Hence present value of £30 000 per annum for 10 years @ six per cent = £30 000 × 7.3602 =	£220 806
To obtain the annual equivalent take interest @ six per cent	0.06
and an annual sinking fund @ three per cent spread over 60 years	0.0061
	0.0661

Annual equivalent of cost of elimination work = £220 806 × 0.0661 = £14 600 per annum.

The credit side is restricted to the site value of the canal—a narrow strip of land normally of interest only to adjoining owners. Hence elimination of the entire length of the Grantham Canal is likely to prove more costly than its retention and conversion to a water channel. Probably the best solution is to eliminate certain stretches of the canal and to retain others as water channel. The British Waterways Board[68] has pointed out that if the upper 8 km of canal were retained as water channel, this length could break even on the water sales accruing from it. It should also be borne in mind that where canal preservation societies are willing to carry out canal restoration work using unpaid voluntary labour, it may be possible to provide a 'cruiseway' at no greater cost than that of obtaining a water channel by orthodox methods.

Set against a background of financial viability, Hadfield's conclusions on the future rôle to be played by canals in the east Midlands are of direct relevance:[69]

The bigger waterways still have a future as large scale carriers of goods. Many of the smaller, those that run quietly through the countryside, see a new life opening in cruising, fishing and the pleasure of those that walk beside them. Others, still useful to the community, will end their days as channels for storing and moving water wherever it may be wanted.

CHILDREN'S PLAYGROUNDS

Considerable difficulty has been experienced in attempting to apply cost-benefit analysis to children's playgrounds. It is relatively easy to calculate the annual costs of providing and operating a playground but the benefits are much more difficult to identify and once identified cannot be evaluated with any degree of realism—they are truly imponderables.

Annual cost of providing and maintaining a typical children's playground	£
Loan charges on land: total cost 0.1 ha @ £10 000/hectare = £1000. Loan charge based on six per cent interest and three per cent sinking fund:	66
Annual equivalent of cost of equipment, etc. spread over its life (15 years) £1200 × 0.11	132
Operating and maintenance costs (with full time attendant or playleader)	1 200
Annual cost of typical playground (1970 figures)	1 398
say	£1 400

Benefits flowing from children's playground

(1) Children play in relative safety off roads with much reduced risk of becoming road casualties.

(2) Suitable outlet for high spirits of older children which might otherwise result in vandalistic or delinquent behaviour.

(3) Opportunity for children to take part in healthy outdoor exercise and help in development of bodies.

(4) Opportunity for children to get together and to learn to stand on their own feet.

CONCLUSIONS

Prest and Turvey[70] and Lewis[71] have emphasised the difficulties inherent in the application of cost-benefit analysis and the danger of putting it forward as a more powerful and accurate tool than it really is. Difficulties have been experienced in attempting to apply the technique to outdoor recreational facilities and some of the benefits cannot be evaluated satisfactorily in monetary terms. An alternative approach could be to adopt ranking procedures under a number of heads when making a choice between different locations but it is unlikely that all the heads will be of equal importance.

Economic considerations alone will rarely justify the provision of public open space as against residential, commercial or industrial uses of the land. Social and aesthetic aspects must be given full consideration in order to produce well planned towns which will provide attractive, healthy and satisfying environments. On the other hand, regard to economic principles can result in the location of open space in such a way that it maximises benefits to the community. These studies have also highlighted the need to ensure the fullest utilisation of recreational resources compatible with the conservation of their natural qualities, and have demonstrated the desirability of experimenting with charging policies for facilities which have hitherto been largely unpriced.

REFERENCES

1. OUTDOOR RECREATION RESOURCES REVIEW COMMISSION. *Economic Studies of Outdoor Recreation.* Study report 24, Washington D.C., (1962)

2. DAVIS, R. K. Recreation planning as an economic problem. *Natural Resources Journal*, **3.2,** (1963)

3. CLAWSON, M. (1963). *Land and Water for Recreation*, Rand McNally, Chicago

4. ROBINSON, W. C. The simple economics of public outdoor recreation. *Land Economics*, **43.1,** (1967)

5. ROLPH, E. (1956). Pp. 20–22 in *The theory of fiscal economics*, University of California Press

6. WENNERGREN, E. B. Valuing non-market priced recreational resources. *Land Economics*, **40.3,** (1964)

7. PEARSE, P. H. A new approach to the evaluation of non-priced recreational resources. *Land Economics*, **44.1,** (1968)

8. MISHAN, E. J. A survey of welfare economics, 1939–1959. *Economic Journal*, **70,** (June 1960), 197–265

9. PREST, A. R. and TURVEY, R. Cost-benefit analysis: a survey. *Economic Journal*, **75,** (December 1965), 683–735

10. PETERS, G. H. *Cost-benefit Analysis and Public Expenditure: Eaton Paper 8.* Institute of Economic Affairs, (1966)

11. MCKEAN, R. N. (1958). *Efficiency in Government through Systems Analysis*, John Wiley, New York

12. ECKSTEIN, O. (1961). A survey of the theory of public expenditure criteria. *Public Finances: Needs, Sources and Utilization*, Princeton University Press

13. COBURN, T. M., BEESLEY, M. E. and REYNOLDS, D. J., *The London-Birmingham Motorway: Traffic and Economics. Road Research Laboratory Technical Paper 46*, H.M.S.O., (1960)

14. BEESLEY, M. E. and FOSTER, C. D. The Victoria Line: Social benefits and finances. *Journal of Royal Statistical Society*, **128.1,** (1965)

15. LICHFIELD, N. Cost-benefit analysis in town planning: A case study: Swanley. *Urban Studies*, **3.3,** (1966), 215–249

16. LICHFIELD, N., *Cost-benefit Analysis in Town Planning: A Case Study of Cambridge*. Cambridgeshire County Council, (1966)

17. LICHFIELD, N. (1965). Spacial externalities in urban public expenditures: A case study, in *The Public Economy of Urban Communities* (Ed. Margolis, J.), John Hopkins Press, Baltimore

18. LICHFIELD, N. Cost-benefit analysis in urban expansion. A case study: Peterborough. *Regional Studies*, **3.2,** (1969)

19. INSTITUTE OF MUNICIPAL TREASURERS AND ACCOUNTANTS, *Cost-benefit Analysis*, (1968)

20. HENDER, J. D. Introduction to cost-benefit analysis. *Cost-benefit Analysis*, Institute of Municipal Treasurers and Accountants, (1968)

21. WILSON, A. G. The technique of cost-benefit analysis. *Cost-benefit Analysis*, Institute of Municipal Treasurers and Accountants, (1968)

22. PESTON, M., Cost-benefit values. *Town and Country Planning*, (December 1969), 563–565

23. STOCKS, N. R., Cost-benefit analysis. *The Chartered Surveyor*, (April 1966), 547–551

24. RESOURCES FOR TOMORROW CONFERENCE. Water Workshop B Benefit-cost analysis. *Proceedings of Resources for Tomorrow Conference, Montreal,* (1961)

25. CRUTCHFIELD, J. A. Valuation of fishery resources. *Land Economics,* **38.2,** (1962), 145–154

26. MACK, R. P. and MYERS, S. (1965). Pp. 71–116 in *Outdoor Recreation. Measuring Benefits of Government Investments.* (Ed. Dorfman R.), Brookings Institution, Washington D.C.

27. TRICE, A. H. and WOOD, S. E., Measurement of recreation benefits. *Land Economics,* **34.3,** (1958), 195–207

28. CLAWSON, M. and KNETSCH, J. L. (1966). *Economics of Outdoor Recreation,* John Hopkins Press, Baltimore

29. KNETSCH, J. L. Economics of including recreation as a purpose of eastern water projects. *Journal of Farm Economics,* **46.5,** (1964)

30. DAIUTE, R. J. Methods of determination of demand for outdoor recreation. *Land Economics,* **42.3,** (1966)

31. PREWITT REPORT. *An Economic Study of the Monetary Evaluation of Recreation in the National Parks.* U.S. Dept. of the Interior, National Park Service and Recreational Planning Division, (1949)

32. CLAWSON, M. *Methods of Measuring the Demand for and Value of Outdoor Recreation.* Reprint No. 10, Resources for the Future, Washington, (1959)

33. KNETSCH, J. L. Outdoor recreation demands and benefits. *Land Economics,* **39.4,** (1963)

34. MEREWITZ, L. Recreational benefits of water resource development. *Water Resources Research,* **2.4,** (1966)

35. BOYET, W. E. and TOLLEY, G. S. Recreation project based on demand analysis. *Journal of Farm Economics,* **48.4,** (1966), 984–1001

36. WENNERGREN, E. B. Surrogate pricing of outdoor recreation. *Land Economics,* **43.1,** (1967), 112–116

37. WOOD, D. F., The distances-travelled technique for measuring value of recreation areas: an application. *Land Economics,* **37.4,** (1961), 363–369

38. MANSFIELD, N. W., Recreation trip generation. *Journal of Transport Economics and Policy,* **3.2,** (1969)

39. BURTON, T. L. and WIBBERLEY, G. P. (1965). *Outdoor Recreation in the British Countryside,* Wye College, University of London

40. ROAD RESEARCH LABORATORY. (1965). *Research on Road Traffic,* H.M.S.O.

41. NORTON, G. A. *An Economic Analysis of Outdoor Recreation as a Rural Land-using Activity in North Wales.* Private communication, Department of Agriculture, University College of North Wales, (1968)

42. AUTOMOBILE ASSOCIATION. *Schedule of Estimated Running Costs.* Technical Paper 9, (1967)

43. RILEY, C. S. *Motivational Aspects of Car Use,* Ministry of Transport

44. OUTDOOR RECREATION RESOURCES REVIEW COMMISSION. *Outdoor Recreation for America.* Report to President and Congress of United States, Washington D.C., (1962)

45. SECKLER, D. W. On the uses and abuses of economic science in evaluating public outdoor recreation. *Land Economics,* **42.4,** (1966)

46. CLAWSON, M. Recreation as a competitive segment of multiple use. *Land and Water Use,* American Association for the Advancement of Science, (1963)

47. STATE OF CALIFORNIA. *California Public Outdoor Recreation Plan,* (1960)

48. STATE OF OHIO. *State Park Survey, Fees and Charges,* State of Ohio, Division of Parks, Department of National Resources, Columbus, (1962)

49. BROOM, E. The great outdoors. *Sport and Recreation,* **7.4,** (1966)

50. PEPPIATT, W. D. The pricing of sea-side facilities. *Essays in the Theory and Practice of Pricing,* Institute of Economic Affairs, (1967)

51. SMITH, R. J. and KAVANAGH, N. J. *The Measurement of Benefits of Trout Fishing: Preliminary Results of a Study at Grafham Water, Great Ouse Water Authority, Huntingdonshire.* Studies of recreational demand No. 4. Faculty of Commerce and Social Science, University of Birmingham, (1969)

52. RODGERS, H. B. Leisure and recreation. *Urban Studies,* **6.3,** (1969)

53. COUNTRYSIDE COMMISSION. *Methods of Charging at Rural Car Parks,* (1969)

54. KNETSCH, J. L. Land values and parks in urban fringe areas. *Journal of Farm Economics,* **37.4,** (1961), 1718–1726

55. KITCHEN, J. W. and HENDON, W. S. Land values adjacent to an urban neighbourhood park. *Land Economics,* **42.3,** (1967), 357–360

56. NATIONAL RECREATION AND PARK ASSOCIATION. (1966). *Outdoor Recreation Space Standards,* NRPA, New York

57. KNETSCH, J. L. The influence of reservoir projects on land values. *Journal of Farm Economics,* (February 1964), 231–243

58. CIRIACY-WANTRUP, S. V. The 'new' competition for land and some implications for public policy. *Natural Resources Journal,* **4.2,** (1964), 264–266

59. NISBET, J. Cost planning in relation to landscape. *Journal of Institute of Landscape Architects,* (November 1962), 10–14

60. WILSON, P. M., Marinas: development and economic factors. *The Appraisal Journal,* (April 1967), 199–222

61. BRITISH TRAVEL ASSOCIATION/UNIVERSITY OF KEELE, *Pilot National Recreation Survey. Report No. 1,* (1967)

62. BURTON, T. L. and FULCHER, M. N. Measurement of recreation benefits—a survey. *Journal of Economic Studies,* **3.2,** (1968)

63. MANAGEMENT ACCOUNTING UNIT, H. M. TREASURY. *Seminar on the Treatment of Land, Infrastructure and Amenity in Cost Benefit Studies,* Sunningdale, (1969)

64. GOLF DEVELOPMENT COUNCIL. *Elements of Golf Course Layout and Design*

65. SEELEY, I. H. (1967). *Municipal Engineering Practice,* Macmillan

66. DEPARTMENTAL COMMITTEE OF INQUIRY INTO ALLOTMENTS. *Report: Cmnd. 4166,* H.M.S.O., (1969)

67. BRITISH WATERWAYS BOARD. *Annual Report and Accounts 1968,* H.M.S.O., (1969)

68. BRITISH WATERWAYS BOARD. *The Facts about the Waterways,* (1965)

69. HADFIELD, C. (1966). *The Canals of the East Midlands,* David and Charles

70. PREST, A. R., and TURVEY, R. Cost-benefit analysis: a survey. *Economic Journal,* **75,** (1965), 683–735

71. LEWIS, J. P. *Mis-used Techniques in Planning : Occasional Paper No. 2—Cost-benefit analysis*. University of Manchester, Centre for Urban and Regional Research, (1969)

72. MANSFIELD, N. W. The estimation of benefits from recreation sites and the provision of a new recreation facility. *Regional Studies*, **5.2,** (1971)

4 REVIEW OF RESEARCH METHODS IN OUTDOOR RECREATION

THE LAST DECADE has seen a rapid growth in research work in outdoor recreation in Great Britain. An effective incentive was given by the work of the Outdoor Recreation Resources Review Commission in America, published in 1962.[1] Few would advocate the wholesale application of the American findings to this country, nevertheless, the general predictions of doubling or even trebling of demand by the year 2000, the dominance of casual and water based activities, and the important influence of population, income, education, leisure time and mobility factors on demand have been generally accepted as valid for Britain.[2] Indeed these findings were largely confirmed in the Pilot National Recreation Survey undertaken in the United Kingdom in 1965.[3]

Another reason for the recent growth of research interest probably stems from the multi-disciplinary and inter-disciplinary nature of the subject matter of recreation and the scope it offers for a variety of approaches: geographical, town planning, sociological, economic, biological and physical education. Hence in British universities alone there were forty-four separate departments listed in the Countryside Commission's Research Register No. 2 as supervising individual and team research study on recreation in 1969.[4] Another important incentive to the growth of research effort, and recognised by Greaves[2] has arisen particularly in local and central government, where the need to plan for recreation in a more positive way has been clearly established. Heavy pressures on some recreational resources, traffic congestion near the sites, conflict between users and, in some cases, physical and biological deterioration of the resources themselves, has demonstrated the need for a sounder basis for the selection, design and management of recreational resources.

RESOURCE SURVEYS

The first national inventory studies of outdoor recreation facilities were undertaken in the United States by the Outdoor Recreation Resources Review Commission.[5-7] Of particular interest is Study Report 8 which examines potential recreation sites of 12 ha or more, in private ownership and located in the ten densely populated north-east States of America.[7]

The Sports Council from its inception recognised the need for a stocktaking of recreational resources and facilities, embracing those provided by local authorities as well as commercial and private facilities. Hence the regional sports councils each undertook initial appraisals of the major facilities in their regions and the majority of the reports were published in 1967.[8] These appraisals have varied in range and depth and have indicated the need for further studies in demand. Surveys of existing facilities indicate the number, size and location, and nature of provision of recreation resources in a prescribed area. They will assist in showing local or sub-regional deficiencies, or excesses of provision, and the general pattern of distribution. Surveys of this type are an essential prerequisite to more detailed studies into patterns and intensity of use and assessment of demand. Furthermore, they need periodic updating to incorporate facilities of recent origin.

ASSESSMENT OF DEMAND

Clawson and Knetsch[9] have shown how an understanding of present demands and the manner in which they are changing over time has become of immense importance in recreation resource planning and policy formulation. Furthermore, available data concerning recreation use are often seriously deficient in the United States and even more so in Great Britain.

The volume of demand for a particular type of facility needs to be known in order to assess the adequacy of present provision and probable future requirements. Both demand and capacity must be measured in the same terms and, as suggested in the Cheshire recreation study,[10] the participations per unit facility per year system has much to commend it. A person's demand for recreation has been found to be largely determined by personal circumstances —age, income, level of education, family circumstances, and other factors. Recreational activities present barriers to participation in the form of monetary costs, time and energy. Each person will choose to participate or otherwise according to the significance of the restraints to him. The demand for an activity generated by a certain population will be largely influenced by its age structure, income level and distribution, proportion of children, and so on.

This requires a great detail of quantitative data of which little is at present available. The Pilot National Recreation Survey No. 1[3] is helpful but has limitations due to the small size of the sample and is not specifically concerned with urban recreation as such. The Government Social Survey on Planning for Leisure[11] is particularly concerned with the present pattern of participation in outdoor and physical recreation and the frequency and manner of use of public open spaces in urban areas of England and Wales, and should provide a useful basis for assessment of demand. The author will draw extensively upon the results of the survey for comparison purposes in later chapters. Practical difficulties arise in undertaking surveys aimed at providing a basis for assessment of demand. The high cost necessitates sampling, with the result that the statistics are frequently restricted to a very small proportion of the population and, with minority activities, the sample is insufficient as a base for the measurement of present and future participation.

It is difficult to isolate the effect of supply on participation, so that the measurement of present demand may simply reflect the presence or absence of suitable facilities and have little relationship to the personal circumstances of the participant. 'Latent' or 'deferred' demand may also exist through lack of suitable facilities. Furthermore, reasons for participation involve the complexities of human behaviour and this is also difficult to assess. We are also concerned with potential demand which may become effective at some future date if certain conditions change, for example, increase in purchasing power or leisure time.

Tanner[12] in his study of coastal recreation, also concluded that 'the assessment of demand for recreational facilities is a very complex problem'. Little is known about the numbers of participants, the precise nature of their demands or the catchment areas for different activities or types of facility. Cesario[13] postulated that the number of visitors to a park in unit time was determined by several different factors: accessibility of park (joint function of population and distance), attractiveness of park, competition of other parks, and a saturation function. These investigations also serve to illustrate the complexities of demand assessment.

The American Outdoor Recreation Resources Review Commission[14] has shown that participation in outdoor recreation by American adults is remarkably widespread. About ninety per cent engage in one or more outdoor recreation activities in the course of a year. More than sixty-six per cent participate in driving for the purposes of sightseeing and picnicking. Water sports are also becoming increasingly popular with forty-five per cent swimming, forty per cent fishing and thirty per cent boating. The American study also found that many people desire to engage in more outdoor recreation activity but are prevented from doing so mainly by lack of time and to some extent by lack of money. Since incomes are likely to rise and leisure time may also increase, some growth in participation rates seems reasonably certain.

In contrast the Government Social Survey on Planning for Leisure[11] asserts that except amongst the very young, active participation in sports and games seldom occupies more than a very small proportion of people's leisure time. On the other hand twentieth century technical innovations have created a host of new recreation activities—ranging from pleasure motoring to water skiing, and gliding to sub-aqua activities.

RECREATIONAL STANDARDS AND CAPACITIES

Open space standards in general use were discussed in chapter 2 and it was evident that standards based upon population have limited validity. Sessoms[15] asserts that standards for intelligent recreational planning must consider socio-economic conditions, minority situations and especially the function of, and the need for, types of recreation. He saw the need for the application of some new concepts and ideas to recreation systems planning. Clawson and Knetsch[9] emphasised the need to determine the carrying capacity of various kinds of areas for different kinds of uses, and that capacity is closely related to the concept of optimum intensity of use. As described in chapter 2, it is important that optimum use should be made of recreational resources subject to avoidance of physical overcrowding, conflict between different users and site erosion. The Nature Conservancy[16] is actively investigating the biotic effects of public pressures on the environment and has already formulated some valuable guidelines.

The Sports Council is mindful of the need for research into determining the maximum capacity of facilities and into ways of restricting use to a desirable level, as little positive work has been done in this field. Capacity has been defined as the number of participations a facility can accommodate at a given time. In practice it normally varies over a period of time. The capacity of a facility is influenced by the following factors:

(1) *Spatial needs:* with team games—tennis and bowls—the space requirements of players can be readily calculated, but with more informal pursuits—such as golf and swimming—the space standards of participants have still to be defined.

(2) *Time requirements:* the shorter the time spent by each participant the greater the numbers that can be accommodated over a specified period. With more formal activities such as football, playing time is regulated. Hours of opening also affect the capacity.

(3) *Maintenance requirements:* some facilities need closing periodically to allow essential maintenance work to be performed and this may reduce the capacity of the facility.

Cheshire County Council[10] produced a schedule of capacity standards for various outdoor recreational activities. In this schedule the main activities are listed together with the minimum number of participants per facility unit, such as a cricket pitch, and the average time of a game. The maximum possible number of participations by players per annum is found by multiplying the number of participants by the number of available hours (6 days of 8 hours per week for 52 weeks less maintenance periods) and dividing by the number of hours occupied by an average game.

Many of the stated capacities expressed in participations per year are wholly unrealistic. For instance, 10 240 participations of cricket per year assumes 1.6 games of cricket per day throughout the whole year (less Sundays and maintenance periods). Most facilities show maximum use at weekends and intermittent use throughout the week, so that actual use would be quite a small percentage of the full theoretical capacity.

TABLE 4.1

RECREATION CAPACITY USE STANDARDS

Activity	Space standard per unit of facility (in metres)	Type of facility unit	Min. no. of participants per unit	Av. session time per participant occupying one unit (hours)	Necessary maintenance (days)	Capacity in participations per year assuming facility available 8 hours per day: 6 days per week
Cricket	137 diam.	1 field	22	5	21	10 240
Association football	110 × 73	1 pitch	22	3	51	15 290
Hockey	40 × 18	1 pitch	22	3	51	15 290
Bowls	40 × 40	1 green	2	3	51	1 380
Rugby league	123 × 69	1 pitch	24	3	51	16 700
Rugby union	146 × 69	1 pitch	30	3	51	20 880
Golf (18-hole)	—	1 hole	2	0.2	21	23 280
Archery	30 × 4	1 range	1	3	21	750
Outdoor tennis (hard)	36 × 18	1 court	2	2.5	42	1 730

Source: Cheshire County Council, *Recreation in Cheshire* (1968)

SURVEY METHODS

A variety of survey methods have been employed to collect data relating to the use of recreational facilities. Burton and Noad[17] have classified these data collection techniques into six categories: use of physical evidence; mechanical and electronic devices; use of available documentation; observation; self-administered and postal surveys; and interview surveys. Each of these methods and their uses will now be considered.

Physical Evidence

This approach investigates physical traces surviving from past behaviour and events. The most relevant aspect in recreational resources is erosion, where the degree of wear and tear on vegetation serves as a measure. Studies by the Nature Conservancy[16] have shown the effect of public pressures on vegetation, and in some cases the rate of deterioration has been measured at fixed points along survey lines at regular intervals. In the case of the Cairngorms, the damage to the soils and vegetation near the ski-lifts is so extensive that the erosion shows clearly on aerial photographs. Such photographs provide a useful basis for before-and-after studies. Physical evidence measures may prove useful in supplementing information on recreational use obtained in other ways.

Recording Devices

Mechanical and electronic devices may be used for recording data, and their primary use is for counting the number of vehicles passing a specific point over a given period of time. A survey of visitors to the Wye and Crundale National Nature Reserve[18] made use of a stile where pressure of a visitor on the lowest bar activated an electro-mechanical counter, which thus recorded the number of visitors entering the reserve. The value of such devices is rather limited and they operate mainly as supplementary processes to other research methods.

Documentary Evidence

Recreational researchers often have recourse to public and private records such as census tables, club membership lists, ticket sales, and so on, which can help in establishing demand trends. A study of the Norfolk holiday industry used records of bread sales in the county as a means of measuring the seasonal flow of holiday makers.[19] Furthermore electoral lists have often been used as sampling frames for interview surveys. In some recreation studies time-budget or time-use diaries have been employed. Respondents are supplied with a blank diary form covering an allotted period, often one week, and each day is sub-divided into convenient time periods (half-hour or one-hour intervals) and the respondents are asked to record all activities undertaken during each time period.

The BBC survey of people's activities[20] produced detailed records of the activities of 2353 persons aged 15 and over and resident in Great Britain in the late spring of 1961. Time-use diaries were designed to show what people do at each half-hour from 6.30 a.m. to midnight on all days of the week. The social class of the respondent was subjectively assessed by the interviewer and occupation was also recorded, pre-retirement or marriage, where appropriate. It is worthy of note that the sample originally selected for enquiry consisted of 4026 names and addresses picked at random from electoral registers. The reduction to 2353 arose from a variety of causes—death, illness, removal, absence or lack of cooperation.

The composition of the respondents is shown below in brackets as percentages:

Sex: males (48), females (52)

Age group: 15–24 (15), 25–44 (39), 45–64 (35), 65 and over (11)

Social class: upper middle (6), lower middle (29), working class (64), unclassified (1)

Educational groups: F/T education to 17 or over (13), 15 or 16 (34), 14 or less (53)

Occupational groups: Professional, managerial and highly skilled (20), moderately skilled and clerical (47), semi-skilled and unskilled (28), unclassified (5)

Age of family groups: Parents of children under 5 (17), 5–14 (20), remainder (63)

Average percentage participation by the respondents in outdoor sports is illustrated in the following schedule.

	Weekday	Saturday	Sunday
Mid-morning	1	2	4
Mid-afternoon	2	7	10
Mid-evening	2	3	5

These figures show the peak activity period on a Sunday afternoon. It must be borne in mind that the sample is very small to cover the whole country and that people's outdoor activities do vary in extent in different parts of the country. Unfortunately, activities relating to recreation, apart from sports, are nowhere clearly distinguished.

Robinson and Converse[21] in their contribution to the cross-national time-budget study coded activities on a diary day into ninety-six basic activity groups, all of which fell into one or other of two main categories—obligatory or non-leisure activities and leisure or spare time activities. They produced an average figure of about twenty-three activities per person per day covering sleeping, eating, travel, work, personal hygiene, shopping and a wide range of spare time activities.

Another American time-budget study was made by Chapin and Hightower[22] in which they established nine major categories of activities divided into sixty-two sub groups. The major groupings were:

(1) Income-producing and related activities.

(2) Child-raising and family activities.

(3) Education and intellectual development.

(4) Religious and human welfare activities.

(5) Social activities.

(6) Recreation and relaxation.

(7) Participation in club activities.

(8) Participation in community service and political activities.

(9) Activities associated with food, shelter, medical and similar needs.

As Burton and Noad[17] have emphasised, the time-diary studies to date have been to some extent experimental but they do offer a valuable means of obtaining information on leisure and recreation habits. The main problems are securing an adequate response rate, determining the time period and intervals to be used and formulating satisfactory coding and grouping of activities.

Observation

Observation has been defined as 'the purposeful and selective watching and counting of phenomena as they take place'. It is of value as a complementary technique to interview surveys but has a number of deficiencies. There are severe limitations to its application, it is not easily combined with sampling procedures and permits far too readily the exercise of the subjective influence of the investigator.

Limited use has been made of observation techniques in recreation research. Hole[23] adopted this approach in his investigation of children's play on new housing estates because of the difficulties inherent in interviewing young children. It is worthwhile to examine Hole's methods in some detail:

A layout plan of each estate was divided into a series of observation areas. Each area was one which an observer could conveniently view from a single spot and note any children who might be there at the time of the visit. Each child's activity and where he was playing was noted as at the moment of observation; subsequent changes which occurred while the observer was still at a particular observation point were ignored. If the same child appeared later in another observation area or was still in the same observation area when the observer returned for a second visit, he was noted again. Each observation area was visited in strict rotation during a walk-round which covered a whole estate. These walk-rounds were repeated at intervals throughout the day.

Hole aimed at achieving a systematic observational situation but the report does not show whether the observations themselves were systematic. The use of a check list, for instance, is an aid to uniformity but may give rise to difficulties in recording activities which do not appear on the check list. Winterbottom[24] organised a physical survey of the use of several open spaces in Colchester. The survey was carried out on two weekends and two weekdays during the summer of 1965, when it was hoped that there would be maximum use of all open space facilities. The purpose of the study was to arrive at a standard for provision of public open space by means of observed usage.

To this end, counts were made at approximately hourly intervals from 10.0 a.m. to 8.0 p.m. at weekends and 12 noon to 2.0 p.m. and 4.0 p.m. to 8.0 p.m. on weekdays. Difficulties were encountered in establishing the numbers of persons engaged in specific activities and recorded usage was therefore classified under 'organised games' and 'other activities.' Winterbottom concluded that on the basis of his investigations the provision of just over 1 hectare of open space per 1000 population appeared adequate. It is doubtful whether these investigations proceeded over a sufficiently long period to give conclusive results.

A survey of use of county open spaces in Hampshire[25] in 1966 used half-hourly counts of vehicles and people to supplement the information obtained on questionnaires, and the author adopted the same procedure in use surveys of Nottingham parks and lidos which are described in chapters 6 and 8. Observation techniques are frequently employed in traffic counts to avoid obstructing the flow of traffic. Ross[26] used this method to assess the volume of pleasure traffic using the main roads out of Newcastle-upon-Tyne on a Sunday morning in September, 1965. Furmidge[27] described how aerial surveys by helicopters, coordinated by radio with ground interview teams, were used in east Sussex to record by observation and photographs the extent and nature of day-trip activity in the summers of 1967 and 1968.

Postal Surveys

With this type of survey questionnaires are sent by post to respondents whom, it is hoped, will complete and return them without the assistance of an interviewer. Burton and Noad[17] described them as self-administered surveys. This method has advantages in terms of cost and convenience of operation but there is the accompanying disadvantage of low response rates possibly leading to bias in the findings. Response rates are often as low as thirty per cent and a return of fifty per cent is usually regarded as good. The people who return questionnaires may not be wholly representative of the whole sample and, even if they are, the findings may be distorted significantly by the degree of non-response. Finally, respondents may misread or misinterpret questions as there is no interviewer available to assist them.

An effort must be made to secure a high response rate by arousing interest in the subject amongst recipients, by keeping the questionnaire as concise and simple as possible and by enclosing a stamped addressed envelope for its return. Seitz[28] asserts that the use of postage stamps on reply envelopes is more effective than reply-paid envelopes, and Clausen and Ford[29] suggest that the covering letter is best separated from the questionnaire itself.

Gray and Corlett[30] obtained an increase in response from thirty-eight to seventy per cent by sending follow-up letters. Other investigators[31] have not secured such dramatic increases and this latter experience is shared by the author who found that responses in the order of thirty to thirty-five per cent increased to forty-five to fifty per cent as a result of follow-up letters. Views differ as to the advisability of offering some inducement to respondents. One local authority has suggested the payment of 50p to each respondent who completes a questionnaire on an interview recreation survey. In a Newcastle-upon-Tyne theatre survey, the numbers of completed questionnaires were placed in a lottery for a prize of free tickets for the theatre.

Use has been made of postal surveys in recent recreation research. The initial appraisals of facilities for sport and recreation made by the ten regional sports councils were all based on postal surveys of local authorities, and they secured a very high response rate. Cullen[32] in his industrial recreation survey sent questionnaires to all industrial organisations with 1000 employees or more and obtained a thirty-nine per cent response. The author has used postal surveys to obtain information from sporting organisations and allotment holders in Greater Nottingham and the analysed results are given in chapters 6, 7 and 8.

Interview Surveys

Interview surveys have been the principal method used to collect information on people's behaviour in recent years. They have the great merit of flexibility and also secure a high response. The possibility of misunderstanding of questions inherent in the postal survey is removed, and results are likely to be more accurate. The interviewer can make sure that the respondent understands the questions and can also obtain supplementary information, although some degree of bias may arise. Recreation interviews are usually based on standardised techniques—obtaining similar information from each respondent. They can be conducted in homes (household surveys) or on recreation sites (on-site, user or turnstile surveys).

The big advantage of household surveys is that they embrace a good cross-section of the community and are not confined to participants in any particular activity. They are, however, very expensive to operate and need to cover a large number of respondents to provide a satisfactory sample and give meaningful information on minority activities. The practical application of both types of survey is now investigated.

User Surveys

Burton and Hills[33] organised a user survey of Windsor Great Park on two successive Sundays in June, 1966, between the hours of 12 noon and 6.0 p.m. The numbers of visitors entering the park at selected points were counted and interviews conducted at random with a proportion of the visitors by sixteen London university graduates. Information was obtained on points of origin of visitors, method of travel, composition of visiting parties, length of stay, intended pursuits, frequency of visits and preferences for additional facilities. The questionnaire was much shorter than that used by the author in his surveys of Nottingham parks and a comparison of the findings of the two surveys will be made in chapter 6.

Hampshire County Planning Department[25] carried out a user survey of four major county open spaces on Sundays in August and September, 1966, from 2.0 p.m. to 6.30 or 7.0 p.m. The survey technique consisted of interviews with visitors using questionnaires, and information was obtained on origin of visitors and distance travelled, activities pursued and visitor preferences. In the Netherlands, Heytze[34] conducted a survey of recreationalists using the State Forest at Nunspeet and spread his enquiries over 28 days during July and August, 1966 (7 Sundays, 7 Saturdays and 14 weekdays) when weather conditions were considered suitable (temperature of about 18°C, no rainfall and not too damp in the woods). Each interview took about half an hour and questions covered social criteria, recreational needs, measure of appreciation and activities pursued.

Duffell and Goodall[35] organised 1700 interviews on ten recreational sites in Worcestershire and Staffordshire in the summer of 1966. The information was obtained by on-site interviews of car drivers with the use of questionnaires. Interviewing was carried out between 11.0 a.m. and 7 or 8 p.m. with days split into three periods—morning, afternoon and evening. Interviews proceeded for a maximum of 2 hours at each site, when interviewers moved to the next site, and on the next occasion the sites would be visited in reverse order working on a 4-day rota system. It was intended to carry out as many interviews as possible at weekends but the programme was upset by the weather.

The objectives of the survey were stated as:

(1) to collect data to assist in quantifying the demand by car-borne visitors to recreational areas of different types being at varying degrees of accessibility from population centres;

(2) to determine trip-generation rates to these sites in relation to degree of accessibility;

(3) to establish the parking duration, activities engaged in and routes used by car-borne visitors; and

(4) to counsel the public's views on facilities, improvements, parking charges, etc.

Straw[36] organised a questionnaire survey of twenty-nine sites visited by the public in the Lincolnshire Wolds and adjoining fringe areas. The interviews were conducted by pupils from eight secondary schools on a Saturday and Sunday in July, 1967, between 10.0 a.m. and 12 noon and 3.0 p.m. and 5.0 p.m. The purpose of the survey was to determine the extent and nature of recreational use in the Wolds area, the places of origin of visitors and the use made of the area by coastal holiday makers.

In 1964, the former London County Council conducted surveys in thirteen parks, where a sample of approximately 160 adult visitors to each park was interviewed at 15 minute intervals. Interviewing took place at the times when the parks were most used; 12.00 a.m.–1.15 p.m., 1.30–2.45 p.m., 3.45–5.00 p.m. and 5.15–6.30 p.m. The questions asked related to all characteristics of the visit, opinions on the park visited and on facilities which might be provided, and a large number of profile characteristics of the respondent. The results have been published by the Greater London Council.[37]

These surveys show a surprisingly wide variation in method of execution—varying lengths of survey period, months of year, days of week, times of day and categories of person interviewed—and this makes for difficulties in comparing results.

Household Surveys

The Pilot National Recreation Survey[3] investigating national and regional patterns of recreation, involved household interviews of 3167 respondents: 2839 adults aged 17 years and over, and 328 children aged between 12 and 16 years. A random sample was attempted, intended to be representative of the total population of the country. At least twenty sampling points were selected within each region with approximately equal regional sub-samples. At each sampling point a random starting point was taken on the electoral register and every tenth address thereafter with no substitutes being permitted. At each address the selected respondent was to be the youngest person over the age of 12 years who was present at the time of the call, to guard against under-representation of young people who are those most frequently away from home.

The representation of the younger age groups (12–16 and 17–24 years) corresponded well to the proportions in the national population, while the age group 65 years and over included only ten per cent of respondents compared with fifteen per cent in the national population. The sample has proved inadequate for analytical work on socio-economic aspects, regional variations and minority activities. Rodgers[38] has recognised its shortcomings and it was described as a pilot survey from the outset.

The Government Social Survey[11] is concerned with the recreation of urban populations and is orientated especially towards physical recreation and formal sport. The sample consisted of 2682 persons aged 15 years and over living in urban areas with a minimum total population of 6000 households and a minimum density of fifteen persons per hectare at the 1961 census. The sample was also devised to enable the results from the New Towns, Inner London and the remainder of urban England and Wales to be analysed separately. Forty persons were selected at random from the electoral register for each area. If the person selected was the head of the household then all other persons aged from 15 to 20 years were also interviewed. As the survey aimed at obtaining a higher proportion of younger persons in the sample, fifty rateable units were chosen at random from the valuation list for each area, at which all persons aged 15 to 30 years only were interviewed. There was a ten per cent refusal rate in the national sample and a further nine per cent could not be contacted.

National Opinion Polls were commissioned by the North Regional Planning Committee to carry out an investigation into outdoor leisure activities in the northern region.[39] The data was obtained by interviews of a representative sample of 3828 residents aged 12 years and over during June and July, 1967. One hundred administrative district sampling points were selected with probability of selection proportionate to their population, and at each sampling point forty-four households were selected from the electoral register. At each household, a systematic procedure was adopted to select a person aged 16 or over for interview: children aged 12 to 15 inclusive were interviewed only at households where an adult had been interviewed. The survey results were suitably weighted to correct the over sampling of children.

Questionnaires were sub-divided into three sections:

(1) Personal characteristics of the respondent.

(2) Leisure activities in each of two previous weekends in quasi-diary form.

(3) Normal leisure pursuits—not necessarily those of the two previous weekends.

The North West Sports Council[40] advocated a survey of 1700 households in the north-west region in 1967, representing a sampling fraction of 1:1250. It was envisaged that the survey would involve at least three visits to each household and together with data processing would cost £17 800 (approximately £10 per household).

The former London County Council conducted a home interview survey of 2015 adults chosen from electoral registers by a systematic sample from random starts in 1964. The results are published by the Greater London Council.[37] Respondents who had visited an open space in the previous week were asked detailed questions about each of their visits. Those who had not visited in the previous week but at other times in the previous month were asked a number of questions about each of their last two visits. Less frequent visitors were asked why they did not visit spaces more often. The whole sample was also questioned on attitudes to open spaces, sports activities, leisure trips out of London, play characteristics of any children in the household under 10 years and a wide variety of profile data. A number of the questions or concepts used in this survey proved unsatisfactory in operation and this highlights the complexities inherent in recreational surveys and the desirability of running pilot surveys in advance of the main investigation. These aspects will be considered further in chapter 6.

Griffiths[41] has investigated the leisure activities of post-school adolescents. A ten per cent sample of secondary modern, technical, grammar and direct grant schools in south-east Lancashire was taken and all leavers in those schools interviewed on recreational habits. Two years later the same respondents were again interviewed in order to examine the factors which affect the physical recreation patterns of adolescents.

Kent County Council[42] undertook a social survey in 1962 covering over 20 000 persons. Trained investigators using questionnaires interviewed housewives or householders in respect of all members of the household, on a wide range of questions including playing of games. The results of this survey will be examined in chapter 7. Duffell and Goodall[43] undertook a recreational survey in the Northfield district of Birmingham in 1966. They adopted a one per cent sample of households obtained by a systematic random sampling technique, using the electoral register as a basis. In most cases the head of the household was interviewed but in some cases the wife answered the questions. The survey covered social data, town entertainments, country pursuits and demand for leisure around the conurbation. The total number of households investigated was 184 and there must be some doubt as to the adequacy of the sample.

Burton and Noad[17] have emphasised the need for comparability of data as between different surveys. An analysis of six major recreational surveys in Britain showed that they could be compared on only four items of profile data. For this reason the author conferred with the Sports Council and the Central Council of Physical Recreation prior to finalising questionnaires for use on his case studies, in an attempt to ensure maximum comparability with other studies. Subsequently the Countryside Commission[66] formulated a set of suggested standard classifications for use in questionnaire surveys which should do much to secure increased uniformity of approach.

SAMPLES

Sampling has been defined as 'the selection of part of an aggregate of material to represent the whole aggregate'. It involves identifying the sampling units which may be natural units, such as individuals, or aggregates of them, such as families or households. The sampling units must be clearly definable within a recognised frame, of which the electoral register is the most common. The main aim in sampling must be to avoid bias. This may arise through errors in the selection of the sample or through chance differences between persons in the sample and those not included. Difficulties arise in determining the size of the sample and in ensuring that the sample selected is truly representative of the total population that is the subject of the study.

With recreation surveys problems of sample size are accentuated by reason of the diverse nature of recreational pursuits. It is evident from the studies undertaken by the BBC,[20] the British Travel Association (now British Tourist Authority),[3] the Department of Education and Science[11] and the North Regional Planning Committee[39] that the percentage of total population participating in any particular recreational activity is not very high. There are many pursuits in which only one per cent or less of the population takes part. Furthermore, there are numerous pursuits for which participation is confined to specific age groups, for example, many sports are taken up mainly by persons between the ages of about 12 and 25 years. Unless the sample is relatively large, a household survey is unlikely to include sufficient numbers of persons who take part in minority pursuits to make subsequent analysis statistically valuable.

In the Pilot National Recreation Survey[3] a sample of 3167 persons is taken from a total population aged 12 years and over of about 44 million in England, Wales and Scotland—this is equivalent to a ratio of about 1:13900 and is incredibly small. It would need at least a tenfold increase in sample size to pick up sufficient pony-trekkers, water skiers and gliding enthusiasts to draw significant conclusions about their characteristics. The information obtained is also inadequate for many other minority pursuits where the response was less than ten per cent, such as motor or motor cycle racing, sailing, boating, rowing, underwater swimming, archery, winter sports and go-karting. The deficiences are accentuated many times when investigating the relationship between recreational activities and such aspects as age, income, occupation and education.

The North Regional Planning Committee survey[39] of outdoor leisure activities took a sample of 3828 residents aged 12 years and over representing a total population of over 2 million, giving a ratio of about 1:530. This, although showing a vast improvement on the Pilot National Recreation Survey, is still too small to give reliable forecasts for those activities which have very low participation rates. With these deficiencies in mind, the author decided at an early stage in his research that it would be impracticable to carry out a worthwhile household recreational survey in the Nottingham area. Further evidence of an inadequate sample is shown in the Government Social Survey[11] where only three out of the twenty-four sports and games listed show regular participation by ten per cent or more of respondents. It is very doubtful whether the majority of the comparisons between Inner London and the New Towns participation rates in various activities are of any real value.

DATA PROCESSING

The processing of data emanating from large numbers of recreational questionnaires poses problems and it is important that these problems should be anticipated at the outset and the questionnaires framed to meet them. If the total number of completed questionnaires is unlikely to exceed 100, it is probable that manual processing, by tabulating the information on specially prepared schedules, will be the cheapest and quickest method. Where larger numbers are involved, the use of punched cards and computers is almost indispensable.

The normal punch card contains eighty columns with ten numbered spaces in each column (800 characters in all). This means that up to eighty answers can be picked up on a single punch card and up to ten alternatives for each question. There is, however, a limiting factor in that each column can only be holed once, and if a number of answers can be applied to a question then each will have to be allocated a separate column on the punch card. Reference to the questionnaires contained in appendixes 1 to 4 inclusive will serve to illustrate this. All punch card entries should be verified by a second operator.

When processing punch cards for questionnaires relating to recreation sites, it is helpful to reserve columns 79 and 80 for code numbers representing the site and the day of the week, for purposes of identification. The punch cards have to be handled with care to avoid any damage to edges and they need to be stored at a uniform temperature, preferably about 18°C, to prevent deterioration of the cards. In the absence of a computer, mechanical sorters can be employed to separate cards containing like information.

Computers can be programmed to produce print-outs on which the numbers of respondents answering each question or part of a question can be totalled. Furthermore, matrixes can be produced showing correlations between various factors contained on the questionnaires. Once successfully programmed, the computer can produce a wealth of information both speedily and accurately. Not only will its use permit a vast saving in time, but where many thousands of questionnaires are involved the computer alone makes analysis possible. On the other hand it seems that difficulties can arise in the processing of data, as the Government Social Survey[11] makes reference to delays in publication of the report due to protracted difficulties experienced with the computer and the agency used for processing the data!

PROJECTION AND PREDICTION TECHNIQUES

One of the major needs in recreation research is to devise satisfactory ways of predicting future trends. Predictions of this type are both difficult and hazardous, involving as they do changing habits and tastes. Various American studies and a number of British ones have shown that income, occupation and education have an important influence on the amount of time and money that people will spend on recreational pursuits. It is considered desirable to define some of the more commonly used forecasting terms to avoid any possible confusion.

Forecasting Terminology

'Projection' was defined in a Countryside Commission seminar[44] as 'a forecast based on the extrapolation, to some future date, of the controlling variables thought to influence conditions'. Thus if the population is to double in size then, all other things being equal, the rates of participation in recreation activities will also double. 'Extrapolation' is the calculation of future conditions on the basis of past trends, while a 'forecast' is a statement about a future situation and an 'estimate' is a forecast based on informed judgement. Before-and-after studies enable past experience at similar sites offering similar recreation opportunities to be used as a basis for extrapolation.

'Prediction' is the process of combining variables in a way which allows the interaction of the variables upon each other to be seen, and which makes possible systematic differentiation of groups within the population, about whose likely behaviour meaningful statements can be made.[17] 'Regression analysis' indicates the way in which one variable changes in response to change in two or more other variables. Individual forecasts for the controlling variables are regressed together to assess their combined effect on the demand for outdoor recreation as a whole, and for groups of activities and individual activities.[67] Where changes in one variable affect another, duplication of these effects on the demand for recreation can be avoided by using multivariate analysis. 'Multivariate analysis' is used to estimate the separate effect of one variable while all other variables are held constant, and also the effect of different combinations of variables.[44]

Forecasting Methods

Clawson and Knetsch[9] distinguish five methods of forecasting demand:

(1) Extrapolation of past trends in the use of recreation areas, where past trends have been relatively stable, and could be useful for forecasting up to 5 years ahead.

(2) Projection of controlling variables provided all the variables and their relationships to each other and to demand are known and measurable.

(3) Application of the 'satiety principle' by establishing a saturation point representing the maximum participation rate for each activity.

(4) Prediction based on the relationship between socio-economic variables and rates of participation.

(5) Judgement based on available information and individual experience.

Some of the more widely used methods and their applications are now explored.

Demand Curve Analysis

Clawson[45] has shown how curves could be constructed and used in forecasting demand at Yosemite National Park, as described in chapter 3. Knetsch[46] suggests that the demand curve approach can be extended to take into account the effects of controlling variables other than population size and accessibility, for example, the substitution of demand, effects of congestion and changes in structure of demand over time. The results of demand curve analyses at recreation areas could be used to infer values at other existing or proposed areas. Kavanagh[47] applies demand curve analysis to a hypothetical situation of the demand for boating on a reservoir. He recognises that the demand for a commodity is influenced by many factors, and especially that rising incomes may well bring about changes in the type of recreation demanded.

Regression Analysis Techniques

In predicting levels of participation in different recreational pursuits it is advisable to group individuals, as in sociological analysis it is easier to make relatively accurate predictions about groups than it is about individuals. Burton and Wibberley[48] point out that if a way could be found of grouping the population in terms of its leisure and recreation patterns, we should be in a better position to make valid statements about the ways in which recreation demands are generated by these identifiable groups and so forecast future needs. In Britain these groups have been identified entirely upon the basis of socio-economic characteristics. Thus the population is usually divided into five social classes, or seventeen socio-economic groups, or two marital status groups; although even these have not been standardised.

The most comprehensive prediction model yet developed is that outlined by the Outdoor Recreation Resources Review Commission.[49] This attempted forecasts of demand for selected recreation activities for the years 1976 and 2000, using the findings of other studies of the Commission for its base data. It estimated the gross effects on rates of participation in sixteen activities, of each of five socio-economic factors, the estimates being calculated by re-weighting the 1960 rates according to projected distributions of the population by each of the five factors: family income, education, occupation, place of residence and age-sex. The gross effects were then reduced to a net basis by adjustments developed through a multivariate analysis devised at the Survey Research Center of the University of Michigan.[14]

One weakness in this approach is the basic assumption that the correlations between activities and the five socio-economic factors that were calculated for 1960 would remain constant in the future. This concept is capable of being tested by projecting backwards to find what levels of participation in certain activities would have been, say,

10 years ago on the basis of the current values of the correlation coefficients, and then to compare these with actual levels of participation at the time. Variations in demand arise from many factors including changes of fashion. This is well illustrated by the rise and fall of numbers of club members participating in tenpin bowling: 1963—10 000, 1964—25 000, 1965—15 000.[48]

In addition to grouping the population on the basis of socio-economic characteristics, it is also possible to group the recreational activities. Proctor[50] formulated four basic groupings—backwoods recreation; boat culture; country club and picnic area recreation; and passive outdoor recreation. The purpose of this grouping was to identify a method for determining similarities between individuals in their leisure patterns, using a factor analysis applied to data collected for the American National Recreation Survey.[51] Proctor calculated a 'score' for each respondent to the survey which reflected his level of participation in each of fifteen activities. An attempt was then made to 'predict' what his score ought to be, by identification and analysis of thirty background variables, which statistically 'explained' a significant part of the variance in 'activity scores'. The data were thus arranged to give an index of the extent to which participation in any one activity was related to participation in others and to the possession, in varying degrees, of the thirty background variables.

More recently, the North Regional Planning Committee[39] has endeavoured to forecast future outdoor leisure activities in the northern region. This study used the technique of discriminant analysis to isolate the most important of eleven variables, which influenced rates of participation in various activities. A computer programme was designed to sieve out the variables in order of importance and to build up a matrix of associations between the variables and the participation rates for each activity. Forecasts for the relevant variables were then used to predict the future rate of participation. It provides an interesting approach although the sample of 3828 respondents was insufficient to give reliable forecast rates for activities with very low participation rates.

Analysis of User Preferences

Sociologists and behavioural scientists have adopted a different approach to the problem of forecasting demand. Reid,[52] for instance, identifies four methods of forecasting demand:

(1) Attendance-counting studies involve extrapolating results to some future date and take no account of changes in taste, preferences, opportunities, and social and economic factors.

(2) Activity participation studies are based on extrapolating participation rates for individual activities and modifying these by social and economic factors.

(3) User preference and satisfaction studies assess visitor opinion about existing opportunities and attempt to show their relative desires for opportunities as yet unprovided. There is a danger that visitor opinions express wishful thinking rather than intended action.

(4) Behavioural characteristics studies assume that persons holding identical values, having similar motivations and seeking like ends, can be assigned to identifiable groups which can be used as a basis for forecasting.

Reid considers that user preferences are key elements in forecasting demand but techniques for obtaining information on visitor opinions need testing. He suggests that preference studies should seek to obtain information on the identity of a respondent, his past and current actions and his desire to adjust to a different situation in the future, given specified alternatives and costs.

Taylor[53] outlined a Canadian approach which involved a series of related studies:

(1) Survey of present use of parks.

(2) Inventories of recreation opportunities, measuring land capabilities for alternative purposes and identifying potential areas for recreation development.

(3) Surveys of visitor characteristics and behaviour at different types of recreation opportunities.

(4) Analysis procedures to identify the relationship between use and supply.

Factors Affecting Participation in Recreation

The American report[14] has identified the following factors as preventing participation in a desired outdoor recreation activity:

TABLE 4.2

FACTORS PREVENTING PARTICIPATION IN RECREATION ACTIVITIES

Factor	Percentage reporting the factor
Lack of time	52
Lack of money	17
Age	11
Family ties	11
Lack of available facilities	9
Lack of car	5
Lack of equipment	4

Admittedly the percentage weighting of the factors could be appreciably different in Great Britain and there could be significant variations if consideration was confined to urban recreation activities.

Burton and Noad[17] and Tanner[12] have identified the five main background variables which affect rates of participation in recreation activities as population, economic growth, car ownership, education, and leisure time.

Difficulties in Forecasting Demand

Sessoms[15] postulated that:

Recent trends have indicated clearly that all standards are relevant only to the time in which they are prepared. . . . The arbitrary drawing of a circle with a specific radius, and the enumerating of so many facilities and hectares per thousand population when planning for the provision of recreation is as antiquated a planning concept as is the gridiron street pattern for proper subdivision traffic control.

The random provision of, say, tennis courts at an overall standard of so many courts per 1000 population can be a wasteful form of provision, compared with the skilful siting of groups of six courts. Burton and Wibberley[48] favour the provision of neighbourhood recreation centres.

After the establishment of the present relationship between participation in an activity and the personal circumstances of a participant, the usual method of projecting demand into the future is to project personal circumstances and, from this projection, predict future demand. There are, however, problems which must throw doubt upon the validity of the conclusion. The method assumes that whatever the participation pattern of a particular type of population now, it will apply to a population of the same type in the future. Changes in fashion or the introduction of a new form of recreation could invalidate the predictions. Some activities may be substitutes for others and changes in demand may occur between them unpredictably. Furthermore, there may be a saturation level where any extra leisure time ceases to be used for, say, sport or physical recreation.[10] Burton and Wibberley[48] have emphasised the weaknesses of forecasting land requirements for leisure in Britain.

OTHER RESEARCH ACTIVITIES

Research is proceeding into a number of related aspects and a brief résumé follows.

Economics of Recreation

Chapter 3 covered many of the problems involved and examined various approaches that have been adopted in the last decade or so. The problems stem from the difficulty of defining and assessing the value of land devoted to outdoor recreation. Knetsch[54, 55] has made a number of studies in measuring such values and has suggested that the basis of measurement is what people are willing to give up. Many researchers have asserted that travel-cost may be substituted for missing entrance prices in calculating recreation benefits.[45, 56, 57] While not entirely satisfactory, the method does offer an economically rational basis for the measurement of recreation benefits, exclusive of those benefits which may arise from any enhancement in neighbouring land values due to the provision of the recreation facility.[58]

An excellent general examination of the problem of the economics of outdoor recreation is given in the Outdoor Recreation Resources Review Commission Study Report 24[59] and in studies by Clawson and Knetsch.[9] They cover both theoretical and practical approaches to some basic problems of recreation development including those of investment, pricing, timing, cost-benefit evaluation and the relationship of public and private investment. They also indicate the scope available to the private investor to make available facilities which central and local government are not prepared to provide.

Pricing Policies

Clawson and Knetsch[60] have postulated that the use of outdoor recreation areas and facilities is always priced; the price ranging from zero to the maximum net revenue point. They assert that zero is still a price, and the decision to charge a zero price is as much a decision as that to charge any other price. Probably as important as the level of prices charged is the method of levying them and numerous systems are possible. Possibly the simplest is to make a single charge to each person admitted to an area or obtaining a service. Another variant is a windscreen sticker which operates for a limited period or even a whole season. Yet another approach is to permit free entry into the recreation area, but to charge for various activities ranging from car parking to swimming or boat launching.

Research is needed to test the effect of pricing methods, examining such aspects as relationship between charging and use of recreation area, effect on various socio-economic groups, forms of administration, levels of maintenance, revenue, and so on. Research could also be directed to the use of pricing as a means of securing more efficient use of recreation resources. It could, for instance, show how far public action—in permitting free use or in setting prices far lower than many users would be willing to pay—is encouraging types and levels of use seriously incommensurate with the capacity of the area to support on a sustained yield basis.

Young[61] advocates practical and constructive experiments designed to show whether and when and who will pay for various facilities. It is proposed that some of the new country parks should be designed with this principle in mind. Foster[62] advocates research into the application of differential pricing systems. They can take many forms:

(1) Entrance fees charged for certain facilities at weekends, but not on weekdays, to spread use peaks.

(2) Parking or camping charges imposed in heavily used areas but not in lightly used ones.

(3) Charges imposed for camp ground use beyond the first week to discourage longer stays.

Thus many forms of differential charging are possible, mostly with the objective of influencing visitors as to areas or times of use, activities undertaken, modes of conduct and the like. The charges are only likely to be effective if they are high enough to place a real burden on the payee and to provide a sufficient advantage to the user who avoids them. With the increasing pressures on recreation resources, comprehensive investigations into pricing methods and their likely effects should have high priority.

Landscape Evaluation

In recent years increased attention has been devoted to the conservation of attractive landscapes and to the need to assimilate satisfactorily any new uses into the landscape. A recent research exercise by a multi-disciplinary team operating in an area of outstanding natural beauty in east Hampshire[63] is worthy of consideration. The team attempted to identify the rural resources, types of land use and management, and to assess their relative importance and interrelationships as a basis for ensuring that demands on the countryside are capable of maximum fulfilment, in so far as they are compatible with other demands and are in accord with national and regional policies. The team was primarily concerned with:

(1) Natural resources such as physical land quality, wild life and landscape.

(2) Land uses such as agriculture, forestry, recreation and mining.

(3) Physical development such as power lines, building and roads.

(4) Management practices such as drainage and use of toxic chemicals.

In the evaluation of wild life, the habitat zones were given a value of a 5-point scale based on species diversity and national and local rarity. The highest value was accorded to semi-natural vegetation and woodland. In evaluating the landscape, four grades were established by analysing the extent to which a basic set of features which make attractive landscape were present on a 0.25 km² grid, and weighting these by the presence of features detracting from the scene. The basic criteria used were: topography (horizontal or vertical emphasis or strong contrasts, leading to high values); care of farmland; proportion of woodland; and simplicity of patterns and special features, such as parkland. The detractors were elements such as power lines, refuse tips, and derelict structures, which were either definite eyesores or locally out of place. In evaluating agriculture, five groups were established based mainly on national levels of production. Forestry evaluation was based on the degree of management, and although sporting and recreation value was recognised it was not capable of accurate assessment for inclusion in this classification. Interactions between the different land uses were then analysed to form a basis for determining rural land use policies.

MAIN RESEARCH NEEDS

Supply/Demand Relationships

The ultimate aim of much of the recreational research being undertaken is to enable an assessment to be made of future patterns of recreation and to examine ways in which available resources can best be deployed to satisfy future demand. The planning of a new facility takes place within the framework of government decisions as to the total resources available for investment in recreation which, in turn—in the view of the Sports Council—should involve consideration of the rôle of recreation in the lives of people. Those responsible for recreational planning are concerned first with the problem of allocating the available resources between various kinds of facility. Then matters of scale, location and kind of provision as well as organisational and administrative aspects all have to be examined.

It is important that some research should be directed towards determination of supply and demand at both national and local levels, so that the significance and interrelationships of a wide variety of factors can be studied and methodological problems investigated. An important feature of such a study would be an assessment of the significance of a wide variety of sociological, economic and environmental factors which appear to influence patterns of recreation. For a wide range of recreational activities the Sports Council sees an urgent need for studies covering the quantity, quality, design and costs of facilities; the extent and pattern of their use and the characteristics of the users; the financial and administrative arrangements relating to the facilities; and the desirability and feasibility of increasing the supply. It is hoped that the present study will go some way towards meeting this need. Palmer[58] emphasises the importance of measurement of demand, for without it realistic planning is impossible. Existing knowledge is only sufficient to make forecasts of short-term needs and long-term demand requires far more detailed study.

Studies are needed to examine ways of assessing the maximum capacity of facilities and of restricting use to a desirable level. This is particularly difficult of assessment in connection with countryside facilities and involves major problems of recreational resource management. There is a need for research into the factors which influence the individual's use of leisure time and of the possible classification of groups of activities within which recreation may be regarded as an acceptable substitute for any other.

Burton[64] has outlined an approach for equating supply and demand for recreational facilities:

(1) Establishing nature and extent of existing provision.

(2) Determination of present and future needs.

(3) Investigation of conflicts within recreation and between recreation and other pursuits.

(4) Assessment of future resource requirements.

(5) Assessment of effect of changes in supplies of facilities upon demands.

The British approach is not very different from that outlined in the American recreation report[1] which sees the need for a systematic and continuing programme of recreational research to provide a basis for wise decisions and sound management. This report suggests that the research can conveniently be sub-divided into three main categories:

(1) Data collection, inventory and fact finding.

(2) Applied management research, for example, determining carrying capacity of recreation areas.

(3) Fundamental research—for example, finding out where recreation fits into social values of our society; what substitutes, if any, exist for outdoor recreation; and future trends.

A Canadian conference[65] suggested the compiling of a recreation land use inventory and a recreation land use capability inventory as background material for recreational planning.

Present Deficiencies

Clawson and Knetsch[9] have described the inadequacies of much of the data prepared by public authorities administering outdoor recreation areas. Much of the data on numbers of sites, areas, personnel and expenditures are more descriptive than analytical and are collected primarily to meet the administrative needs of the respective bodies. Comparability between specific facilities is difficult or impossible, owing to the wide variety of definition. Problems resulting from the form of publication are even greater, as often the only information available is contained in an annual press release which rarely makes reference to previous years' figures and is seldom preserved.

Palmer[58] has highlighted the need for standard definitions and methods of working at local, regional and national levels to facilitate the making of comparisons. Greaves[2] has described how, in spite of a growing number of registers, directories and data banks, both research workers and recreation planners suffer from poor channels of communication. It becomes increasingly difficult either to avoid duplication of ideas or to learn or build on research from elsewhere, and this leads to large gaps and inconsistencies in the information available for planning. The research register issued by the Countryside Commission[4] has provided, for the first time, a reasonably comprehensive record of current recreation research in Britain, although since 1970 this has been confined to countryside recreation.

There are serious deficiencies in many of our present approaches to recreational planning problems, often stemming from a lack of knowledge and understanding of the underlying factors. For instance, Greaves[2] has drawn attention to the need for more research into identifying the qualitative and quantitative changes on sites, the nature and scale of conflicts between users, and the effects of different management methods designed to increase capacity. There is, as yet, no clear knowledge of what environmental factors are the best and most easily measured indicators of site damage or repair. Similarly, unless there are more attempts to measure the economic costs and benefits of recreation to both users and providers, not only will there be no development of methods for doing so, but regional and local investment decisions will continue to be made—as now—on a basis of inadequate information. Burton and Noad[17] have set apart three broad groups of problems to form the subject of field studies:

(1) Establishing methods for the classification and analysis of recreation data in such a way that projection and prediction of future trends becomes possible.

(2) Determining the kinds of profile data that are needed about the subjects of recreation studies, so as to secure greater comparability between studies.

(3) Examination of alternative methods of securing recreation data, especially the potential value of such procedures as the secondary analysis of previous recreation studies and the use of time-budget diaries.

In conclusion, it seems evident that considerable research into recreation is needed in order to deal effectively with the problems of recreation which are likely to become increasingly more complex. There is a need also for a better clearing house for recreation research arising from the fragmentation and diversification of the activities in this field, although it is recognised that the Countryside Commission is providing a valuable service.

REFERENCES

1. OUTDOOR RECREATION RESOURCES REVIEW COMMISSION. *Outdoor Recreation for America,* Washington D.C., (1962)
2. GREAVES, J. (1968). *National Parks and Access to the Countryside and Coast: Trends in Research,* Countryside Commission
3. BRITISH TRAVEL ASSOCIATION/KEELE UNIVERSITY. *Pilot National Recreation Survey Report No. 1,* B.T.A., (1967)
4. COUNTRYSIDE COMMISSION. *Research Register No. 2,* (1969)
5. OUTDOOR RECREATION RESOURCES REVIEW COMMISSION. *Public Outdoor Recreation Areas—acreage, use, potential. Study Report 1,* Washington D.C., (1962)

6. OUTDOOR RECREATION RESOURCES REVIEW COMMISSION. *List of Public Outdoor Recreation Areas—1960. Study Report 2,* Washington D.C., (1962)

7. OUTDOOR RECREATION RESOURCES REVIEW COMMISSION. *Potential New Sites for Outdoor Recreation in the North-east. Study Report 8,* Washington D.C., (1962)

8. SPORTS COUNCIL. (1969). *The Sports Council: a review 1966–69,* Central Council of Physical Recreation

9. CLAWSON, M. and KNETSCH, J. L. (1966). *Economics of Outdoor Recreation,* John Hopkins Press, Baltimore

10. CHESHIRE COUNTY COUNCIL. *Recreation in Cheshire: Technical Studies No. 1: Provision for Urban Recreation,* Cheshire County Council, (1968)

11. SILLITOE, K. K. (1969). *Government Social Survey: Planning for Leisure,* H.M.S.O.

12. COUNTRYSIDE COMMISSION. *Coastal Recreation and Holidays: Special study report Vol. 1,* H.M.S.O., (1969)

13. CESARIO, F. J. Operations research in outdoor recreation. *Journal of Leisure Research,* **1.1,** (1969), 38

14. OUTDOOR RECREATION RESOURCES REVIEW COMMISSION. *Participation in Outdoor Recreation: Factors Affecting Demand among American Adults. Study Report 20,* Washington D.C., (1962)

15. SESSOMS, H. D. New bases for recreation planning. *Journal of the American Institute of Planners,* **30.1,** (1964), 26–33

16. NATURE CONSERVANCY. *The Biotic Effects of Public Pressures on the Environment: Monks Wood Experimental Station Symposium No. 3,* Natural Environment Research Council, (1967)

17. BURTON, T. L. and NOAD, P. A. *Recreation Research Methods: A Review of Recent Studies. Occasional Paper No. 3,* University of Birmingham, Centre for Urban and Regional Studies, (1968)

18. HAMMOND, E. C. *A Survey of Visitors to Wye and Crundale National Nature Reserve.* Nature Conservancy. Private communication, (1965)

19. NORFOLK COUNTY COUNCIL. *Report on the Norfolk Holiday Industry.* Norfolk County Planning Department, (1964)

20. BRITISH BROADCASTING CORPORATION. *The People's Activities,* (1965)

21. ROBINSON, J. P. and CONVERSE, P. E. (1966). *Sixty-six Basic Tables of Time-budget Data for the United States.* University of Michigan Survey Research Center

22. CHAPIN, F. S. and HIGHTOWER, H. C. (1966). *Household Activity Systems—a pilot investigation,* University of North Carolina Urban Studies Research Monograph

23. HOLE, V. *Children's Play on Housing Estates. National Building Studies Research Paper 39,* H.M.S.O., (1966)

24. WINTERBOTTOM, D. M. How much urban space do we need? *Journal of Royal Town Planning Institute,* **53.4,** (1967), 144–147

25. HAMPSHIRE COUNTY COUNCIL. (1966). *The Use of County Open Spaces,* Hampshire County Planning Department

26. ROSS, J. B. (1966). *Tourism in Northumberland,* Northumberland County Council

27. FURMIDGE, J. Planning for recreation in the countryside. *Journal of Royal Town Planning Institute,* **55.2,** (1969), 62–67

28. SEITZ, R. M. How mail surveys may be made to pay. *Printer's Ink,* **209,** (1944)

29. CLAUSEN, J. A. and FORD, R. N. Controlling bias in mail questionnaires. *Journal of the American Statistical Association,* **42.240,** (1947), 497–511

30. GRAY, P. G. and CORLETT, T. Sampling for the social survey. *Journal of the Royal Statistical Society A.2,* (1950), 150–199

31. MOSER, C. A. (1958). *Survey Methods in Social Investigation,* Heinemann

32. CULLEN, P. Whither industrial recreation? *Sport and Recreation,* (October 1966 and January 1967)

33. BURTON, T. L. (1967). *Windsor Great Park: A Recreation Study,* Wye College, University of London, Department of Economics

34. HEYTZE, J. C. (1969). *Recreation in the Forestry of Nunspeet,* State Forest Service of the Netherlands, Utrecht

35. DUFFELL, J. R. and GOODALL, R. G. Worcestershire and Staffordshire recreational survey 1966. *Journal of Royal Town Planning Institute,* **55.1,** (1969)

36. STRAW, F. I. (1967). *Lindsey Countryside Recreation Survey: A Survey of the Public Use of the Lincolnshire Wolds and Adjacent Areas.* Lindsey County Council and University of Nottingham

37. GREATER LONDON COUNCIL. Research Paper No. 2. *Surveys of the Use of Open Spaces 1,* Greater London Council Planning Department, (1968)

38. RODGERS, H. B. Leisure and recreation. *Urban Studies,* **6.3,** (1969), 368–384

39. NORTH REGIONAL PLANNING COMMITTEE. *Outdoor Leisure Activities in the Northern Region,* (1969)

40. NORTH WEST SPORTS COUNCIL. *The Case for a Leisure Activities Survey* (1967)

41. GRIFFITHS, I. (1968). *Study of Leisure Activities of Post-school Adolescents,* University of Manchester, Department of Physical Education

42. KENT COUNTY COUNCIL. *Social Survey,* (1962)

43. DUFFELL, J. R. and GOODALL, G. R. Leisure in town and country—results of a home interview survey at Northfield, Birmingham. *Surveyor and Municipal Engineer,* (13 January 1968), 32–37

44. COUNTRYSIDE COMMISSION. *Seminar on Demand for Outdoor Recreation in the Countryside:* Introductory paper, (15 January 1970)

45. CLAWSON, M. *Methods of Measuring the Demand for the Value of Outdoor Recreation.* Reprint No. 10, Resources for the Future, (1959)

46. KNETSCH, J. L. Outdoor recreation demands and benefits. *Land Economics,* **39.4,** (1963), 387–396

47. KAVANAGH, N. J. The economics of the recreational uses of rivers and reservoirs. *Water and Water Engineering,* (October 1968), 401–408

48. BURTON, T. L. and WIBBERLEY, G. P. (1969). *Forecasting Land Requirements for Leisure. Proceedings of Conference on Regional Planning and Forecasting, University of Sussex,* Regional Studies Association

49. OUTDOOR RECREATION RESOURCES REVIEW COMMISSION. *Prospective Demand for Outdoor Recreation. Study Report 26,* Washington D.C., (1962)

50. PROCTOR, C. *Dependence of Recreation Participation on Background Characteristics of Sample Persons in the September 1960 National Recreation Survey.* Appendix A to Outdoor Recreation Resources Review Commission, Study Report 19, Washington D.C., (1962)

51. OUTDOOR RECREATION RESOURCES REVIEW COMMISSION. *National Recreation Survey,* Study Report 19, Washington D.C., (1962)

52. REID, L. M. Utilizing user preferences in predicting outdoor recreation demand. *Recreation Research.* American Association for Health, Physical Recreation and Education (1966), 86–92

53. TAYLOR, G. D. (1969). *History and Techniques of Demand Prediction. Proceedings of Congress for Recreation and Parks, Chicago,* Research and Planning Branch, Department of Tourism, Winnipeg, Manitoba, Canada

54. KNETSCH, J. L. Economics of including recreation as a purpose of water resources projects. *Journal of Farm Economics,* (December 1964)

55. KNETSCH, J. L., Land values and parks in urban fringe areas. *Journal of Farm Economics,* **44,** (1963), 1718–1726

56. WOOD, D. F. The distances travelled technique for measuring value of recreation areas—an application. *Land Economics,* **37.4,** (1961)

57. BURTON, T. L. and WIBBERLEY, G. P. (1965). *Outdoor Recreation in the British Countryside,* Department of Agricultural Economics, University of London.

58. PALMER, J. E. Recreational planning—a bibliographical review. *Planning Outlook.* **2,** (1967)

59. OUTDOOR RECREATION RESOURCES REVIEW COMMISSION. *Economic Studies of Outdoor Recreation. Study Report 24,* Washington D.C., (1962)

60. CLAWSON, M. and KNETSCH, J. L. Outdoor recreation research: Some concepts and suggested areas of study. *Natural Resources Journal,* **3.2,** (1963), 268–271

61. YOUNG, M. The way ahead: Planning for the changing countryside. *Report of Conference of Rural Research Workers,* Royal Town Planning Institute, (1967)

62. FOSTER, J. Provision for countryside and coast: National Parks, *Paper to Course on Recreation and Leisure,* York Institute of Advanced Architectural Studies, (23 to 27 October 1967)

63. HAMPSHIRE COUNTY COUNCIL. *East Hampshire—area of outstanding natural beauty: a study in countryside conservation,* (1968)

64. BURTON, T. L. The classification of recreation demands and supplies. *Planning for Recreation in the West Midlands. Research Memo. 1,* University of Birmingham, Centre for Urban and Regional Studies, (1967)

65. PIGOTT, A. V. Devising and implementing programs for more effective utilization of renewable resources. Recreation workshop B. *Resources for Tomorrow Conference, Montreal, Canada,* (1961)

66. COUNTRYSIDE COMMISSION. *Outdoor Recreation Information: Suggested Standard Classifications for use in Questionnaire Surveys,* (1970)

67. DEPARTMENT OF THE ENVIRONMENT/NORTH WEST SPORTS COUNCIL. *Leisure in the North West* (1972)

5 BRITISH OUTDOOR RECREATION POLICIES AND EXPERIENCE IN THE TWENTIETH CENTURY

THIS CHAPTER SEEKS to portray the main recreational developments that have taken place in Great Britain during the present century and to explore the motivating factors. Events in the latter part of the nineteenth century are examined briefly and some comparisons are made with developments in the United States.

Living and Working Conditions

It is important to consider recreation provision against the background of the great social changes which took place in the nineteenth century. The rapid development of industry drew workers from the countryside to the towns, and this, together with a rising population, caused serious problems stemming from overcrowding and the unsatisfactory and often wretched condition of the dwellings. Of the wretchedness there can be no doubt. The early reports of the Health of Towns Commission[1] bore testimony to the insanitary condition of the towns. Dwellings were built at excessively high densities and often on the most unsuitable sites, adjoining factories or on low marshy ground. Gibbon and Ball[2] have described the deplorable state of much of the housing development in London in the middle of the century, and the position with regard to water supply and sanitation was no better.[3] Ferguson[4] has drawn attention to the high rate of deaths among children at the time, particularly those in one-roomed houses.

Chambers[91] has described how Nottingham in 1830 consisted of a 'chequerboard of mean streets, alleyways and courts, and a byword for filth and misery beyond relief', leading in 1832 to an outbreak of Asiatic cholera. Nottingham became notorious for its 8000 back-to-back houses. During the period 1840–43 the mean age at death in Nottingham was about 25 years and over thirty-three per cent of city children died before they reached 4 years of age. Bryant[101] has summed up the situation very aptly: 'Nearly all the social troubles and divisions from which we suffer today stem from that fatal social division, that appalling neglect of and blindness to human well-being which the land and its use should serve'.

Working conditions were no more satisfactory than the deplorable living conditions. Women and children worked excessively long hours in factories and coal mines, sometimes in appalling conditions. The Royal Commission on Mines (1840–50) found that women pulled coal trucks on their hands and feet and children of 5 years worked alone in the darkness. The use of little boys in sweeping soot choked chimneys was not checked until 1875.[5]

By the end of the century the worst of the deficiencies in housing and sanitation had been removed. A housing survey in London at the time[6] stated:

the once familiar narrow courts, approached under archways from main streets, sorely lacking in light and air with their damp, dilapidated and insanitary rooms, gradually disappeared from view; back-to-back houses diminished greatly in London.

In addition, substantial progress had been made with town water supplies, sewerage and drainage, paving of streets and scavenging, and in the erection of baths and washhouses. There remained, however, many serious obstacles to healthy living in the towns. Low real wages which restricted nutrition and failed to provide any margin for sickness or the recurrent bouts of unemployment; a low level of general education which, together with poor working conditions, encouraged alcoholism and deterred from thrift; this was the picture for the mass of urban workers.[7] The Boer War had revealed startling physical deficiencies in prospective recruits (forty per cent were unfit for service) and this led to the setting up of an Interdepartmental Committee on Physical Deterioration.

Open Space Provision

As towns grew in the nineteenth century so the open countryside receded as both open fields and common lands were built over. Thus the inhabitants were often deprived of their rightful access to commons for healthy exercise and recreation. Compulsory education was first introduced in 1870 and prior to this the majority of children worked long hours in factories and mills and when not so employed ran wild or played in the streets in dirty and often insanitary conditions. Most of the early elementary schools had small playgrounds which were used for 'drill' and free play in break periods. Teachers were instrumental in organising football matches and sports meetings between one school and another, and this led to the formation of School Sports and Games Associations. Funds were obtained by individual subscriptions from local supporters and school boys also contributed their farthings and pennies.[7]

The Public Health Act, 1875, was the first major statutory provision enabling local authorities to provide and maintain 'public walks and pleasure grounds' and to make byelaws regulating their use. The Act was silent as to their use for the playing of games and it was found necessary to give such a use in later statutes which empowered local authorities to set aside parts of such lands for the playing of games. On the other hand, as described by Roddis,[8] there had been for centuries the use of village greens and commons for such purposes and many ancient municipal corporations had put corporate property to such use for centuries. Provision could also be made in Parish Enclosure Acts and Awards for the allotting of land to be set aside as places for exercise and recreation.

The Public Health Acts Amendment Act, 1890, extended the powers of a local authority in regard to the closing of public walks and pleasure grounds for limited periods and to charges to be made for admission; the provision and regulation of boating pools and boats on lakes; and the making of contributions towards the purchase and laying out of public walks and pleasure grounds provided by others.

Three other acts were passed in the nineteenth century with the object of making open space available to the public for certain specific purposes, but the powers were little used in the last century.

(1) The Recreation Grounds Act, 1859, empowered trustees to hold lands as open public grounds for playgrounds for children and youth and for resort and recreation for adults. It is interesting to note that in later times, most of the land owned by the National Playing Fields Association is vested in that body under the provisions of the 1859 Act.

(2) The Town Gardens Protection Act, 1863, enabled local authorities to protect and, if desired, take charge of enclosed gardens or ornamental grounds set aside for public enjoyment and use.

(3) The Public Improvements Act, 1860, was an adoptive Act enabling ratepayers to purchase or lease lands and accept gifts and grants of lands for the purpose of forming public walks for exercise or playgrounds, and to levy rates for their maintenance. The greatest obstacle to the successful working of this Act lay in the fact that prior to the rate being levied, a sum of not less than one-half of the estimated cost of the improvement had to be raised, given or collected by private subscription or donation.

Law[9] saw two principal motivating forces at work in park provision in the last century—philanthropic/moral issues and the design element. The first approach is exemplified in a report of the Select Committee on Public Walks in 1833 which stated that it was important for the working classes to enjoy fresh air on their day of rest, that if they had parks to walk in with their families they would tend to dress soberly and neatly and that this incentive to be clean and properly clothed would be an inducement to greater productivity in industry. It was suggested in 1834 that the provision of parks would help to alleviate drunkenness. The second major influence is seen as the design element, in which parks constitute an enhancement to the urban 'environment' and a structural component of towns and cities. In the present century these latter two functions have often been interlinked as in the Garden Cities and New Towns and in the concept of green wedges or walkways joining town and country.

In London, as in many British towns and cities, the provision of public open space occurred in a very piecemeal way. The Crown parks were gradually turned over to use by the public and a number of large parks, including Victoria and Battersea parks, were provided between 1840 and 1860. The majority of parks in London were not originally designed for use by the public. No positive steps were taken to rationalise the provision of open space and this resulted in a gross imbalance in the spatial distribution of the facilities.[10] It is only in the last 40–50 years that local authorities have attempted to meet recreation and environmental needs by the conscious planning of open spaces, probably prompted by the growing enthusiasm for the benefits of physical recreation and the increasing concern over the effects of city living on health.

Developments in America

A study of the history of municipal recreation in the United States during the last century shows a striking resemblance to progress at local level in Britain. Land was purchased for Central Park in New York City in 1853 and the first purchase of land for playground use was at Brookline, Massachusetts in 1872. By 1892, 100 American cities had acquired parks but few were used for active recreation.[11] In 1895, the first state legislation was passed for the establishment of a county park system in Essex County, New Jersey.[12] At national level however, progress was made in the United States in the provision of national parks. The first to be established was the Yellowstone National Park in 1872, followed by Sequoia, General Grant (now part of Kings Canyon) and Yosemite National Parks in 1890.[13]

PLAYING FIELDS AND CHILDREN'S PLAYGROUNDS

Historical Background

We have seen that in the first half of the nineteenth century the rapidly growing towns sprawled over the surrounding countryside eliminating many of the areas previously available for play and recreation. Few gave any thought to the need for playing fields for recreation in leisure hours, and for the majority of people there was very little leisure time except on Sundays, when the playing of games was not permissible. During the second half of the nineteenth century there was an upsurge of interest in organised sport. Clubs for all kinds of games came into existence and governing bodies were formed for association football (1863), rugby football (1871) and athletics (1880), but opportunities for play were extremely limited.[14] Little use was made by local authorities of the 1859 and subsequent acts and the bulk of the population, concentrated in the overcrowded towns, had completely inadequate facilities for sport and exercise.

The National Playing Fields Association

It was necessary that both Government and people alike should realise the importance to the country as a whole of outdoor recreation for the ordinary citizen, in order that effective pressure should be brought to bear upon local authorities to provide the necessary facilities. Little real progress was made until the formation of the National Playing Fields Association in 1925, following a mass meeting in the Royal Albert Hall on 8th July. The Duke and Duchess of York were present and the Duke agreed to act as President. A resolution was carried:

That this meeting, recognising the vital importance of playing fields to the physical, moral and mental welfare of the youth of the country, deplores the widespread and increasing shortage of recreation grounds, and urges all Local Authorities, Sports Governing Bodies, Societies and members of the public interested in the matter to co-operate with the National Playing Fields Association, in order that, by their united efforts, the deficiency may be met.[15]

Progress of the Association after formation was very encouraging and it received many gifts of money and land, following the example of King George V who presented two of the royal paddocks at Hampton Court as children's playgrounds, and personally headed the appeal to the Lords Lieutenant to form branches of the Association in their counties. Local authorities were brought into the scheme by invitations to the chairmen of parks committees to sit on the council of the Association. Within 3 years of inauguration the Association had received £330 000 and 136 hectares of land. By 1933, with the encouragement, advice or financial assistance of the Association, 1200 new playing fields, covering 4040 hectares, had been made available for public use, quite apart from many other schemes carried out by local authorities with their own resources. In 1932 the Association received a Royal Charter. As described in chapter 2, the Association formulated a minimum standard of 6 acres (2.4 hectares) of playing space per 1000 population, although it is rarely achieved. After the death of King George V it was decided that—apart from a statue in London—the national memorial should consist of playing fields throughout the country to be known as King George's Fields. A capital sum of £496 000 became available from the National Memorial Fund for that purpose. The King George's Field Foundation was dissolved in 1965 after making grants from the National Memorial Fund for almost 500 playing fields.

The current aims and objects of the Association are:

(1) To secure adequate playing fields available to the public, and facilities for open air and indoor recreation for the present and future needs of all sections of the community.

(2) To assist in the development of existing recreational facilities where needed.

(3) To cooperate with local authorities in making the fullest use of their powers when preparing town planning schemes to ensure that ample playing space is secured.

(4) To secure properly equipped playgrounds for the use of children and to press for facilities to be made available where required.

(5) To encourage the training and appointment of playleaders for children's playgrounds.

(6) To cooperate in saving threatened recreational facilities.

(7) To act as a centre of advice and assistance for local authorities, sports clubs and other interested organisations on all matters connected with the acquisition, layout and use of grounds and buildings set apart for the purpose of recreation.

(8) To provide and maintain a technical service of high standard to form the complete counterpart in the counties of the National Sports Council Technical Service.

(9) To raise money so that financial assistance, by way of grants and loans, may be given where needed for recreational facilities.[16]

The National Association, whose President is now the Duke of Edinburgh, works through county associations, on whom it relies for information and guidance. In order to provide service at local level, each county has its own autonomous association or representative. Most county associations depend almost entirely on the voluntary service of their members. Applications for loans or grants will always be dealt with in the first instance by the county association. The National Association has published a wide range of literature and issues a very useful quarterly journal. By 1969, facilities provided with assistance from the National Playing Fields Association included: 2160 football pitches, 1817 cricket grounds, 2168 tennis courts, 381 netball courts, 408 bowling greens, 283 hockey pitches, seventy-one running tracks, twenty-one squash courts, 849 changing accommodation schemes, 3908 children's playgrounds, 109 play leadership schemes and forty-six adventure playgrounds. Since the last war there has been considerable emphasis on the provision of children's playgrounds, particularly on new housing estates.

Central Council of Physical Recreation

The provision and equipment of playing fields is not the complete solution. If maximum pleasure and value are to be obtained from games, people must be taught effectively how to play them. The Central Council of Physical Recreation was formed in 1935 to meet this need. It is supported by government grants and voluntary subscription, and recognised as a charity, and has as members the governing bodies of no less than 195 national organisations concerned with physical recreation. Its primary task is to train coaches and instructors in all forms of recreation from folk dancing to tennis and skiing, and this it does at three National Recreation centres, in Berkshire, Shropshire and North Wales. The Council is interested in breaking new ground by publicising and providing instructors for outdoor activities that were once considered beyond the reach of the ordinary man and woman, such as horsemanship, yachting and climbing. The Government was in 1972 considering the place of the Central Council of Physical Recreation in relation to the reorganised Sports Council.

Other Legislation

The Open Spaces Act, 1906, enables local authorities to use former burial grounds as public open space. The National Playing Fields Association[17] describes how small grounds of up to about 0.5 hectare can make useful children's playgrounds or courts for tennis or basketball and many churchyards of this size are in the heart of large towns where the need for play space is greatest. The legal preliminaries and the actual task of conversion are often difficult and expensive, but the effort and cost may frequently be worthwhile in built-up areas.

Under later Public Health Acts (1907, 1925 and 1961), a local authority may prescribe a part of a park or ground for the purpose of cricket, football, or any other game or recreation, and exclude the public from the area set apart while it is in use for that purpose, together with the whole or any part of a pavilion, convenience, refreshment room or other building, subject to such charges and conditions as the local authority thinks fit. The authority may not, however, permit the exclusive use to clubs or other bodies of more than one third of the area of any park or pleasure ground or more than one quarter of the total area of all parks and pleasure grounds under its control.

The Physical Training and Recreation Act, 1937, marked the beginning of a new era in the provision of playing fields, gymnasia, swimming baths, holiday camps and camping sites—all far removed from the public walks and pleasure grounds of Victorian times. It has been subsequently amended by the Education Act, 1944, and the Local Government Acts of 1948 and 1958. The Department of Education and Science is empowered to make grants towards the expenses of voluntary organisations (non-profit making) in providing facilities for physical training and education and for the training and supply of teachers and leaders. Local authorities may provide gymnasia, playing fields, holiday camps or camping sites or contribute towards expenses of other local authorities or voluntary organisations in providing them if they will benefit inhabitants in the area of the contributing authority.

The Physical Training and Recreation Act, 1937, is still the main vehicle for direct central government assistance to sport and recreation, and was founded on the twin objectives of physical training and recreation. However, as Molyneux[18] has shown, a close study of the debates on the various readings of that Bill indicates quite clearly that the emphasis was much more on physical training than on recreation.[19] However, the stimulus given by the report of the Wolfenden Committee[20] in 1960 led to debate, discussion and—in 1963—to direct central government participation in sport and recreation: an involvement recognising the importance of recreation in its own right.

EDUCATIONAL PROVISION OF PLAYING FACILITIES

Early Developments

At the beginning of the present century physical exercise in elementary schools was still continuing as formal drill, and schools were actually encouraged to use trained army instructors for this purpose. In 1904, an Inter-departmental Committee on Physical Deterioration strongly advised: methodical physical training to improve health and physique; and medical inspection of all school children.

In 1907 a Medical Department was established at the Board of Education which issued its first report in 1908, and this emphasised the need for physical exercise in gymnasia or the open air as a vital contribution to good health, growth and a strong physique. It also stressed the important part that games, dancing, athletic sports and swimming should play in the educational work of the schools and the effort needed to provide the facilities.

The National Playing Fields Association[5] has traced effectively subsequent developments in schools and the immense difficulties that were experienced against a general background of dirt, disease, malnutrition, bad housing, poor sanitation and poverty:

In 1909 a syllabus was introduced including free standing exercises (no apparatus was yet feasible) some running, jumping, dance steps and playground games—not much activity it is true, but an advance for teachers of general subjects who had never tackled anything of the kind before. This syllabus was revised in 1919 giving more emphasis to activity and games and still further expanded in 1933 to include coaching of games and school athletics and teaching of dancing and swimming. Little though the general public, or even some of the experts realised at the time, the pattern of 'physical recreation' for all was starting at school level, and children who had previously spun their tops and played marbles or hopscotch in the streets, were now learning team games and other skills in the playgrounds, parks and recreation grounds in town and country. As was foreseen, there was yet a long way to go. Playgrounds were too small for the size of the classes who needed to use them; teachers unaccustomed to handling children 'in action' feared accident or undiscipline and took the safer line of formal drill; there were few playing fields to which the schools could have access; there was seldom any indoor accommodation in wet weather other than the classroom; children's shoes and clothing were far from suitable for exercise.

The first course for the training of men teachers in physical education was established at the SW Polytechnic, Chelsea, in 1908. Later courses were established at Sheffield Training College (1919), Carnegie College of Physical Education, Leeds (1933), Loughborough College (1935) and Goldsmith College, London (1937). In the country as a whole there was growing enthusiasm for recreational activities of all kinds organised by voluntary agencies—the Boy Scout Movement was founded in 1908 and the Girl Guides followed in 1910. The Scout Movement is also concerned with promoting improved physique, character building and citizenship training, and owed its beginnings to Baden-Powell's love of camping, tracking and the outdoors in general. A broader conception of physical education and recreation emerged in the Education Act, 1918, which extended the powers of local authorities to include the provision of holiday and school camps, playing fields, swimming baths and other facilities for social and physical training in schools and for young persons up to the age of 18 or over, attending educational institutions. School buildings came under careful review and considerably improved standards were prescribed for facilities of all kinds for physical education and recreation, including the size and equipment of gymnasia, playgrounds and playing fields, bearing in mind the age of the children and the number requiring to use them. It was emphasised that the area of playing fields should be adequate for every child in the school, if medically fit, to play regularly, and hockey pitches for girls' games as well as boys' football pitches should be provided in the mixed schools.

After the passing of the 1918 Act, physical education facilities began to improve, particularly in the newer schools with their more generous provision for a wider programme of activities. In towns and cities where schools had only very small playgrounds, many authorities began to acquire outlying fields to which the children were taken by tram or coach.

The Education Act, 1944, and Subsequent Regulations

The 1944 Act reaffirmed the wide powers already conferred upon local education authorities by earlier Acts—to provide facilities, such as camps, playing fields, play centres, gymnasia and swimming baths, for recreation and social and physical training. It placed on every local education authority the duty of securing adequate facilities in all primary and secondary schools and in further education establishments. From this stemmed more varied programmes of vigorous activities in the majority of junior schools, including as they do the use of portable and fixed apparatus of many kinds, such as climbing frames, nets, ropes, bats, balls and hoops. There have also been marked changes in recent years in the activities pursued by the older school children. Free choice is being increasingly offered in the less familiar individual and group activities such as judo, fencing, cycling, hiking, sailing, canoeing, pony-riding and rock climbing, with a view to interesting pupils in some activity that they can continue after leaving school.

Building Bulletin 26[22] suggests that there are three main aspects of physical education in secondary schools and these need to be welded together into a balanced programme:

(1) Experience and understanding of movement which is achieved through dancing, drama and gymnastics.

(2) Training and practice in specific skills through team games, games for small groups or athletics.

(3) Participation in activities such as cycling, camping, climbing and sailing which for the most part will take place outside the school site.

Current school playing field requirements are prescribed by The Standards for School Premises Regulations 1959 (S.I.890) which are often referred to as The Building Regulations, although this latter term could give rise to confusion with The Building Regulations 1965 formulated under the provisions of the Public Health Act, 1961, and controlling all building work in the provinces. The playing field space standard varies with the type and number of pupils and is well tabulated in Building Bulletin 28[21] and the upper and lower limits of the ranges are given in table 2.6. Unfortunately, many local education authorities have been unable to meet the statutory requirements relating to playing field space, particularly with older schools situated in built-up areas. Sillitoe[23] in his survey for the Department of Education and Science found that fifty-three per cent of boys' schools and forty-three per cent of girls' schools in Inner London did not have playing fields of their own, although in the majority of cases they shared the use of some other facility, compared with one per cent and six per cent respectively in the New Towns. Deficiencies in Nottingham's school playing field provision (examined in chapter 7) are probably typical of most large cities. Nicholson[24] writing in *The Guardian* in 1969 described how the Inner London Education Authority had provided a ring of ten sports centres, nine of which were located outside its administrative area and the largest being at Epsom with an area of 53 hectares, to try and meet the physical education needs of its pupils. The annual cost incurred by the Authority in transporting children to these facilities was approaching £0.5 million.

Latest Trends

The National Playing Fields Association has for many years advocated the fuller use of school playing fields by children and youth organisations outside school hours, with a view to reducing the widespread shortage of recreational facilities. Local education authorities have, over the years, advanced a number of objections to more extensive use of playing facilities outside school hours:

(1) Facilities already used by youth clubs and old pupils' associations.

(2) Turf cannot stand up to any more wear.

(3) Without adequate supervision damage could occur and is it possible to provide the supervision?

The National Playing Fields Association[25] emphasises that the use must be discriminate and adequately supervised and they consider that much could be done to improve the wearing qualities of turf and to secure closer cooperation between public authorities. The Association has also suggested the use of playleaders for supervision and increased provision of all-weather hard porous playing surfaces, preferably floodlit. In a survey undertaken by the Association in 1964,[26] it was found that thirty-nine per cent of county councils and thirty-two per cent of county borough councils did not encourage or permit any form of dual use. More recently, regional sports councils have undertaken surveys in their regions to determine the extent of dual use of facilities.

In 1964 a joint ministry circular[27] advised local authorities in assessing local needs and resources to consider how far facilities for sport and physical education already provided, or in course of provision, at schools and other educational establishments can be shared with other users, or can be economically expanded to meet the needs. In planning new or re-planning existing sports provision for educational establishments, the needs of the community generally for both outdoor and indoor sports facilities should be borne in mind. The concept of joint provision and use of sports centres permits the supply of superior facilities available to many more people with economies in construction, maintenance and operation. Some examples of combined sports centres are described in chapter 7.

INDUSTRIAL AND PRIVATE PROVISION OF PLAYING FACILITIES

As indicated in chapter 1 not all recreational facilities are provided by public authorities, and numerous facilities are supplied by industrial organisations for the benefit of their employees, private sports clubs and commercial organisations on a profit making basis. Cullen[28] has shown that on a national scale there is a decline in interest in industrial sports clubs on the part of both management and employees, with smaller firms in particular using or selling the playing fields for building development as the level of interest in the sports activities has dwindled. A relatively small proportion of private sports clubs own their own grounds and some of these have been obliged to disband their clubs and sell their land as membership has continued to decline. The majority of the more recently founded sports clubs rely upon hiring the necessary playing facilities from local authorities.

It seems likely that there will be increased provision of recreational facilities by commercial organisations in the future. This is particularly the case with water based recreation where the demand is rising sharply but for which the supply of resources is restricted, and participants are often willing to spend considerable sums on the pursuit. The construction of marinas and acquisition of sailing, water skiing, angling and similar rights could well prove sufficiently attractive to the commercial operator. It has been suggested that farmers and landowners in attractive areas of the countryside could become recreational managers by providing and operating various facilities such as restaurants, hostels, camping sites and car parks. In America the provision of recreational facilities is regarded as 'big business', and as incomes rise and people spend more time in leisure pursuits in this country, so the opportunities for the profitable provision of resources by commercial operators may also increase.

GREEN BELTS

A green belt is an area of land, near to and sometimes surrounding a town, which is kept in agricultural use by permanent restriction on building. The form it takes depends upon the purposes it is intended to serve. It may take the form of a wide wedge or belt between two nearby towns to prevent them coalescing or, more frequently, it provides a continuous belt around a town to limit its growth.[29] Richardson[30] sees a green belt as a clearly defined area of rural land surrounding a large town or group of towns, marking their limit of growth and providing not only an area where agriculture can continue in stability, but also where the town dweller can enjoy the pleasures of the countryside.

There is little doubt that green belts often possess high recreational value, by providing the town dweller with the opportunity to escape from the noise, congestion and strain of town life and to obtain recreation in the countryside. Green belts may provide facilities for organised games or sports or opportunities for scientific or artistic study. More frequently they provide the means for rambling or riding with no other object than to enjoy the scenery, fresh air and sunshine, although the inclusion of land in a green belt does not give the public any rights of access which they would not otherwise enjoy.

The most extensive example in this country is the green belt encircling Greater London, which occupies about 14 300 hectares and was established under the Green Belt (London and Home Counties) Act, 1938. Green belts have also been established around the majority of the larger English cities. For instance Nottingham green belt proposals aim at separating Nottingham from Derby, Mansfield and a number of scattered colliery villages. The latest Nottinghamshire and Derbyshire sub-regional study proposals[31] provide for an arrangement of recreational facilities in strips or belts of country, termed 'greenways', which link regional parks to one another and to the towns. It is further suggested that recreational facilities provided within the greenways might include picnic places, country parks, scenic drives, museums, cafés, riding schools, beauty spots, playing fields, boating and fishing, and possibly camping sites.

A World Health Organisation expert committee[32] envisaged green belts as performing two main functions—protective and recreational. The protective belts would separate residential areas and industry; protect against noise and fumes from vehicles; control expansion and divide urban areas from one another; and act as a microclimate regulator against the dangers of pollution. At the recreational level, green belts should be provided for a wide variety of recreational needs from children's playgrounds to parks and open spaces around schools, hospitals and health centres. The Committee held the view that green belts, green streets and open spaces of all kinds lead logically from the home, the neighbourhood and the city to the country and they advocated studies evaluating more exactly the effects of different kinds and configurations of open space and their psychological and economic benefits.

An interesting extension of the green belt concept is being carried out in the German Ruhr where, under a creative policy of conservation and reclamation, green areas of leisure parks, farmland and forest are expanding throughout this intensively developed industrial area. The area contains an average of 1235 persons per km² and contains twelve cities with a population of 100 000 or more. The coal pit closures have been largely counteracted by the establishment of new industries. The Ruhr Planning Authority—the Siedlungsverband Ruhrkohlenbezirk—has as one of its primary functions the environmental preservation and improvement of the area.

The Authority designates 'green areas' and protects them against urban encroachments in a complex region of conflicting local authority ambitions. As a result of this policy, the cities in the Ruhr are separated from one another by 'green wedges', which prevent the fusion of conurbations and bring the countryside right into built-up areas. In this heavily industrialised area it is quite remarkable that no less than 53.6 per cent is still farmland, 15.9 per cent woodlands, 2.3 per cent water and two per cent open space (mainly parks and playing fields), with only 23.7 per cent built-up land. Each year the Authority spends about DM 1.5 million on conservation of woodlands and other landscape, the same amount on securing and renewing regional open space and more than DM 5 million on provision of recreational sites. Reclamation of derelict land is proceeding at an impressive rate and mine owners are compelled to backfill their wastes underground.[33]

NATIONAL PARKS

Prior to the last war there was relatively little use made of the countryside for casual, and even less for active, recreation. The recreational use was largely confined to a minority of dedicated ramblers and our network of footpaths and minor roads was well able to satisfy their needs. *De facto* access rights existed over much moorland, foreshore and common, and there were no serious pressures on beauty spots, farmland or water resources. The few recreational facilities in existence were the product of private or club investment. After the war fears of uncontrolled urban sprawl, memories of agricultural depressions and probable increased recreational needs in the future, prompted the move towards more positive protection of the countryside and, in particular, those areas of outstanding scenic quality.[34]

101

National Parks and Access to the Countryside Act, 1949

Dower[35] prepared a report for the Minister of Town and Country Planning on national parks in 1945 in which a national park was defined as:

an extensive area of beautiful and relatively wild country, in which, for the nation's benefit and by appropriate national decision and action, (a) the characteristic landscape beauty is strictly preserved, (b) access and facilities for public open-air enjoyment are amply provided, (c) wild life and buildings and places of architectural and historic interest are suitably protected, while (d) established farming use is effectively maintained.

This concept was accepted by the Hobhouse Committee[36] in 1947 together with Dower's proposal for the setting up of a National Parks Commission implementing 'a progressive policy of management designed to develop the latent resources of the National Parks for healthy enjoyment and open-air recreation to the advantage of the whole nation'.[36]

Under the National Parks and Access to the Countryside Act, 1949, the Government made the newly constituted local planning authorities responsible for the national parks, although where a park lay in the area of more than one authority provision was made for the establishment of a joint planning board, with joint advisory committees as an exceptional alternative. In practice due to the strenuous opposition of local authorities only two joint boards have been set up. Four parks have joint advisory committees as well as separate park planning committees in each of the constituent local authorities. The remaining four parks lie wholly within the area of a single local authority and are administered by a local authority committee.[37]

A National Parks Commission was also established with mainly advisory functions. It had a general duty to advise the Minister on matters affecting the natural beauty of the countryside—primarily but not exclusively in national parks and other 'areas of outstanding natural beauty'. Its main executive function was concerned with the selection and operation of national parks but it could only make recommendations to planning authorities and representations to the Government. A detailed account of the work of the National Parks Commission has been given in the annual reports, the last of which (the nineteenth) was issued in December, 1968,[38] when the National Parks Commission was superseded by the Countryside Commission.

The National Parks Commission had a duty to promote the provision of facilities for open air recreation within the parks and the Act created two legal instruments to assist in implementing this aim. They were *access agreements* made between the landowner and Park Planning Authority to permit public access to the land covered by the agreement, and *access orders* which provide the same facilities but are made unilaterally by the Park Planning Authority subject to right of appeal by the landowner to the Minister.[39] A seventy-five per cent grant was available from central government funds for the provision of recreational facilities but the scale of provision has been disappointing. Davidson[34] holds the view that this stems largely from a lack of initiative, guidance and even identifiable need. The larger park authorities could afford the twenty-five per cent they had to contribute while the smaller authorities experienced difficulties. In 1968–69, forty-five per cent of all expenditure occurred in two of the parks (Peak District and Lake District).

The total gross expenditure on national parks in 1968–69 amounted to £599 000.[38] Administrative costs represented appreciably more than fifty per cent of the total expenditure, whilst expenditure on positive action under the Act fell by approximately 10.5 per cent, compared with the previous year, to £260 000.[40] This presumably reflects the restrictions on expenditure imposed by the Government and is particularly noticeable in relation to the provision of accommodation, camping and caravan sites, car parks and lay-bys, and on the restoration of derelict land, which is unfortunate at a time when the demand for car parks, camp sites and similar facilities is increasing. Hence the National Parks Commission tended to concentrate on development control, particularly in the giving of advice and resisting proposals such as pipelines and power stations. Much was done on the publicity side with the issuing of leaflets, the formulation of the 'country code' and the setting up of information centres, but the publicity was mainly geared towards preservation rather than enjoyment in the recreational sense. Finally, progress was made in the formulation of access orders and agreements and work commenced on the establishment of a network of long distance footpaths.

Nature and Distribution of National Parks

The Standing Committee on National Parks[41] considered that the primary function of national parks was to provide an opportunity for the predominantly town dwelling people of Britain to enjoy the beauty and quiet of the most dramatic scenery and wild country of England and Wales. Large numbers of young people visit the national parks for more adventurous types of activity such as rock climbing, mountaineering, hill walking, cycling, pony-trekking, canoeing, boating and fishing. The national parks also constitute a valuable reserve of nature and wild life.

As Foster[42] has emphasised, a national park in Britain is very different to one in the United States or Canada— remoteness is only relative and the land remains largely in many different private ownerships without any implied right of access.[44] Nevertheless, there is a common theme—the inclusion of the best in the characteristic natural landscape beauty of the country which is to be protected for the enjoyment of present and future generations. It is interesting to note that the planning aim for French national parks is threefold:[43]

(1) To protect the natural environment (flora, fauna and site) in a condition worthy of interest.

(2) To safeguard the traditional ways of life wherever possible.

(3) To preserve local interests and yet encourage tourism and the recreational interest of land.

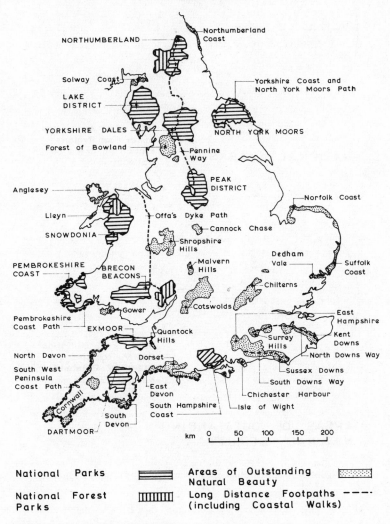

Figure 5.1 National Open Spaces

The national park authorities have wide powers to provide accommodation of all kinds where a known need is not being met adequately by private agencies, and all the authorities have made some provision, although as shown by Foster[45] the needs of the motor car seem to claim first priority. Some of the more unusual types of facility that have been provided include holiday chalets in Llanrwst in Snowdonia; the conversion of old mine buildings into climbing huts in the Lake District; and in the Peak District the provision of a public ski run, the purchase of a grit-stone outcrop for climbing and the acquisition of a length of old railway track for walking and pony-trekking.

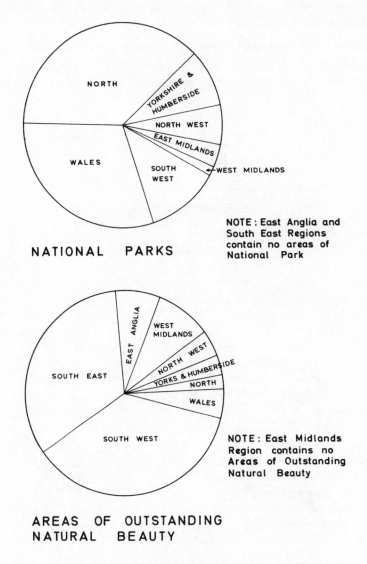

Figure 5.2 Distribution of National Open Spaces by Regions

Table 5.1 lists the national parks that have been designated with their areas: their geographical locations are illustrated in figure 5.1, and their spatial imbalance in relation to population is clearly demonstrated in figure 5.2.

TABLE 5.1

NATIONAL PARKS

National parks	Date of designation		Area (km²)	Population in millions within 2 hours driving time of park in 1971
Peak District	28 December	1950	1404	18.7
Lake District	30 January	1951	2245	10.2
Snowdonia	6 February	1951	2188	6.6
Dartmoor	15 August	1951	946	1.8
Pembrokeshire Coast	20 December	1951	583	0.9
North York Moors	12 February	1952	1432	7.5
Yorkshire Dales	7 December	1953	1761	14.4
Exmoor	27 January	1954	686	3.4
Northumberland	20 September	1955	1032	4.0
Brecon Beacons	20 September	1955	1344	7.3

Problems in Operating National Parks

A wide range of problems has been encountered in operating the national parks and it would seem advisable to examine these under a number of separate heads.

Traffic problems

At weekends in the summer and on bank holidays there is a very heavy influx of private motor cars into the national parks. It is difficult to provide adequate facilities for parking and servicing all these vehicles and to adapt highways to accommodate them without altering the character of the parks so radically as to destroy much of the natural beauty and the opportunities for public enjoyment of all kinds, including even the pleasure of motoring. On the other hand, the lack of facilities for vehicles to pass and turn also has a detrimental effect on amenities and reduces the enjoyment by all sections of the community.[41] Recent research in Devon has shown that the capacity of Dartmoor and Exmoor national parks has been restricted by narrow bridges, the appearances of which are essential to the distinct character of the national parks, and which are listed buildings or ancient monuments in their own right. The capacity of one-way systems and their practicability is now being considered, and the end result could be the establishment of the capacity of day visitors into the two parks and a positive management scheme to limit visitors to these numbers.[46]

The Ramblers' Association[47] asserts that 'there is a grave danger that the more popular National Parks will be overwhelmed by the sheer number of vehicles crowding into them', and Foster[45] has emphasised that traffic management must be tackled to deal with this situation. In the case of the Peak District national park there are over 2 million private cars within 100 km of the park. The Lake District national park is already experiencing weekend pressures from a distance and the M6 will bring people from Manchester and Merseyside into the park for tea on Sundays. Few people who visit The Peak or The Lakes on a bank holiday can really enjoy sitting in a 5 km queue waiting to pass through Bakewell or Windermere.

The Peak Park Planning Board has produced a motorists' map which aims at encouraging motorists to leave the class I roads, which they are often reluctant to do, and to travel on good secondary roads where traffic is light and the views are magnificent. Both the Peak and Lakes Planning Boards are studying various management techniques, including closing valley culs-de-sac and high pass routes at busy times through the introduction of terminal car parks and mini-bus services; one-way traffic systems and low speed limits on minor roads at weekends; establishment of scenic clearways; published and signposted routes; and eventually electronically controlled barriers limiting the number of vehicles on a particular length of road.[121]

Conflict between uses

Conflicts can arise between the need to provide facilities for the enjoyment of national parks and the intention to preserve and enhance their natural beauty. Indeed, Longland[107] saw that one of the main problems in operating

105

national parks would be how best to marry the twin objectives of landscape conservation and recreation provision. The increasing traffic congestion and the mounting demand for caravan and camping sites and other forms of accommodation, and for facilities for gregarious recreation, threaten to destroy the beauty, disturb the quiet, and tame the wild nature of the countryside, which are the principal attractions of a national park. The Town and Country Planning Association[48] saw the overriding need in national parks as one of 'promoting the creative enjoyment of their scenic qualities and natural features while at the same time conserving these'. To secure this objective it is necessary to obtain improved access to almost all the parks, both for those who wish to drive to the picnic areas, scenic view points, or bases for short walks, and for those who wish to walk, ride, climb or study the natural life of a park. We have seen that a great deal of imaginative planning is needed to absorb and guide the increasing number of cars. Car parks, caravan and camping sites may be objectionable in visual terms, yet the aim must be not to keep them out but to accommodate them in a way that is not too repressive to the motorist, caravanner or camper, nor too depressive to the lover of fine scenery and solitude.

Davidson[34] sees conflicts in the use of national parks developing in three main ways:

(1) The effects of recreation on other land uses: trespass, pollution of water supplies, disturbance of wild life, fires, erosion and other factors.

(2) The effects of other users on recreation: loss of access by intensification of agriculture and forestry, and reservoir and other developments.

(3) Recreational use on the recreationalists themselves: crowding, noise, congestion, and physical interference between participants in different activities.

As the demand for recreation increases so will the need for improved management techniques to resolve conflicts in the use of the facilities.

Education of visitors and the country code

One of the most pressing and delicate problems in the operation of national parks is how to make land available for recreational purposes without prejudicing its other uses and disturbing unduly the lives and livelihood of the men who own it. The editor of *The Field*[49] has illustrated some of the problems very forcibly:

The growth of private motoring has brought an influx of people some of whom show little respect for the needs of the landowners. It is no use preaching to a farmer about the need to share our limited heritage of wild country when he is contemplating the havoc done to his stock by broken bottles, broken walls, open gates and other examples of mindlessness exhibited by a minority.

Others have emphasised the need to establish in the public mind the connection between farming and food.

There is an evident need to educate the public in the use of our natural resources for recreational purposes. The country code has been given extensive publicity and is a code of conduct for the guidance of visitors to the countryside. It sets out ten simple maxims for good country manners to avoid damage to farm property, stock or crops: 'guard against fire risks; fasten all gates; keep dogs under proper control; keep to paths across farmland; avoid damaging fences, hedges and walls; leave no litter; safeguard water supplies; protect wild life, wild plants and trees; go carefully on country roads; and respect the life of the countryside'.[50]

Foster[45] has stressed the need for more to be done to safeguard the interests of national parks and high amenity areas, particularly by raising the climate of public opinion by a better knowledge and understanding of the countryside and its problems. Much can be learnt from the information or interpretive services operated in the American national parks, which include talks, lectures, guided tours, natural history trails and an immense museum and information centre programme to cater for both adults and children, with national park officers to answer questions and provide educational programmes or itineraries. In the British national parks some excellent work has been done in the appointment of full time wardens and the provision of information centres, but the interpretive services need to be extended and improved. Heus[114] has described how display cases can be of metal, concrete or synthetic construction.

Public access

As described earlier, the land occupied by national parks (which embraces nine per cent of England and Wales) is under public control, but little of it is in public ownership. The Countryside Commission, which superseded the National Parks Commission in 1968, aims at achieving maximum public access for recreation compatible with the interests of other land users. Denman[51] has indicated how public access to private land can be obtained in one of four ways:

(1) By compulsory purchase by a central or local government department or public body.

(2) Compulsory compliance with rights imposed on a general and arbitrary principle.

(3) Compliance with access orders and arrangements made with the majority consensus of local voluntary opinion.

(4) Spontaneous voluntary invitation.

Denman favours the last approach where agreement can be reached between landowners and other interests. In practice the third procedure will often be adopted with proposals being formulated at local level.

Industrial developments

Cullingworth[37] has drawn attention to the dangers to amenity stemming from developments by government departments and statutory undertakers. By their very nature national parks are ideally suited for military training; they contain valuable mineral deposits; some of them can provide unrivalled water resources; and the development of electricity transmission networks and road improvements exerts pressures on the land in the parks. A nuclear electricity power station at Trawsfynydd in Snowdonia—with its accompanying network of transmission lines on pylons and two oil refineries and an oil terminal at Milford Haven astride the eastern boundary of the Pembrokeshire Coast park—are bound to injure amenities on account of their enormous size, although considerable efforts were made to reconcile these structures with their surroundings. Electricity boards are often requested to re-route overhead transmission lines or to lay them underground, but the latter procedure is very expensive. For instance, it cost more than £2 million to 'bury' an electricity transmission line across the Peak District park. Water authorities are often requested to re-site or adequately landscape new reservoirs. The Peak Park Planning Board, which already has its share of large reservoirs serving Manchester and Sheffield, is currently resisting approaches from the Trent River Authority and has suggested what it considers to be suitable alternatives outside the park.[52] As the Water Resources Board estimates that the demand for water will double by the end of the century, impounding reservoirs cannot meet all foreseeable needs and water authorities must inevitably look to other processes, such as de-salinisation, the re-use of cleansed water and estuarial storage.

Major road proposals can also have serious effects on the landscape in a national park. Proposals for a new major traffic route from Sheffield to Manchester is causing the Peak Park Planning Board great concern as they wish to keep all through traffic to roads on the periphery of the park. To protect the skyline by constructing part of the motorway underground might cost an extra £10 million.[53] Extractive industries leave terrible scars on the landscape and the North York Moors Park Planning Committee is strongly resisting potash mining while the Peak Park Planning Board seems to be fighting a losing battle as the extraction of limestone and fluorspar, which is important to the local economy, produces large ugly scars with dust hanging over the quarries and whitening the surrounding countryside. Robinson[108] has described how mineral workings nearly always involve some measure of noise, dust and traffic in the countryside, quite apart from the damage they may do to the scenery. Another major dispute has centred on the Army's use of 10 000 hectares on Dartmoor for which the leases expired in 1970. Both the Countryside Commission and the National Trust pressed for military exercises to cease in 1975 with a phased withdrawal planned over the intervening years, but this proved unacceptable to the Army.[52]

Administration and finance

The greater measure of success secured by the two joint planning boards in the Peak District and the Lake District, demonstrates clearly that where a national park extends beyond the boundaries of a single county, the single and autonomous planning authority is more efficient than the alternative system, under which authority is exercised by committees of the several county councils.[41] The Town and Country Planning Association[48] has also pointed out that there is often a real conflict between local and national interests which cannot satisfactorily be resolved within the local committees and boards as at present constituted.

The Hobhouse Committee[36] envisaged expenditure on the national parks in the first 10 years at £17 million, whereas it only amounted to about £1 million. The annual report of the Countryside Commission in 1968[38] stated that positive action had been much restricted by financial stringency and that a more than usually large number of projects had been unavoidably postponed. The annual expenditure on national parks for the year ended 30th September 1968 was £601 076 as compared with about £50 million for national parks in the United States. In 1972 the Government announced its plans for the integration of the national parks into the new local government structure. The Royal Institution of Chartered Surveyors[115] believed that the successful development of national parks had been prejudiced by lack of positive policy coupled with insufficient financial incentives and recommended that the Government should provide 100 per cent subsidies.

Use of the National Parks

The intensity of use of national parks varies from park to park and is influenced by the characteristics of the park itself and its location in relation to large centres of population. The Lake District, Peak District and Yorkshire Dales national parks are conveniently situated in relation to the conurbations of Merseyside, Manchester and the West Riding and with access much improved since the construction of the M6 motorway. On the other hand, the national parks in Wales and south-west England are far more remote from the main centres of population and are far distant from any motorways, and their main use is likely to be confined to summer holiday visits. The extent and type of use made of the Peak District and Dartmoor national parks will now be considered.

The British Travel Association Gallup Poll Survey estimated that about 4 million people visited the Peak District national park in the summer of 1963 using 1.3 million cars for travelling, and Foster[45] has suggested that these figures could increase to 8 million people and 3 million cars in the early seventies. The Peak caravan information centre is used by over 40 000 people each summer and 100 000 copies of a calendar of events are issued annually. The majority of visitors come to enjoy the countryside and fresh air and participate in some form of outdoor recreation. The natural qualities of the area—its beauty, quietness and combination of moorland and dales, together with particular places of interest, constitute the main drawing power of the park. Mosley[92] has described how the chief features exciting the interest of the walker are the gorges of the limestone dales and the cloughs and plateau tops of the gritstone country. There were, however, sizeable minority groups interested in specialised pursuits such as hill walking, climbing, potholing and caving, fishing, cycling, pony-trekking, gliding, skiing, swimming and golf, although the preponderance was under 30 years of age. The origins of day visitors by regions of residence were north-east—forty per cent; north-west—sixteen per cent; Midlands—thirty-four per cent; other regions—ten per cent. The east Midlands study[54] describes how the pleasure traffic tends to produce a few periodic peaks which give rise to short period needs for lay-bys, car parks and refreshment facilities. The Peak Park Planning Board has discussed with local water authorities the possibility of providing for the recreational use of reservoirs in the park, and Edwards[55] sees the need for a field study centre in a park which embraces such highly diversified landscape types; which is an unusually rich area for field studies in the natural sciences; and is surrounded by a large number of higher educational establishments.

A survey of Dartmoor national park indicated that about 3 million day visitors went to the park in 1967, and that on peak Sundays in 1968 as many as 55 000 visitors arrived in some 15 000 cars.[56] The survey indicated that about twenty-five per cent of visitors stayed in or beside their cars, some forty to fifty per cent engaged in activities such as picnicking, strolling, sightseeing or sunbathing, and the remainder engaged in more active pursuits or in water activities (swimming, paddling, scrambling on river boulders and fishing), although the proportions varied considerably from one location to another.

Hookway[57] has emphasised the need for public authorities to exercise control over the number and activities of visitors if the efficiency of the established uses of farming and forestry is not to be diminished. Other writers have drawn attention to the need for capacity standards related to physical, ecological and psychological aspects. Another problem lies in finding the best organisational methods of securing cooperation between landowners and public authorities, where the most promising solution seems to be the development of 'management agreements'. Hookway[58] has also stressed the desirability of greater cooperation with private investors—either by the management authority seeking to persuade them to do more than they had contemplated doing or, alternatively, by persuading private enterprise to do something the authority decides is needed and which could be a profitable activity. A good example would be the provision of a camping site, picnic area or car park by an entrepreneur in conjunction with a small petrol service station and refreshment room, with the buildings possibly screened by stone walls or some other structure of local material consistent with the profiles of land form and texture.

AREAS OF OUTSTANDING NATURAL BEAUTY

Both the Dower and Hobhouse reports proposed that, in addition to national parks, certain areas of outstanding landscape beauty should be subject to special protection. It was thought that these areas did not require the positive management which would be a feature of national parks but 'their contribution to the wider enjoyment of the country-side is so important that special measures should be taken to preserve their natural beauty and interest'.[36] The National Parks and Access to the Countryside Act, 1949, gave the National Parks Commission (now superseded by the Countryside Commission) power to designate 'areas of outstanding natural beauty' and provided for exchequer grants on the same basis as for national parks. Generally, areas of outstanding natural beauty are smaller than national parks—some are of small extent such as the 67 km^2 of Cannock Chase, and others, such as west and south Dorset, covering 1040 km^2, are as large as some of the national parks. There is also a wide diversity of landscapes from attractive coastlines and reclaimed or natural salt marshes to forests, moors and downs. The administration of these areas is the responsibility of the local planning authorities, but despite the exchequer grant-aid which is available, many authorities seem reluctant to make use of their powers.[37] The location of the areas of outstanding natural beauty is illustrated in figure 5.1 and their distribution by regions in figure 5.2. In 1970 they occupied 7.3 per cent of the total area of England and Wales.

NATIONAL TRUST

The National Trust was founded in 1894 as a limited liability company by Miss Octavia Hill, and it became a statutory body in 1907 by Act of Parliament. It is an independent society, receiving no regular financial support from the Government and it depends on subscriptions from its members and voluntary gifts from the public. The Trust is essentially a property owning body with the primary aim of preserving places of historic interest or natural beauty for the permanent enjoyment of the nation. While promoting public access to its properties where possible, it regards the preservation of scenery as its primary task. For instance, not all of the Trust's farmland is open to the general public for recreational purposes, although in most cases footpaths have been provided which enable the public to pass through the land. From its initial preoccupation with unspoilt natural scenery, the National Trust became more concerned with preserving important historical buildings, particularly country houses. Since 1965 the emphasis has been on coastal protection: at that time the Trust controlled 282 km of coastline and the Enterprise Neptune campaign (towards which the Government has contributed £250 000) aimed at bringing a further 240 km of coastline under the Trust's protection.

The National Trust protects 170 000 hectares of land in England, Wales and Northern Ireland and is one of the country's largest landowners. It also protects more than 200 houses and other buildings of architectural or historic importance; 2000 farms; mills and abbeys; Roman and other archaeological remains; islands and fenland (Farne islands and Wicken Fen); whole villages (Styal, Lacock and West Wycombe); lengths of canal (Stratford-on-Avon canal); and nearly 480 km of unspoilt coastline.[59] An excellent example of a National Trust park is Clumber Park in north Nottinghamshire which occupies a well wooded estate of over 1500 hectares, which was formerly the seat of the Dukes of Newcastle. It draws and is able to cater for many thousands of visitors each weekend because of its concentrated and artificial attractions—its lake, church and woodland drives. Owing to its extensive forests and well drained soils it is able to absorb a very large number of parked vehicles on natural standings, without giving the feeling of overcrowding and without spoiling the appearance of the grounds by hard standings.[41]

COUNTRY PARKS

Country parks found their origins in a government white paper, *Leisure in the Countryside,* in 1966,[60] to augment the national parks. The proposals entered the statute book in The Countryside Act, 1968, which also created the Countryside Commission and gave local authorities powers to provide camping and picnic sites and to secure public access to woodland and waterways. The Countryside Commission is mainly an advisory body but with responsibility for the whole of the countryside of England and Wales, and a duty to keep under review all matters relating to:

(1) The provision and improvement of facilities for the enjoyment of the countryside.

(2) The conservation and enhancement of the natural beauty and amenity of the countryside.

(3) The need to secure public access to the countryside for the purpose of open air recreation.

Country parks will vary greatly in size and character but will be strategically placed in attractive countryside and reasonably accessible to major towns and cities. They will provide a variety of recreational facilities for the family and so draw people away from high quality agricultural land. The Countryside Commission has deliberately avoided precisely defining country parks and, as Crossley[109] indicated, they could be of many types, some impressive open moorland and others catering to greater or lesser degrees for varied activities by the public but all providing places where people can enjoy themselves in real contact with the country. Hookway[61] has suggested that they 'will serve as "honeypots", drawing off some use from those areas at present overcrowded or otherwise vulnerable, and at the same time filtering traffic off the main day-trip routes'. White[105] sees the main functions of country parks as meeting some of the urgent needs of recreationalists and permitting the rational use of scarce resources.

Within country parks, local authorities are empowered to provide facilities for the enjoyment or convenience of the public, including meals and refreshments, car parks, shelters and lavatory accommodation, for which seventy-five per cent grants are available from the Countryside Commission. Where the country park incorporates stretches of water, the local authority may provide facilities for sailing, boating, fishing and bathing. The 1968 Act also contains powers to provide increased facilities on commons which may be managed as country parks. Davidson[34] has drawn attention to the loose definition of a country park in the 1968 Act and has described how the Countryside Commission is becoming more selective in its approach to country park applications from local authorities and how the Commission takes into account such factors as distance from large towns, variety of facilities to be provided, probable demand in the area and other local provision.

The Countryside Act states that a country park is 'a park or pleasure ground for the purpose of providing or improving, opportunities for the enjoyment of the countryside by the public'. The Countryside Commission has extended the definition in the Act to: 'an area of land, or land and water, normally not less than 25 acres (10 hectares) in extent, designed to offer to the public, with or without charge, opportunity for recreational activities in the countryside'.[62] The purpose of specifying a normal minimum area of 10 hectares is to distinguish small country parks from large picnic sites. To be recognised by the Commission a country park must also be readily accessible for motor vehicles and pedestrians; have an adequate range of facilities, including car parks and lavatories, and a supervisory service; and be operated and managed by statutory bodies or private agencies or a combination of both. Gillespie[110] has expressed the view that there is likely to be variable provision of country parks throughout the country as some local authorities are more enterprising than others and the amount of grant aid may not be sufficient for the poorer authorities. In 1972 country parks on average were costing £640/ha to acquire and develop.[124]

A good example of a country park is Elvaston Castle country park near Derby which was opened in 1970 (purchase price—£129 730).[104] The Castle, which dates substantially from 1817, comprises about 160 hectares of ornamental gardens, parkland, farmland and lake. The scheme provides for camping and tourist caravan sites, car parks, toilets, a café and information centre, 6 km of cinder surfaced horse riding track and large areas for unorganised family activities. Picnickers and ramblers have access to extensive woodlands and the castle will house a conservation museum and hostel accommodation. Other possibilities are the provision of a field study centre in the Castle and a permanent nature trail. The lake will be preserved exclusively for wild fowl of which there are already more than thirty varieties present there.[116] During the first year of operation the park was visited by about 160 000 people.[123]

Nottinghamshire County Council submitted three country park schemes with widely differing characteristics to the Countryside Commission:

(1) Rufford Abbey (52 ha) with its lake will serve a dual rôle as a quiet 'lung' for town dwellers and as a nature reserve.

110

(2) Sherwood—Edwinstowe—(35 ha) around the Major Oak is a great attraction of international repute and was visited by about 30 000 people on the 1969 late summer bank holiday. Approved in 1970.

(3) Holme Pierrepont (93 ha) will include a rowing course designed to Olympic standards, water sports and picnic sites. This scheme is described in chapter 8.

COMMONS

For land to be legally a 'common', there must exist commoners' rights over it which may be enjoyed by owners of particular houses or land in the parish or manor or by particular persons who have the right to pasture cattle on it or to take furze, bracken or heather from it. Other rights include the taking of underwood for fuel and other domestic uses such as repairing fences, the cutting of turves or the extraction of stone or gravel. Roddis[8] explains that the recreational use of commons is often subject to there being no detriment to the exercise of common rights by the persons entitled to them. The right to play games is not in law a right of common and is often either a customary right or a statutory right.

Common land is to be found in moorland, marsh and fen, among rich pastures and fertile arable lands and in the heart of cities and suburban expansion. Denman[63] has described how the uniqueness of commons lies in the history and complexity of the land tenure of common land and in the conflict of interests to which the tenure gives rise. On common land, unlike land held in exclusive freehold, all traces of ownership are frequently lost. Restrictions imposed by statute law, common law and custom have made profitable exploitation of the land difficult, if not impossible, for the landowners. Commons are open land and are normally unfenced. Denman asserts that whether as a village green or wider manorial common, the public at large has always had ready access to them as of right.[63] Some commons are completely wild, and wide open stretches—unfenced and inviting to the motorist, picnicker and hiker—are in consequence a characteristic of many commons. The Commons Registration Act, 1965, gave all county councils and county borough councils the responsibility of compiling registers to record applications for the registration of common and greens, rights of common over such land, and ownership of the registered land, following the report of the Royal Commission on Common Land.[64]

It has been estimated that there are still 600 000 hectares of common land in England and Wales.[64] The most extensive areas of common land are located in the highlands, although there are many smaller commons scattered throughout the country. Nearly half the common land in lowland England is within 80 km of Greater London, the larger part being to the south of the capital on the heathlands of Surrey and Hampshire.[65] Figure 5.3 shows the relative distribution of common land in England and Wales.

The recent history of common land is one of increasing public interest in and control over the use of what was described by the Royal Commission as 'the last reserve of uncommitted land'.[64] It has been the intention of much of the legislation on common land since the Metropolitan Commons Act, 1866, to preserve commons for the purpose of exercise and recreation. Wager[66] considers that the general public has a legal right of access to only 130 000 hectares of common land. This is made up of commons lying wholly or partly within a borough or urban district; rural commons for which the owner has made a deed of dedication; and commons owned by the National Trust.

Wager[66] conducted a survey in 1962–63 of the public use of thirty commons situated in various parts of England. This survey showed that the majority of users visited common land to enjoy the natural attractions and take physical exercise. The motor car was the focal point for nearly fifty per cent of the recreational activity and many visitors can satisfy their recreational needs within a few metres of a parked car or by remaining inside it. It is evident that common land contributes extensively to the recreational use of the countryside and in towns it often brings a sense of the country into the town—the riverside commons at Cambridge being an excellent example. Wager[66] draws a number of conclusions from his survey:

Many 'commons' are visited by the public only occasionally and most public use occurs on a limited number of particularly attractive and conveniently situated 'commons'. Even on those, intensive recreational activity is concentrated on the accessible margins. Much common land in upland Britain is used little more than other areas of rough grazing, which are not subject to common rights. In the future, common land may be expected to absorb an increasing volume of outdoor recreation, but there will always be some 'commons' for which the general public have little need and upon which agriculture and forestry can continue undisturbed.

111

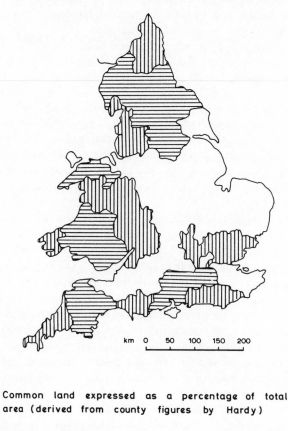

Common land expressed as a percentage of total
area (derived from county figures by Hardy)

☐ Less than 1 per cent

▥ 1 - 5 per cent

☰ Greater than 5 per cent

Figure 5.3   Relative Distribution of Common Land in England and Wales

COASTAL RECREATION

The coastline of England and Wales occupies 4387 km.[73] As a recreational outlet, the coastline performs a dual rôle, providing both holiday resorts by the sea and stretches of undeveloped coastline for quiet enjoyment. Approximately twenty-five per cent of the coastline is either built-up or already committed for development and, of the remainder, there are some 1400 km of cliffs above 15 metres in height, 845 km of shingle, 370 km of sand dunes and 450 km of marsh.[68] Much of this land is protected from development either through public ownership or by means of planning policies. An important coastal landowner is the National Trust which, in 1965, launched a project (Enterprise Neptune) to bring more land into its ownership or, alternatively, to ensure its protection by covenants. The National Trust owned 245 km of coastline in 1969 and local authorities owned a further 175 km. Of the protective planning policies, national parks and areas of outstanding natural beauty embrace no less than thirty-nine per cent of the coastline of England and Wales.[67]

The beauty of the coastline is marred by the presence along many stretches of a wide variety of developments, including defence installations, power stations and scattered caravans and chalet sites. The Ministry of Defence is one of the worst offenders and it has been estimated that the Government owns some five per cent of the coastline of England and Wales and from which the public are excluded.[67] Pressures for new developments of all kinds are increasing and the demand for 'second homes' for weekends and holidays from a more prosperous and leisured society may have a heavy impact on the coastline unless rigidly controlled.

The Institution of Municipal Engineers[69] considers that local authorities will be able, through a controlled policy of land use, to prevent further destruction of coastal beauty. The Institution feels that a much fuller assessment is needed of the future increase and distribution of population, the current and future patterns of holiday requirements and travel, and the transport and parking facilities which will consequently be needed.

Tanner[70] in his report to the Sports Council has shown that on the greater part of the coast, existing recreational facilities do not even match present demand. The main problem of congestion stems from a shortage of permanent facilities and the concentration of demand on to certain parts of the coast, particularly that of south-east England. The most critical problem is seen as the shortage of facilities for boats of all kinds, and particularly moorings for keelboats. In the long term, it seems that this problem can only be solved by the development of marinas. Conflict can occur between most water based activities, but is usually most serious when it concerns water skiing and motor boating, and may involve zoning of activities.

Different people have different recreational needs to be satisfied. Some just want a stretch of sand on which the children can play. Some are looking for all the facilities of a popular resort. Others simply need moorings for their boats. And yet others ask for nothing more than the peace and quiet of some unspoilt scenery. The satisfaction of one need encroaches upon another, so there will have to be a great deal more regulation if the opportunities of the coastline are not to be destroyed in the attempt to enjoy them.

The Countryside Commission has suggested the setting up of a national resorts development agency to sponsor new coastal holiday villages; long sections of 'heritage' coast where controls would be especially strict; an inquiry into Ministry of Defence landholdings; the removal of eyesores; and the setting up of regional parks to complement country and national parks.[111] The suggested designation of heritage coast would occupy more than thirty possible areas covering 1175 km or twenty-seven per cent of the coastline of England and Wales, mainly located between Pembrokeshire and the Isle of Wight.[112]

FORESTRY COMMISSION

The Forestry Commission was established in 1919 and is the government organisation concerned with forestry in Great Britain. The Commission manages the national forests where its prime consideration is the production of timber, but it must have regard to amenity, recreation and wild life. There are 760 000 hectares of plantations under Commission ownership and 480 000 hectares in grant-assisted and agreed management schemes on private estates. Commission planting proposals aim to add a further 200 000 hectares by 1978, while private planting is expected to produce a further 80 000 hectares.[71]

Garthwaite[72] has described how the preoccupation with timber production—with its attendant problems of fear of fire and lack of access—prevented the large scale development of other uses until quite recent times. The first forest park was opened in Argyll in 1936, and others were established in Snowdonia and the Forest of Dean before the last war. Four more forest parks were opened between 1943 and 1955 to give, with the New Forest, nearly 160 000 hectares of forest and moorland available for public enjoyment. But these offered few facilities other than access, the main attraction being the open mountain which was too high to plant.

In the past decade the Forestry Commission has paid far more regard to the ways in which forests can contribute to wild life habitats, landscapes and public enjoyment. By 1972 the Commission had provided 213 picnic sites, eleven camp sites, twenty information centres and 208 forest trails. It also provided observation towers, car parks and toilets.[73] Garthwaite[72] has described how the forests have become 'reservoirs' for wild life, compensating substantially for the loss of habitat due to the removal of hedgerows from agricultural land. The Commission has many areas managed under special agreement with the Nature Conservancy and County Naturalists' Trusts, with the primary objective of conserving existing sites of special scientific interest within the forest. Wherever possible brakes of natural vegetation—birch, alder and oak—are left beside streams and, in replanting old woodland areas, clumps of broadleaved trees and patches of scrub are retained to form ecological reserves to enrich the wild life of the new plantations.

All the measures taken to conserve wild life also contribute to the landscape and to the amenity of forests, and conversely nearly all improvements in landscape create better wild life habitats. Garthwaite's[72] conclusions are extremely relevant:

It is when foresters have learned to integrate their silviculture and forest management, with consideration for landscape, wildlife conservation and recreation that the forest reaches its full potential in the land use pattern of this country. The future pattern that is likely to emerge is a series of new forest parks, smaller, more compact and more accessible to large centres of population than the existing ones.

In the Forestry Commission's 49th annual report[90] the commissioners laid the strongest possible emphasis on the conservation of amenity and the provision of recreational facilities in the belief that, so far from amenity and recreation being incompatible with commercial forestry, they are permanent and integral elements in its practice. The forest parks are attracting the public in ever growing numbers, and increasing use is also being made of the picnic places and forest walks which have been created. It is probable that the number of forest parks will be increased covering relatively small areas of land on similar lines to the country parks. In European Conservation Year, the Forestry Commission issued three brochures aimed at publicising the recreational aspects of forests.[94-96] Wibberley[103]—while accepting the fact that forest areas offer many benefits to soil and climate, fauna and flora, to amenity and rural incomes, for recreation and solitude—is nevertheless disturbed by the possibility of large areas of conifer mono-culture dominating parts of the hills and uplands while hedgerows, single trees and the small copse could continue to disappear before the spread of large scale commercial mechanised arable farms.

It is evident that greater consideration is now being given universally to the recreational use of forests and a practical example is the recreational facilities provided in Nunspeet Forest in the Netherlands, described in chapter 2. In Britain Mutch[74] carried out surveys of the recreational use of some of the national forests in 1963 and 1964, in view of the fact that the Commission's revenue from public recreation is limited to camp and caravan site charges, while direct expenditure is incurred in providing access and other facilities, and there will inevitably be some reduction in the amount of timber grown. Hence Mutch sought information on the quantity of recreational use, the nature of the demand and the value of the recreational opportunity. The main reasons for visiting were picnicking, pleasure driving, walking and climbing. Ninety three per cent of all the visitors interviewed came by car and the average distance travelled was 40 km. Sixty-six per cent of the visitors wanted improved facilities, particularly in relation to sanitation, picnic tables, water points, shelter huts and restaurants. The majority of visitors found the conifers attractive and claimed unconcern at travel costs.

Mutch[74] estimated that demand for tourist access to national forests is increasing rapidly and could be as high as forty-five per cent per annum in some forests. Most of the visitors are seeking seclusion, quietness and freedom to wander and there is a great need for private cars to be able to penetrate the forests. Mutch recommended the provision of a car park with services such as lavatories, an information bureau and even a café-restaurant at the entrance to each forest. Gravelled one-way tourist routes could penetrate the forests with chains of small parking areas which could serve as picnic spots and from which visitors could penetrate the forest on foot. He also saw a need for better sign-posted paths and the supply of maps. Sidaway[106] estimated that 150 concentrated forest sites received 4–8 million visits for the period June–September 1968, and dispersed use probably accounted for double those figures. Richardson[97] favoured the extension of recreational facilities in forests to include hotels, restaurants and public houses, possibly museums, zoos, game parks, marinas, intensive fishing, pleasure parks, car and motor cycle race tracks, and even discotheques, dance halls and striptease shows. Present recreation activities include walking, picnicking, camping, natural history study and photography, shooting, car rallying, orienteering, fishing, pony-trekking, deer stalking and wildfowling.

PICNIC AREAS

The government white paper, *Leisure in the Countryside*,[60] stressed that there will be places in the countryside and on the coast where a country park would not be justified, but something better than a lay-by is needed by the family who want to stop for a few hours—perhaps to picnic, explore the footpaths, or simply to sit and enjoy the view and the fresh air. Subsequently, the Countryside Act, 1968, empowered local planning authorities and rural district councils to provide picnic sites, and such expenditure is grant-aided (up to seventy-five per cent). The Countryside Commission[62] has laid down certain minimum requirements for a picnic site:

(a) an area of land generally between 1 and 25 acres (0.4–10 ha);

(b) an area set aside for picnicking in attractive surroundings close to the parking area;

(c) car parking area, well-drained, with a surface which may be natural or artificial in keeping with the surroundings, which withstands wear;

(d) safe vehicular access;

(e) provision for removal of litter; and

(f) signs to indicate transit site (for those breaking a long journey).

The difference between a country park and a picnic site is essentially one of scale. Compared with a country park, a picnic site would be smaller, simple and informal, and provide for less variety of recreational activities. The facilities which might be provided on the most intensively used picnic sites include tables and chairs, benches, refreshment hut, shelter hut, fireplaces, supervisory service and nature trails.[62] Some sites will be suitable for picnicking to take place beside the car. Picnic sites averaged 6 ha and cost about £7500 each to acquire and develop in 1972.[124]

The Countryside Commission can make grants to private persons for the provision of picnic sites. In considering applications the Commission will encourage the provision and improvement of sites where the need is greatest, such as in areas subject to great pressures; where recreational use is causing damage to the landscape; and on waste land. Brancher[75] has made the point that every half-hour spent at a view point or picnic site means a car less on every 15–25 km of road, and money saved on capacity improvements. Bonsey[102] has shown that we have much to learn in making picnic areas convenient and comfortable, while retaining a natural and unspoilt appearance, and has advocated the use of a collection of small grassed areas, sheltered by informal groups of trees and bushes, termed 'nesting sites'.

LONG DISTANCE FOOTPATHS AND DISUSED RAILWAY LINES

The National Parks and Access to the Countryside Act, 1948, required county councils to make surveys of footpaths and bridleways but by 1964 only half the councils had published definitive maps.[60] The pattern of footpaths has largely been determined by ancient rights of way and it is no longer suited to present day needs. Lord Robens[76] has stressed the need to devise a new network of pathways linking parking and picnic areas, because if these are not planned they may develop haphazardly to the detriment of farmer and visitor alike.

The Countryside Commission, like its predecessor, the National Parks Commission, is responsible for proposing long distance footpaths. Table 5.2 lists the routes approved and progress achieved by March 1969, together with the numbers of local authorities involved; and their locations are illustrated in figure 5.1. The designation of the routes has been a difficult and lengthy process. The two Commissions have been the initiating bodies—making the proposals, discussing them with the local authorities concerned and presenting a report to the Minister. The report shows the route, together with existing public rights of way, and may contain proposals for the improvement of paths and the provision of new paths, ferries, accommodation, meals and refreshments. However, in spite of the Commissions' technical contribution and financial assistance from the Government, implementation of the proposals rests with the local authorities, and progress has been slow.[37]

The Countryside Commission has endeavoured to accelerate the administrative work by seconding staff to local authorities for short periods. The difficulties of coordinating the work of so many local authorities (thirty-three were concerned with the Pennine Way alone) has been one of the major causes of delay, apart from the many discussions which have to take place with ramblers' organisations, landowners, farmers and other interested parties.[77] Millar[78] has described how the numerous district councils are often inadequately staffed and their officers have not always had the time to ascertain ownerships and make the necessary personal approaches to landowners, write to their representatives, and hold discussions with various public bodies, including the county council, district valuer and government departments. Furthermore, delay in completing statutory county footpath maps makes it uncertain whether a right of way exists or not.

The exceedingly slow rate of progress in establishing one of the most attractive long distance routes—the Pembrokeshire Coast path—is described by Barrett.[79] The completely inadequate sum of £800 (about £4 per km)

TABLE 5.2

LONG DISTANCE FOOTPATHS

Route	Date approved by Minister	Length (km)	New Rights of Way needed		Number of local authorities concerned	Time lag (years)
			At approval stage (km)	Still to be negotiated in March 1969 (km)		
Pennine Way	6.7.51	400	113	—	33	14
Cornwall—North Coast	7.4.52	217	72	8	13	16
Pembrokeshire Coast	3.7.53	269	106	14	9	15
Cornwall—South Coast	18.4.54	214	69	20	12	14
Offa's Dyke Path	27.10.55	270	72	23	36	12
Devon—South Coast	22.6.59	150	29	21	16	9
Somerset and North Devon	13.1.61	132	43	32	9	8
South Downs Way	28.3.63	129	14	1½	12	6
Dorset Coast Path	4.4.63	116	8	5	8	5
Yorkshire Coast and North York Moors	11.2.65	150	23	½	15	4
Totals:		2047	549	125	163	

Source: MILLAR T. G., *Britain's long-distance paths.* Town and Country Planning, March 1969.

has been made available for its maintenance. Establishing the path was also difficult where it traversed thickets of gorse and bramble, steep screes, boggy bottoms and long lengths which were remote from even a small lane. One cannot help but be entranced by the diversity and splendour of the scenery with its cliffs, coves and raised beaches; its unbroken geological succession over 2000 million years; the vivid colours of countless varieties of wild flowers; the Welsh gorse and heather and the abundance of wild life; and historical associations going back 10 000 years—embanked fortifications, castles and small quays. Some of the long distance routes, like the North Downs Way which was approved in July 1969, will provide many stretches of gentle family style walking. Much the same applies to the Dales Way which will link the West Riding and the Lake District, and the Wolds Way which will traverse the little known but scenically first-class country in the East Riding. The local groups of the Ramblers' Association who have planned these routes have had the wants of casual walkers as much in mind as the needs of the 'tigers'.[80]

Considerable attention has been directed towards the recreational use of disused railways for walking and horse riding—and, to a much less extent, cycling—since many attractive lines have closed in recent years. There seems to have been a total lack of any sort of national policy on their future use, and only comparatively short sections have been sold to local authorities, landowners, and other bodies. Such piecemeal disposal loses an opportunity to provide new facilities for the general public, particularly in the recreational field. Appleton[93] has also shown the unsatisfactory nature of the procedure for disposal of disused railways in the countryside. Probably the most extensive project is a 48 km route in the Peak District from Cromford to Parsley Hay and from Ashbourne through Hartington towards Buxton, of which an 18 km stretch, the Tissington Trail, is now operative. Topsoil has been spread over the ballast and seeded for walking and pony-trekking. It is proposed to develop picnic areas, car parks, and tourist caravan and camping sites to serve this route. A Nottinghamshire proposal utilising the Farnsfield to Southwell line produced strong protests from farmers who feared damage to crops and stock. The Cyclists' Touring Club has also expressed considerable concern that cyclists are being excluded from these routes and has suggested that the tracks should be surfaced with shale or similar hard material which would be more serviceable in bad weather, reduce maintenance costs and be suitable for all types of user.[81]

Not all of the 7200 km of disused railways will be suitable for conversion to recreational use. The old lines must generally be attractive in themselves, give views over pleasing countryside and fit into an overall footpath scheme with suitable access points for cars and bus services. A good example is the Thetford/Bury St. Edmunds branch line in East Anglia which passed through arable farmland and breckland heath of considerable natural beauty, but the lack of variation and exceptional views resulted in the abandonment of the proposal for a long distance walk.[122] A Lindsey county survey[117] identified certain sections of disused lines as having potential for recreation or nature conservation and as being worthy of acquisition. Although the purchase price is sometimes relatively low, the cost of maintenance can be formidable. A viaduct can cost up to £600 per annum to keep in sound condition; drains and culverts are costly to maintain; and maintenance of hedges, fences, accommodation bridges and crossings to farmland may prove to be a heavy liability. Further expenses stem from the provision of car parks, camping sites, toilets, information boards, signposts, picnic areas and sometimes countryside wardens to patrol paths.[113] The Countryside Commission[118] has published details of disused railways converted or proposed for conversion to recreational use.

RECLAMATION AND CONSERVATION

Dereliction problems and the pressing need for extensive reclamation and increased conservation were examined in chapter 2. Hilton[82] has suggested that a government fund of £1 million a year for 20 years should be set up for land reclamation purposes. There are approximately 40 000 hectares of derelict land in England and Wales of which probably about fifty per cent is reclaimable. Others have suggested the payment of a 100 per cent government grant and the streamlining of administrative procedures to speed up the reclamation of derelict land, some of which is ideally suited for recreational use.

European Conservation Year, 1970, increased public awareness of the grave dangers of pollution of land, water and air, and of the need to establish policies to conserve and improve the environment and to devise the best ways of implementing them. With the increased use of inland waters for recreational purposes, great concern is being shown at the heavy pollution of the water by sewage works effluents, industrial wastes and agricultural fertilisers. A Countryside Commission report[83] has described the enormous pressures on the coast from cars and caravans to power stations, ports, oil refineries and the armed forces, and states:

Important sites and the habitats which they provide for plants and animals are likely to be eliminated, while the value of others may be greatly reduced. It must be appreciated that each natural habitat has a definite and limited capacity to withstand use. Beyond a certain point, the recuperative powers of the vegetation are unable to function and degradation and erosion set in.

On the other hand, cooling water from power stations, barrages and reclamation schemes can, if wisely and imaginatively planned, offer excellent opportunities for positive conservation by creating new habitats for wild life.

Hookway and Davidson[84] have drawn attention to the wide variety of ecological, scenic, economic, social and political effects which accompany increased leisure activity. The more obvious deleterious effects are threefold:

(1) The interference caused to established rural activities.

(2) The physical disturbance to fragile areas of the countryside, expressed visually and ecologically.

(3) The conflicts that exist between different leisure interests that compete for resources.

Environmental conservation which is concerned with both quantity and quality aims to harmonise resource interests, with the minimum of conflict. The application of conservation principles is essential if the problems resulting from increased leisure activity in the countryside are to be solved.[84]

Both Lindsey County Council[98] and Coppock[99] have found that lines of contact between land and water or between one kind of vegetation and another—for example, on the margins of woodland or at the junction between heath and grassland—are of the greatest popularity for recreation and this is where the highest concentrations of recreational use seem to occur. There is also a very close relationship between pressure and motor car access, pressure tending to be inversely proportional to the distance from the car park. The effects of public pressure can be categorised under two main heads—inevitable effects such as wear and tear on vegetation, disturbance to wild life and soil erosion, effects which can often be minimised by positive management; and unnecessary threats to environment and amenity such as the dropping of litter and vandalism, problems which might be substantially eliminated through education.[98]

Stoddart[100] advocates the development of three lines of action to maintain the present concern with environment:

(1) Popular support must be maintained.

(2) The values and assumptions on which concern for environmental quality depends must be more clearly

defined and built in to theoretical and factual bases on which prescriptions for the future can be based.

(3) Geographers and ecologists must participate at levels where decisions are made and carried out.

NATURE CONSERVANCY

The Nature Conservancy was established in 1949 and has, since 1965, been a component body of the Natural Environment Research Council.[85] Much of its effort has been devoted to the selection and establishment of national nature reserves and the notifying of planning authorities of more than 2000 sites of special scientific interest. In its research, the Nature Conservancy has inevitably become concerned with the total pattern of vegetation and fauna; the factors that control this pattern; and the likely consequences of the changing demands of society, including those for recreation, on the coast and countryside.[86]

Research and conservation are the prime functions of the national nature reserves. On these areas experimental work can be conducted which will enable the Conservancy to advise planners and land managers on suitable techniques for maintaining plant and animal communities, especially on the wild lands which are so important for recreation. The Conservancy makes national nature reserves accessible for recreation wherever possible and provides facilities for such activities as nature study and bird watching, wildfowling, rock climbing, caving and skiing. Wherever practicable, the effects of these activities are monitored so that research and survey information is collected which may have much wider application.

The Nature Conservancy conducts three main types of recreational study:

(1) The effects of recreational impact on different habitat types.

(2) The management of wild life populations of value for recreation, for example, deer, grouse and wildfowl.

(3) The value of different areas for nature conservation and the reconciliation of this interest with recreational development plans.

Some of the Conservancy's research programmes were outlined in chapter 2. Furthermore, the regional staff of the Conservancy are intimately concerned with recreational planning and development and are represented on the technical panels of the regional sports councils. Increased attention is being paid to the effects of large scale projects, such as barrages, and to the creation and management of habitats valuable for both wild life and recreation. Finally, the Conservancy is conscious that the observation and study of wild life is one of the fastest growing forms of recreation, and it is constantly trying to evaluate and improve the effectiveness of the facilities—such as nature trails and reserve centres—which encourage people to study and enjoy wild nature on the reserves.[86]

SPORTS COUNCIL

The Sports Council is an advisory body which was appointed by the Government in 1965; it operates through separate Sports Councils for Scotland and Wales and has nine regional sports councils in England. Its main functions were defined as:

(1) To advise the Government on matters relating to the development of amateur sport and physical recreation.

(2) To foster cooperation among statutory bodies, local authorities and voluntary organisations to increase opportunities for participation in sport and physical recreation.

The Council has initiated surveys of existing major recreational facilities, promotes improved access to resources and develops research programmes. In the research programmes, the Council has relied extensively on outside organisations, particularly university departments. Some regional sports councils have undertaken studies in depth into specific recreational pursuits or problems.[87] The establishment of the Sports Council has undoubtedly given a new impetus to the provision of sports facilities. Direct grants from central government funds to national voluntary bodies and local voluntary sports clubs have increased substantially. In 1965–66 total expenditure in grants in England, Scotland and Wales amounted to £1 335 735, and in the year 1968–69 this had increased to £2 325 558,[88] despite the fact that the country had been suffering from acute economic difficulties with a consequent restriction on public expenditure.

118

In 1971 the Government announced its intention to enhance the status of the Sports Council, to give it executive powers and widen its responsibilities, whereby it would become an independent body responsible for grant aiding functions with increased finances.[119] It was hoped that the Sports Council would get the most out of existing facilities; bring into fuller use under used natural resources; apply the latest technological advances to sports and recreational needs; and involve the private sector.[120]

RECENT DEVELOPMENTS AND TRENDS

Urban outdoor sports are, with few exceptions, holding their own and in some—such as archery, rugby football and golf—there is marked growth which is more than commensurate with population increase. The growth in golf since the mid-fifties has been very great indeed and the game's large land requirements has made it the subject of special regional and national studies.[18] In some parts of the country the use of industrial recreational clubs is declining and there is a disturbing tendency to use industrial sports grounds for building development. The growth of indoor sports is often retarded by lack of facilities. With open country activities there has been a rapid upsurge of active participation since the mid-fifties, with the one exception of cycle touring.

The changing pattern of recreational demand is creating a new emphasis in terms of space and complexity of facilities which must result in increased provision by public bodies, particularly local authorities. The Sports Council considers that the larger authorities should accept responsibility for developing major facilities of a sub-regional or regional nature, such as multi-purpose sports centres; large swimming pools; golf courses and countryside facilities (including water centres); in addition to assuming a coordinating rôle in planning and integrating the contributions from private, industrial, commercial and public sectors. Grants have been made by the Department of Education and Science for a number of large scale projects where at least fifty per cent of the members of the management committee are representatives of voluntary organisations. Examples of projects of this type are the sports centres at Harlow, Basingstoke, Poole, Folkestone and Dawley.[88]

Since the issue of the joint circular in 1964,[27] the Department of Education and Science has endeavoured to encourage authorities to achieve the best use of available resources by the joint planning and dual use of sports facilities. By October 1969, approval had been given to some thirty schemes of dual provision in England and Wales, thereby combining a local education authority's resources with those of one or more local authorities to provide a sports facility to serve both educational and community needs. Some of these schemes are described in chapter 7, and they are often the means of providing a valuable amenity in a community, which otherwise would be unobtainable. The concept of dual use applies not only to sports facilities owned by local education authorities, but also by universities, some of which are now encouraging sports associations to make use of their modern well equipped sports halls and swimming pools.[88]

Water recreation activities, as a group, show greater relative growth than other sports, and this was clearly demonstrated in the Countryside Commission report on coastal recreation.[70] The Transport Act, 1968, placed on the British Waterways Board a new and positive duty to maintain some 1770 km of cruising waterways in a condition suitable for cruising, fishing and other recreational purposes, and this involves a substantial grant in aid from the Government. A joint circular in 1966[89] drew the attention of water undertakers to the growing demand for water recreation and suggested a review of existing arrangements for public access to reservoirs and gathering grounds. Of 120 undertakers who have opened reservoirs and gathering grounds, eighty-one reported the use of water resources for the following types of recreation: sailing forty-five, canoeing sixteen, water skiing two, bathing one, sub aqua nine and angling seventy-four. Of 108 undertakers the following have permitted the recreational use of gathering grounds: ornithology sixty-three, rambling sixty-four, camping seven, rock climbing six, picnicking twenty-seven, shooting eighteen and car parks nineteen.[88]

Anglers are by far the largest users of inland waters in Great Britain. They prefer undisturbed use of the water they fish and, owing to conflict with other water users, it is sometimes necessary to operate some system of zoning or time-tabling. A useful resource for water recreation is that of gravel pits, as almost sixty per cent of these are wet workings. They are mostly to be found in a triangular area stretching from Weymouth to the south-east of London and up to the Midlands. When extraction is completed these pits, suitably landscaped, form attractive lagoons for all types of water recreation. Some of the larger workings offer new and large areas of water which may be of regional

119

or even national significance and the following examples serve to illustrate this:

(1) The Lea Valley which is being reclaimed and developed by the Lea Valley Regional Park Authority as a major recreational centre to the north of London. The proposals include a rowing and canoeing regatta centre between Cheshunt and Broxbourne.

(2) The Cotswold Water Park, a country park, planned by Gloucestershire and Wiltshire county councils in the upper Thames valley, which includes deep water filled gravel pits and these will accommodate a variety of water sports.

(3) Colwick Park and Holme Pierrepont Water Park (Nottinghamshire) where a series of lagoons will be developed as an extensive water park on either side of the River Trent within about 4 km of the centre of Nottingham. It will incorporate facilities for specialised activities, a 2000 metres rowing and canoeing regatta course, a water ski area and a sailing lagoon. The proposals are illustrated in figures 8.2 and 8.3 (chapter 8).

Regional sports councils are establishing priorities based on their initial appraisals of facilities, and local authorities are advised to consult with them before embarking on detailed planning. As Molyneux[18] has stressed:

Future planning for recreation should recognise the inter-penetration of town and country for different recreational functions. Society has moved to a time when leisure is with us in greater abundance and, for this is the major element in the recreation explosion, when education, higher standards of living and mobility are broadening the total spectrum of recreational activity. These developments should be regarded by society as presenting opportunities to widen social and community life and to extend human experience. It is a challenge to create an increasing range of opportunities through positively generated policies. The challenge is as much the structure and framework for recreational policies as it is of directing public investment into the provision of facilities of the right type, in the right place and in the right proportion.

REFERENCES

1. SMITH, T. S. *First Report of the Commissioners for Inquiring into the State of Large Towns and Populous Districts, Vol. 1,* (1844)
2. GIBBON, G. and BALL, R. W. *A History of the London County Council,* London, (1939)
3. DALEY, A. and BENJAMIN, B. London as a case study. *Public Health and Urban Growth.* Centre for Urban Studies, Report 4, University College, London, (1964)
4. FERGUSON, T. Public health in Britain in the climate of the nineteenth century. *Public Health and Urban Growth.* Centre for Urban Studies, Report 4, University College, London, (1964)
5. CLARKE, E. R. and CLARKE, W. S. Children's recreation in the United Kingdom. *Statutes and Constitutions.* National Playing Fields Association
6. SMITH, Sir H. L. (Ed.). *New Survey of London Life and Labour,* London, (1930)
7. BENJAMIN, B. The urban background to public health changes in England and Wales, 1900–50. *Public Health and Urban Growth.* Centre for Urban Studies, Report 4, University College, London, (1964)
8. RODDIS, R. J. (1970). *The Law of Parks and Recreation Grounds,* Shaw
9. LAW, S. (1967). *Planning for Public Open Space in Greater London. Proceedings of Conference on Planning for Recreation,* York Institute of Advanced Architectural Studies
10. LONDON COUNTY COUNCIL. *Parks for Tomorrow,* (1964)
11. BUTLER, G. B. (1959). *Introduction to Community Recreation,* McGraw Hill
12. MEYER, H. D. and BRIGHTBILL, C. K. (1964). *Community Recreation: A Guide to its Organisation,* Prentice-Hall
13. CLAWSON, M., HELD, R. B. and STODDARD, C. H. (1962). *Land for the Future,* John Hopkins Press, Baltimore
14. NATIONAL PLAYING FIELDS ASSOCIATION. *Outdoor Recreation in Great Britain*
15. NATIONAL PLAYING FIELDS ASSOCIATION. *Grounds for Action: A Description of the Work of the National Playing Fields Association*
16. NATIONAL PLAYING FIELDS ASSOCIATION. *About Our Work,* (1969)
17. NATIONAL PLAYING FIELDS ASSOCIATION. *Disused Burial Grounds as Playgrounds and Playing Fields,* (1965)
18. MOLYNEUX, D. D. Working for recreation. *Journal of Royal Town Planning Institute,* **54.4,** (1968)
19. HANSARD PARLIAMENTARY DEBATES, Official Report. Fifth Series. 1936–37. Vol. **322,** cols. 193–284, Vol. **324,** cols. 2173–2192
20. CENTRAL COUNCIL OF PHYSICAL RECREATION. *Sport and the Community,* (1960)
21. DEPARTMENT OF EDUCATION AND SCIENCE. *Playing Fields and Hard Surface Areas,* Building Bulletin 28, H.M.S.O., (1966)
22. DEPARTMENT OF EDUCATION AND SCIENCE. *Secondary School Design: Physical Education,* Building Bulletin 26, H.M.S.O. (1965)
23. SILLITOE, K. K. *Planning for Leisure,* H.M.S.O., (1969)
24. NICHOLSON, G. Team games in decline amid the quiet revolution. *The Guardian,* (15 November 1969)
25. NATIONAL PLAYING FIELDS ASSOCIATION. *Making the Most of School Playing Fields,* (1960)
26. NATIONAL PLAYING FIELDS ASSOCIATION. *School Playing Fields—dual use policies in operation,* (1964)

27. MINISTRY OF HOUSING AND LOCAL GOVERNMENT (Circular 49/64) and DEPARTMENT OF EDUCATION AND SCIENCE, *Provision of Facilities for Sport,* (1964)

28. CULLEN, P. Whither industrial recreation now? *Sport and Recreation,* **7.4,** (1966), 16–22 and **8.1,** (1967), 10–15

29. MINISTRY OF HOUSING AND LOCAL GOVERNMENT. *The Green Belts,* H.M.S.O., (1962)

30. RICHARDSON, T R. Green belts—past, present and future. *Journal of Institution of Municipal Engineers,* **86.10,** (1959)

31. NOTTINGHAMSHIRE/DERBYSHIRE SUB-REGIONAL PLANNING UNIT. *Nottinghamshire and Derbyshire Sub-Regional Study,* (1969)

32. WORLD HEALTH ORGANISATION EXPERT COMMITTEE. Technical report 297. *Environmental Health Aspects of Metropolitan Planning and Development,* World Health Organisation, Geneva, (1965)

33. BARR, J. Planning for the Ruhr. *Geographical Magazine,* (January 1970), 280–289

34. DAVIDSON, J. M. The Countryside Commission. *Proceedings of Conference on Recreation in the Countryside,* Loughborough University, (1969)

35. NATIONAL PARKS IN ENGLAND AND WALES. (Dower Report), *Cmd. 6628,* (1945)

36. REPORT OF THE NATIONAL PARKS COMMITTEE (ENGLAND AND WALES). (Hobhouse Report), *Cmd. 7121,* (1947)

37. CULLINGWORTH, J. B. Planning for leisure. *Urban Studies,* **1.1,** (1964)

38. COUNTRYSIDE COMMISSION. *Nineteenth Report of the National Parks Commission and First Report of the Countryside Commission,* H.M.S.O., (1968)

39. BURTON, T. L. and WIBBERLEY, G. P. (1965). *Outdoor Recreation in the British Countryside,* Department of Economics, Wye College, University of London

40. FULL, H. F. National Park Authorities' Statistics, 1968–69. *County Council's Gazette,* (November 1969), 328–330

41. STANDING COMMITTEE ON NATIONAL PARKS. *The future of National Parks and the countryside.* Study No. 2

42. FOSTER, J. National Parks and in particular the Peak District National Park. *Land and People,* British Broadcasting Corporation, (1966)

43. CLOUT, H. Planning National and Regional Parks in France. *Town and Country Planning,* (December 1969), 560–563

44. COPPOCK, J. T. The recreational use of land and water in rural Britain. *Tijdschrift voor Economische en Sociale Geographie,* **57.3,** (1966)

45. FOSTER, J. Provision for countryside and coast: National Parks. *Course on Recreation and Leisure,* York Institute of Advanced Architectural Studies, (1967)

46. COUNTRYSIDE COMMISSION. Recreation research in Devon. *Recreation News, No. 14,* (January 1970), 3

47. RAMBLERS' ASSOCIATION. *Motor Vehicles in National Parks,* (1962)

48. TOWN AND COUNTRY PLANNING ASSOCIATION. A policy for countryside recreation in England and Wales. *Town and Country Planning,* (December 1965), 473–481

49. THE FIELD EDITORIAL. Opening the paths in Snowdonia. *The Field,* (17 April 1969)

50. COUNTRYSIDE COMMISSION. *The National Parks of England and Wales,* H.M.S.O.

51. DENMAN, D. R. Public access to private land. *Chartered Surveyor,* (August 1968), 77–80

52. HAWTHORNE, G. Threat to National Parks grows. *The Guardian,* (14 November 1969)

53. ARDILL, J. Outcry looms on Park Plan. *The Guardian,* (19 March 1970)

54. EAST MIDLANDS ECONOMIC PLANNING COUNCIL. *The East Midlands Study,* H.M.S.O., (1966)

55. EDWARDS, K. C., Peak District—museum of the outdoors. *Nottingham Evening Post and News,* (13 September 1968)

56. JOINT SCHOOLS SURVEY. People at play in Dartmoor National Park. *Geographical Magazine,* (January 1970), 266–279

57. HOOKWAY, R. J. S. (1968). *Planning for Leisure and Recreation,* Countryside Commission

58. HOOKWAY, R. J. S. (1968). *Investment in Recreation in National Parks,* Countryside Commission

59. NATIONAL TRUST. *The National Trust: Some Facts and Figures,* (1969)

60. LEISURE IN THE COUNTRYSIDE (ENGLAND AND WALES). *Cmd. 2928,* (1966)

61. HOOKWAY, R. J. S. (1968). *Planning of Land Resources: Recreation in the Countryside,* Countryside Commission

62. COUNTRYSIDE COMMISSION. *Policy on Country Parks and Picnic Sites,* (1969)

63. DENMAN, D. R. Five crucial years in the destiny of common land, 1965–1970. *The Countryside in 1970, Second Conference,* (1965)

64. REPORT OF ROYAL COMMISSION ON COMMON LAND, *1955–58 Cmnd. 462,* H.M.S.O.

65. HARDY, D. *The Use of Land for Recreation with Special Reference to an Area near Brentwood, Essex.* Private communication, Department of Geography, University of Exeter, (1969)

66. WAGER, J. Outdoor recreation on common land. *Journal of the Royal Town Planning Institute,* (November 1967), 398–403

67. COUNTRYSIDE COMMISSION. (1968). *The Coasts of England and Wales: Measurements of Use, Protection and Development,* H.M.S.O.

68. TURNBULL, P. Planning for the holidaymaker—the next ten years. *Journal of the Royal Town Planning Institute,* (July/August 1962)

69. INSTITUTION OF MUNICIPAL ENGINEERS. Preliminary memorandum on coastal preservation and development to National Parks Commission. *Journal of Institution of Municipal Engineers,* (May 1967)

70. TANNER, M. F. Coastal recreation in England and Wales. *Coastal Recreation and Holidays: Special study report Vol. 1,* Countryside Commission, H.M.S.O., (1969)

71. EDLIN, H. L. Creating forests. *The Guardian,* (19 August 1969)

72. GARTHWAITE, P. F. Enjoying the wildlife. *The Guardian,* (19 August 1969)

73. COUNTRYSIDE COMMISSION. *Digest of Countryside Recreation Statistics,* (1969)

74. MUTCH, W. E. S. *Public Recreation in National Forests : A Factual Survey.* Forestry Commission Booklet No. 21, H.M.S.O., (1968)

75. BRANCHER, D. M. *Scenery, Roads, Cars and Cost.* Proceedings of Third Annual Study Conference, University of Wales, Council for the Protection of Rural Wales, (1969)

76. LORD ROBENS. *The Use and Development of the Nation's Resources.* Proceedings of Annual Conference of Royal Institution of Chartered Surveyors, University of Nottingham, (1966)

77. HAWTHORNE, G. Two more long routes ready for walkers. *The Guardian,* (10 April 1969)

78. MILLAR, T. G. Britain's long-distance paths. *Town and Country Planning,* (March 1969), 103–107

79. BARRETT, J. H. Progress on a coastal path. *Geographical Magazine,* (January 1970), 292–303

80. HALL, C. Up on the Downs. *Town and Country Planning,* (November 1969), 512–513

81. CYCLISTS' TOURING CLUB. *Disused Railway Lines.* Press notice, (October 1969)

82. HILTON, K. H. (Ed.). (1967). *The Lower Swansea Valley Project,* Longmans

83. COUNTRYSIDE COMMISSION. (1970). *Nature conservation at the coast,* H.M.S.O.

84. HOOKWAY, R. J. S. and DAVIDSON, J. (1970). *Leisure : Problems and Prospects for the Environment,* Countryside Commission

85. NATURE CONSERVANCY. (1968). *The Nature Conservancy Handbook 1968,* H.M.S.O.

86. COUNTRYSIDE COMMISSION. *The Nature Conservancy. Recreation News No. 10,* (1969)

87. COUNTRYSIDE COMMISSION. The Sports Council. *Recreation News No. 7,* (1969)

88. CENTRAL COUNCIL OF PHYSICAL RECREATION. *The Sports Council : A review 1966–69,* (1969)

89. MINISTRY OF LAND AND NATURAL RESOURCES/DEPARTMENT OF EDUCATION AND SCIENCE. Joint Circular 3/66 : 19/66. *Reservoirs and Gathering Grounds,* (1966)

90. FORESTRY COMMISSION. *Forty-ninth Annual Report and Accounts, 1967–69,* H.M.S.O., (1970)

91. CHAMBERS, J. D. Modern Nottingham in the making. *Nottingham Journal,* (1945)

92. MOSLEY, J. G. *The Peak District National Park : A Regional Study of an Amenity Area.* Private communication, University of Nottingham, Department of Geography, (1955)

93. APPLETON, J. H. (1970). *Disused Railways in the Countryside of England and Wales,* Countryside Commission, H.M.S.O.

94. FORESTRY COMMISSION. *See Your Forests,* (1970)

95. FORESTRY COMMISSION. *The Forestry Commission and Conservation,* (1970)

96. FORESTRY COMMISSION. *Forestry Commission Camping and Caravan Sites,* (1970)

97. RICHARDSON, S. D. Forestry planners must include recreation. Address to British Association. *The Guardian,* (9 September 1970)

98. LINDSEY COUNTY COUNCIL. *Countryside Recreation : the Ecological Implications,* (1970)

99. COPPOCK, J. T. Reconnaisance study of the impact of outdoor recreation on the countryside of Central Scotland. *Royal Town Planning Institute Research Conference : Planning for the Changing Countryside. Paper 32,* (1967)

100. STODDART, D. R. Our environment. *Area 1.* Institute of British Geographers, (1970)

101. BRYANT, A. The best use of our land. *Chartered Surveyor,* **103.3,** (1970)

102. BONSEY, C. C. *The Rising Tide of Outdoor Recreation.* Proceedings of Annual Conference of Royal Institution of Chartered Surveyors, University of Warwick, (1970)

103. WIBBERLEY, G. *Rural Conservation.* Proceedings of Annual Conference of Royal Institution of Chartered Surveyors, University of Warwick, (1970)

104. COUNTRYSIDE COMMISSION. Elvaston Castle Country Park. *Recreation News, Supplement 1,* (1970)

105. WHITE, J. The provision of country parks; a critique. *Town and Country Planning,* **38.6,** (1970)

106. SIDAWAY, R. M. Estimation of day use recreation by the Forestry Commission. *Recreation News,* **20,** (1970)

107. LONGLAND, J. Role of the Countryside Commission. *Conference of National Park Authorities, Sheffield,* (1970)

108. ROBINSON, K. Address to *Annual Conference of National Park Authorities, Aviemore,* (1969)

109. CROSSLEY, H. Elvaston Castle. *County Councils Gazette,* **63.6,** (1970)

110. GILLESPIE, W. Rural parks. *Journal of Institute of Landscape Architects,* **90,** (1970)

111. COUNTRYSIDE COMMISSION. (1970). *The Planning of the Coastline,* H.M.S.O.

112. COUNTRYSIDE COMMISSION. (1970). *The Coastal Heritage.* H.M.S.O.

113. CHRISTIAN, R. New uses for old railways. *Country Life,* (25 June 1970)

114. HEUS, C. DE. The manufacture of orientation tables for recreation areas. *Recreation News Supplement 4.* Countryside Commission, (1971)

115. ROYAL INSTITUTION OF CHARTERED SURVEYORS. *Memorandum of Evidence to National Parks Policies Committee,* (1972)

116. ELVASTON ESTATE JOINT MANAGEMENT COMMITTEE. *Elvaston Castle Country Park 1969–71,* (1971)

117. SELLORS, M. R. (1972). *Disused Railways in Lindsey,* Lindsey County Council

118. COUNTRYSIDE COMMISSION. *Schemes for the Recreational Use of Disused Railways,* (1970)

119. DEPARTMENT OF THE ENVIRONMENT. Press notice 357, *Reorganisation of Sports Council,* (1971)

120. DEPARTMENT OF THE ENVIRONMENT. Press notice 375, *Major Objectives for New Sports Council,* (1971)

121. FORSTER, R. Case Studies in Recreational Traffic Management. *Proceedings of Conference on Outdoor Recreation,* Department of Surveying, Trent Polytechnic, (1972)

122. WALDEN, R. G. The redevelopment of disused railways in East Anglia. Private Communication. Department of Surveying, Trent Polytechnic, Nottingham, (1973)

123. GARTON, K. The Development of Elvaston Castle Country Park. *Proceedings of Conference on Outdoor Recreation*, Department of Surveying, Trent Polytechnic, (1972)

124. PHILLIPS, A. A. C. British Outdoor Recreation Policies. *Proceedings of Conference on Outdoor Recreation*, Department of Surveying, Trent Polytechnic, (1972)

6 PARKS AND GARDENS

THIS CHAPTER IS sub-divided into three sections concerned with public parks, children's playgrounds, and allotment gardens.

SECTION 1: PUBLIC PARKS

This first section explores the types, functions and standards of provision of public parks in urban areas. Methods of undertaking user surveys of public parks are examined, and the findings of Nottingham park surveys are compared with the results of park user studies undertaken in other parts of the country. Finally the needs of park visitors are critically examined.

Park Types

Town parks can be classified in three ways:

(1) By the type of visitor for whom they cater, such as parks for adults and families with sufficient facilities to meet a wide range of tastes, and rest gardens for elderly visitors providing for quiet relaxation in pleasant surroundings. Some of the larger parks provide a wide range of facilities catering for both active and passive pursuits.

(2) By the location of the facility, such as large parks providing facilities for visitors from the entire city or even a region, to neighbourhood, district or local parks which are designed to cater for the needs of people in a certain residential neighbourhood. The latter type of facility is particularly relevant to areas of high density residential development.

(3) By the form or arrangement of the park, such as intensively cultivated parks comprising floral displays and ornamental gardens, to areas of 'natural' mown grassland and trees.

The Greater London Council[1] conducted surveys of the use of London parks and suggested a hierarchial structure of park provision which takes account of both types of visitor and desirable locations:

(1) Local parks to cater for young children and very old people situated within 0.2–0.4 km of every home and with a minimum area of 2 ha.

(2) Parks with an area of not less than 20 ha and situated within 1.2–1.6 km of every home. This type of park would cater for the more specialised needs of weekend users, more infrequent visitors, sports activities and family visits.

(3) Parks of at least 60 ha in size and catering for the more specialised needs of persons living up to 8 km distant from the park.

Taylor[2] has described how recreation can take place in all parks, but not all recreation *need* take place in parks as, for instance, team games on separate playing fields. In Victorian times the function of a town park was to provide facilities for rest, relaxation and association with natural beauty and it normally incorporated attractively landscaped areas often enclosed within wrought iron railings. Later parks often devoted some space to accommodating organised games. Jellicoe[3] in his analysis of London parks aptly describes how they bring the best of the English countryside of trees and grass and peaceful lakes to the doorstep of the Londoner.

Butler[4] sees the American large town park as the means of giving the city dweller the opportunity to get away from the noise and the rush of traffic and to enjoy contact with nature. He also saw as a primary function the provision of a pleasant environment for engaging in a variety of recreational activities, and considered that the desired park effect can seldom be achieved on less than 40 ha. Butler advocated that a large part of these parks should be woodland, open lawn meadows and glen but with provision for picnic areas and boating and such facilities as day camps, zoological gardens, botanical gardens and nature museums.

Butler[4] holds the view that neighbourhood parks should be landscaped with trees, shrubs and grass as places for quiet, informal recreation but often with facilities for younger children. He views their primary function as a breathing spot in a business district or congested residential neighbourhood or as a setting for a civic centre, and suggests a size range of 1–20 ha. Liverpool Corporation's Planning Officer[5] considered that local parks require space for flowers; grass for casual games; corners for quietness or for watching others; with, possibly, facilities like tennis courts and bowling greens; and containing a minimum area of 4 ha.

STANDARDS OF PARK PROVISION

In Britain the usual recommendation for park provision is a minimum of 0.4 ha per 1000 population, based on the National Playing Fields Association's suggestions. The demand for this type of open space will vary with the size and character of the town. The South Hampshire Plan[6] refers to the almost complete lack of research on the land needs for town parks, and concludes that 0.4 ha per 1000 population is the lowest level of provision adequate to meet people's general recreation needs. Studies in Lancashire[7] revealed that larger towns had higher levels of provision than small towns, possibly stemming from the relative ease of access to the countryside and smaller funds available in the case of the small towns. Lancashire County Council suggested the following range of provision as a result of the surveys made of existing facilities in the country.

Town population	Area of parks and gardens per 1000 population in ha
10 000	0.70
50 000	0.85
100 000	0.90
250 000	1.00
500 000	1.10
1 000 000	1.15

Butler[8] in his investigation of the recreation space needs of American cities has shown how varying local conditions, topography, climate, population density, available funds and other factors influence the amount and types of recreation space that are required or that are possible of attainment in a particular city or neighbourhood. Standards, he postulates, are designed to indicate a norm or a point of departure; as such they afford a basis for the intelligent development of local plans. Standards also need to be reviewed and appraised from time to time and to be modified whenever changing conditions make revisions necessary.

USER SURVEYS OF PARKS

On-site user surveys were organised by the author in five Nottingham parks in the summer of 1968 with the main objectives of determining the numbers and types of visitor, and use patterns and catchment areas of the selected parks. The five selected parks, which varied from 9 to 210 ha in area, gave a good range of park types as well as having a good geographical spread.

After consultation with the local education authority, it was arranged for fifteen lower VI city grammar school children to help with the surveys. The interested pupils attended a briefing meeting, following which a tentative programme was prepared. Consent forms were signed by the pupils' parents or guardians and each helper was supplied with an authorisation letter and a survey team identification disc and received 75p per day for their services. The survey period extended from 11.00 a.m. to 7.00 p.m. for 3 separate days at each park, and included at least one

Saturday or Sunday in each case.

In the surveys, the author and the helpers distributed questionnaires of the type shown in appendix 1 and assisted in the completion of the questionnaires where necessary. Assistance of this kind was generally needed with children under the age of 11, elderly people and foreign visitors. A letter attached to the questionnaire explained the purpose of the survey. In addition a record was kept of the weather, and of the approximate numbers of people and cars at half-hourly intervals throughout the survey period.

By way of contrast, Burton[9] in his survey of Windsor Great Park had the services of sixteen graduate students from Wye and Imperial colleges and the survey period was from 12 noon to 6.00 p.m. on two successive Sundays in June, 1966. In the surveys of London parks undertaken by the Greater London Council,[1] 150 interviews were allocated to each of the majority of selected parks, with equal numbers of interviews carried out on the Tuesday, Thursday, Saturday and Sunday of the survey week in July, 1964, between the hours of 12 noon and 6.30 p.m. Interviews were carried out at park gates at pre-determined intervals, with the first person entering or leaving the park, excluding children under 15 years of age.

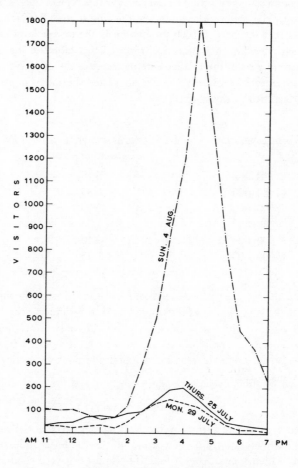

Figure 6.1   Visitors to Highfields Park, Nottingham

TRAVEL AND VISITING CHARACTERISTICS OF PARK VISITORS

Numbers of Visitors

The numbers of visitors to an outdoor recreational facility are influenced by a variety of factors, of which the most important are the weather conditions and the day of the week. Peak attendances occur on warm, sunny Sundays

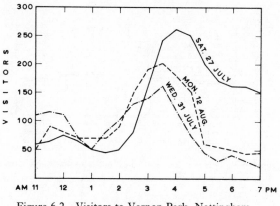

Figure 6.2   Visitors to Vernon Park, Nottingham

during the summer months. Figures 6.1 and 6.2 show the approximate numbers of visitors to two Nottingham parks (one large and one small) during the survey periods in 1968. In all cases the peak attendance of the day occurred at around 4.00 p.m. and the favourite day for family outings was Sunday. A survey of open spaces in Hampshire[11] also showed a peak visiting period around 4.00–4.30 p.m. Five times as many visitors were attracted to Wollaton Park, Nottingham, on a moderately fine Sunday as on a weekday with ideal weather conditions.

Mode of Travel

The mode of travel to an urban park is influenced considerably by the location and nature of the park. The smaller parks, possessing a rather restricted range of facilities and with quite extensive residential areas in close proximity to the park, receive a high proportion of visitors on foot. Thirty-five to seventy-six per cent of the visitors to the smaller Nottingham parks walked to them, whereas with the larger and better equipped parks it dropped to a range of ten to twenty-six per cent. In direct contrast, the proportion of visitors travelling by car or motor cycle to the larger parks ranged from fifty to seventy-five per cent compared with six to fifty-seven per cent to the smaller parks. The higher percentages in both cases occurred on Sundays with family expeditions.

The larger parks also attracted much higher proportions of visitors by bus (seven to twenty-two per cent) and on one weekday twelve per cent of the visitors to Wollaton Park, Nottingham, travelled by coach on trips arranged by schools. The proportions of visitors travelling by bicycle varied considerably within a range of from one to fifteen per cent and there was no significant difference between the larger and smaller parks. It is interesting to note that practically all visitors classified as employers, self-employed persons, managers or foremen travelled to the parks by car.

By way of comparison the Government Social Survey[10] found that approximately sixty-five per cent of visitors to all forms of urban open space walked to the facilities and about twenty-two per cent travelled by car. A survey of London parks[1] indicated that seventy-eight per cent travelled on foot, eleven per cent by bus, eight per cent by car and the remaining three per cent by tube, cycle, train and other forms of transport. At the other extreme Burton's survey of Windsor Great Park[9] revealed that an overwhelming proportion of visiting parties to the park travelled by car (ninety-three to ninety-four per cent).

Extent to which Children are Accompanied by Parents

In the larger and more remotely sited parks a higher proportion of children were accompanied by parents, generally about twenty-five to forty per cent. With the smaller parks, situated in much closer proximity to residential areas, the proportion of accompanied children dropped to about ten to twenty per cent.

Distance Travelled to Parks

Figures 6.3, 6.4 and 6.5 show in the form of histograms the distance travelled by visitors to three of the selected Nottingham parks during the survey days. The smaller parks have a predominance of visitors from the immediate

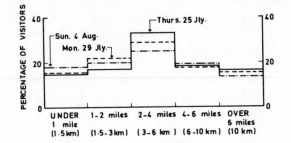

Figure 6.3   Distance travelled to Highfields Park, Nottingham

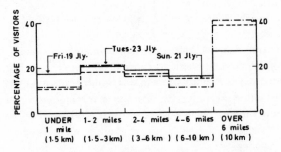

Figure 6.4   Distance travelled to Wollaton Park, Nottingham

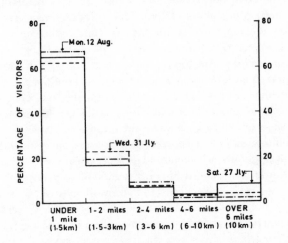

Figure 6.5   Distance travelled to Vernon Park, Nottingham

vicinity of the park (within 1.5 km), whereas the larger Highfields Park draws similar proportions of visitors from each of the five distance groupings, but with a ten per cent rise in the intermediate category (3–6 km). On 2 of the 3 survey days the very popular Wollaton Park attracted about forty per cent of its visitors from localities in excess of 10 km from the park.

The survey of London parks[1] also showed that people were prepared to travel greater distances to larger parks accommodating a larger range of facilities. In the London study it was found that sixty per cent of the visitors to parks of less than 1 hectare in area travelled less than 0.4 km and eighty-four per cent less than 1.6 km. Whereas with large parks in excess of 20 ha, the proportion of visitors travelling less than 0.4 km dropped to thirty per cent and the proportion journeying less than 1.6 km was about sixty per cent, indicating that people in the London area generally travel much shorter distances to urban parks than people in the Nottingham area. In direct contrast, Burton's investigations of Windsor Great Park[9] indicated that over sixty per cent of visitors to the park on a typical summer Sunday travelled over 16 km. The Government Social Survey on Planning for Leisure[10] analysed travel to public open spaces by time according to type of transport, average figures being: foot—10 mins; car—18 mins; public transport—24 mins.

FREQUENCY OF PARK VISITS AND LENGTH OF STAY

Frequency of Visits

People visit the smaller Nottingham parks far more frequently in both summer and winter than the larger parks (in summer the proportion of persons visiting the smaller parks more than twenty times per month is in the range of twenty-four to forty-six per cent). Another noticeable characteristic is that the proportion of persons visiting at the high frequency rate is halved during the winter months, and this is confirmed by Masser's findings in the Birmingham area.[14] With the larger parks thirty-three to fifty per cent of the visitors do not visit the park more than once a month in the summer and this proportion is increased to between sixty and seventy per cent in the winter. Of the parkgoers interviewed, sixteen per cent visited Nottingham parks on not more than one occasion per month in the summer, whereas thirty per cent visited parks more than twenty times per month during this time of the year. In winter the position was almost reversed with thirty-seven per cent visiting not more than once a month and fifteen per cent visiting more than twenty times per month. Men tend to visit parks more frequently than women and the frequency of visits is in direct proportion to distance travelled, with a large reduction in visiting frequency once the distance exceeds 1.5 km. The Government Social Survey[10] also showed that increases in travelling time result in a reduction in visiting frequency. The Greater London Council Survey[1] limited its investigation of the frequency of visiting patterns to information about the previous last visit to the park.

Length of Stay

In all types of park a considerable proportion of visitors stayed from 1 to 2 hours at the park. In the smaller parks the proportion of visitors in this category was generally in the order of forty to sixty per cent increasing to fifty to sixty per cent in the larger parks. The proportion of short-term visitors staying less than an hour does not often exceed fifteen per cent: at the other extreme, all-day visitors rarely exceed ten per cent of all visitors.

By comparison, in the Hampshire County Council survey of open spaces,[11] sixty-three per cent of the visitors to Old Winchester Hill interviewed and forty-one per cent of the visitors to Abbotstone Down interviewed, stayed less than 1 hour. In contrast to urban open spaces, the majority of the visitors travelled about 15 km to the open space although there are no special facilities provided at the sites. Both of these factors would tend to reduce a visitor's period of stay. In Burton's survey of Windsor Great Park[9] about eighteen per cent stayed less than 1 hour and about sixty per cent stayed for a few hours, showing a greater similarity with the Nottingham findings.

ACTIVITIES PERFORMED BY VISITORS TO NOTTINGHAM PARKS

With the larger parks the most popular pastime is strolling, whilst in the smaller parks the playing of games (pitch and putt, cricket and bowls and children's ball games) are rather more popular than strolling. Half the visitors to the larger Nottingham parks were interested in the trees and flower displays, whilst fifteen to twenty-two per cent of the visitors to neighbourhood parks exercised their dogs in the parks. The 210 hectare Wollaton Park was by far the most popular park for picnicking purposes and thirty-three per cent of the people interviewed were taking a picnic. Playing games and sitting in the open were both popular pursuits and visitors who sat inside cars parked in the open space never exceeded fifteen per cent. The majority of children use playground equipment wherever it is provided.

It was also found that only a very small proportion of persons over the age of 35 play games, and that the popularity of strolling and interest in the general scenery tends to increase with age. These latter findings are also supported in the survey of London parks[1] and the Government Social Survey.[10] In the Lincolnshire countryside recreational

129

survey[12] it was found that on the Lincolnshire Wolds active recreation (strolling and playing games) formed only twenty-five per cent of the total number of recreational activities recorded, whereas passive recreation (sitting in the car, or in the open or picnicking) was far more popular. In the Forestry Commission survey of the use of national forests,[13] the most popular activity was pleasure driving, followed by walking and picnicking.

FACILITIES VISITORS WOULD LIKE PROVIDED IN PARKS

The greatest demand from visitors to Nottingham parks is for children's playgrounds (formal and adventure types), paddling pools, tennis courts, pitch and putt courses, boating facilities, better seating provision, more shelters and cafés, and pets' corners. Floral displays and increased provision of grassed areas for play received surprisingly little support.

In the London parks survey[1] the greatest demand was for ample provision of general scenery, followed by space and facilities for children; more seating; sports facilities, especially swimming and tennis; and refreshment facilities. The Government Social Survey[10] found that on a national scale there was an evident need for more and improved public lavatories and children's facilities.

SOCIO-ECONOMIC AND OTHER CHARACTERISTICS OF PARK VISITORS

On weekdays in the summer, children and students accounted for just over fifty per cent of all visitors and this dropped to an average of thirty-two per cent on Saturdays and Sundays, when most adults were free from work. On weekdays in the smaller parks, children under 11 years of age accounted for twenty to thirty per cent of all visitors. At the other end of the age range, retired persons comprised between two and nine per cent of all visitors and so constituted a rather smaller group than might have been expected. Employees accounted for almost forty per cent of all visitors at summer weekends. The supervisory and executive categories of employer, self-employed, manager and foreman collectively never account for more than 4.5 per cent of all visitors and are usually well below this percentage.

Children in the 11–14 years age range visit the parks in considerable numbers on weekdays in the summer holidays (fifteen to thirty-six per cent of all visitors), while the 15–19 years age range shows a wider variation in the proportion of total visitors (eight to thirty per cent) and the sharp distinction between numbers visiting on weekdays and at weekends is no longer apparent. As a general rule the proportion of visitors in the 20–54 years age range is higher at weekends than during the week.

On all survey days there was a predominance of men completing the questionnaires which might be interpreted as indicating that more men visit parks than women. The higher figures for male visitors may be influenced to some extent by the greater reluctance of wives to complete questionnaires in the presence of their husbands. In the majority of cases single visitors far outnumber married ones but the relatively high proportion of children must distort the figures.

An attempt was made to determine whether there was any significant relationship between park visits and the absence of home gardens. There is no evidence that persons who have no garden at home visit public parks more frequently than those who have their own gardens. The proportion of people without gardens visiting the small Vernon Park is higher than for other parks, mainly because many of the houses around Vernon Park have no gardens. In general, more people without gardens visit parks on Sundays than on other days of the week.

The Government Social Survey[10] indicated that on a national scale over the age of 15 years, the 23–30 years age group made the most visits to public open spaces, but this is not borne out by the Nottingham surveys. The London parks survey[1] confirmed the Nottingham findings that there is no great divergence between the activities and wishes of persons in the different occupational groupings.

MAIN NEEDS OF PARK USERS

In the surveys of Nottingham parks visitors were asked to comment on the park facilities. The items in the five selected parks receiving the greatest number of mentions were toilet provision, refreshment facilities and children's playground equipment. Considerable concern was expressed at the inadequacy of the toilets, the general lack of washing facilities and the unsatisfactory state in which the toilets were often maintained. This is not an unusual comment as surveys of Chilterns beauty spots,[15] the Government Social Survey,[10] the study of Windsor Great Park[9] and surveys of national forests[13] all emphasised the need for improved toilet facilities. Drainage problems sometimes restrict the locations in which toilets can feasibly be provided, yet it is evident that the public generally is requiring higher standards of provision and hygiene. The increased demand for refreshment facilities in even the smallest parks is a product of rising prosperity and this also features high in the list of items wanted by visitors in other parks throughout the country. The demand for more children's playground equipment is generally aimed at securing a greater variety in provision, by incorporating such features as climbing frames, sandpits, paddling pools and cradle swings.

The next features in order of demand were requests for greater control of dogs, the banning of transistor radios and increased provision of litter receptacles. All these requests are aimed at making the parks pleasant places for general enjoyment and indicate the extent to which the public is becoming increasingly concerned with pollution and noise aspects. The remaining items aim at increasing the public's use and enjoyment of public parks through the provision of more shelters and seats; more facilities for family use; more flower displays in smaller parks; more drinking fountains; better signposting and naming of trees and plants; provision of adventure playgrounds and model boating pools; and greater control of motor cycles, scooters and cycles. All of these suggestions involve additional expenditure in their provision at a time when local authority funds available for recreational facilities are subject to severe restrictions. Shelters and seats are often the subject of severe vandalism, and local authorities may be reluctant to increase their provision for this reason alone.

The surveys of London parks[1] have confirmed the view that the majority of park visitors engage in passive pursuits, with only a minority taking part in activities of a specialised nature such as sport, entertainments or watching birds or animals. Law[1] in her attempt to assess the needs of park visitors, built up seven 'demand groups'—mothers with young children; families with children; children 5–14; young people pre-marriage; sportsmen aged 15–44; men and women aged 35–64; and older people over 64. In considering the requirements of these demand groups, two principal elements emerged, namely the distance which a visitor is prepared or able to travel and the function which a park is called on to fulfil. Each individual has a different series of requirements at different times and each park can fulfil a range of functions, only limited by its physical size and components and defined by the life styles of the community at any one time. In the London study demand curves were drawn for a number of size ranges in which distance travelled represented the 'price' element and the proportion of opportunities taken up represented the 'demand' element. The data used for constructing the curves was drawn from a household interview survey. By the use of this approach the Greater London Council was able to formulate a hierarchy of open spaces based on park size and probable catchment areas as described earlier in the chapter.

Over the past two decades, the public's tastes and activities have developed and changed at an increasing rate. This process must have its effect on the uses to which parks are put and some adaptions are vitally necessary. The former London County Council[16] drew attention to the need for a face lift in many of the London parks; the re-planning of park entrances on contemporary lines; the transplanting of large trees from their 'serried ranks' into more informal groups; and the floodlighting of flower gardens. It suggested the provision of heated and covered swimming pools; artificial skating rinks and ski slopes; simulated rock faces for climbing; enlarged sailing lakes; itinerant zoos and ambitious aviaries; more pony- and horse-riding; model villages; hobby centres; observation towers; camp sites; restaurants; reading rooms; children's nurseries and clinics; and old people's homes on the edge or just within a park. It is evident that we need to liven up our parks and provide many more facilities for old and young alike who possess a variety of interests and needs. Certainly the needs of elderly people in the winter months must not be overlooked and it is at this time of the year that the parks are so grossly under utilised.

Nevertheless, although many of the features listed are needed in our cities, provision for walking, sitting and feeding the ducks is no less important. Nottingham, in common with most other cities, does not possess such an abundance of parkland that it can afford to encroach substantially upon it with buildings. As postulated by Dower,[17] the main emphasis within the parks must still be on a quiet landscape. Many visitors to the Wollaton and Highfields parks in Nottingham admired the natural beauty and avoidance of over commercialisation of these parks, and their comments indicate how vital it is to maintain a satisfactory balance in future park developments. Buildings, facilities for more active pursuits and larger car parking areas may be introduced in moderation, but in many cases it will be necessary to acquire new sites—possibly alongside existing parks in some cases—to accommodate these 'harder' features. Beazley[18] has shown with first-class illustrations how a wide variety of structures can be designed to blend in with natural surroundings.

This section examines the different types and standards of playgrounds; provision of playgrounds in Greater Nottingham; and use patterns, travel characteristics and play needs and preferences of children.

TYPES OF PLAYGROUNDS

The form and layout of a children's playground is influenced considerably by the age of the children for whom it is provided. Furthermore, an examination of playgrounds reveals three different types of facility which will hereafter be described as 'orthodox', 'imaginative orthodox' and 'adventure'.

Play Needs at Different Ages

For every child play is growth, expansion, discovery of the world and of himself. It is the introduction to physical and mental activity and the basis for creative ability and work.[19] Children need space and opportunity for active play outdoors and they also need protection from dust and excessive noise. It has also been stressed that a playground should be relaxing as well as stimulating and that children should have opportunities for resting and daydreaming. Small children, including those of pre-school age, have a right to play in safe and pleasant surroundings.[20]

For children of 2–5 years of age, play space should be provided close to children's homes because of the dangers of straying.[5] The stages of development in these early years are well described in *Play with a Purpose*.[21] At 5–7 years of age children need space to run, jump, skip, climb and engage in imaginative play. Children in the 7–11 years age range often want to engage in some form of physical activity and they require space, equipment and opportunity to meet this need. Larger playgrounds are needed to accommodate a wider range of activities and the children are able to travel greater distances from home.

A marked change in children's interests often occurs at about 11 years of age. They display more physical energy and tend to play in groups or gangs with an increasing need for comradeship.[22] By the late teens the playground activities have been entirely replaced. At Liverpool[5] stress has been laid on the desirability of grouping the facilities to serve the different age ranges on a continuous site to permit easy graduation. This arrangement also produces economies in staffing and maintenance but requires careful planning to prevent one set of activities interfering with another.

Neighbourhood Playgrounds

Butler[23] has postulated the need for neighbourhood playgrounds in America each with an area of 1.5–3 ha, preferably sited near the centre of the neighbourhood and adjacent to a primary school site, to serve the interests and needs of children but also to afford limited recreational opportunities for all people of a residential neighbourhood. In this way the neighbourhood playground can become a centre where the residents of the neighbourhood can find recreation and relaxation with families, neighbours and friends. In direct contrast, in Great Britain, Oldham[24] sees the need for large numbers of toddlers' play areas in residential districts, playparks to serve children of 5–15 years of age primarily in residential areas, and a good distribution of 'kickabout' areas, possibly sited on school playing fields. Butler's neighbourhood playground would appear to be well suited to meet weekend family needs, whilst Oldham's wider provision would cope more effectively with the day-to-day needs of children of all ages.

Orthodox Playgrounds

The earlier children's playgrounds almost invariably contained orthodox equipment and their primary objective was to prevent children having to play in the street. Horizontal bars, swings, slides (preferably constructed on bank slopes), merry-go-rounds and plank swings are popular features, and their space requirements are given elsewhere by the author.[25] Cradle type swings are invaluable when catering for children in the 2–5 age group, although they are sometimes subject to misuse by older children, and ought ideally to be set apart from the equipment provided for older children. Sandpits are also welcomed by the younger children but provision must be made for periodic changing of the sand.

Traditional playgrounds have been the subject of considerable criticism in recent years. The main criticisms have centred around the uninspiring playground arrangements set in a 'sea' of asphalt in which children soon become bored and their natural instincts are thwarted.

Imaginative Orthodox Playgrounds

From the author's investigations described later in this chapter, it seems evident that many children would like livelier and more imaginatively planned playgrounds. Added interest and enjoyment can stem from a varied range of less orthodox features assisted by a well landscaped, undulating site. The National Playing Fields Association[27] has made suggestions for a variety of features of improvised equipment for children's play and many of these features have been incorporated in children's play areas in different parts of the country and are extremely well illustrated in *Design for Play*.[20] The suggested items comprised piles of logs bearing upon one another in a horizontal plane and fixed at intersections; log piles fixed in a more irregular arrangement; climbing net on a timber frame; log cabin; timber clamber pen or stockade; tree butt steps; plank walk supported on two logs; pipe tunnels; irregularly arranged climbing bars; cross pole and tyre swing; grass mounds with stone fort, pole swing and pipe tunnel caves; dwarf walls; climbing tree; tree trunk; climbing blocks; stepping stones; play rocks; mock-up boat; and mock-up engine. Tree trunks up to 1.5 m in diameter and 6–14 m long can be used for clambering over when laid on the ground. They can be propped up at one end on a solid section of oak or elm, or can be supported by a reinforced concrete frame.[32]

The incorporation of novel features is particularly advantageous as these represent aspects of everyday life or

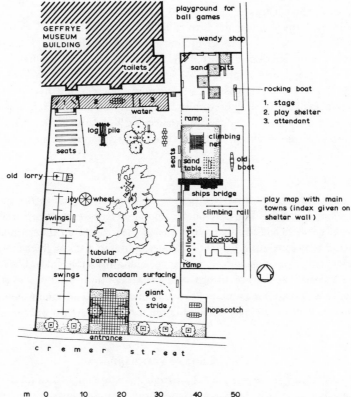

Figure 6.6 Geffrye's Garden Playground, Shoreditch

fiction which are of special interest to children. They offer endless scope for the designer to introduce new and original ideas. Gooch[27] has suggested an imitation harbour or quayside complete with warehouse, bollards and boat tied up alongside. Other suggestions include an old car or bus, a space ship, model planes in which children can sit, a castle or fortress and possibly some form of play sculpture. Play sculptures can be decorative additions and can also provide children with the fun of rock climbing and hiding in caves.[26] In the Heiligfeld playground in Zurich,[28] standard concrete sections are used in the most ingenious ways. Concrete sewer pipes are made into a train, bridging sections into a stepping stone surround and circular tanks into a series of paddling pools at different heights which overflow into one another. Figure 6.6 illustrates a varied arrangement at Shoreditch.

Adventure Playgrounds

Adventure playgrounds differ from orthodox playgrounds in that there is an absence of standard playground equipment and usually the only play facilities are those created by the children themselves out of waste material on the site or arising out of the terrain of the playground itself. Nicholson[29] sees an adventure playground as 'one where most of the site can be used by children for games and work of their own invention; where a variety of tools and materials are provided; and where the children can rely on the backing of a capable and friendly adult'. Lady Allen of Hurtwood[30] would like to see adventure playgrounds offering a rough playground and the opportunity for children to do tough jobs of real work such as building houses; digging and cultivating gardens; keeping pets; making fires; damming streams; building dirt tracks; carving and shaping wood; moulding clay; and digging wells and caverns. Advocates of adventure playgrounds believe that through decision making being in the hands of the users the instinctive adventurous spirit and ingenuity of youngsters can be nurtured towards social awareness, thus reducing boredom and frustration which leads to vandalism.

These suggestions stem from the writings of a Danish landscape architect, C. T. Sörenson, as long ago as 1931 when he mentioned his idea of a 'sort of junk playground in which children could create and shape, dream and imagine, and make dreams and imagination a reality'.[31] Subsequently the Emdrup playground was opened in 1943 in a new housing estate outside Copenhagen during the German occupation. Since 1943 many adventure playgrounds have been provided on the Continent and in America, but their development in Britain has been slow and in 1960 the National Playing Fields Association knew of only thirteen such ventures. Considerable opposition was raised to their provision mainly on the grounds of their unsightly appearance and the dangers from fires and other play activities. The first British adventure playground was provided by a voluntary association at Camberwell in 1948.

Playgrounds for Blocks of Flats

In high density residential developments there is often too little attention paid to the provision of play space for children and outdoor relaxation for adults. The Liverpool Corporation Report on Open Space[5] advocated the provision of carefully designed roof play decks and ventilated lobbies and play rooms on intermediate floors of tall blocks of flats. It was also considered that competing demands for space around flats might necessitate the use of roofs of garages for play space and, with ground moulding, roof space could resemble ground space. In addition balconies could be designed for use by small children by incorporating panels of unbreakable glass at child's eye level, so that he can look out rather than over. Flats on the ground floor could have a small area immediately outside their windows, surrounded by a low fence or wall, where very small children can play together without danger of straying.[34]

PLAYGROUND STANDARDS

The National Playing Fields Association[33] has emphasised the difficulties in attempting to lay down hard and fast standards for playground provision. Many of the existing playgrounds are unattractively designed and fail to draw as many children as perhaps they ought. Table 6.1 incorporates a schedule prepared by the National Playing Fields Association giving suggested minimum space standards related to numbers of children resident in the catchment area, suitably metricated.

TABLE 6.1

SUGGESTED MINIMUM PLAY SPACE STANDARDS

Age groups	Minimum allowance per child m²	Minimum size of playground (excluding landscaping) m²	Maximum number of children served by minimum size of playground	Remarks
2–5 years	3.5	125	37	Little space needed, most games usually of 'let's pretend' variety. Ball games not popular but a proportion of hard surface essential for wheeled toys
5–10 years	8.5	335	40	Attracted by equipment. Chasing, hunting, climbing, acrobatics, and make believe and ball games popular. Provision of a natural undulating grass area with trees most important
9–15 years	12.5	670	53	For various kinds of ball games. Owing to other pursuits the proportion of children using the playground at any one time is likely to be much lower than for the other two groups

Source: National Playing Fields Association, *Playgrounds for Blocks of Flats*[33]

It is useful to compare this standard with that suggested by the National Recreation Association[8, 23] in America. The Association related play space provision to neighbourhood population in the manner indicated below:

Population of neighbourhood	Size of playground needed
3000	1.6 ha
4000	2.0 ha
5000	2.4 ha

This amounts to approximately 0.50 ha per 1000 population and is about 2.5 times greater than the British recommendation of 0.20 ha per 1000 population based on present age structure. The larger space allowances probably stem mainly from the inclusion of playing fields and landscaped areas.

PLAYGROUND PROVISION IN GREATER NOTTINGHAM

The locations of children's playgrounds in Greater Nottingham are shown on figure 6.7 and circles of 400 m radius have been drawn around each playground to indicate the limits of recommended desirable catchment areas. In some cases, however, physical constraints such as the River Trent, heavily trafficked roads and steep gradients prevent the whole circle being effective. In some of the newer housing areas there is a considerable overlap of catchment areas based on the 400 m radius circles, whilst in the older residential areas there is considerable under-provision and in some districts children would have to travel as much as 1300 m to reach a playground.

A comparison of playground provision in the different administrative areas shows some surprising variations, ranging from 854 children (between 2 and 15 years of age) per playground in Carlton urban district to 1745 children per playground in Arnold urban district. These figures can, however, be very misleading owing to the different methods of playground provision by the various authorities and the geographical scatter of the playgrounds. For instance, most of the Nottingham city playgrounds occupy quite small enclosures without large grassed areas for ball games and over fifty per cent of them are on independent sites and do not form part of public parks or recreation grounds. By comparison, all the playgrounds in Beeston and Stapleford form part of recreation grounds and often incorporate considerable areas of grass which are available for ball and other games.

135

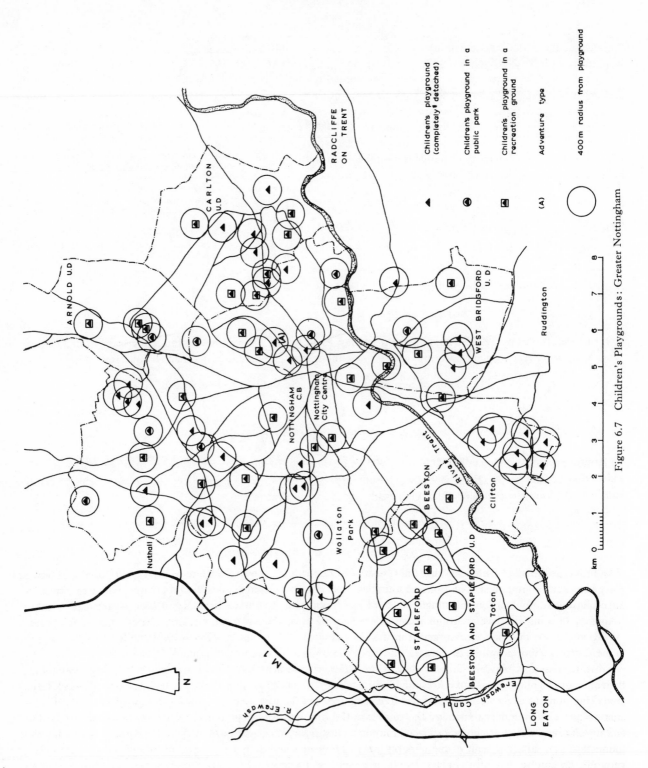

Figure 6.7 Children's Playgrounds: Greater Nottingham

On account of the practical difficulties involved in interviewing children on the playgrounds themselves, arrangements were made with the Nottingham city and Nottinghamshire county education authorities to visit selected schools and interview a ten per cent sample of the pupils, amounting in all to 1082 pupils. The aim was to secure a good cross-section of children in the survey area with all age groups between 5 and 14 years of age uniformly represented. In general, the children in the primary schools were interviewed in groups of ten to twelve pupils and the author completed the questionnaires, whilst the pupils in the secondary schools completed individual questionnaires of the type shown in appendix 2 with the author explaining the purpose of the survey and ensuring common interpretation of the questions. The majority of pupils were quite enthusiastic, particularly when it was explained that they might be able to influence future children's playground provision.

PATTERN OF USE OF NOTTINGHAM PLAYGROUNDS

Table 6.2 shows the use characteristics of Nottingham playgrounds by the children interviewed, sub-divided into three age groupings.

TABLE 6.2

CHILDREN'S PLAYGROUNDS: USER CHARACTERISTICS

Age group	Number of visits per month in summer				Normal length of stay in hours			
	0–5	6–10	11–20	over 20	under 1	1–2	2–3	over 3
5–7 years	33.8	10.3	14.3	41.6	36.4	17.6	42.3	3.7
7–11 years	25.5	9.3	10.9	54.3	28.7	21.9	42.4	7.0
11–14 years	26.4	23.0	17.3	33.3	21.8	42.1	25.6	10.5

Note: all figures are expressed in percentages of children interviewed in each age group

Approximately twenty-five per cent of all the junior and secondary school children interviewed did not visit a children's playground more than once a week in the summer, and the proportion increased to thirty-three per cent with primary school children, mainly because parents or older brothers and sisters were not prepared to take them. The highest proportion of frequent visitors was in the 7–11 years age group where over fifty per cent asserted that they visited playgrounds more than four times a week. This is probably explainable by the fact that the majority of items on playgrounds attract children of this age range and quite a high proportion of these children are able to visit playgrounds unaccompanied. The frequency of visits by children of all ages is surprisingly high and lends support to the Liverpool study[5] contention that fifty per cent of children in a residential area could be playing on children's playgrounds at any one time. The London study[1] also found that children of 13 years of age or over visited parks and open spaces less frequently than younger children. In Nottingham there was no evidence of any relationship between frequency of visits and availability of facilities or class of residential district.

Over forty per cent of children aged from 5 to 11 years considered that they normally spent 2–3 hours on a visit to a children's playground, equivalent to most of a morning, afternoon or evening. With older children the most popular duration of visit was 1–2 hours. Over thirty-three per cent of the infant school children normally stayed less than an hour at a playground and correspondingly smaller proportions of older children paid short visits. The London study[1] found that forty-two per cent of children spent between 1 and 2 hours in parks and open spaces, whereas this study indicates that children visiting playgrounds in Greater Nottingham tend to spend rather longer periods at the facility. Hole and Miller's study of children's play on housing estates,[35] investigating the play activities of 365 children, found that over sixty per cent of the children spent less than 20 minutes at the playground, indicating some wide variations in children's visiting habits. In Greater Nottingham in general it was found that girls tended to be less frequent visitors to children's playgrounds than boys and also stayed for shorter periods.

TRAVEL CHARACTERISTICS—NOTTINGHAM PLAYGROUNDS

Table 6.3 shows the form of travel and proportion of accompanied children related to the three main age groupings.

TABLE 6.3

CHILDREN'S PLAYGROUNDS: METHOD OF TRAVEL

Age group	Usual method of travel to playground			Mostly go alone	Mostly accompanied by older person
	car	cycle	on foot		
5–7 years	19.5	12.1	68.4	39.4	60.6
7–11 years	16.2	12.8	71.0	56.0	44.0
11–14 years	4.0	21.9	74.1	72.0	28.0

Note: all figures are expressed in percentages of children interviewed in each age group

There is a steady decline in the number of children visiting playgrounds with increasing age; whilst the proportions cycling and walking increase. The proportion of children travelling alone to playgrounds increases rapidly with age: about forty per cent in the 5–7 years age range rising to seventy-two per cent of 11–14 year olds. A much higher proportion of boys than girls cycled to playgrounds and this was also borne out in the London survey of open spaces.[1] The London investigations also showed that approximately sixty-six per cent of the children went to parks on foot. The majority of children tended to favour the use of the nearest playground to their homes, although in districts where there was a deficiency of playgrounds children tended to visit several playgrounds on the periphery of the neighbourhood, with older children journeying up to 1.5 km from their homes.

The Council for Children's Welfare[36] study of children's play at playgrounds in Brent, Bristol, Camden, Leicester Liverpool, Newcastle-upon-Tyne, Southampton, Southwark, Stockholm, Swansea and Worcester, showed that there is a higher proportion of boys than girls travelling distances up to 1.5 km to playgrounds. The study also revealed that well over fifty per cent of the children travelled less than 400 m but more than twenty-five per cent exceeded 800 m, and the overall Nottingham pattern would not be too dissimilar. Another interesting finding of the study was that the distance children travelled varied very little with their age. Playgrounds in parks and recreation grounds received more children than independent playgrounds containing similar equipment, largely because the parks and recreation grounds serve larger areas of cities than do playgrounds sited on their own.

TABLE 6.4

CHILDREN'S PLAYGROUNDS: FACTORS PREVENTING MORE FREQUENT USE

Age group	Jobs at home or errands	Need to be accompanied by older people	Dogs on playgrounds	Insufficient equipment on playground	Playground too far from home	Need to cross busy roads	Need to climb steep hills	Rough older children at playground	Parents	Other activities	Looking after younger children
5–7 years	2.9	11.8	2.2	—	1.5	18.7	—	1.5	4.8	2.2	3.3
7–11 years	9.2	6.1	—	5.9	4.5	13.9	2.8	9.4	2.8	2.8	6.6
11–14 years	1.2	—	1.4	3.5	12.2	1.7	—	3.7	1.7	2.0	2.6

Note: all figures are expressed as percentages of children interviewed in each age group

Table 6.4 lists the main factors which have prevented Nottingham children from visiting playgrounds more frequently. The largest single deterrent to attendance at playgrounds by children up to 11 years old is the need to cross busy roads, and this underlines the importance of this aspect in selecting sites. Nearly twelve per cent of the children interviewed in the 5–7 years age group visited playgrounds less than they would wish because they needed older people to take them and the latter were not always available. The proportion was halved in the 7–11 years age group and disappeared altogether with the oldest children. The 7–11 years age group was more adversely affected than other age groups by having to do jobs at home or run errands and looking after younger children, and seemed more worried about rough treatment on the playground sites by older children. This particular age group was also more concerned about the inadequacies of equipment at playgrounds.

CHILDREN'S NEEDS AND PREFERENCES

Table 6.5 indicates some of the children's main preferences in Greater Nottingham.

TABLE 6.5

CHILDREN'S PLAYGROUNDS: MAIN PREFERENCES

| Age group | In favour of play-leaders | In favour of adven-ture play-grounds | Features preferred in usual playgrounds | | | | | | | | | |
			play leaders	equip-ment	playing games	nearest play-ground	adven-ture activities	sand play	water play	meet friends	don't know	no feature in parti-cular
5–7 years	41.5	61.9	4.8	65.4	56.6	56.6	10.3	19.8	1.8	43.0	0.7	2.9
7–11 years	35.7	85.0	2.1	58 2	60.6	43.0	12.0	10.1	4.2	42.1	7.0	2.1
11–14 years	27.6	82.0	6.0	27.4	33.8	21.6	26.4	2.6	9.4	45.5	10.2	15.9

Note: all figures are expressed as percentages of children interviewed in each age group

These investigations indicate that a higher proportion of younger children prefer playleaders to organise their games for them, but as they grow older they tend to want to become more independent and play amongst themselves. Many of the children interviewed had no direct experience of playleaders and the proportions favouring their services would possibly have been higher had all seen them operating at first hand. There is widespread support for adventure playgrounds but the percentages are rather suspect as the majority of children interviewed associated adventure playgrounds with the more imaginatively planned playground at Wollaton Park, Nottingham, and not a junk yard. Nevertheless, the statistics show a strong desire by children for facilities different to the normal standard equipment. The children interviewed were also asked to state the features on their usual playground which they preferred the most. Features such as playleaders, adventure activities and water play received limited support mainly because these facilities were not available on the majority of playgrounds. There is a sharp decline in interest for equipment with the increasing age of children; for instance the playing of games is very popular with 5–11 year olds but its popularity drops considerably with the 11–14 years old group. The younger children place more emphasis on the 'nearest play-ground' and this gives support to the recommended spacing of playgrounds at 800 m in residential areas, with possibly a closer spacing of toddlers' play spaces. Sand play is a popular activity amongst the younger children and the use of the playground as a place for meeting friends is equally popular at all ages. Table 6.6 also assists in defining children's preferences.

These figures show that as a general rule the popularity of standard equipment falls with the increase in age of the children. One noticeable exception was the swings, where the 11–14 years age group displayed very high interest, particularly amongst the girls. A Ministry of Housing and Local Government survey at Paddington found swings and slides to be the most popular items of conventional equipment.[38] It should not, however, be concluded that girls are only interested in passive pursuits, as they also liked tree climbing and wanted more climbing frames. Many of the older girls would like to see netball posts provided and boys wanted more goal posts. The provision of grassed areas for games arouses little interest with the 5–7 years age group but becomes an item of major importance with the older children, contradictory to the findings of the Ministry of Housing and Local Government survey of children's play at Paddington which seemed to indicate that children of all ages favoured provision for ball games.[38] There is a constant and relatively high demand for aerial ropeways, and observations at the playground at Wollaton Park,

139

TABLE 6.6

CHILDREN'S PLAYGROUNDS: FAVOURITE ITEMS OF EQUIPMENT

Favourite item of equipment	Age groups		
	5–7 years	*7–11 years*	*11–14 years*
Merry-go-round	4.5	4.0	3.6
Seesaw	12.4	1.8	1.2
Aerial ropeway	9.4	22.2	16.8
Trampoline	1.5	1.1	0.7
Trees for climbing	3.4	6.8	4.2
Tree house	7.5	6.2	0.6
Climbing frame	4.1	12.6	7.0
Grassed area for games	0.4	5.3	26.0
Ropes	4.1	5.3	4.0
Swings	21.2	13.8	25.4
Slide	22.9	14.8	9.5
Ocean wave	1.5	2.9	1.0
Maypole	—	0.4	—
Logs	—	0.2	—
Plank swing	—	0.4	—
Paddling pool	4.9	0.2	—
Wendy house	—	0.2	—
Maze	—	0.7	—
Concrete tubes	1.5	1.1	—
Boating pool	0.3	—	—
Sandpit	0.4	—	—

Note: all figures are expressed as percentages of children interviewed in each age group

Nottingham confirm their popularity with children of all ages. Similarly, children of all ages like to have climbing facilities and ropes for swinging. The demand for paddling pools and sandpits is confined to the younger children.

Hole[37] investigated the use of equipment on children's playgrounds on twelve housing estates (nine in London and three in provincial cities), and the author recorded the numbers of children playing on the various items of equipment in the Nottingham playgrounds when visiting the sites in the summer of 1967. It should however be borne in mind that Hole's use investigations proceeded over a longer period than those of the author, and this could in part account for the consistently higher Nottingham figures. Furthermore, the Nottingham figures were also inflated by the introduction of playleaders on to some of the playgrounds, in 1967, which attracted large attendances. Table 6.7 tabulates the two sets of findings.

TABLE 6.7

CHILDREN'S PLAYGROUNDS: INTENSITY OF USE OF EQUIPMENT

Item of equipment	*Average number of children using equipment as recorded by Hole[37]*	*Average number of children using equipment in Nottingham playgrounds (summer 1967)*
Slide	2.3	3.5
Climbing frame	2.7	4.2
Sandpit	4.7	5.2
Merry-go-round	2.9	4.5
Seesaw	2.3	2.5
Ocean wave	3.4	6.2
Concrete tubes	2.5	2.0
Swings	60% utilisation	62% utilisation

Hole[37] confirms the author's findings in that up to fifty per cent of the children on a playground at any particular point in time are not using the equipment but are sitting, chatting and reading comics. Hole's observations also showed that swings, slides, climbing frames and sandpits tend to obtain a relatively high rate of utilisation. Analysis of the data collected by the Council for Children's Welfare indicated that swings, climbing frames and tunnels were significantly popular with children. Best attendance/cost ratios were obtained on sites where there was neither a playleader nor an attendant, but where there was instead an abundance of equipment.

SECTION 3: ALLOTMENT GARDENS

The author believes that gardening is an important form of outdoor recreation despite the declining interest in allotment gardening. The final section of this chapter sets out to trace the historical background to allotment provision; to examine allotment standards and methods of provision; to investigate in some depth the use of allotments in Nottingham; and finally, in the context of the report of the Departmental Committee of Inquiry into Allotments,[39] to consider possible future trends. Garner[40] traces the origins of allotments to the enclosure movement and refers particularly to numerous private Acts of Parliament in the seventeenth and eighteenth centuries. These acts allocated small parcels of land to individuals in compensation for rights to graze a cow or a few geese on the former common field of the village or township. Some local enclosure acts created 'fuel allotments' and 'field garden allotments' for the benefit of the poor of the parish.

By the nineteenth century the provision of allotments as a form of poor relief had become well established, although both Garner[40] and Nelmes[41] have emphasised that allotments at that time were essentially a feature of the countryside, of the village or small town. In 1834, the Poor Law Commissioners reported:

The day is not long past, since in every industrious cottage family the wheel and the distaff, the shuttle and knitting needles, were in full activity. At present, to compete with machinery, would be a useless waste of time, money and labour. We must however see if the hours formerly devoted to manufacture may not be profitably applied, and habits of industry created. We cannot suggest any mode of doing so more profitable to the agricultural labourer and his family than the cultivation of exactly that quantity of land which will occupy these hours as well as his own spare time. This quantity is calculated to be the 1/16 part of an acre, or ten lug or rods to each individual capable of work.

The Poor Relief Act, 1819, empowered churchwardens and overseers of the poor to provide land for the employment of poor persons at reasonable wages and also to let it to poor persons for cultivation at reasonable rates.

The Small Holdings and Allotments Act, 1908, repeated the duty of allotment authorities to provide allotments for the labouring population, where a need had been established. A considerable improvement was secured by the Allotments Act, 1922, when tenants of allotment gardens received some measure of security and compensation rights on termination of a tenancy. Further improvements in security and compensation rights, albeit insufficient, became operative with the passing of the Allotments Act, 1950.

An examination of the historical development of allotment gardening shows the prime motivating force to be economic and certainly not recreational. The nineteenth century labourer's main concern was to produce as much food as he could for his family and in doing so he increased his self-respect. These factors remained relevant throughout the early part of the present century, although during the two world wars, a new incentive of patriotism was introduced. Allotments made a valuable contribution to the nation's food supply in both wars; and in 1941 the Ministry of Agriculture assessed the total annual production from allotments at over 1.3 million tonnes,[42] following the Minister's appeal for half a million more allotments and his launching of the Dig for Victory campaign.

An allotment garden is defined in the Allotments Act, 1922, as 'an allotment not exceeding 40 poles (1012 m²) in extent which is wholly or mainly cultivated by the occupier for the production of vegetable or fruit crops for consumption by himself or his family'. The upper limit of area is four times that of the customary 10 rod plot. This definition appears to preclude the right of the occupier to sell produce from an allotment garden. The town allotment is not precisely defined in the Allotments Acts.[40]

The National Allotments and Gardens Society is the only organisation which claims to represent the allotments movement nationally in England and Wales. The great majority of its members are acquired by the affiliation of numerous local allotments associations and the membership was around 170 000 in 1970. Its main objects are stated to be 'securing the co-operative organisation of allotment, cottage garden, village produce, horticultural, small livestock and social welfare societies; the securing of improved legislation and the promotion of education'.[43]

METHOD AND STANDARD OF PROVISION OF ALLOTMENTS

Allotments may be provided by private landlords or trustees, who rent plots of land direct to tenants; allotment associations, who either own land themselves or rent it and sub-let it as allotments to individuals; and local authorities.

The local authorities with allotment responsibilities up to April 1974 were borough, urban district and parish councils, and district and parish councils thereafter. As a general rule rural district councils had no allotment functions, whilst county councils had default powers under section 24 of the Allotments Act, 1908. Allotment authorities have the power to take a lease of, or to purchase land for, allotments, either by agreement or compulsorily. County councils were empowered to make compulsory purchase orders on behalf of parish councils. An allotment authority may provide and maintain fences, roads and drains, and may also provide amenities in the form of water supplies, tool sheds on individual plots, and communal store sheds, which they may let to an allotments association. On the financial side, an allotment authority may spend on its allotments a sum not exceeding the product of a twopenny (83p) rate. However the Committee of Inquiry's investigation of allotment expenditure in 1965–66 of twelve towns of varying size revealed that the average rate expenditure was 6p and the highest did not exceed 17p.[39]

As quoted in the Committee of Inquiry's report[39] three classes of allotment land have become widely accepted, although not specified in legislation:

(i) Land of which the freehold was vested in the allotments authority, and which had either been originally purchased for allotments or had subsequently been appropriated to allotment use, became known as *statutory* allotment land.

(ii) Land which was either rented by the allotments authority on lease or tenancy, or, being owned by the authority, was destined ultimately for some other use, became known as *temporary* allotment land.

(iii) Land which was neither owned nor administered by the allotments authority in whose area it was situated, became known as *private* allotment land.

The National Allotments and Gardens Society in its evidence submitted to the Committee of Inquiry[44] stressed that private owners of allotment land are becoming increasingly conscious of high land values, particularly where planning permission for residential development is obtainable, and thus private allotments might not offer occupiers much in the way of security of tenure. The view has also been expressed that statutory allotments were only permanent if they were fully tenanted and there was no pressure for other civic needs.[41] Yet, security of tenure is of vital importance to an allotment holder who has spent considerable sums of money on manures, fertilisers and in other ways.[44]

The author[46] once stated:

One of the main obstacles to the taking of an allotment plot is insecurity. Transfer to another plot is not a satisfactory solution even though it be offered rent free for a period. Apart from the physical problem of breaking in a new plot a Nottingham gardener held the view that it would take at least five years to appreciate the natural deficiencies of the soil and the type of crops that would grow successfully. Compensation is nearly always unsatisfactory; the removal of sheds, greenhouses, etc. is a major problem for the plotholder but rarely is it considered important to the owner of the site.

In the past, standards for the provision of allotments have been expressed in acres or hectares per 1000 population. For instance, the National Allotments Society has advocated provision of 0.8 ha per 1000 population. This approach can at best be only a very rough guide and some regard should be paid to the size of allotment plots and the varying needs in different areas. The Committee of Inquiry[39] found that in the twenty largest towns in England and Wales, excluding London, average allotment provision fell from 0.6 ha per 1000 population in 1952 to 0.4 ha per 1000 population in 1967.

TRENDS IN ALLOTMENT USAGE

Thorpe[45] stated that over the 10 year period prior to 1969 the number of allotments in England and Wales fell at the rate of nine per cent each year and that there is no sign of this slackening off over the country as a whole. There were in 1969 some 600 000 plots of all classes (local authority, private and railway) occupying approximately 25 000 ha. Furthermore about twenty per cent of the remaining plots are unoccupied at a time when land is a scarce commodity. Table 6.8 indicates the extent of the decline in allotment provision between 1950 and 1967, and shows that it has gathered momentum in the latter part of the period, particularly in the private sector.

TABLE 6.8

PERCENTAGE DECLINE IN NUMBERS AND AREA OF ALLOTMENTS, 1950–67: ENGLAND AND WALES

| Period | *Number of plots* | | | | *Area of plots* | | | |
	Local authority	Private	Railway	*All*	Local authority	Private	Railway	*All*
1950–60	22.6	23.8	28.4	23.3	18.7	21.3	25.9	19.8
1960–67	21.6	49.0	50.4	31.0	17.9	30.4	47.7	23.1
1950–67	39.3	61.1	64.5	47.1	33.3	45.2	61.3	38.3

Source: Departmental Committee of Inquiry Report into Allotments, Cmnd. 4166

PROVISION OF ALLOTMENTS IN GREATER NOTTINGHAM

In Nottingham there were, during the seventeenth and eighteenth centuries, several areas of gardens detached from houses, which are shown on detailed plans of the city dating from 1740.[39] By 1844, Nottingham possessed many allotment gardens and these were later augmented as a result of the Enclosures and became a feature and tradition of the city.[48]

Hudson and Edwards[49] have given an interesting account of the origins of rose culture and allotment gardening in Nottingham.

It was in the district called Hunger Hill to the north-east of the city that Nottingham's rose culture originated just over a century ago. At that time rose-growing was a favourite spare-time pursuit of 'stockingers' (hosiery workers) and other artisans. Hunger Hill, then just outside the town, became especially noted for its little rose gardens and in the early 'sixties some cultivators started to grow them under glass and soon earned fame in many parts of the country for their early and elegant blooms. In April 1859 what may be claimed as the first rose show in England was held in an inn near Hunger Hill by a group of 'stockingers'. Dean Hole, whose early home was at Caunton Manor, near Newark, was invited to this exhibition and, greatly impressed, insisted on seeing the gardens. In his famous work, 'A book about roses', he wrote of Hunger Hill: 'These are tiny allotments on sunny slopes just out of the town, separated by hedges and boards, in size about three to the rod, such an extent as a country squire in Lilliput might be expected to devote to horticulture'. The exhibition, known as 'St. Ann's Rose Show', named from that part of the town, became an annual event and did much to stimulate the development of rose culture in the surrounding area.

Large numbers of allotments were acquired under the various Enclosure Acts and were classified by Nottingham Corporation as 'statutory allotments' up to 1964, then as 'permanent allotments' and in 1969 the classification was changed again, this time to 'temporary allotments', indicating that Nottingham allotment holders now have little security of tenure. The total area of all classes of allotment dropped from 360 ha in 1949 to about 230 ha in 1969, a decrease of thirty-six per cent.[50] In 1969, Nottingham Corporation owned 4805 allotment plots of which 987 (20.5 per cent) were vacant. At the same time there were seventy-two persons on a waiting list, being people who resided in areas where there were either no vacancies or no allotments. The distribution of both public and private allotments throughout Greater Nottingham is illustrated in figure 6.8.

The ratios of allotment plots to population in the various administrative areas in Greater Nottingham are listed in table 6.9. The proportion of allotment plots vacant ranged between 16.3 and 20.6 per cent in the five local authority areas and was remarkably consistent.

In 1969 the author sent questionnaires to 100 allotment holders on each of four Nottingham city sites and to fifty occupiers of each of four sites in the neighbouring urban districts, to obtain basic information about the working of plots. The form of questionnaire used is shown in appendix 4.

SOCIO-ECONOMIC AND OTHER CHARACTERISTICS OF NOTTINGHAM ALLOTMENT HOLDERS

The majority of the Nottingham city allotment gardeners covered by the survey lived in houses with no gardens, whereas the majority of those occupying plots in the surrounding urban districts lived in houses with small back

143

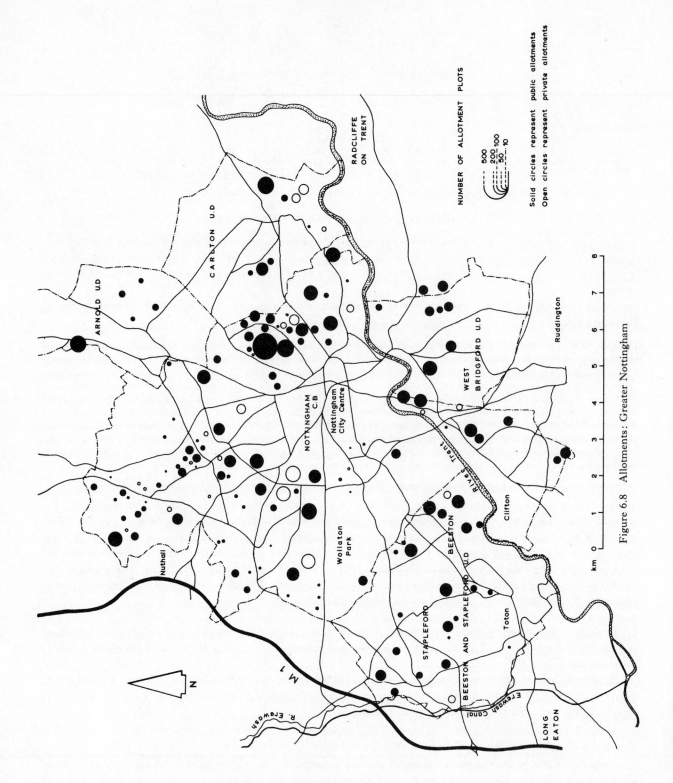

Figure 6.8 Allotments: Greater Nottingham

TABLE 6.9

ALLOTMENT PROVISION IN GREATER NOTTINGHAM (1969)

Local authority	Number of public allotment plots per 1000 population	Number of allotment plots of all categories per 1000 population	Area of public allotment plots per 1000 population (in hectares)	Area of allotment plots of all categories per 1000 population (in hectares)
Nottingham CB	15.9	19.2	0.60	0.75
Arnold UD	6.4	6.4	0.18	0.18
Carlton UD	9.3	12.8	0.31	0.50
Beeston and Stapleford UD	16.0	16.9	0.49	0.52
West Bridgford UD	13.3	13.3	0.62	0.62
Greater Nottingham	14.5	17.1	0.53	0.65

gardens (up to 80 m²). Very few allotment holders had large back gardens (over 320 m²) at their homes. About twenty-five per cent of the city gardeners owned cars compared with about fifty per cent of those in the suburbs, while the evidence submitted by the National Allotments and Gardens Society to the Committee of Inquiry[44] indicated that about twenty per cent of allotment holders nationally owned cars. Contrary to general belief quite a high proportion of allotment gardeners participated in other outdoor recreational activities, for instance sixteen per cent in both swimming and angling, which is all the more surprising when the relatively elderly age structure of plot holders is taken into account.

Over fifty per cent of all allotment holders in Greater Nottingham were manual workers compared with forty-five per cent in the Committee of Inquiry report[39] and over twenty-five per cent were retired persons compared with twenty per cent in the national inquiry. About twenty-five per cent of the allotment gardeners who completed questionnaires from Arnold and West Bridgford were classified as professional or managerial persons. Less than ten per cent of Nottingham allotment holders were under 30 years of age, about seventy per cent were 45 years and over and twenty-five per cent exceeded 65 years of age, indicating a very elderly age structure indeed for this particular activity. These proportions were largely supported by the report of the Committee of Inquiry which showed seventeen per cent under 40 years of age and twenty per cent of 65 years of age or over. A survey of Brent allotment holders[47] showed about twenty per cent under 40 years of age and twenty-eight per cent over 60 years of age.

OPERATIONAL CHARACTERISTICS OF NOTTINGHAM ALLOTMENTS

The prime reason given for allotment gardening was the production of fresh produce; next came love of gardening; the opportunity to secure plenty of fresh air; relaxation; exercise; and, last of all, the 'family retreat'. On the basis of these replies it seems a little doubtful whether the majority of existing allotment holders would favour the Committee of Inquiry's 'leisure garden' concept.

It is worthy of note that about twenty-five per cent of the city plotholders taking part in the survey were prepared to travel in excess of 1.60 km to plots, and sixty per cent of the city plotholders and fifty per cent of those in the suburbs were prepared to travel further than the limit of 0.8 km suggested by the National Allotments and Gardens Society. In a survey of allotments in the London Borough of Brent,[47] it was found that forty per cent of allotment gardeners travelled more than 0.8 km to their plots, but the report points out that the majority do so because there is no other site nearer to them: motivation by necessity rather than choice.

Nottingham allotment gardeners receive a substantial amount of help from their wives on their plots, and to a considerably lesser extent from children and other relatives. Under ten per cent of allotment holders took over allotments from relatives or shared their allotments with other persons. On six sites out of eight, over seventy-five per cent of the allotment holders taking part in the survey belonged to a local allotment association. It is evident that many allotment holders pursue this activity over long periods of time, as half of those completing questionnaires in Nottingham had occupied their plots for 10–20 years and thirty-three per cent had occupied them for over 20 years.

The visiting patterns of the allotment holders on the different sites are similar, except for the Arnold site where the much reduced frequency of visits stems from its rather remote location in relation to residential areas. Nearly sixty-six per cent of allotment holders visit their plots over twenty times a month in the summer but this reduces to about five times a month in the winter. Very few allotment gardeners visit their plots less than twice a week in the summer but in the winter about twenty-five per cent visit once a week at most. The report of the Committee of Inquiry[39] found that the average allotment holder in England and Wales visited his plot five times per week in the summer, four times in autumn and spring and once in the winter. The most popular length of stay on the plot is 2–3 hours and this is confirmed in the report of the Committee of Inquiry.[39]

The majority of allotment holders had erected garden sheds on their sites, and a high proportion of the enclosed city plots (but comparatively few of the open suburban plots) contained greenhouses. The majority of allotment holders with enclosed plots grew soft fruit and flowers and about half of those occupying open plots, showing that the popular idea of allotment holders growing only cabbages and turnips is not borne out by the facts. The size of allotments varied considerably but the majority came within the range of 250–500 m², whilst on a national scale about fifty per cent of allotment plots were 200–300 m² in area.[39]

ALLOTMENT HOLDERS' COSTS AND RETURNS

The Committee of Inquiry[39] found that the majority of urban allotment holders pay less than 75p for a plot of about 250 m² and the Committee considered this level of payment to be unrealistic. The average rent on the Nottingham city plots was £2.56 but this covered a larger than normal plot with a number of amenities, and was further complicated by reason of the fact that old aged pensioners paid a reduced rent. The average rent on the suburban plots was about £1. The average annual cost of seeds, fertilisers, manures, and other outlays was calculated at £7.50 and the average annual value of produce (based on shop prices) was estimated at £33. A survey undertaken by the National Allotments and Gardens Society in 1965 attracted 1000 returns which showed that the average annual value of crops from a 250 m² plot was £42.90.

MAIN PROBLEMS AND NEEDS

One-half of the allotment holders who completed questionnaires complained of vandalism. In some cases the damage had been very extensive with sheds destroyed or damaged; glass to greenhouses smashed; tools stolen; and crops pulled up or trampled; and one plotholder described how his shed had been forced open on four occasions in 9 months. Furthermore, the incidence of trespass and damage or theft seems to be increasing and this is causing many gardeners to become despondent. More locked gates to allotment sites could act as a deterrent. The National Allotments and Gardens Society[44] have estimated that fifty-seven per cent of allotment sites are troubled with vandalism. A few allotment gardeners complained of the poor quality of their sites—particularly those which were low lying with liability to flooding and damage from late spring frosts. A frequent complaint concerned the increasing number of uncultivated plots which resulted in the spread of weeds. On sites without a piped water supply, the allotment holders were virtually unanimous in their request for a supply. Insecurity was another major worry to allotment holders. There were also requests for toilet facilities, better access roads and paths, communal huts and availability on hire of rotavators and similar mechanical equipment.[51]

These problems and needs were also revealed in the report by the Committee of Inquiry.[39] The Committee also made some criticisms of the allotment holders themselves with regard to lack of corporate spirit on some sites and the untidy and unattractive appearance of many plots and of the buildings erected on them. Both the Committee of Inquiry[39] and the National Allotments and Gardens Society[44] have referred to the poor relationships which sometimes exist between local authorities and allotment holders and their associations. One common complaint is that local authorities fail to give publicity to vacant plots. Thorpe[45] considers that low rents for plots contribute to the charitable image of allotment gardening, whilst local authorities insist that they cannot provide good amenities from such low income. Thorpe also expressed the view that 'to many local authorities allotment sites are nothing more than an eye-sore and a nuisance and to many planners half-derelict allotment sites in dense urban areas seem a criminal waste of land'.[45]

POSSIBLE FUTURE TRENDS

Increasing leisure time and the need for outlets from the mounting strain of modern life and working conditions could result in a reversal or, at any rate, a slowing down of the present decline in demand for allotments. The National Allotments and Gardens Society has frequently expressed the view that the building of high rise residential accommodation without gardens would inevitably result in increased demand for allotment plots, although there is little evidence of this in Nottingham.

The Committee of Inquiry[39] viewed the present deteriorating situation with some dismay and believed that there is a need to develop a system of better-class gardens. The Committee recommended that allotment gardening should in future be considered primarily as a recreation, and that the Allotments Acts should be repealed and replaced by a Leisure Gardens Act. A leisure garden was defined as 'one of a group of contiguous plots of land, each not exceeding 20 poles in extent and not attached to a rateable dwelling provided by a leisure gardens authority for recreational gardening by the occupier and his family'. Established leisure garden sites should be provided to the extent of 0.20 ha per 1000 population, although both established and non-established gardens could be provided in excess of this standard if there were sufficient demand. Every leisure gardener should be urged to make his plot attractive by incorporating flowers or flowering shrubs at strategic points.

Thorpe[45] sees the need for greater security of tenure for the plotholder, increased capital expenditure by local authorities and a readiness by societies and plotholders to improve the appearance of sites. He also advocated the implementation of new designs for fully landscaped sites incorporating interesting groupings of plots, public walkways, communal areas and imaginative planting schemes, preferably close to other recreational open space. There are excellent examples in Holland, Denmark, Sweden and Western Germany of attractively planned plots with a neat wooden summerhouse, lawn or patio, flowers, ornamental shrubs, fruit trees and discreetly screened areas of vegetables. It remains to be seen, however, whether today's allotment gardeners in Great Britain are prepared to accept these proposals.

REFERENCES

1. GREATER LONDON COUNCIL. *Surveys of the Use of Open Spaces. Vol. 1,* Research paper No. 2, (1968)
2. TAYLOR, G. D. An approach to the inventory of recreational lands. *The Canadian Geographer,* **9.2,** (1965), 84
3. JELLICOE, G. The London park—yesterday, today and tomorrow. *The Architect's Journal,* **148.38,** (1968), 563–571
4. BUTLER, G. B. (1959). *Introduction to Community Recreation,* McGraw-Hill
5. LIVERPOOL CORPORATION. *Report No. 15 of City Planning Officer on 'Open Space',* (1964)
6. SOUTH HAMPSHIRE PLAN ADVISORY COMMITTEE. *South Hampshire Plan: Study Report No. 5: Recreation,* (1969)
7. LANCASHIRE COUNTY COUNCIL. *Preliminary Report: Survey of Existing Facilities for Sport and Physical Recreation,* (1967)
8. BUTLER, G. B. Standards for municipal recreation areas. *Recreation,* New York, (July/August 1948)
9. BURTON, T. L. (1967). *Windsor Great Park: A recreation study,* Wye College, University of London, Department of Economics
10. SILLITOE, K. K. (1969). *Planning for Leisure: Government Social Survey,* H.M.S.O.
11. HAMPSHIRE COUNTY COUNCIL. *The Use of County Open Spaces*
12. LINDSEY COUNTY COUNCIL/UNIVERSITY OF NOTTINGHAM. *Lindsey Countryside Recreational Survey: A Survey of the Public Use of the Lincolnshire Wolds and Adjacent Areas,* (1967)
13. FORESTRY COMMISSION. *Public Recreation in National Forests: A Factual Study,* H.M.S.O., (1968)
14. MASSER, I. The use of outdoor recreational facilities. *Town Planning Review,* **37.1,** (1966), 45
15. CHILTERNS STANDING CONFERENCE. *Recreational Survey, 1968: Public Gathering Points,* (1969)
16. LONDON COUNTY COUNCIL. *Parks for Tomorrow,* (1964)
17. DOWER, M. Fourth wave: The challenge of leisure. *The Architect's Journal,* **141.3,** (1965)
18. BEAZLEY, E. (1969). *Designed for Recreation,* Faber
19. WORLD ORGANISATION FOR EARLY CHILDHOOD EDUCATION. *Space for Play: the Youngest Children,* (1964)
20. LADY ALLEN OF HURTWOOD. (1965). *Design for Play,* The Housing Centre Trust
21. MINISTRY OF HEALTH. (1960). *Play with a Purpose,* H.M.S.O.
22. MINISTRY OF EDUCATION. (1963). *Out of School,* H.M.S.O.
23. BUTLER, G. D. (1960). *Playgrounds: Their Administration and Operation,* Ronald Press, New York
24. OLDHAM, S. A. J. Open air recreation. *Park Administration* **34.3** and **4,** (1969)
25. SEELEY, I. H. (1967). *Municipal Engineering Practice,* Macmillan
26. AARON, D. and WINAWER, B. P. (1965). *Children's Play: A Creative Approach to Play Spaces for Today's Children,* Harper and Row, New York
27. GOOCH, R. B. (1963). *Selection and Layout of Land for Playing Fields and Playgrounds,* National Playing Fields Association
28. ARCHITECT AND BUILDING NEWS. Playground at Heiligfeld, (7 October 1959)
29. NICHOLSON, M. (1964). *Notes on Adventure Playgrounds,* National Playing Fields Association

30. LADY ALLEN OF HURTWOOD. (1965). *Adventure Playgrounds,* National Playing Fields Association
31. BENJAMIN, J. (1966). *In Search of Adventure: A Study in Play Leadership,* National Council of Social Service
32. LADY ALLEN OF HURTWOOD. (1966). *New Playgrounds,* The Housing Centre Trust
33. NATIONAL PLAYING FIELDS ASSOCIATION. *Playgrounds for Blocks of Flats,* (1961)
34. HOUSING CENTRE TRUST. *Two to Five in High Flats,* (1961)
35. HOLE, W. V. and MILLER, A. Children's play on housing estates—a summary of two Building Research Station studies. *Building Research Current Papers Design Series 46,* Building Research Station, (1966)
36. COUNCIL FOR CHILDREN'S WELFARE. *The Playground Study: Preliminary Analysis,* (1966)
37. HOLE, V. *Children's Play on Housing Estates,* National Building Studies, research paper 39. Building Research Station, (1966)
38. SHARP, A. (1970). *Survey of Paddington Schoolchildren,* Sociological Research Section, Ministry of Housing and Local Government
39. DEPARTMENTAL COMMITTEE OF INQUIRY INTO ALLOTMENTS. *Report:* Cmnd. 4166, H.M.S.O., (1969)
40. GARNER, J. F. (1963). *The Law of Allotments,* Shaw
41. NELMES, W. *Allotment Gardens in the Urban Landscape.* Proceedings of Annual Conference of National Allotments and Gardens Society, New Brighton, (1969)
42. STAMP, L. D. (1962). *The Land of Britain: Its Use and Misuse,* Longman
43. NATIONAL ALLOTMENTS AND GARDENS SOCIETY LTD. *Rules,* (1965)
44. NATIONAL ALLOTMENTS AND GARDENS SOCIETY LTD. *Evidence Prepared for Submission to the Committee of Inquiry into Allotments*
45. THORPE, H. *Address to Annual Conference of National Allotments and Gardens Society, New Brighton,* (1969)
46. SEELEY, I. H. *Recreational Needs in an Urban Environment.* Proceedings of Annual Conference of National Allotments and Gardens Society, New Brighton, (1969)
47. LONDON BOROUGH OF BRENT, PLANNING AND RESEARCH DEPARTMENT. *Allotments in Brent: Report of Survey, 1965/66,* (1966)
48. FISHER, R. E. *Allotments and Gardens in the City of Nottingham.* Private communication, School of Town and Country Planning, Nottingham College of Art and Design (Trent Polytechnic), (1967)
49. HUDSON, J. P. and EDWARDS, K. C. (1966). *Horticulture: Nottingham and Its Region.* British Association for the Advancement of Science, Nottingham
50. LITTLE, F. M. (1966). *An Interim Assessment of Allotment Land in Nottingham,* Nottingham Corporation
51. SEELEY, I. H. *Problems in the Location, Provision and Utilization of Allotment Gardens.* Proceedings of Annual Conference of National Allotments and Gardens Society, Skegness, (1972)

7 SPORTING ACTIVITIES

THIS CHAPTER IS sub-divided into four sections concerned with team sports; tennis and bowls; golf; and other sporting activities. Water sports are considered in chapter 8.

SECTION 1: TEAM SPORTS

This section is concerned with the principal organised games of football, rugby, hockey and cricket. They differ from other sporting activities like tennis, bowls, archery, swimming, golf and sailing, in that they cannot be undertaken by people in small groups but need teams of eleven to fifteen people who require fixtures with other teams for matches. Another essential difference is that team sports require much larger areas of land than the majority of other land based sporting activities, with the exception of golf, and they often attract a considerable number of spectators particularly with games involving professional players. An investigation is made of methods and standards of provision, and sports clubs in Greater Nottingham are examined and compared with those in other parts of the country. Finally, dual use of school playing fields, the provision of all-weather playing surfaces and combined sports centres are considered in relation to the overall problem of supply of adequate playing facilities.

METHODS OF PROVISION OF PLAYING FACILITIES

Sports facilities are provided by three main types of agency: the public authority; commercial organisation or business firm; and privately.[1] Table 7.1 prepared by Willis[2] relating to the ownership of sports pitches in the London New Towns and two old towns in 1964–65, shows that less than half the cricket, rugby and hockey pitches were in public ownership, and only with football pitches was there a majority for hire. As industrial organisations with over 1000 employees were more likely to provide their own sports grounds, larger towns generally have more of these facilities.

TABLE 7.1

OWNERSHIP OF SPORTS PITCHES IN LONDON NEW TOWNS AND TWO OLD TOWNS—1964–65

Ownership	Football pitches		Cricket pitches		Rugby/hockey pitches		Total	
	New towns %	Old towns %	New towns %	Old towns %	New towns %	Old towns %	New towns %	Old towns %
Local authority	66	63	47	45	42	34	58	47
Employer	27	30	35	32	19	22	28	28
Private	7	7	18	23	39	44	14	25
Total per cent	100	100	100	100	100	100	100	100
Number of pitches	161	27	74	31	36	32	271	90

Source: M. Willis, Town Planning Review, **38.4**, (1968)

By way of contrast, the Government Social Survey[3] investigated sports provision and participation nationally, in Inner London and in eight New Towns. This survey found that in all three cases local authorities were the chief providers of facilities for physical and outdoor sports and games. Private clubs were important providers of cricket facilities and employers' clubs made their largest contribution in the provision of facilities for football and cricket.

It should, however, be borne in mind that the data in this latter survey gave only the proportions of participants who used facilities operated by local authorities, clubs and employers: not the proportion of facilities provided by local authorities compared with private clubs and companies.

Provision by Local Authorities

Many of the limitations and restrictions imposed on local authorities in the provision of sports fields were removed in the Public Health Act, 1925.[4] This Act was itself repealed by the Physical Training and Recreation Act, 1937, whereby local authorities were empowered to provide playing fields and also centres for the use of clubs, societies or organisations having athletic, social or educational objects. By virtue of the Local Government Act, 1933, local authorities are authorised to accept gifts of land upon trust for purposes of recreation. The Local Government Act, 1966, introduced exchequer grants to local authorities (fifty per cent of loan charges) for the provision of public open spaces and reclamation of derelict land, and the laying out of playing fields can be included under both heads.[5] Furthermore, under the provisions of the Education Act, 1944, local education authorities were required to provide adequate facilities for recreational and social and physical training—including playing fields—for all receiving primary, secondary and further education. The advantages to be gained from dual use of these facilities will be considered later in this chapter.

Provision by Industrial Organisations

Cullen[6] has aptly described how the company sports ground is today a fairly familiar feature of our industrial landscape. It is estimated that there are at present approximately 1300 industrial clubs in the United Kingdom. In these clubs, football and cricket are by far the most popular pursuits. There are, however, severe operational limitations in that while company owned facilities are usually available to an employee's wife or family, relatively few companies extend their use to the general public in spite of pressure to do so, and clubs usually limit outside membership as much as possible. A strong case could be made for some form of dual use of under utilised industrial sports fields.

Cullen[6] has described how there is a diminishing interest in many industrial clubs on the part of both management and employees. Management seems not quite so sure now about the place of sport and welfare in industry, while in the clubs themselves there is frequently apathy among the membership, resulting in the organisation being left to a handful of people and less than ten per cent of employees using the club facilities. Some smaller companies, unable to maintain an acceptable level of interest in their sports facilities, have sold or used the land for building development. Some larger companies, after analysing the costs and benefits of their playing facilities, are also opting for development of the sites.

Provision by Private Clubs

Willis[7] conducted a survey of sports clubs in ten New Towns and two established towns and found that a large number of clubs would prefer a ground of their own, almost all of those at present using a private ground and forty-one per cent of those in New Towns playing on a public park or playing field. The principal reasons given were the desire to be independent and the sole user of the ground and pavilion at the time of play, rather than one of a number using a group of pitches and sharing the facilities; and to be able to have their own clubhouse, improve the facilities and build up a club spirit. For most of these clubs the choice has little relevance as they will have to continue to use local authority grounds for financial reasons. Almost all the private men's hockey and rugby clubs and a majority of the cricket clubs covered by the survey opted for a ground of their own, but the football clubs seemed less interested in a private ground. There is often a town football ground but few other football clubs seem to require separate accommodation. Most other large football clubs are attached to industrial firms and are able to use an industrial sports ground, while many private clubs run only one team and have a rapid turnover so that hiring a ground is more practical.

McPartlin[8] asserts that, with very few exceptions, the day of provision by private specialist sports clubs of large scale facilities must be considered over, and the future lies in partnership between such clubs and the local authority as far as local provision is concerned, and in cooperation between the headquarters of governing bodies and the appropriate ministries where the provision of national facilities is concerned. Grants are available to amateur sports clubs from the Department of Education and Science (through the Sports Council) provided club membership is open to the public in general.

STANDARDS OF PROVISION

The existing pattern of sporting activities reflects local deficiencies of facilities, local traditions and the current level of promotion and encouragement. The future influence on this pattern of improved health, longer active age span, increased affluence and mobility, and different forms of promotion and fashion are difficult to predict with accuracy.[11] These factors make the formulation of a nationally applicable playing space standard unrealistic. Nevertheless, the National Playing Fields Association[12] laid down a recommended standard of 2.40 ha (6 acres) of permanently preserved playing space per 1000 population in addition to school playing fields, and in 1956 the Ministry of Housing and Local Government stated that 'no better assessment of need has so far been put forward'.[10] This standard includes children's play space; general recreational areas; privately owned sports grounds; such areas of school playground or playing fields that are in regular use out of school hours and during weekends and school holidays; and miniature and par-3 golf courses, driving ranges and associated car parking space. It is accordingly very difficult to apply.

The National Playing Fields Association has suggested the following scale of provision of playing facilities to serve a population of 60 000:

Football: 20–30 pitches (proportion of rugby to football pitches to be determined by local requirements)

Hockey: 2–5 pitches (men and women)

Cricket: 8–15 pitches (at least half of these should be accommodated between winter games pitches)

This standard is a shade low when compared with the Department of the Environment yardsticks of one cricket pitch per 4500 persons and one winter sports pitch (football, rugby and hockey combined) per 1800 persons.

The former Ministry of Housing and Local Government[13] undertook a study of the provision, use and ownership of pitches for organised games in ten New Towns, and two established towns. Football pitches were, in every town, the most numerous, but the provision of rugby pitches was noticeably affected by regional differences. Hockey appeared to be a minority sport, with fewer pitches generally and none at all in the smallest towns. The provision of cricket pitches varied between towns, indicating possible regional or traditional differences. The extent to which cricket outfields are on land used for winter games will affect the area of pitches in a town. The investigation showed that a provision of about 0.60 hectares of playing area per 1000 population seemed adequate and where it fell below 0.40 hectares per 1000 population it became inadequate. It is suggested that possible factors in determining demand for pitches could be size of town; age and marital status of population; socio-economic groupings; regional differences; type of clubs; and organisation of sport. The pitch requirements will also be affected by the number of games played on each pitch per season. In the ministry study the average number of games on football pitches ranged from twenty-two to fifty-six, rugby pitches from twenty-two to thirty-nine, hockey pitches from thirteen to forty-six and cricket pitches from twenty-one to fifty-one, with consistently higher numbers of games on private pitches.

Figure 7.1 shows the spatial distribution of both publicly and privately owned cricket, football, rugby and hockey pitches in Greater Nottingham with each symbol representing a pitch.

DEVELOPMENT OF TEAM SPORTS

During 1969 the author undertook a survey of sporting organisations in Greater Nottingham, with the aid of postal questionnaires. The form of the questionnaire is shown in appendix 5. Questionnaires were accompanied by explanatory letters and stamped addressed envelopes, for return of completed questionnaires, and were sent to the honorary secretaries of all affiliated clubs in the area.

Table 7.2 shows the historical development of sports clubs in Greater Nottingham and illustrates how the winter sports have developed during the present century, whereas the development of cricket clubs can be traced back to the middle of the last century. With cricket, rugby and men's hockey the major growth period was from 1920 to 1965,

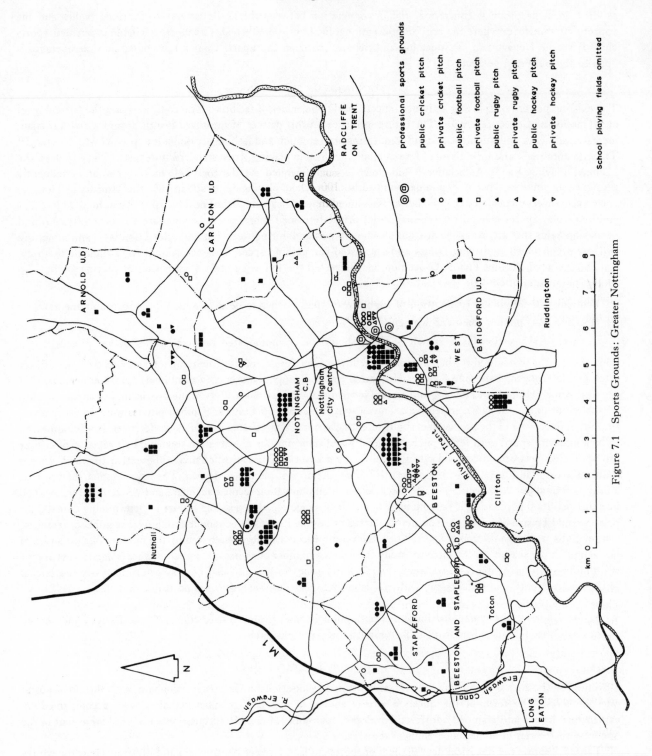

Figure 7.1   Sports Grounds: Greater Nottingham

whilst the main impetus in the development of women's hockey came rather later and was more spasmodic. In the case of football, interest has been increasing steadily from 1920 onwards with a tremendous growth in the number of clubs since 1960.

TABLE 7.2

DATE OF ESTABLISHMENT OF SPORTS CLUBS IN GREATER NOTTINGHAM

Type of Club	Number of clubs founded													
	Pre-1851	*1851–60*	*1861–70*	*1871–80*	*1881–90*	*1891–1900*	*1901–10*	*1911–20*	*1921–30*	*1931–40*	*1941–50*	*1951–60*	*1961–64*	*1965–69*
Cricket	1	2	3	1	2	4	2	4	11	9	9	9	4	1
Football	—	—	—	—	—	1	5	3	8	8	13	18	33	47
Rugby	—	—	—	—	—	1	—	—	2	1	—	2	2	—
Hockey (men)	—	—	—	—	—	—	1	—	3	—	1	3	1	1
Hockey (women)	—	—	—	—	—	—	—	1	—	1	2	—	1	3

An analysis of Nottingham club membership numbers over the period 1950–69 shows a decline in the case of cricket, football and rugby and an increase in the case of hockey. The large increase in the number of clubs—particularly football clubs—if in excess of real demand, could result in a reduction in the membership of individual clubs. On the other hand there was no real evidence of shortage of members: none of the cricket or men's hockey clubs investigated had waiting lists and this also applied to ninety-six per cent of the football clubs, eighty-eight per cent of the rugby clubs and ninety-one per cent of the women's hockey clubs. By way of comparison table 7.3 shows the position with regard to the number of affiliated clubs at national level.

TABLE 7.3

AFFILIATED SPORTS CLUBS, 1950–69

National organisation	Numbers of affiliated clubs				
	1950	*1955*	*1960*	*1965*	*1969*
National Cricket Association	Figures for earlier years not available owing to recent formation of National Association				20 000
Women's Cricket Association	147	178	131	83	65
Football Association	not available		22 680	25 217	32 234
Rugby Football League	461	349	372	337	351
Rugby Union (includes Schools section)	1298	1678	1775	2309	2541
Hockey Association	1298	1576	1684	1967	2300
All England Women's Hockey Association	853	901	829	890	865

These figures show considerable variations over the period under examination but generally appear to indicate that football, rugby and men's hockey are growing in strength. It has been estimated that the number of school rugby clubs has doubled since the last war.[15] The large increase in football clubs between 1960 and 1969 is largely accounted for by the fact that since 1960 the Football Association recognised, for the first time, teams which played the game on Sundays and the majority of new members were Sunday clubs affiliated to county Associations. Attendances at sports fixtures have declined considerably in the last 20 years—for instance football league attracted about 40 million spectators in 1949–50, and this dropped to about 33.5 million in 1958–59 and to 28 million in 1960–61. Similarly, the total annual gates in the county cricket championship dropped from their peak of 2 126 000 in 1949 to 1 641 000 in 1955 and the decline continues.[14]

Table 7.4 shows the extent to which various facilities are available to sports clubs in Greater Nottingham. This table shows that there is a wide variation in the scale of provision of the various facilities as between the different sports. For instance, nearly twice as many cricket grounds have pavilions as football grounds, and rugby and hockey fall in between. Apart from rugby clubs relatively few sports clubs possess a club room. Changing rooms are provided on the majority of sports grounds, but the provision of showers is much more variable. Most sports grounds have

TABLE 7.4

SPORTS CLUB FACILITIES IN GREATER NOTTINGHAM

| Type of Club | Percentage of clubs with each facility | | | | | | | | | | | |
	Pavilion	*Changing rooms*	*Club room*	*Showers*	*Toilets*	*Bar*	*Restaurant*	*Wives' club*	*Spectator accommodation*	*Car park*	*Owned*	*Rented*
Cricket	63.0	80.0	15.4	50.6	70.7	12.3	3.1	—	3.1	49.2	33.9	66.1
Football	36.3	93.7	21.9	66.5	90.4	8.0	2.3	2.3	3.4	56.7	19.8	80.2
Rugby	44.4	88.8	44.4	77.7	88.8	55.6	—	—	11.1	55.6	50.0	50.0
Hockey (men)	58.4	100.0	25.0	83.4	100.0	16.7	8.3	—	8.3	66.7	33.3	66.7
Hockey (women)	55.6	88.8	22.2	55.6	77.7	22.2	—	—	—	66.7	22.2	77.8

toilets although about thirty per cent of cricket grounds and over twenty per cent of women's hockey pitches are deficient in this respect. Apart from rugby clubs, few sporting organisations have their own bars. There are very few restaurants or wives' clubs and little spectator accommodation. Between fifty and sixty-six per cent of the clubs possess car parks. Fifty per cent of the rugby clubs own their own facilities, whilst in other sports the proportion of clubs owning the grounds varies between twenty and thirty-three per cent.

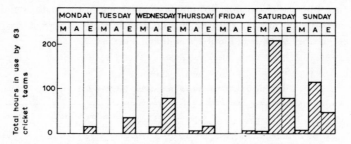

Figure 7.2　Intensity of Use of Cricket Pitches in Greater Nottingham

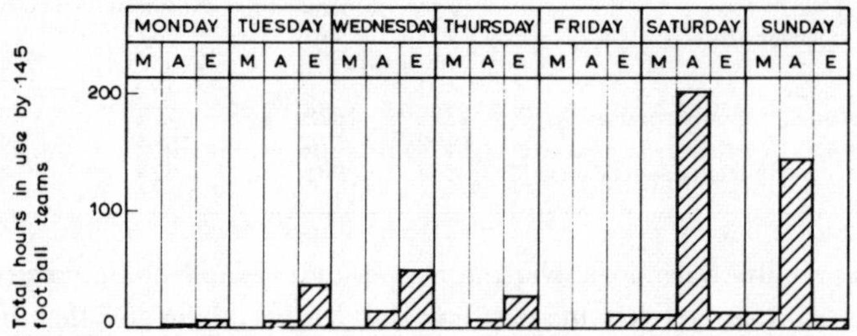

Figure 7.3　Intensity of Use of Football Pitches in Greater Nottingham

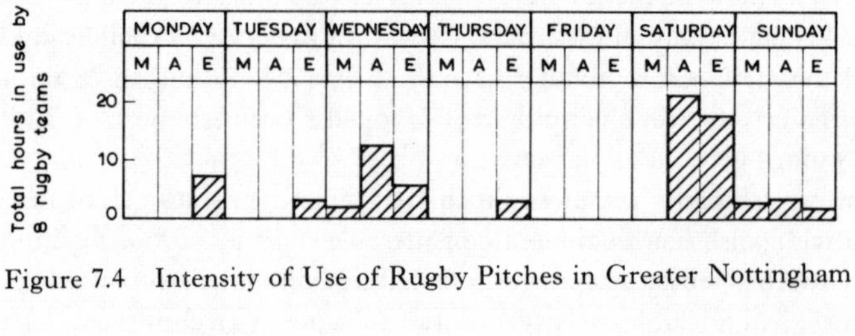

Figure 7.4　Intensity of Use of Rugby Pitches in Greater Nottingham

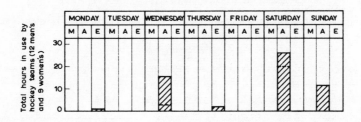

Figure 7.5   Intensity of Use of Hockey Pitches in Greater Nottingham

NOTE

M = morning   — men's teams
A = afternoon   -- women's teams
E = evening

INTENSITY OF USE OF PITCHES

The pattern of use of sports pitches in Greater Nottingham is portrayed in figures 7.2–7.5 inclusive. With all four sports the peak period is Saturday afternoon, with Sunday afternoon also proving very popular except in the case of rugby and women's hockey. Saturday evening is also becoming a popular time for rugby matches on floodlit pitches. Activities during the week are minimal except on Wednesdays, when the increased use is mainly by students of higher educational establishments. A greater spread of games throughout the week would permit much greater utilisation of playing pitches. The average number of hours of sport per week during the playing season obtained by clubs varies considerably between different sports: Cricket—9.6 hours; football—3.8 hours; rugby—10.2 hours; men's hockey—4.7 hours; and women's hockey—2.5 hours.

Figure 7.6 illustrates how the provision and use of Nottingham public sports pitches have changed during the period 1949–69. The provision of hockey pitches has remained virtually constant throughout the 20 year period; cricket pitch provision has increased by seventeen per cent although it reached its peak in 1959–60 with a twenty-six per cent increase and has since declined; and football facilities show the most spectacular rise with an increase of ninety-five per cent. However, the increased supply of pitches has not been matched by a corresponding rise in use. In the case of football the total number of matches played in 1968–69 was six per cent less than in 1949–50 when there were only half as many pitches. There has been a significant decrease in the number of games played per pitch per season. In 1949–50 the number of games played on football and hockey pitches was well in excess of 100 per season and those on cricket pitches was not far short of this figure. By 1968–69 the number of games per pitch had dropped to twenty-six for cricket, sixty-five for football and forty-five for hockey. Figure 7.6 shows diagrammatically the reduced usage of public pitches in the three sports in Nottingham over the 20 year period. Cricket shows a fairly constant decline in use of pitches while the football and hockey usage is far more erratic.

The Central Council of Physical Recreation survey[16] of recreation in local authority parks indicates average rates of usage far in excess of those operating in Nottingham, but these figures are not supported by Willis[2] whose investigation of New Towns shows usage rates not greatly in excess of those operating in Nottingham; indeed Nottingham's football participation rates are higher. This possibly indicates some over provision of facilities in Nottingham and/or insufficient spread of times when games are played with excessive concentration on Saturday afternoons. Where local authorities restrict the playing of games on Sundays this tends to aggravate the situation. The number of school bookings in each of the three sports has fluctuated considerably over the 20 year period but the number of games played in 1968–69 showed striking reductions on the 1949–50 figures: cricket—seventeen per cent of 1949–50 total; football—thirty-five per cent; and hockey—twenty-four per cent. As new schools are built with ample playing fields, so the demand for use of public sports grounds by school pupils during school hours diminishes.

AGE AND SOCIAL COMPOSITION OF MEMBERS

Table 7.5 shows the age composition of the membership of sports clubs in Greater Nottingham.

TABLE 7.5

AGE COMPOSITION OF MEMBERSHIP OF SPORTS CLUBS IN GREATER NOTTINGHAM

Type of sports club	Under 20	20–24	25–29	30–34	35–44	45–54	55–64	65 and over
Cricket	16.2	17.7	20.7	21.1	16.8	5.6	1.6	0.3
Football	24.7	43.0	19.0	8.0	3.6	1.3	0.3	0.1
Rugby	44.5	29.6	12.4	7.0	4.5	1.1	0.8	0.1
Men's hockey	25.4	38.9	18.9	9.7	5.3	1.8	—	—
Women's hockey	36.2	24.0	16.8	16.3	6.3	0.4	—	—

Note: all figures are expressed in percentages

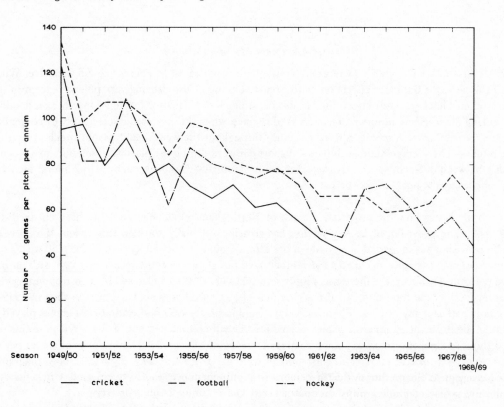

Figure 7.6   Number of games per pitch on public sports fields in Nottingham: 1949 to 1969

This table shows some striking variations in age groupings of club members in the various sports. The winter sports have a more youthful following than the summer sport of cricket, probably influenced by the more exacting nature of the winter sports, with sixty-six per cent of the members under 25 years of age as compared with only thirty-three per cent of cricket players. The very high proportion of rugby players under 20 is largely accounted for by the fact that thirty-three per cent of the teams are composed of students in higher educational establishments. In cricket alone is there any really significant proportion of members over the age of 34.

The Government Social Survey[3] also shows a predominance of single persons under the age of 23 participating in football and rugby, and some extension of the age range with cricket. Table 7.6 shows the percentage of males in various age groupings participating in the three main team sports in New Towns[17] and these display some marked variations from the Nottingham pattern.

TABLE 7.6

PERCENTAGE OF MALE PARTICIPANTS IN SPORTS IN NEW TOWNS
IN VARIOUS AGE GROUPS

Age group	Football	Rugby	Cricket
15–19	13.7	1.0	3.0
20–29	11.5	1.5	4.9
30–44	3.1	0.2	2.8
45–59	—	—	0.7

Source: Central Council of Physical Recreation: Planning for Sport

Table 7.7 shows the social composition of the membership of sports clubs in Greater Nottingham. This indicates some interesting and significant variations between the different sports. For instance, twenty-five per cent of cricket club members are in professional or managerial posts and this proportion is almost halved with football clubs, whilst rugby and men's hockey clubs lie in between the two extremes. Just over fifty per cent of the membership of cricket and football clubs are manual workers, and the proportion drops to around ten per cent for rugby and men's hockey clubs. Rugby and hockey clubs in contrast to the other two sports contain a large proportion of students in their organisations. Non-manual workers (mainly clerks and typists) account for a quite consistent proportion of club members in all sports (twenty-three to thirty-one per cent). The composition of women's hockey clubs is quite different to that of men's hockey clubs owing to the higher proportion of office workers and a considerable number of housewives.

TABLE 7.7

SOCIAL COMPOSITION OF MEMBERSHIP OF SPORTS CLUBS IN GREATER NOTTINGHAM

Type of sports club	Professional	Managerial	Skilled manual	Non-manual	Semi-skilled manual	Unskilled	Non-employed	Students
Cricket	18.4	7.1	18.4	30.8	9.6	4.5	0.1	11.1
Football	7.5	5.3	25.1	24.0	17.2	9.2	0.1	11.6
Rugby	6.2	11.7	7.6	31.4	1.1	—	—	42.0
Men's hockey	13.0	7.1	8.0	23.0	3.7	—	—	45.2
Women's hockey	6.1	3.9	4.4	30.0	1.1	—	18.4	36.1

Note: all figures are expressed in percentages

In the Government Social Survey,[3] 5735 persons were interviewed from a national sample and they were subdivided into five socio-economic groups. In cases where five per cent or more of a group participated at least once a month in a particular activity, these were recorded as shown in the following schedule (the response in both rugby and hockey was insufficient for them to register).

Group	Cricket	Football
1. Employers and managers in large establishments, and professionals	—	—
2. Employers and managers in small establishments, and intermediate non-manual workers	5	—
3. Supervisors and foremen (manual) and skilled manual workers	6	12
4. Junior non-manual workers	12	12
5. Semi-skilled and unskilled manual workers	8	10

157

This schedule confirms the Nottingham finding of greater participation by managerial and professional groups in cricket as compared with football, and vice-versa with the semi- and unskilled manual workers. A Ministry of Housing and Local Government Open Space Survey[13] also indicates how different sports attract players from different socio-economic groups. In the ministry study of both old and new towns, skilled manual workers accounted for about fifty per cent of the football players and showed far less non-manual footballers than that in Greater Nottingham. As at Nottingham, cricket and rugby appealed rather more to non-manual workers and hockey was mainly the preserve of non-manual workers and students.

DISTANCE TRAVELLED TO SPORTS GROUNDS

Members of Nottingham sports clubs often travel several kilometres from their homes to the club's home ground. There are a number of reasons for this:

(1) Figure 7.1 shows a predominance of sports grounds, both public and private, in the south-western sector of the city and its environs.

(2) Approximately twenty-five per cent of the playing facilities are provided by employers with the playing fields in one specific location and the homes of employees dispersed over a wide area.

(3) The majority of players belong to private sports clubs and if and when they change their place of residence they tend to stay with the same club.

(4) Many sports clubs hire local authority pitches and there are not always pitches available in reasonable proximity to the members' homes.

The majority of the Nottingham clubs seem to draw their members from a surprisingly wide area and the average distances travelled to home grounds by club members in the various sports are as follows: cricket—6.6 km; football—5.8 km; rugby—9.2 km; men's hockey—8.2 km; and women's hockey—6.4 km. This seems to substantiate the findings at Crystal Palace,[18] that hockey and cricket appear to attract users from wider areas than football. The much smaller number of rugby and hockey pitches must result in a more restricted choice of site for prospective players and would, of necessity, often involve a longer journey in consequence. In the Government Social Survey[3] sixty-two per cent of the cricket players travelled by private transport but only forty-four per cent of football players, and this is largely explainable by socio-economic factors. The average length of time of journey was 13 mins for cricket, 13 mins for football and 16 mins for rugby, which bears a reasonable relationship with the Nottingham findings.

PROBLEMS OF SPORTS CLUBS

The main problems of Nottingham cricket clubs were concerned with restrictions on Sunday play, inadequacy of facilities and difficulty of recruiting younger members. Football clubs seem to experience far greater difficulty in securing pitches as required; many of them hire local authority pitches on an annual basis and there is no certainty that their applications for pitches will be accepted, regardless of league and other commitments. Summer training facilities are hampered owing to the closure of Nottingham parks in the summer and in some cases no Sunday matches are permitted. Many football clubs would like a clubhouse which could assist socially by providing facilities for table tennis, snooker and billiards, in addition to giving indoor training facilities. Some clubs complain about the quality of the hired pitches and their standard of maintenance and some pitches can be out of use for up to 4 weeks at a time during periods of heavy rain. Changing facilities are barely adequate on some sports grounds, and on one site ten clubs have to share the changing rooms at the same time.

Many football clubs described the difficulty of raising sufficient funds to meet rising operating costs; the hire of a pitch is often in the order of £1.60 per fixture which amounts to about £45 per season, to which has to be added league fees, insurance and laundry bills. One club secretary described how his club remains solvent mainly through the efforts of committee members who ensure that players turn out in reasonable kit and use their own cars to transport players to various grounds, in addition to providing facilities at their homes for committee meetings.

The principal complaint of rugby and hockey clubs was the poor state of pitches, often due to ineffective surface drainage, and inadequate changing facilities. It was emphasised that additional matches and training would be

158

possible with floodlighting.

In the Government Social Survey,[3] complaints were often made in relation to changing accommodation and washing facilities. Seven per cent of football players and three per cent of cricket players had no changing facilities, and eight per cent of football players and three per cent of cricket players were without washing facilities. A few had no toilets at their usual sports grounds and over thirty per cent wanted improvements to the basic facilities. Hence the complaints of the Nottingham clubs on these aspects are not exceptional. Willis[19] in her survey of sports ground provision in both old and New towns found that the main items of dissatisfaction amongst sports clubs were the poor changing accommodation and standard of pitches and their maintenance.

DUAL USE OF SCHOOL PLAYING FIELDS

The Sports Council[17] has defined 'dual use' as the long-term regular use—on an organised basis—of facilities, particularly those financed from public funds, by the general public either as members of groups or clubs or as individuals, for whom the facility was not primarily intended. This concept is particularly applicable to educational facilities; although possibly 'multi-use' would be a better term.

The National Playing Fields Association[22] has for many years strongly advocated the more extensive use of school playing fields out of school hours. Objections often raised include the following:

(1) The ground is already being used out of school hours by organised bodies, such as youth clubs and old pupil's associations.

(2) The turf cannot stand up to the increased wear.

(3) Additional supervision is needed.

Obviously dual use demands a good quality turf maintained to a high standard, close cooperation between local authorities and adequate supervision. In 1964 a joint circular from the Ministry of Housing and Local Government and the Department of Education and Science,[23] advised local authorities in assessing local needs and the resources to match them, to consider how far facilities for sport and physical education already provided—or in course of provision—at schools and other educational establishments can be shared with other users, or can be economically expanded to meet the needs. The Sports Council[24] and the Wolfenden Committee[9] have emphasised that the concept of dual use applies not only to sports facilities owned by local education authorities, but also by universities, some of which are now encouraging sports associations to make use of their modern well equipped sports halls and swimming pools.

Howell, when Minister with special responsibility for sport,[25] effectively expounded the feelings of the regional sports councils in an address in 1966:

We want joint planning and 'dual use' to make more sense in the future. It is nonsense to shut school fields at 4.00 p.m., and not to use them to their full capacity. . . . We are particularly interested in hard surfaces and floodlighting and will urge seven-day opening. I believe that we can get a much greater use of facilities for a very small increase in annual expenditure.

Furthermore, the concept of dual use could with advantage be extended to under utilised industrial sports grounds.

ALL-WEATHER PLAYING SURFACES

The National Playing Fields Association[26] has campaigned for the wider use of all-weather pitches of hard surface, which will withstand an intensive programme of team games. This would be of particular value in areas where land is scarce. The benefits can be further increased by the installation of floodlighting so that games and athletics training can be continued through winter evenings. This policy also has the support of the Sports Council[17] who favour their use on school playing fields. The extra cost of construction over turfed pitches may be compensated for by community use during evenings, weekends and holidays.

The building regulations relating to schools[20] permit the provision of a hard porous surface in place of up to one-half of the grass area for the playing of hockey, football or other appropriate games, and that part may be deemed to be three times its actual area. The main advantages are the provision of a playing surface which is suitable in all weathers, with a greater wearing quality and enabling economy in playing field areas.

COMBINED SPORTS CENTRES

The joint circular on Provision of Facilities for Sport[23] strongly advocated that in planning new, or re-planning existing, sports provision for educational establishments, the needs of the community generally—as well as of pupils and students—for both outdoor and indoor sports facilities should be borne in mind. Better value for money, and a wider range of facilities, may be obtained if combined provision can be made in an integrated scheme. The Sports Council[17] has shown how it is possible to plan the entire physical education accommodation of a large new school for shared use with the community, the result being a sports complex comprising pool, sports hall, gymnasia, squash courts and social provision. Other schemes range from swimming pools or sports halls down to small improvements such as the provision of floodlighting for a hard porous area, which may nevertheless add materially to the amenities of a community.

The school use and community use are complementary, as schools mostly want facilities during weekdays and the public in the evenings, weekends and holidays. Ideally the building complex, containing sports hall/gymnasium, swimming pool(s), squash courts, catering and social amenities, and other facilities, should be surrounded by hard playing areas such as a floodlit hard porous pitch, floodlit hard tennis/netball courts, a floodlit athletics training area and cricket practice pitches. Soft areas of grass for football, cricket and hockey should also be included according to the combined requirements of school and community. Finally, the programming of the facilities should be undertaken by an independent manager holding a joint appointment to secure a satisfactory use allocation.[27]

Nottinghamshire County Council has collaborated with a number of district or borough councils to provide combined sports centres alongside large new comprehensive schools. Some of the main advantages stemming from this arrangement are that the County Council is able to offer a site and car parking space free of charge; free architectural and quantity surveying services; and the reduced prices obtainable with large contracts. Moreover, the roads, sewers and landscaping are in the school part of the building contract.[21] The first of the Nottinghamshire schemes at Bingham was opened in 1969 at a cost of £200 000; £130 000 to be borne by the Rural District Council and £70 000 by the County Council. Annual running costs were estimated at £30 000 and on opening times (up to 11.0 p.m.) the County Council would have forty per cent use and the Rural District Council sixty per cent use. It was finally decided, under pressure from the Rural Council, to share losses on a fifty per cent basis although it is hoped that net profits will accrue in the future.[28] None of the Nottinghamshire schemes are costing more than £230 000, and even the addition of hidden benefits including land will not push the total figure beyond £300 000 (1969 prices). This latter figure is about the cost of a pools complex for most authorities, but in the Nottinghamshire schemes, there is also a sports hall, squash courts and a floodlit all-weather pitch.

SECTION 2: TENNIS AND BOWLS

These two sporting activities have been grouped together because their land requirements and form of use have similar characteristics, although admittedly they mainly serve people of different age ranges. Methods and standards of provision of facilities and extent of support for these activities are investigated. The results of surveys of facilities and clubs in Greater Nottingham are then considered and compared with statistics from other sources. Finally, an attempt is made to analyse the main problems and needs of participants in these two activities.

TABLE 7.8

OWNERSHIP OF TENNIS AND BOWLS FACILITIES IN GREATER NOTTINGHAM

Type of facility		Local authority	Private club	Employer
Tennis	hard	61.2	16.7	22.1
	grass	26.4	21.8	51.8
Bowls		58.7	16.0	25.3

Note: all figures are expressed in percentages

Sporting Activities

METHOD OF PROVISION

The Government Social Survey[3] revealed that the majority of players of tennis and bowls interviewed on a national basis used facilities provided by local authorities. Other sources were private clubs and employers. The proportional supply of facilities in Greater Nottingham by the three sources is given in table 7.8. The number of private clubs with tennis courts has dropped since the last war as some of the smaller sites have been developed for residential purposes.

STANDARDS OF PROVISION

The National Playing Fields Association standard of 6 acres (2.40 ha) of permanently preserved playing space per 1000 population,[12] in addition to school playing fields, includes facilities for both tennis and bowls. Liverpool Corporation[11] favours the grouping of local facilities—in order to ensure economic use of land, be functionally effective and provide a reasonable range of activities—in units of at least 5.80 ha and including 0.8 ha of tennis courts and bowling greens. It was envisaged that units of this scale would serve a population of about 8000, although this ratio must be affected by the population density.

The former Ministry of Housing and Local Government suggested certain yardsticks for guidance purposes, namely: one tennis court per 2000 persons and one bowling green per 7000 persons.[30] They can at best be only rough guides because of different regional and sub-regional patterns of play and levels of interest. The National Playing Fields Association[29] suggested twenty–thirty hard tennis courts and eight–twelve bowling greens to serve a population of 60 000 (the design population of many of the first generation New Towns). This produces standards of one tennis court per 2000–3000 persons and one bowling green per 5000–7500 persons. The Association, however, advises each community to carry out its own participation survey and to take into account: local traditions; the age structure of the population; the extent of Sunday football; type of school provision; demand from boys and youth clubs; whether dual use of school facilities is permitted; nature of soil and climate; proximity of countryside pursuits such as climbing rambling, sailing, rowing and golf; and whether the town is inland or seaside.

The Central Council of Physical Recreation undertook a survey of sports provision by local authorities in twelve large county boroughs in 1966.[16] The average population per tennis court was 3620 but this covered public provision only. The Council held the view that this could mean a generous provision if evidence from the Ministry of Housing and Local Government's survey in New and old towns[31] was accepted, as this suggested that in old towns the proportion of public courts is less than thirty-three per cent of all tennis court provision. In all the towns surveyed there was a reasonably consistent reduction in demand for lawn tennis over the period 1958–65. There is little doubt that the demand for tennis is affected by factors other than the extent of facilities. The location, environmental qualities and standard of playing surface must influence demand. The Central Council of Physical Recreation[16] recommends the development of the use of public tennis courts along club lines and the provision of suitable changing, social and ancillary facilities.

The Central Council of Physical Recreation survey[16] showed an average provision of one public bowling green per 16 382 persons in twelve county boroughs, although there were wide variations (7875–41 750 persons). The Ministry of Housing and Local Government yardstick is one bowling green per 7000 persons[30] and the same Ministry also suggested that about fifty per cent of the greens in old towns would be in public ownership.[31] On the basis of these suggestions the local authority provision of bowling greens seems low. Once again the Central Council statistics[16] show a fairly consistent decline in demand for bowls over the period 1958–65, although it is nowhere near as marked as in the case of lawn tennis, and two of the boroughs held their own. Probably the most important factor affecting demand for bowls is the quality of the turf and its maintenance and preparation is a demanding activity. Many bowling clubs play regularly on local authority greens. Many local authorities offer special concessions to old-age pensioners but there is no evidence that this had led to increased demand.

The distribution of tennis courts in Greater Nottingham is illustrated in figure 7.7. Public provision is concentrated in five main centres with the largest single provision in University Park (twenty-four hard courts and twelve grass courts). Private provision is concentrated in The Park and the northern part of West Bridgford with further concentrations on the sports grounds of two major industrialists. Over sixty-six per cent of all tennis courts in Greater

161

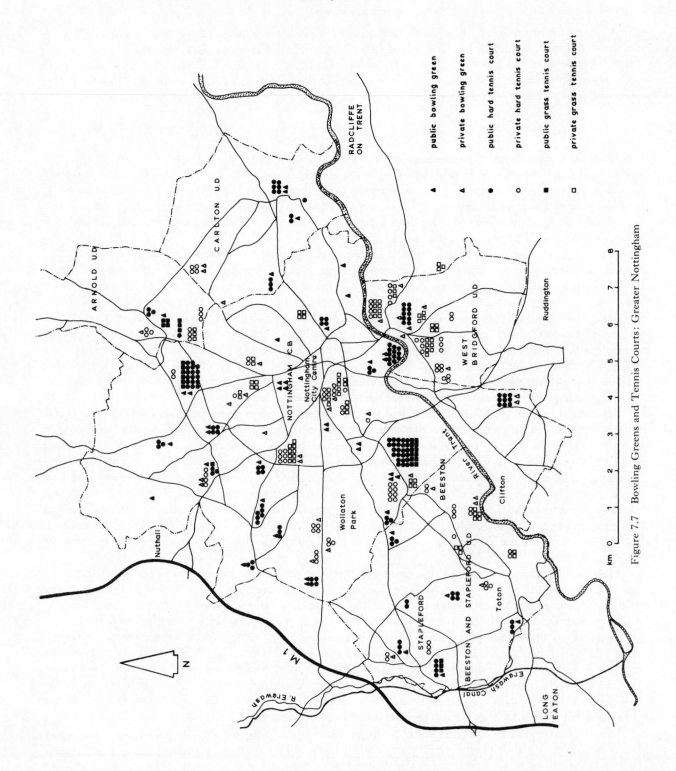

Figure 7.7 Bowling Greens and Tennis Courts: Greater Nottingham

Nottingham are hard courts and over sixty per cent of these are in public ownership. In direct contrast nearly seventy-five per cent of grass courts are privately owned. The overall provision of one court per 1322 persons compares favourably with the ministry yardstick of one court per 2000 persons.[30]

The distribution of bowling greens in Greater Nottingham is also illustrated in figure 7.7 and the greens are widely dispersed throughout the area. Nearly sixty per cent of greens are in public ownership which is rather higher than the proportion of fifty per cent encountered in the ministry survey.[31] The overall provision of one green per 6260 persons is slightly in excess of the ministry yardstick of one green per 7000 persons.[30]

CLUB, MEMBERSHIP AND PLAYING TRENDS

Table 7.9 shows the pattern of development of tennis and bowling clubs in Greater Nottingham during the present century. The rate of formation of new clubs has been surprisingly constant with 1951–60 as the only period when there was a marked divergence between the rate of establishment of tennis and bowling clubs. The first lawn tennis club covered by the completed questionnaires was founded in 1880 and the first bowling club in 1848.

TABLE 7.9

DEVELOPMENT OF TENNIS AND BOWLING CLUBS IN GREATER NOTTINGHAM

Type of club	up to 1900	1901–10	1911–20	1921–30	1931–40	1941–50	1951–60	1961–69
Tennis	17.6	11.8	11.8	23.5	5.9	11.8	—	17.6
Bowls	3.0	18.2	12.2	15.1	9.1	12.2	15.1	15.1

Note: all figures are expressed in percentages

At national level the statistics in table 7.10 give some guidance as to developments in these two activities over the last 20 years. Interest in bowls seems to be steadying while that in tennis is probably declining nationally but the spectacular increase in school tennis clubs may cause this trend to be reversed in the future.

TABLE 7.10

AFFILIATED TENNIS AND BOWLS CLUBS, 1950–69

Type of affiliated club	Number of clubs				
	1950	1955	1960	1965	1969
Tennis clubs	2739	3687	3748	3197*	2970
School tennis clubs	385	733	1034	1447	1611
Bowling clubs	2117	2375	2470	2603	2618 (1968)

* Reduction stemmed largely from new system of payments by players
Sources: Lawn Tennis Association and English Bowling Association

The Sports Council[1] reports several signs of declining participation in tennis. Returns from the parks departments of several large cities confirm the marked and continuing fall in the numbers using public courts. The Council attributed the decrease—at any rate in part—to: increased subscription rates; termination of leases; acquisition of land for redevelopment; amalgamations; and inability of clubs to develop their facilities, particularly social amenities, to modern requirements.

The Sports Council[1] also reported that figures from parks departments in large towns and cities throughout the country reflected a marked decline during the 10 years prior to 1966 in the use of public bowling greens. The English Bowling Association on the other hand was still growing and in 1965 reported a total membership of all its clubs exceeding 110 000, while membership of the Scottish Bowling Association was 60 000. The Government Social Survey[3] indicated that about five to six per cent of the population participated at least monthly in tennis and bowls; while Burton[32] estimated that in the early sixties some seven per cent of people in Great Britain played tennis at least once a year, six per cent in Sweden and less than one per cent in the United States.

An analysis of the returns from tennis clubs in Greater Nottingham shows an average club membership of ninety-six persons per club, fifty-five per cent of the members being female. Those clubs which have membership records available for the period 1950–69 show an average increase in membership over this period of twenty per cent, indicating that interest in tennis in the Nottingham area has been increasing over the last two decades as far as club membership is concerned, although this may be partially offset by the closing of a few small club facilities and the transfer of the members to other clubs. However, of the clubs investigated, eighty-six per cent have some spare capacity and only eleven per cent admitted to having a waiting list for new members.

The position with regard to bowling clubs is quite different. The thirty-seven clubs submitting returns show an average club membership of forty-three persons per club and female members account for nineteen per cent of the membership. Furthermore, of the clubs investigated, thirty per cent have less than thirty members. Those clubs which have membership records available for the period 1950–69 show an average decline in membership of thirteen per cent, indicating that interest in bowls has been falling over the last two decades as far as Nottingham club membership is concerned, although it is necessary to consider also other factors such as increased provision of facilities, greater population and the more elderly age structure of the population. Of the clubs investigated, eighty-eight per cent have some spare capacity and only sixteen per cent admitted to having a waiting list for new members.

The Nottingham public tennis courts were used about fifty per cent of the time in the early fifties but were barely used for twenty-five per cent of the time in the late sixties (a reduction of 900 to 400 players per court per annum). The declining use of public facilities by schools also illustrates the desirability of joint provision. There has been a continuous decline in the use of public bowling greens in Nottingham over the last two decades. The reduction in the number of hourly tickets issued is nowhere near as great as the fall in season tickets which is now only thirty-three per cent of the number issued in the early fifties, resulting in considerable under utilisation of resources.

Table 7.11 shows the extent of provision of club facilities by the tennis and bowling clubs in Greater Nottingham that submitted returns.

TABLE 7.11

TENNIS AND BOWLING CLUB FACILITIES IN GREATER NOTTINGHAM

Type of club	Percentage of clubs with facilities										
	Pavilion	Changing rooms	Club room	Showers	Toilets	Bar	Restaurant	Wives' club	Spectator accommod.	Car park	Owned ground
Tennis	95	100	50	50	89	39	6	—	22	44	44
Bowls	89	63	37	13	79	32	3	16	11	47	24

The majority of clubs completing questionnaires possessed a pavilion or shelter and it became apparent that tennis clubs regarded the provision of changing rooms as essential. It was surprising to find that not all tennis or bowling clubs have toilets and that a higher proportion of tennis clubs than bowling clubs had club rooms. As was to be expected, a much higher proportion of tennis clubs had showers and also owned their own grounds. Just under fifty per cent of both types of club had their own car parks which were now becoming increasingly important.

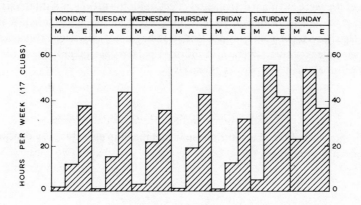

Figure 7.8   Intensity of Use of Tennis Courts in Nottingham

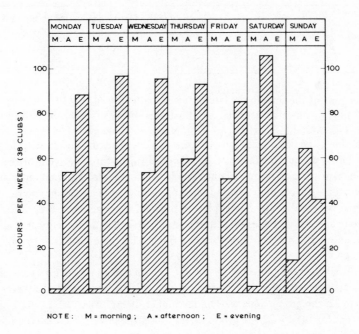

NOTE: M = morning ;   A = afternoon ;   E = evening

Figure 7.9   Intensity of Use of Bowling Greens in Nottingham

INTENSITY OF USE OF FACILITIES

Figures 7.8 and 7.9 show the pattern of use of tennis courts and bowling greens by clubs in Greater Nottingham. Little use is made of either facility during mornings except on Sundays. With tennis courts the peak periods of use are Saturday and Sunday afternoons with considerable use on all evenings of the week. With bowling greens the period of greatest use was Saturday afternoon closely followed by evenings on all weekdays. Considerable bowls playing also takes place in afternoons so that in general bowling greens are subjected to heavier use over longer periods than tennis courts. This greater use of bowling greens outside evenings and weekends doubtless stems from the quite high proportion of retired persons who make up the membership of some of the bowling clubs. There was no evidence that the longer periods of use were having a detrimental effect upon the greens as with the six rink greens it is possible to change the direction of the greens from time to time. Only eight out of eighteen tennis clubs attracted spectators and their numbers averaged seven per club ground. With bowling clubs only eight clubs out of thirty-nine recorded having spectators at their greens with an average of fourteen persons per green. Hence these activities arouse little interest amongst persons other than the players themselves.

AGE AND SOCIAL COMPOSITION OF MEMBERS

Table 7.12 shows the proportions of members of the tennis and bowling clubs in Greater Nottingham who completed questionnaires in selected age groupings.

TABLE 7.12

AGE COMPOSITION OF MEMBERSHIP OF TENNIS AND BOWLING CLUBS IN GREATER NOTTINGHAM

Type of club	Age Groupings							
	Under 20	*20–24*	*25–29*	*30–34*	*35–44*	*45–54*	*55–64*	*65 and over*
Tennis	31.9	16.6	13.2	12.2	14.9	7.3	3.4	0.5
Bowls	0.8	1.2	2.3	4.2	8.3	25.4	25.6	32.2

Note: all figures are expressed in percentages

This table shows striking age differences between the players of tennis and bowls. Tennis is essentially a game for the under 40's and bowls a game for the over 40's. Indeed thirty-three per cent of the members of the bowling clubs in Greater Nottingham were 65 or over; hence bowls is often described as an old man's game, and it confirms the Sports Council view that 'the game draws its following from a wide age range, more particularly from the over forties and among retired people'.[1] Many bowls players pursued more active sports in their earlier years, and took up bowls when increasing age dictated a less exacting pastime. It is also noteworthy that about thirty-three per cent of tennis players were under 20 and this is doubtless influenced by the increased tennis facilities which are now available at secondary schools.

The Government Social Survey[3] indicated that eight per cent of the men interviewed between the ages of 15 and 18, fourteen per cent between 19 and 22 and seven per cent between 23 and 30 played tennis at least once a month. For women up to 22, the proportions were much higher, being twenty-three per cent for the 15–18 years age group and twenty per cent for the 19–22 age group. With bowls the government survey indicated that five per cent of men between 31 and 45 years of age, and nine per cent between 46 and 70 played the game at least once a month. It also indicated that five per cent of all females in the sample play tennis at least monthly and that six per cent of all males play bowls just as frequently.

The Pilot National Recreation Survey[34] largely supports the author's findings in Nottingham as it showed a sharp drop in interest in tennis after the age of 20 with a hard core of five per cent in the 30's. It also found that men and women followed the sport in similar proportions, although more girls than boys participated in it at school. It was also felt that it was something of a status sport. Bowls was referred to as an 'elderly sport'. Of the adults interviewed four per cent would like to take up tennis and three per cent would like to play bowls. These percentages may not however, have very much significance as many people claim to have an interest in activities which they will never pursue for one reason or another. The survey of outdoor leisure activities in the northern region[33] also referred to higher participation levels in tennis amongst young, single people.

Table 7.13 shows the social composition of the membership of the tennis and bowling clubs who submitted returns in Greater Nottingham.

TABLE 7.13

SOCIAL COMPOSITION OF MEMBERSHIP OF TENNIS AND BOWLING CLUBS IN GREATER NOTTINGHAM

Type of club	Professional	Managerial	Skilled manual	Non-manual	Semi-skilled manual	Unskilled	Non-employed	Students
Tennis	21.8	13.1	4.8	22.4	1.5	0.2	3.0	33.2
Bowls	6.4	9.4	22.1	20.6	9.9	2.9	28.7	—

Note: all figures are expressed in percentages

These analyses show that the majority of tennis players are either students or professional, managerial and non-manual workers, and confirm the Pilot National Recreation Survey view that tennis is a status sport. Bowling embraces a much wider range of social groups with approximately thirty-three per cent manual workers and about thirty-three per cent retired persons. The remaining players are made up of professional, managerial and non-manual workers, which in tennis accounted for over fifty per cent of all players.

The Government Social Survey[3] also shows the highest participation in tennis amongst employers, managers, professionals and non-manual workers whilst bowls are played by five per cent or more of supervisors, skilled, semi-skilled and unskilled workers, non-manual workers and employers, and managers of small establishments. The Pilot National Recreation Survey[34] also indicated that the playing of bowls was practised by persons earning less than £850 per annum in 1967 and could not therefore be regarded as a rich man's sport. Another survey[35] indicated that of the single men interviewed between 15 and 24 years of age, twenty-eight per cent of the middle class respondents and ten per cent of the working class played tennis regularly, whilst with women the percentages were forty-seven per cent middle class and nineteen per cent working class. The northern region survey[33] showed that sixteen per cent of the respondents who played tennis were employers or professional workers and the proportion of this group who played bowls dropped to four per cent.

DISTANCES TRAVELLED

Tennis and bowls players travel considerably shorter distances than participants in team games, but this is to be expected with the wider scatter of facilities and the fact that these activities are very much user-orientated. The average distance travelled by tennis players from homes to courts from the clubs investigated in Greater Nottingham was approximately 5 km and that of bowls players was just over 3 km. The members of about thirty per cent of both types of club did not travel more than 1.5 km, but a few clubs drew their members from a very wide area.

The Pilot National Recreation Survey[34] recorded journeys by duration and not distance and found that average travel times were 13 mins for tennis and 16 mins for bowls. It is probable that tennis players are more likely to travel by car or cycle than bowls players and hence their average travel times could be less even though they travel longer distances, as was found in the Nottingham study. This also demonstrates the weakness of using travel times as opposed to distances. The Government Social Survey[3] also gives an average travel time of 13 mins for tennis players with sixty-two per cent of the players using private motorised transport. The same survey shows an average travel time of 9 mins for bowls players, being a rather wide variation from the national pilot study, with only thirty per cent of the players using private motorised transport.

PROBLEMS AND NEEDS

The tennis clubs in Greater Nottingham completing questionnaires seemed to have few problems except for one club with four grass courts which was founded in 1922 to serve the needs of a trade union of public employees. This particular club was experiencing financial problems and club members were compelled to carry out grass cutting, marking of courts and general repairs, as the club could no longer afford to employ a groundsman. Another club held the view that it was deplorable that a city the size of Nottingham had no indoor facilities for tennis. A number of clubs restricted play by juveniles to a single court during busy periods. The Government Social Survey[3] indicated that about twenty-five per cent of tennis players considered the facilities to be very good and, at the other extreme, about 12.5 per cent considered them to be poor or very poor, whilst the majority of players considered the charges to be fair.

Thirty-three per cent of the bowling clubs in Greater Nottingham submitting returns complained of inadequate facilities ranging from the absence of a clubhouse to too restrictive pavilions and poor condition and positioning of toilets. One club secretary described how the pavilion was so small that ladies preparing tea had to leave while the visitors changed into their whites. Others complained of the restriction on activities due to the limited facilities provided on Nottingham Corporation greens. Yet another club described how their 50 year old dilapidated hut without toilets or hot water, was shared with another bowling club and anyone else who wished to use it. A number of bowling clubs experience difficulty in recruiting new members, particularly younger ones. The Government Social Survey[3] indicated that almost fifty per cent of the bowls players interviewed considered the facilities to be very good and another thirty-three per cent assessed them as good. Almost fifty per cent of the players covered by the survey thought the charges to be fair and most of the remainder considered them to be cheap.

SECTION 3: GOLF

The view has been expressed that 'golf probably has the greatest active following of all sports taking place close to population centres'.[36] Although it is an extensive land user (the average size of an 18-hole course is over 50 ha), it does allow for extensive use throughout daylight hours in all seasons and golf courses have high amenity value. In the words of the Sports Council[1] 'Golf now caters for a wide age range, a broad spectrum of ability, is played by both sexes, requires a minimum of pre-arrangement and has a well developed social side'. As such it has an advantage over sports which may demand higher skill, physical fitness, organisation and dedication. Limits to growth are likely to be imposed principally through failure of facilities to match demand.

This section of the chapter is concerned with all types of golf facility: 18-hole and 9-hole public and private courses; par-3 courses; pitch and putt courses; putting greens; driving ranges; and golf centres. Consideration is given to methods and standards of provision, membership trends, club facilities, intensity of use, age and social composition of members, distances travelled by golfers and the main problems and needs.

METHODS OF PROVISION

Golf courses are mainly provided in one of two ways: by private clubs or by local authorities, with a preponderance of private over municipal courses. It seems likely that whether or not the future demand for golf is met will depend to a considerable extent on the initiative of local authorities in this field. In many cases it will not be possible for local authorities to provide courses within their own boundaries as they exist at present, and a high degree of cooperation between different authorities will be needed. The study report on coastal recreation[37] found 175 golf courses located in the coastal areas of England and Wales and described how the post-war growth in the popularity of golf has led to three kinds of pressures on these courses:

(1) Local residents who use courses throughout the year.

(2) People who have purchased second homes in the area and play mainly at weekends.

(3) Visitors who wish to play golf during their annual holiday, often resulting in a doubling of demand.

Boddy[38] has described how play on a municipal golf course is usually less attractive than on a private course, and that there are aspects of design and upkeep, as well as etiquette, which distinguish a course open to all from one with a closed membership. The real enthusiast commonly complains that municipal courses suffer from the greater number of players, the novices and weekend golfers, and the pressure to get on with the game and not hold up play. In 1970 under ten per cent of all golf courses were owned by local authorities,[16] but the majority of pitch and putt courses and putting greens were in public ownership with a concentration of these facilities in the coastal resorts. Furthermore, if some of the new courses are integrated with other recreational facilities, such as country parks, then local authorities could well be the main providers.[39]

Browne[43] has described how in the United States the municipal golf course is one of very few public recreation facilities which not only pays its own way but often produces revenue far in excess of its operating and maintenance costs. In addition it is claimed that municipal courses increase property values in the surrounding areas, attract new industry, stimulate civic pride and create new business. American municipalities planning new golfing facilities can obtain help from the National Golf Foundation which is a non profit making organisation founded in 1936 by the major manufacturers of golf playing equipment.

Eighteen-hole Golf Courses

The Golf Development Council[44] has described how the ideal golf course site should be gently undulating with trees and natural features with a sandy or light loamy soil. The 18-hole golf course is the most popular facility and needs an area of between 40 and 60 ha, although wide variations occur in practice, particularly in rural areas.

An average course comprises:

4 or 5 holes	120 m–190 m	par-3
9 or 10 holes	320 m–430 m	par-4
3, 4 or 5 holes	435 m–500 m	par-5

Nine-hole Golf Courses

There were, however, in 1967 482 9-hole golf courses in the British Isles. When laying out new 9-hole courses it is advisable to provide wherever possible for eventual extension to eighteen holes—once membership reaches 150–200 full-playing members the course becomes badly congested. Nine-hole courses may prove valuable in sparsely populated areas; where there is doubt as to immediate support for eighteen holes; or where the budget is limited and the second phase could be financed out of income from the first nine. Near urban areas the greatest use of the 9-hole course may be as an attachment to an 18-hole course to increase capacity and spread overheads, possibly reducing the length to about 1800 m.[44]

Par-3 Courses

In areas where it is proving both difficult and costly to make adequate provision for golfers, the construction of par-3 courses may help to bridge the gap. They occupy about 6 ha in which holes are between 90 m and 180 m and the total cost excluding land should not exceed £13 000 (1970 prices). The Golf Development Council[44] considers that the best situation for a par-3 course is in conjunction with a driving range. It can then expand the limitations of that field of operation and complement the playing experience which can be gained.

Driving Ranges

A driving range can be provided on an area of grassland 180–230 m in length by 90–180 m in width. Tee mats are generally of rubber separated by safety guards and automatic teeing-up devices are often provided. Other basic equipment includes a small tractor with netting protection for the driver, a ball harvester, ball washing equipment and some form of audible warning. More elaborate installations have a roof over the tee mats and sometimes a second or third tier of mats above ground level. Floodlighting for night play and heating in winter extend potential use. Driving ranges serve as a useful substitute for a practise and tuition ground.[44]

Pitch and Putt Courses

An undulating area of land unsuitable for ordinary games will often prove to be a suitable site for a pitch and putt course. These courses are usually extremely popular and pitch and putt is one of the few games where income can more than offset the operating costs. Holes may range from 35–80 m in length,[47] although 65 m is often regarded as a useful maximum.[44] An 18-hole course requires 3.2–4 ha.

Putting Greens

An 18-hole putting green requires an area of about 1350–1700 m² and a 9-hole course about half this amount. There should be a minimum course width of 12.5 m, and the lengths of holes should vary from 4 to 12 m.

Golf Centres

Golf centres are proving popular in the United States as a means of providing a range of facilities for the whole family. They often combine a par-3 course, driving range, practise green and novelty putting course. It is possible to provide complete golf education for the beginner and scope for the experienced golfer, and the incorporation of floodlighting enables intensive use.

STANDARDS OF PROVISION

The Golf Development Council[49] found that in England in 1965 there were on average nine holes per 26 357 population, and the comparable figure in the United States in 1963 was 20,000, or 17 500 if par-3 courses were included. It was also found that the majority of clubs adjoining built-up areas were full and had waiting lists. Evidence also suggested that public courses were often used to excess and that this led to maintenance problems. In addition to the numbers of rounds played being excessive, it was not unusual for players to be turned away from public courses which were fully used at the time. In some areas, populations as low as 10 000 will support a full scale 9-hole course and it was recommended that 15 000 population per nine holes should be accepted as a desirable standard of provision.[49] Appendix 6 shows English counties ranked by provision of golf courses. The unit of nine holes has been used only because it is the smallest practical development unit.

The Sports Council[1] has suggested that one 18-hole course for 20 000–30 000 persons might be an appropriate level of provision, indicating a range on the generous side of the Golf Development Council recommendation,[49] and calling for a land allocation of 1.6–2.4 ha per 1000 population—a very heavy provision indeed. This suggestion was based on investigations in north-west England where golf facilities satisfied present demand. The average number of rounds per member per annum was forty, about 1.5 per cent of the population in the area were members of golf clubs, and provision was equivalent to one 18-hole course for 27 500 persons. It is interesting to note that the South Western Sports Council[36] recommended a variable provision well below the standards suggested by the Sports Council and the Golf Development Council, namely one 9-hole unit per 32 000 population in densely populated areas, one unit per 24 000 population in urban and semi-urban areas and one unit per 18 000 population in rural areas. It was pointed out that in Somerset the number of 9-hole units would have to be increased from twenty to forty-eight in 1981 (an increase of 140 per cent) to meet the very generous standard suggested by the Golf Development Council.

MEMBERSHIP TRENDS

The national growth in popularity and demand for golf is shown by the fact that it has been estimated that the total number of golfers in Great Britain rose from 450 000 in 1954 to 750 000 in 1963.[50] It has further been estimated that the number of persons playing golf in 1966 was approaching 1 million and could be 2 million by 1974,[51] which is in general agreement with a 1970 estimate that over two per cent of the total population plays golf. The northern region[46] reports an increase in golf club membership in the region of sixty-one per cent between 1958 and 1967. The average membership of clubs in Lindsey increased by eighty-six persons between 1961 and 1967; nine of the sixteen clubs have closed their membership and are operating waiting lists.[42] In the northern region survey[33] four per cent of the respondents were golfers. Of the respondents in the Pilot National Recreation Survey,[34] three per cent were playing golf in 1965, nine per cent said they would like to take it up seriously and ranked first amongst all the activities listed, whilst three per cent said they had definite plans to take it up seriously. On the basis of these findings it seems possible that the demand for golf will increase rapidly in the next decade.

The golf clubs in Greater Nottingham show an increase in membership between 1950 and 1969 of forty-six per cent as compared with increases of over 100 per cent over the same period with clubs in Gloucestershire[39] and Somerset.[36] Furthermore, the majority of Nottingham clubs have a full membership and half of them have waiting lists. The average number of members per club with an 18-hole course was 450 in Greater Nottingham and this is the same as for the east Midlands region,[45] whilst the figure for the northern region was 500.[46] Female golfers accounted for about nine per cent of the membership of the Nottingham clubs. Fifty per cent of the Nottingham golf clubs were founded between 1902 and 1910. By way of comparison, in Somerset and Gloucestershire clubs with 18-hole courses were founded as indicated below with the majority formed before 1910.

County	Percentage of 18-hole clubs founded		
	1880–99	*1900–10*	*After 1910*
Somerset	57	36	7
Gloucestershire	36	46	18

GOLF CLUB FACILITIES

All of the Nottingham golf clubs completing questionnaires possessed a pavilion, changing rooms, club room, showers, toilets, bar, restaurant and ample car parking space, but none had practise grounds and only one had a driving range. Furthermore, all the clubs rented the land from public or private sources. In the Government Social Survey[3] approximately seventy-five per cent of the golfers interviewed considered the facilities provided to be good or very good. In the Gloucestershire survey,[39] forty-five per cent of the clubs had practise grounds, nine per cent had driving ranges, and forty-five per cent considered the clubhouse and car parking space adequate. In the Somerset survey,[36] fifty per cent of the clubs had practise grounds, twelve per cent had driving ranges, and fifty-six per cent considered the clubhouse and car parking space adequate. Car parking space was generally regarded as satisfactory in Gloucestershire when there were 100 or more car spaces available and in Somerset when the ratio of members per car parking space did not exceed six.

INTENSITY OF USE

It was not possible to make a precise assessment of the use of Nottingham golf courses, but it is considered that the 18-hole public golf courses probably withstand about 40 000 rounds per annum. Club secretaries believed that their members generally play about twice a week in the summer and less than once a week in the winter, to which must be added play by non-members. At times of maximum activity, usually Saturdays in the summer, 200 players are likely to use an 18-hole course. The courses are open every day during the hours of daylight and play starts at 8.00 or 8.30 a.m. There are two municipally owned courses in Nottingham on which private clubs are established, and both club members and members of the public can play on the courses. The club is responsible for employing certain staff, for instance, professional and steward, and the corporation employ the remainder. The corporation makes a cash grant each month towards the maintenance of the clubhouse. Over the last two decades the number of tickets issued at the two municipal golf courses in Nottingham has increased substantially.

At the well established and attractive 18-hole pitch and putt course at Woodthorpe Grange Park, Nottingham, the number of tickets issued has doubled over the period 1949–69. In contrast, at a 9-hole course in a post-war local authority residential area to the west of the city, the use has remained fairly constant at about 4500 rounds per annum since it was opened in 1963. It seems likely that pitch and putt courses are better located in the larger public parks than in residential areas.

Over the same 20 year period the number of putting greens in Nottingham increased fourfold from two to eight, and there has been a steady decline in the use of greens in recent years indicating that there may now be some over provision of this facility.

The Golf Development Council[49] has estimated that above 40 000 rounds per year a public golf course is liable to be subjected to excessive use. The calculations on which this conclusion was based are detailed in appendix 7.

The Golf Development Council does not however consider that this high rate of usage would be acceptable on a private course, and factors such as weather conditions and the fact that for the majority of players golf is confined to the weekend, means that there must inevitably be a large gap between the theoretical capacity of a course and the actual use. It is probable that the practical saturation point has already been reached on many courses. A study of Gloucestershire golf courses[39] revealed that nine out of eleven golf courses in the county were already fully utilised and one overcrowded in 1967. Methods adopted by individual clubs to meet the problem of course congestion vary considerably. Some clubs tend to make their green fee charges almost prohibitive to non-members at weekends solely in the interest of their own members. On the Nottingham public courses, a fixed ratio of members to non-members playing on the courses is applied.

A study of golf facilities in an industrial sub-region in north-west England found that the average number of rounds played annually by members on different courses varied widely from twenty-one to 250 on 18-hole courses and from seventeen to 150 on 9-hole courses. This variation is probably associated with the social characteristics of particular clubs, for example, some clubs discourage membership to ensure that there is little or no congestion on their courses. The median number of rounds per member is forty-three per member at 18-hole courses and thirty-seven per member at 9-hole courses. In the same sub-region it was estimated that 1.5 per cent of the population played golf and that existing provision would achieve an average use intensity of 16 500 rounds per course per annum.

The Sports Council[1] has pointed out that to achieve 40 000 rounds per annum with a playing membership of 600 would mean the equivalent of a little over five games a month for each member. In many areas clubs are already closed to further members, often at a figure much lower than 600. Eckhoff[48] has described how the number of rounds of golf played on American public courses each year has reached phenomenal figures. New York city reported that in 1963 annual play ranged from 60 000 to 115 000 rounds on each of its ten 18-hole courses. It seems evident that investigations are needed to determine accurately the use made of public and private golf courses and to lay down appropriate guidelines. Few private clubs appear to have detailed information on the total number of rounds played by members and non-members, and it seems advisable to keep these two categories of user separate and to express them as numbers of members and numbers of green fees. Similar problems arise in respect of municipal courses. Records commonly show the total number of green fees (rounds) per annum together with the number of season tickets. It is often impossible to assess accurately the number of rounds played by season ticket holders.[53]

AGE AND SOCIAL COMPOSITION OF GOLFERS

The age groupings of the members of the Nottingham golf clubs submitting returns are indicated by percentages:

Under 20	*20–24*	*25–29*	*30–34*	*35–44*	*45–54*	*55–64*	*65 and over*
10	5	4	4	39	26	7	5

Sixty-six per cent of the members are aged 35–54 and from these limited statistics it could be postulated that golf is essentially a game for middle-aged persons. The Government Social Survey[3] largely confirms these findings, as of the men interviewed seven per cent in the age group 19–22; nine per cent between 31 and 45; and nine per cent between 46 and 60 played golf at least once a month. The only disparity with the Nottingham findings is the quite large proportion of men between 19 and 22 who played golf. The Pilot National Recreation Survey[34] also found that golf was a sport of middle age, being one of the few sports strongly holding the interest of persons over the 35–65 age range. The Sports Council,[1] although recognising that until recently in England and Wales golf was traditionally a game for those over 30, believes that the age range is being extended.

The social composition of the members of the Nottingham golf clubs submitting returns are indicated by percentages:

Professional	Managerial	Skilled manual	Non-manual	Semi-skilled manual	Unskilled	Non-employed	Students
11	15	9	40	13	—	5	7

This analysis shows sixty-six per cent of golf club members in the professional, managerial and non-manual classifications and only twenty per cent of them are manual workers (skilled and semi-skilled). These findings were also largely supported by the Government Social Survey[3] which showed that of the men interviewed eighteen per cent of the employers and managers of large establishments and professional men; nine per cent of the employers and managers of small establishments and intermediate non-manual workers; and six per cent of the junior non-manual workers played golf at least once a month. In the view of the Sports Council,[1] increased affluence and car ownership are extending the social range from which players are drawn.

The Pilot National Recreation Survey[34] found that the incidence of participation in golf was negligible below the £1200 per annum income bracket and highest among those earning above £2000, suggesting that golf is a sport in which demand is partly limited by cost. It also found that interest in golf tends to be selective by occupations being largely confined to the executive and professional groups. The high social standing of golf was also established in the leisure activities survey in the northern region[33] which found that a man in the managerial, professional or non-manual categories with a car, is about six times more likely to be a golfer than the population in general.

DISTANCES TRAVELLED BY GOLFERS

In the Nottingham investigations it was found that the average distance travelled by members of golf clubs from homes to golf courses was about 6.5 km. A survey of golf facilities in the northern region[46] found that the majority of members lived within 8 km of their home course and few lived more than 16 km distant; in fact less than ten per cent of members lived more than 16 km from urban clubs. In a Somerset recreation survey[36] it was found that on average the catchment areas of golf courses extended over a radius of about 15 km in this sparsely populated part of the country. The Greater London and South East Sports Council[52] in an initial appraisal of sports facilities indicated those areas which were more than 9.5 km from a public or private golf course, in an attempt to establish a maximum distance beyond which it is considered unreasonable to expect golfers to travel.[53]

The Pilot National Recreation Survey[34] found that of the respondents who played golf, seventy-nine per cent used their own transport; ten per cent used public transport; and eleven per cent walked to the golf course. In the Government Social Survey,[3] eighty-nine per cent of the respondents who played golf used private motorised transport; one per cent used public transport; and ten per cent walked or cycled to the golf course. This shows a much reduced number of golfers using public transport than the National Recreation Survey but confirms that the majority of golfers use their own cars.

PROBLEMS AND NEEDS

In some parts of the country, Gloucestershire[39] is a case in point, golf clubs face problems through lack of security of tenure and restricted freedom of action owing to covenants in leases. These problems become more acute on courses located on common land, where use of the commons for grazing animals, riding horses, picnicking and other recreational activities cause problems of conflict with golfers.

Oldham[54] has indicated the need for the greater provision and use of golf driving ranges to match the success achieved with these facilities in Japan and the United States. He also favours the provision, by golf centres, of a range of facilities on one site to cater for all age groups and skills together with the opportunities for ancillary social facilities such as a restaurant. To meet a rapidly increasing demand for golf courses, the coastal recreation report[37] advocated more municipal courses and the provision of par-3 courses, driving ranges and good quality pitch and putt courses, while extensions to 9-hole courses were recommended for the west Midlands in *Regional Recreation*.[41] The Sports Council[1] also recommends the greater provision of golf driving ranges, pitch and putt, par-3 and putting courses.

The Golf Development Council[49] has suggested that an area is in urgent need of additional golf facilities when the following criteria have been met:

(1) Population exceeds 35 000 per nine holes.

(2) Clubs are full and have waiting lists.

(3) Public courses (if any) subjected to excessive use.

(4) Public courses (if any) turning players away.

In practice the number of golfers may increasingly be determined by the capacity of available facilities.[40]

A report of the National Association of Public Golf Courses[49] in 1966 confirmed the considerable increase in demand for golf facilities in recent years (congestion on sixty-seven per cent of public courses at weekends and on thirteen per cent of the courses in mid-week, during the summer months). It also seems likely that with more adequate provision for golf, the demand could rise even more steeply. The Central Council of Physical Recreation[16] has reported that while the amount of congestion varies from one authority to another, this does not appear to follow any regional pattern, and contrasting figures can be found on courses that are adjacent to one another. This would suggest that the environment and condition of the course and possibly the club facilities may, themselves, affect the demand.

Proximity to users is not of overriding importance in locating a new golf course in an urban area, since most golfers are car owners. This permits the location of new courses in the green belt where land is more plentiful and of lower cost, and this new amenity feature will help reinforce the green belt concept. On the other hand, pitch and putt courses, putting greens and driving ranges can be located within the urban area on much smaller sites of vacant land or within existing parks lacking these facilities, where they would be accessible to large numbers of people.

As golf courses occupy such extensive areas of land it would be of great benefit if it could be put to multi-purpose use. The continuous use of golf courses throughout the year and the nature of the land use seems to exclude any other type of recreation. However, as far as conservation and amenity are concerned, golf courses can have a beneficial effect upon ecology and rural character. Nevertheless, attempts must be made to maximise the use of land by the provision of driving ranges, par-3 courses and similar means and by reclaiming derelict land for use as golf courses.

SECTION 4: OTHER SPORTING ACTIVITIES

The final section of this chapter is concerned with a variety of different activities outside the range of normal team sports, tennis and bowls, and golf and water based activities. They range from netball to athletics, cycling, archery and rambling and thus embrace diverse facilities provided in a variety of ways. With the exception of archery and rambling they are primarily activities pursued by younger people, and some of them could be classified as minority sports.

METHOD OF PROVISION

Athletics and Archery

The Government Social Survey[3] indicated that about sixty-six per cent of athletics facilities were provided by local authorities, whereas the proportion of archery facilities provided by local authorities is unlikely to exceed ten per cent. Furthermore, the majority of the users of these facilities considered them to be a good standard. The East Midland Sports Council in its initial appraisal of major facilities for sport and recreation in the region[55] found three sources of provision of athletics tracks:

(1) Local authorities through parks departments.

(2) Education authorities by way of facilities in schools and colleges.

(3) Industrial provision through industrial sports clubs.

Of the thirty-one tracks in the east Midland region detailed in the survey, eighteen were associated with educational establishments, sixteen in public parks and seven were provided by industrial sports clubs.

With regard to athletics, it is the stated aim of the National Playing Fields Association and the Amateur Athletic Association[47] that every town of over 30 000 inhabitants shall have a public cinder running track for training and competition of local clubs and use of schools; and that the larger towns and cities shall have an additional track for every 200 000 inhabitants. Problems arise when this formula is applied to regions and sub-regions made up of interconnected towns of varying populations.

Rambling

To serve the needs of town dwellers, footpaths and cycleways should flow naturally from urban areas into the surrounding countryside. The walker needs accurate maps showing public rights of way and adequate footpath signposting.[56] Surveys of rights of way were introduced under the National Parks and Access to the Countryside Act, 1949, and these were to be followed by the preparation of definitive maps. The Government in its white paper *Leisure in the Countryside*[57] stressed the need to complete the definitive maps as speedily as possible to enable small scale ordnance survey maps to show rights of way. The 5 year review period contained in the 1949 Act has been replaced by a simple revision procedure, whereby disputes about the status of paths are decided by the Minister and his decision is final, by virtue of the Countryside Act, 1968. Public footpaths have to be kept in good repair and free of obstruction by local authorities, preferably always by the lowest tier authorities under any schemes of local government reorganisation.

Collins[58] has described how walking for pleasure is the simplest and cheapest of all outdoor recreation activities. The basic requirements are few: pleasant surroundings, fine weather and an adequate system of footpaths, while the impact upon the countryside is generally minimal. Male,[59] when planning for recreation in Cheshire, suggested that the areas most suitable for hiking were those of attractive landscape within 8 km of urban areas. Some of the more adventurous younger persons are prepared to travel long distances to climb mountains and crags. Climbing is a low density activity which occurs throughout the year but particularly in the summer.

Cycling and Riding

Touring cyclists try to avoid the main roads where possible. Young cyclists visiting the countryside from nearby towns present a traffic hazard, especially during school holidays. If cycling as a recreation is to be encouraged, separate routes for cyclists in the countryside and possibly connecting country parks with separate pedestrian/cyclist routes in urban areas are desirable. Collins[58] has classified routes for cycle racing into two categories:

(1) Massed start routes, where competitors start simultaneously and follow a circuitous route.

(2) Time trial routes, where competitors start individually at intervals and race against the clock.

The main problem arises through conflict with other road users and the best solution would be the establishment of closed circuits for races away from public roads.

Riding is of two basic types:

(1) Intensive use of grass areas for racecourses, polo grounds, paddocks for teaching and jumping practice, and fields for gymkhanas.

(2) The wider use of the countryside for long rides and pony-trekking, galloping and hunting.

In addition to the use of farmland, usually by arrangement with the owners, use is made of bridleways and grass verges adjoining roads. The main problem encountered by riders is the lack of suitable bridleways, forcing riders to use roads and roadside verges, the latter often being obstructed or forbidden to horse riders. As with walking, the main need is for a separate right of way system, clearly defined and maintained, with the emphasis on continuity of routes for long distance trekking. Links from towns to the surrounding countryside are also important.[58] Satow[60] has described how thousands of people ride today for pleasure and how a survey of riding in Greater London showed that 25 000 people ride in that area every week.

CLUB AND MEMBERSHIP TRENDS

Completed questionnaires were obtained from the four archery clubs established in the Nottingham area, also from nine out of twelve cycling clubs and three athletics clubs. The number of athletics clubs has dwindled over the years until only a few remain. An examination of national figures for club membership and numbers of affiliated clubs gives some indication of current trends in the activities under investigation.

Sporting Activities

Lacrosse

The English Lacrosse Union estimates that there has been a five per cent growth every 5 years from.1950 up to the present day, with some 2000 adults playing lacrosse at present and about the same number of juniors and schoolboys. The number of universities playing the game has increased by 100 per cent over the period 1950–69 due to boys from lacrosse playing schools seeking places at universities other than Oxford, Cambridge and Manchester.

Netball

The All England Netball Association was unable to supply figures prior to 1965–66 and the following statistics show developments over a recent 3 year period.

Number of Clubs		Number of Individual Members		Number of Schools		Number of Colleges	
1965–66	1968–69	1965–66	1968–69	1965–66	1968–69	1965–66	1968–69
728	876	7868	11 318	1662	2184	48	66

Athletics

The Amateur Athletic Association reported that in 1969 there were approximately 1200 affiliated organisations and that this figure had remained fairly constant during the post-war years. Approximately 400 of the organisations were athletics clubs and the remainder consisted of business house clubs and associations, services, colleges, youth clubs, and so on. It was estimated that there were over 40 000 active male athletes. The Women's Amateur Athletic Association reported 500 affiliated clubs comprising approximately 10 000 athletes, and the progression since 1950 was estimated at an increase of about fifty per cent.

Cycling

The last two decades have seen a considerable reduction in the number of racing and touring cyclists. No doubt greater affluence, much increased car ownership and increasing congestion on most roads have all tended to reduce the appeal of cycling. Membership of the two main cycling organisations over the last two decades are indicated below:

	1950	1955	1960	1965	1969
British Cycling Federation	66 528	35 536	20 918	15 266	11 292
Cyclists' Touring Club	53 574	40 752	25 786	22 344	20 500

Rambling

Year	Individual members	Affiliated clubs
1950	8 778	367
1955	13 197	366
1960	*11 300	*345
1965	13 771	366
1969	19 443	397

* Increased subscriptions

176

Although interest in cycling may have declined over the last two decades, rambling has gained much increased support and the membership figures of the Ramblers' Association throughout this period are listed. The extremely worthwhile objectives of the Ramblers' Association are 'to encourage rambling and mountaineering, to foster a greater knowledge, love and care of the countryside and to work for the preservation of natural beauty, the protection of footpaths and the provision of access to open country'.

Archery

Archery showed a spectacular increase in support in the 1950's but the rate of growth slowed down in the 1960's.

Clubs affiliated to the Grand National Archery Society

Year	1950	1958	1963	1965
Clubs	85	581	580	655

Club membership was estimated at 8600 in 1967.[61]

Relative Support for Different Activities

The Pilot National Recreation Survey[34] listed cycling for pleasure, athletics and hiking or walking more than 8 km as some of the most common recreational accomplishments, being relatively cheap and needing only simple skills taught at school or during childhood. In the same survey five per cent of the adults interviewed would like to take up archery, and two to three per cent cycling for pleasure, athletics and hiking. Of the teenagers interviewed, eleven per cent would like to take up archery; six per cent cycling for pleasure; and five per cent athletics and hiking. In the northern region outdoor leisure survey[33] of the 3828 people interviewed three per cent were currently participating in athletics and a further one per cent would like to do so; corresponding percentages for rambling were four and two and for cycling six and one. These figures do not indicate a very high popularity rating for any of the three activities. The study report on coastal recreation[37] asserts that all forms of horse riding have become increasingly popular in the last 15 years and that this is reflected in the growth in the number of riding schools.

A survey of the sports interests of school leavers in Brent[62] indicated that the following percentages of boys and girls would like to take part in the activities mentioned after they leave school.

Sport	Boys	Girls
Athletics	17	10
Cycling	10	1
Archery	3	2
Horse riding	1	10

A study of games playing habits of school leavers in Surrey in 1962[64] indicated that about twenty-four per cent of boys and eighteen per cent of girls wanted to continue engaging in athletics after leaving school, but it would appear very unlikely that these proportions could be achieved in practice. There are dangers in asking people what they would like to do in the future as their wishes will not always be matched by performance. The Amateur Athletic Association is concerned at the great wastage between the athletics clubs and the school leavers.

Membership of Nottingham Clubs

A study of membership trends in archery, cycling and athletics clubs in Greater Nottingham over the period 1950–69 shows some growth in archery club membership, reductions in membership of most cycling clubs and limited enthusiasm in athletics clubs. The four archery clubs have an average membership of twenty-six with about twenty per cent female members and considerable spare capacity. Most of the cycling clubs have a membership of between thirty and sixty, although the largest had a membership of 322 in 1969. Female members account for only about five per cent of the membership. The principal athletics club has a membership of 156 centred on the Harvey Haddon stadium in Nottingham. Female members account for over forty per cent of all members of athletics clubs. None of the clubs in any of the three activities has waiting lists.

The dates of founding of the various Nottingham clubs, where available, are shown in table 7.14.

TABLE 7.14

DATE OF ESTABLISHMENT OF ARCHERY, CYCLING AND ATHLETICS CLUBS IN GREATER NOTTINGHAM

Type of club	Periods when established							
	Pre-1900	*1900–10*	*1911–20*	*1921–30*	*1931–40*	*1941–50*	*1951–60*	*1961–69*
Archery	—	—	—	—	—	2	1	1
Cycling	2	—	—	1	3	1	—	1
Athletics	—	1	—	—	—	1	—	—

Table 7.15 shows the extent of provision of club facilities by the archery, cycling and athletics clubs in Greater Nottingham that submitted returns.

TABLE 7.15

ARCHERY, CYCLING AND ATHLETICS CLUB FACILITIES IN GREATER NOTTINGHAM

Type of club	Percentage of clubs with facilities					
	Pavilion	*Changing rooms*	*Club room*	*Showers*	*Toilets*	*Bar*
Archery	50	50	25	50	100	25
Cycling	—	—	78	—	33	11
Athletics	66	100	66	100	100	33

The archery clubs possess limited facilities but all have toilets, whilst all the athletics clubs have changing rooms, showers and toilets and the majority have the use of a pavilion and club room. Cycling clubs' facilities are largely confined to club rooms and these are often centred on public houses or community centres.

USE PATTERNS

The three activities under consideration show quite different use patterns, although they share one common characteristic in that they all operate throughout the whole of the year. The archery clubs operate on average about 16 hours per week with concentrations of activity on Tuesday and Wednesday evenings and all day Sunday. The cycling club members meet much less frequently averaging about 5 hours per week, meeting only in the evenings with Monday evening as the period of greatest activity. The athletics clubs have an average operative period of 14 hours per week with concentrations on Tuesday and Thursday evenings and Sunday mornings.

A Central Council of Physical Recreation survey[16] found that it was difficult to measure the use of athletics tracks with any accuracy. An examination of bookings revealed a wide variety of use varying from club to school and youth group. Each booking varied in the degree to which the facilities were used and bookings alone did not therefore provide sufficient evidence of use. There would seem to be a need for more careful measurement of the use of these tracks, especially when their relatively high initial capital cost is taken into account.

AGE AND SOCIAL COMPOSITION OF MEMBERS

Table 7.16 shows the proportions of members of archery, cycling and athletics clubs in Greater Nottingham who completed questionnaires in selected age groupings.

TABLE 7.16

AGE COMPOSITION OF MEMBERSHIP OF ARCHERY, CYCLING AND ATHLETICS CLUBS IN GREATER NOTTINGHAM

Type of club	Age Groupings							
	Under 20	20–24	25–29	30–34	35–44	45–54	55–64	65 and over
Archery	18.8	13.5	5.8	9.8	35.8	10.7	4.5	1.1
Cycling	31.5	41.3	8.4	4.3	9.3	3.6	0.5	1.1
Athletics	32.7	31.7	15.7	8.7	7.7	1.8	1.7	—

Note: all figures are expressed in percentages

Nottingham archery clubs seem to cater for all ages with the greatest support coming from the 35–44 age range. There is also a surprisingly high participation rate for teenagers and those in their early 20's. Cycling is primarily a young person's sport with nearly seventy-five per cent of the club members under 25 years of age, and athletics is rather similar with almost sixty-six per cent of the members in this lower age range. These participation characteristics are partially supported by the findings in the Government Social Survey[3] which showed that thirteen per cent of males aged 15–18, ten per cent aged 19–22, five per cent aged 23–30 and seven per cent aged 31–45 participate in archery or fencing at least once a month. The same survey found that in the sample of persons interviewed fourteen per cent of males aged 15–18, six per cent aged 19–22 and five per cent aged 23–30 participate in athletics or gymnastics at least once a month.

From a sample of 1500 users of the Crystal Palace National Recreation Centre in 1964,[18] twenty per cent of the men and twelve per cent of the women stated they would like to take up athletics, although their first choice was swimming. It is apparent that fewer people participate in athletics than say they would like to. It is probable that activities entered as second choices do not always materialise due to lack of time. Hence user preference surveys do not form a sound basis from which to estimate potential demand in the planning of facilities, unless supported by other information.

Table 7.17 shows the social composition of the membership of the archery, cycling and athletics clubs that submitted returns in Greater Nottingham.

TABLE 7.17

SOCIAL COMPOSITION OF MEMBERSHIP OF ARCHERY, CYCLING AND ATHLETICS CLUBS IN GREATER NOTTINGHAM

Type of club	Social composition							
	Professional	Managerial	Skilled manual	Non-manual	Semi-skilled manual	Unskilled	Non-employed	Students
Archery	2.5	13.3	41.7	28.7	6.8	—	—	7.0
Cycling	2.0	6.8	25.9	22.2	12.8	5.0	0.8	24.5
*Athletics	40.0	20.0	20.0	10.0	—	—	—	10.0

*(Nottinghamshire Athletic Club)

Note: all figures are expressed in percentages

These figures indicate that persons in a wide range of occupations participate in archery with, surprisingly enough, a predominance of skilled manual workers and very few from the professions. Cyclists show a wide occupational spread with sixty per cent manual workers, whereas the principal athletics club in Nottingham has sixty per cent of its membership in the professional and managerial categories. The Government Social Survey[3] findings on social composition of archery and fencing participants showed ten per cent of employers and managers of large establishments and six per cent of supervisors, foremen and skilled manual workers taking part in one of these activities at least once a month. This shows a greater interest by persons in managerial positions than is indicated by the Nottingham study but is complicated by the inclusion of fencing with archery in the government study.

DISTANCES TRAVELLED

The average distances travelled by club members from their homes to club facilities in Greater Nottingham were 9.5 km for archery clubs, 7.5 km for cycling clubs and 6.5 km for athletics clubs. Members of the majority of clubs are drawn from quite wide areas of the city and its environs because of the limited number of clubs engaging in each activity. The higher average distance travelled by archers stems largely from one of the four club sites being established at Gunthorpe, a village about 13 km north-east of Nottingham. An analysis of the holders of athletes' season tickets at the Harvey Haddon stadium in 1967 showed that fifty-six per cent came from the city of Nottingham, nineteen per cent from the surrounding urban districts and the remaining twenty-five per cent from villages farther afield.

The Government Social Survey[3] indicated that the average travelling time from home to facility was 11 mins for athletes and 20 mins for persons participating in fencing, archery and shooting. The same survey also found that about fifty per cent of athletes and forty per cent of archers and others travelled on foot or by bicycle; twenty-five per cent of athletes and fifty per cent of archers and others travelled by car; and twenty-five per cent of athletes and ten per cent of archers and others journeyed by public transport.

PROBLEMS AND NEEDS

Archery

Most of the archery clubs in Greater Nottingham are restricted for space owing to operation of other sporting activities in the vicinity. One club organises three archery tournaments per annum and the sports field on which they are held has to be booked 1 year in advance. Another club described the dangers inherent in people crossing the flight path to watch aeroplane flying; stray children; and people exercising dogs—indicating the difficulties in operating dual use with this particular sport. The sport seems to have lost some of its appeal to newcomers, possibly because of the high cost of equipment needed for tournaments and because the learner is sometimes discouraged if he thinks he is a second Robin Hood and subsequently finds that archery is far more difficult than it appeared.

Cycling

The majority of cycling clubs in Greater Nottingham expressed the need for a closed circuit free of traffic for road racing. One club suggested the provision of 1.6 km of permanent road in one of the new sports centres which could be used for road racing.

Athletics

Concern has been expressed over the growing individualism in sport, with consequent lack of club spirit. There are insufficient young members joining athletics clubs, possibly due to the wide range of other activities available, many of which do not require the same degree of dedication as athletics. Attention was also directed to the need for all-weather surfaces in preference to cinder tracks.

A committee of enquiry into athletics[63] saw a need for a single governing body for athletics in the United Kingdom; a system of registration of individual participants; more active steps to encourage the young athlete who shows promise in athletics at school to continue with the sport after leaving school; and a well organised scheme of leagues and competitions.

The National Playing Fields Association[12] has stressed the need for planning athletics tracks on the basis of regional or sub-regional requirements rather than on purely local needs. A report of the West Midlands Sports Council[41] points out that the majority of athletics tracks in educational establishments and private ownership are seldom constructed to the requirements of the Amateur Athletic Association for competitive events, although the advantage of allowing school training facilities to be available for public use when not required by the school has been stressed by a number of organisations.

Sporting Activities

REFERENCES

1. SPORTS COUNCIL. (1968). *Planning for Sport : Report of a Working Party on Scales of Provision*, Central Council of Physical Recreation
2. WILLIS, M. Provision of sports pitches. *Town Planning Review*, **38.4,** (1968), 293–303
3. SILLITOE, K. K. (1969). *Government Social Survey : Planning for Leisure*, Department of Education and Science
4. RODDIS, R. J. (1970). *The Law of Parks and Recreation Grounds*, Shaw
5. NATIONAL PLAYING FIELDS ASSOCIATION AND NATIONAL ASSOCIATION OF PARISH COUNCILS. *Land for Play*, (1967)
6. CULLEN, P. Whither industrial recreation now? *Sport and Recreation*, **7.4** and **8.1,** (1966 and 1967)
7. WILLIS, M. The type of sportsgrounds clubs would prefer. *Playing Fields*, **28.2,** (1968), 40–45
8. MCPARTLIN, G. A. Planning for recreation. *Town and Country Planning Summer School*. Town Planning Institute, (1963)
9. WOLFENDEN COMMITTEE. (1960). *Sport and the community*, Central Council of Physical Recreation
10. MINISTRY OF HOUSING AND LOCAL GOVERNMENT. *Open Spaces : Technical Memorandum No. 6*, H.M.S.O., (1956)
11. LIVERPOOL CORPORATION. *Report on Open Space*, (1964)
12. NATIONAL PLAYING FIELDS ASSOCIATION. *Planning for Recreation : Application of N.P.F.A. Standard*, (1967)
13. MINISTRY OF HOUSING AND LOCAL GOVERNMENT. *Open Space Surveys : Provision of Playing Pitches in New Towns*, (1967)
14. MCINTOSH, P. C. (1963). *Sport in Society*, Watts
15. BOW GROUP. (1966). *A Better Country*, Conservative political centre
16. CENTRAL COUNCIL OF PHYSICAL RECREATION. *Recreation in Local Authority Parks*, (1967)
17. SPORTS COUNCIL. (1968). *Planning for Sport*, Central Council of Physical Recreation
18. CENTRAL COUNCIL OF PHYSICAL RECREATION. *A Preliminary Analysis of the Non-residential Use of the Crystal Palace National Recreation Centre*, (1966)
19. WILLIS, M. Are sports grounds meeting the needs of users? *Playing Fields*, **28.3,** (1968), 51–58
20. THE STANDARDS FOR SCHOOL PREMISES REGULATIONS. (1959) *S.1., 1959, No. 890*
21. SPENCER, J. R. Dual schemes a reality. *Sports Development Bulletin No. 8*. Central Council of Physical Recreation, (1969)
22. NATIONAL PLAYING FIELDS ASSOCIATION. *Making the Most of School Playing Fields*, (1960)
23. MINISTRY OF HOUSING AND LOCAL GOVERNMENT/DEPARTMENT OF EDUCATION AND SCIENCE. *Circular No. 49/64 or 11/64 : Provision of Facilities for Sport*, H.M.S.O., (1964)
24. SPORTS COUNCIL. (1969). *The Sports Council : A Review, 1966–69*, Central Council of Physical Recreation
25. HOWELL, D. *Address to 33rd National Conference of Institute of Parks and Recreational Administration*, (1966)
26. NATIONAL PLAYING FIELDS ASSOCIATION. *Grounds for Action*
27. SPORTS COUNCIL. *Working Paper on Sports Halls and Indoor Sports Centres*, (1968)
28. FARRER, J. A modern approach to the provision of a sports centre: An example of co-operation between local authorities. *Proceedings of Conference on Planning for Management : National Playing Fields Association*, (1967)
29. NATIONAL PLAYING FIELDS ASSOCIATION. *Suggested Provision of Recreational Units for a Population of 60 000*
30. MINISTRY OF HOUSING AND LOCAL GOVERNMENT. *Method of Calculation of Minimum Acreage for Sports Grounds*, (1966)
31. MINISTRY OF HOUSING AND LOCAL GOVERNMENT. (1966). *Open Space Survey*, Sociological Planning Research Unit
32. BURTON, T. L. Outdoor recreation in America, Sweden and Britain. *Town and Country Planning*, (October 1966)
33. NORTH REGIONAL PLANNING COMMITTEE. *Outdoor Leisure Activities in the Northern Region*, (1969)
34. BRITISH TRAVEL ASSOCIATION/UNIVERSITY OF KEELE. *Pilot National Recreation Survey : Report No. 1*, (1967)
35. ABRAMS, M. Testing consumer demand in sport. *Sport and Recreation*, **4.7,** (1963)
36. SOUTH WESTERN SPORTS COUNCIL. *Golf : A Somerset Recreation Survey*, (1968)
37. COUNTRYSIDE COMMISSION. (1969). *Coastal Recreation and Holidays : Special Study Report. Vol. 1*, H.M.S.O.
38. BODDY, F. A. Golf course design. *Park Administration*, **33.11,** (1968)
39. SOUTH WESTERN SPORTS COUNCIL. *Major Recreation Survey : Gloucestershire : Golf Courses*, (1967)
40. MALE, K. O. (1968). *Recreation in Cheshire : Survey of Existing Facilities for Sport and Physical Recreation : Golf Courses*, Cheshire County Council
41. WEST MIDLANDS SPORTS COUNCIL. *Regional Recreation*, (1968)
42. STRAW, F. I. Planning for recreation in Lindsey. *Paper to Regional Studies Association, East Midlands Group, University of Nottingham. 12 March 1968*
43. BROWNE, T. B. A concept of total recreation in community development. *Urban Land*, **22,** (1963)
44. GOLF DEVELOPMENT COUNCIL. *Elements of Golf Course Layout and Design*
45. EAST MIDLAND SPORTS COUNCIL. *A Guide to the Provision of Golf Courses in the East Midlands*, (1968)
46. NORTH REGIONAL PLANNING COMMITTEE. *Survey of Golf Facilities*, (1967)
47. NATIONAL PLAYING FIELDS ASSOCIATION. *Selection and Layout of Land for Playing Fields and Playgrounds*, (1963)
48. ECKHOFF, H. C. Trends in municipal golf development and operation. *Urban Land*, **22,** (1963)
49. GOLF DEVELOPMENT COUNCIL. *Preliminary Report on Playing Facilities*, (1966)
50. GOLF FOUNDATION. *Making Room for Golf*, (1963)
51. COATES, U. A. *Planning for Leisure in Lancashire. Proceedings of Conference of Local Authorities/National Playing Fields Association, London*, (1966)

52. GREATER LONDON AND SOUTH EAST SPORTS COUNCIL. *Sports Facilities: Initial Appraisal. Vol. 1,* (1968)

53. SPORTS COUNCIL. *Working Paper on Golf,* (1968)

54. OLDHAM, S. A. J. Open air recreation. *Park Administration,* **34.3,** (1969)

55. EAST MIDLAND SPORTS COUNCIL. *Initial Appraisal of Major Facilities Used for Sport and Recreation,* (1967)

56. MINISTRY OF HOUSING AND LOCAL GOVERNMENT. *Report of the Footpaths Committee,* H.M.S.O., (1968)

57. WHITE PAPER. Cmnd. 2928, *Leisure in the Countryside. England and Wales,* H.M.S.O., (1966)

58. COLLINS, N. R. (1968). *Outdoor Recreation and the Gloucestershire Countryside,* Gloucestershire County Council

59. MALE, K. O. (1968). *Cheshire Countryside: An Interim Report on Recreation,* Cheshire County Council

60. SATOW, D. *The Right to Ride. Proceedings of Conference on Recreation in the Countryside, University of Loughborough,* (1969)

61. MOLYNEUX, D. D. Working for recreation. *Journal of Royal Town Planning Institute,* **54.4,** (1968)

62. LONDON BOROUGH OF BRENT, PLANNING AND RESEARCH DEPARTMENT. *Sports Interests of School Leavers in Brent: Report of Survey,* (1965)

63. AMATEUR ATHLETIC ASSOCIATION AND BRITISH AMATEUR ATHLETIC BOARD. *Report of the Committee of Enquiry in the Development of Athletics,* (1968)

64. SURREY COUNTY COUNCIL (County Planning Department)/MINISTRY OF HOUSING AND LOCAL GOVERNMENT. Correspondence in 1962/63 on *game playing habits of school leavers,* made available to author by Surrey County Council.

8 WATER BASED RECREATION

THE AMERICAN outdoor recreation report in 1962[1] considered that water was the focal point of outdoor recreation. In fact swimming, boating and fishing were each among the ten most popular outdoor activities in the United States. In Great Britain a study of inland waters and recreation in the west Midlands[2] expressed the opinion:

Our investigation shows conclusively that interest and participation in recreation on inland waters have increased very substantially in recent years. It is also strongly suggested that participation would be very much higher, particularly in some sports, if water were available, and that there is a strong social and educational trend towards these activities, which will soon widen the gap between demand and supply.

The Pilot National Recreation Survey[3] showed a growing interest in fishing and sailing.

A variety of resources can be used for different types of water based recreation. Drummond[5] has estimated the inland water resources in England and Wales as:

	hectares
Inland water (non-tidal)	85 000
Tidal water (within river authority areas)	40 000
Total	125 000

This total can be roughly analysed as:	hectares
Reservoirs (potable supply)	16 500
Lake District (natural lakes)	5 300
British Waterways Board (feeder lakes)	1 600
Wet gravel pits	2 800
Rivers (tidal and non-tidal)	80 800
Canals, enclosed waters, etc.	18 000
Total	125 000

Drummond[5] also estimated that an additional 32 000 ha of inland water resources will be created in Britain by the year 2000, roughly made up of fifty per cent reservoirs and fifty per cent wet gravel pits. Thus inland water resources have a total area of about 125 000 ha, while land resources available for public recreation were estimated in 1962 as 1.2 million ha, excluding the enormous length of public footpaths. Yet the view has been expressed that over forty per cent of the population prefer water based activities. Coppock[6] has emphasised a further complication in that most inland waters are privately owned. There are however rights of way on the larger rivers, some 3200 km of canals are vested in the British Waterways Board and over 550 reservoirs are owned by public or semi-public bodies.

The American outdoor recreation report[1] saw the need for the more intensive recreational use of both natural and man made water resources to satisfy increasing pressures in the future. Tanner[7] has echoed the same thoughts in Britain and has emphasised the need for the more efficient use of water resources and yet, at the same time, limiting recreational use to a level which is compatible with the needs of the water authority, amenity and nature conservation.

Rivers and Lakes

There are over 2000 km of broad navigable inland waterways and nearly 200 km of narrow waterways in England and Wales, excluding British Waterways Board canals.[8] The broad waterways can accommodate craft up to and over 2.13 m beam, whereas narrow waterways can take craft of up to 2.13 m beam only. Over thirty-three per cent of the broad waterways are situated in East Anglia and all the narrow waterways are in the west Midlands or south-east England.

Rivers provide a valuable natural environment for many recreational activities but there is, particularly in the case of the larger navigable rivers, strong competition for the water space available. In addition, many rivers are used as sources of public water supply and as conveyers of sewage effluent to the sea. Where serious river pollution exists, fishing is prevented or severely restricted, swimming becomes unpleasant and even sailing, motor boating and pleasure cruising are adversely affected.[9] Motor boats can cause damage to river banks and, in narrow reaches, cause conflict with other uses, whilst access to rivers and lakes may be difficult where the banks are in private ownership.[10] Circular 3/66 from the Minister of Land and Natural Resources stated: 'there is a special obligation (to provide public access to water) where a natural lake, traditionally open to the public, has been brought into use for water supply'. Rivers often provide opportunities for angling, sailing, canoeing, rowing, motor boat cruising, water skiing and wild life— subject to restrictions resulting from limited dimensions, weed growth and tides and currents—while ponds and streams can often support angling and wild life.[11] For some leisure pursuits, such as walking and picnicking, the prime need is a waterside path kept in good repair.[12]

Canals

The Romans in their occupation of Britain used the principal rivers and also built canals for drainage and transport. Fossdyke navigation, used by barges and motor cruisers today, was a former Roman canal. Most British canals were, however, constructed between 1760 and 1840, by which time there was about 6800 km of navigable canals and rivers carrying possibly about 30 million tonnes of goods per year, in addition to passenger services which included night sleeping boats and market boats.[14]

In the 1840's the railways began to compete seriously with canals by cutting coal and merchandise rates against the canals and recouping from passenger revenue, and offering a faster service on a larger network. The result was the steady decline of the canals and, with the advent of the motor lorry in the twentieth century, the process of decay and neglect was hastened. By 1945, there were in Britain a number of large waterways—mainly canalised rivers— carrying large quantities of goods, and a variety of small canals and rivers upon which barges and narrow boats were still struggling with diminishing hope of success to compete with lorry and railway. On to this rather depressing scene came the pleasure boat. In 1944 Rolt[15] described a cruise in a converted narrow boat; this proved to be popular reading and was largely responsible for the formation of the Inland Waterways Association. In addition locks, bridges and a variety of buildings serving the waterborne trade provide features of fascinating interest to the recreationalist.

A report by the British Waterways Board in 1965[16] described the high maintenance costs of canals; the decline in the use of narrow boats; the limiting factors (width, depth and permitted speed) of narrow canals; limited financial returns from recreational uses; and high costs of water channelling and eliminating canals. Whatever is done with them the non-commercial waterways will cost at least £600 000 per year at 1965 prices for water supply and surface water drainage purposes, and to keep open for pleasure cruising all the non-commercial waterways currently available for that purpose would cost a further £340 000. In a white paper on British waterways in 1967[17] the Government recognised an increasing demand by people to use the waterways for spare time relaxation and quiet holidays, and expressed their intention to secure recognition of the recreational purpose of the nationalised waterways by Act of Parliament.

The Transport Act, 1968, placed on the British Waterways Board a new and positive duty to maintain approximately 1750 km of cruising waterways or cruiseways in a condition suitable for cruising, fishing and other recreational purposes, and involving a substantial grant-in-aid from the Government. Together with the 'commercial' navigations, over 2250 km of nationalised inland waterways will be available for powered pleasure cruising. Local authorities were required to examine the 'remainder' waterways with a view to including those lengths which could usefully form cruiseways. Some local authorities and voluntary societies are undertaking useful restoration and improvement work. One particularly interesting canal restoration job was that of the Stratford-upon-Avon canal, where over 20 km of derelict waterway was restored in 1966 after 3 years' work backed by the National Trust. The work included rebuilding thirty-six locks and replacing seventy-two lock gates, 112 paddles and many weirs. The total cost was about £80 000, towards which the Ministry of Transport contributed £20 000; £10 000 was obtained from the Pilgrim Trust; and £50 000 from public subscriptions. The comparatively low cost shows the savings that can be made primarily by using unpaid labour, comprising volunteers and military and prison workers and by limiting the organisation structure to one organiser, a secretary and a foreman.[18]

A Department of the Environment Circular[45] in 1971 recommended that the waterways managed by the British Waterways Board should be handed over to the proposed regional water authorities. The British Waterways Board[46, 49] opposed the proposals, asserting that the fragmentation of administration would result in reduced maintenance, varying policies and less efficient administration. In January 1973, the Government decided that the British Waterways Board should continue with its present functions and responsibilities.

Wet Gravel Pits

The government white paper *Leisure in the Countryside*[12] stated that 'excellent opportunities for the creation of recreational facilities are provided on a substantial scale by disused gravel pits'. Wooldridge and Beaver,[19] in a review of changes in the location of gravel workings from 1920 to 1950, noted the tendency of the industry to move into the valleys to obtain gravels of superior quality and to engage in 'wet working'. Since 1950 this policy has been accelerated. Drummond[13] estimated that of the 1968 annual take of 1400 ha of land in England and Wales for sand and gravel, nearly 1000 ha was wet pits and approximately half of this was new water area. It was also estimated that the 1967 annual output of 65 million m^3 of sand and gravel will probably increase to 115 million m^3 by 1975–80.[20]

Wet gravel pits are suitable for a wide range of recreational uses: angling, sailing, wild life study, canoeing, motor boating, rowing, water skiing and hydroplane racing. Some of these uses are mutually incompatible and limitations on use may also result from weed growth, shape and depth of pits, and location where near to residential areas making noisy activities unacceptable.[11]

The after use of gravel pits would also help to alleviate the serious shortage of water for angling. In many parts of the country wet gravel pits are rented, leased or even owned by angling bodies and it is a proven fact that such water filled pits sustain fish life. They are not so susceptible to floods as rivers and are all-weather fisheries. The users of such waters would obviously be more inclined to stock, preserve and improve the facilities, because fish introduced would remain in the pit unlike those in a river which can swim up or downstream to other people's waters.

Reservoirs

New and large surface reservoirs are constantly being constructed to provide a constant, reliable supply of piped water where it is needed,[21] while others are needed for river regulation or compensation. In *Leisure in the Countryside*[12] the Government expressed the view that with suitable planning, management and supervision, access for such pursuits as angling, birdwatching and some forms of boating may be permitted. Power craft are however rarely permitted because of the danger of pollution.[11]

In 1963, the Institution of Water Engineers issued a report on the recreational use of waterworks.[22] The report emphasised that the prime duty of water undertakers is to provide an adequate quantity of safe and suitable water but that access to many reservoirs and waterworks lands—from which the water is filtered and sterilized—could be permitted if reasonable regulations for control are applied. This generally involves the establishment of clubs for the various activities and the approval of the club rules by the water undertaker; provision and satisfactory maintenance of adequate sanitary accommodation; adequate supervision; ample precautions against fire and vandalism; and allocation of special areas for picnicking.

The number of agreements between water undertakers and sailing clubs is on the increase and in some cases the local education authority is a party to the agreement. Fishing is allowed by most water undertakers, with trout fishing by fly or artificial lure being the most common. Birdwatching is generally permitted but the numbers of watchers are carefully restricted. Agreements with sailing clubs are generally detailed and exacting.

Some of the largest reservoirs in the country—Derwent Reservoir (Durham—Northumberland border) and Grafham Water (Huntingdon), both completed in 1966— are used extensively for recreational purposes. Derwent Reservoir with a water surface area of 400 ha was stocked with 90 000 trout and a computer is used to assess the necessary restocking.[24] There were over 10 000 rods in 1970. A sailing club has been established with over 1000 members and 320 dinghies.[47] There is also a nature reserve occupying 60 ha, picnic areas and viewing points.[25] In comparison, Grafham Water has a surface area of 630 ha. The site contains three picnic areas with car parks to accommodate 1400 cars and a nature reserve of 150 ha. A sailing club has 1500 adult members, 200 junior members and 640 dinghies, whilst the sailing facilities cost £78 500, including £51 000 for the clubhouse. The reservoir was stocked initially with 68 000 brown and rainbow trout, and restocking takes place each year (it cost £37 600 for the period 1966–69). Over 21 000 daily fishing permits have been issued each year.[26] Both schemes were planned with the recreational use in mind from the outset.

Akroyd[50] has described how the reservoir to be built at Empingham (Rutland) for the Welland and Nene River Authority will be the largest man-made reservoir in the country, with a water area of 1350 ha and an estimated cost of £17 million. Recreational provision includes 3000 car spaces—high density on tarmacadam, medium density on gravel, and low density on grass under trees; a sailing centre on long lease to a club; trout fishing; and a nature reserve controlled by the Leicester and Rutland Trust for Nature Conservation.

Barrages

Goode[21] has described how barrage schemes appear attractive because they hold out prospects of storing large quantities of water without directly interfering with existing land use. They also exploit the water resources of the whole catchment since they provide storage at the downstream end of the river system where the run-off is greatest. A barrage may also produce other benefits in road communications, land reclamation and recreation. On the other hand, barrages are very expensive and their merit of providing a very large quantity of water carries with it the disadvantage that whereas high costs have to be incurred during construction, it is likely to be some years before the full yield is available. Construction in the sea involves special problems not encountered with reservoirs built on dry land. The effects of a barrage on land drainage, migratory fish and shipping must be considered, and there are certain to be problems of siltation and changes in the ecology of the neighbourhood. Because of the immensity and complexity of these schemes it does not seem likely that any will materialise before the 1980's but there can be no doubt that they could make a substantial contribution to water based recreation at a time when there will be a serious shortage of resources.

Coast

A report by the Greater London and South East Sports Council[9] states that 'subject to the provision of the necessary land-based facilities and access, the potential use of the sea for sailing, cruising and to a lesser extent canoeing is virtually limitless'. This statement would not be valid for all our coasts and a report on water sports in the northern region[10] brings it into perspective:

In the North-East where the coastline is very open with few sheltered bays a concentration of water sports activity is found at the mouths of the main rivers and at major towns along the coast, often in association with harbours and ports. In some places, however, dangerous winds, tides and currents may prohibit any recreational use.

Tanner[27] has made an exhaustive study of coastal recreation and found increasing demand for canoeing, motor boating, sailing, sea angling, sub-aqua activities, swimming and water skiing. He found the main problems to be insufficient access, conflicts between water based activities, interference with the needs of conservation, shortage of marinas, pollution and water safety. He stressed the need for planning for recreation to be regarded as an integral part of coastal planning.

Outdoor Swimming Pools

Swimming pools may be provided by local authorities for use by the public generally; by private establishments such as hotels and holiday camps where the use of facilities is usually restricted to residents; and on school sites, which may or may not be open to the public outside school hours.

The Sports Council[44] has suggested that open air pools can usefully be sited alongside indoor pools (with the same heating plant serving both), but possibly in urban areas these pools are better sited in parks where temporary changing facilities can be made available and where space can be set aside for sunbathing and general recreation. The dimensions of outdoor pools are less important than for indoor pools, as they are mainly used for play and relaxation rather than for serious swimming.

WATER BASED RECREATIONAL ACTIVITIES

The main requirements of the principal water based recreational pursuits are now considered, together with current trends in these activities.

Motor Boating and Cruising

The expression 'cruising' comprises the movement of boats by water from place to place, requiring overnight mooring places. It covers all forms of powered boats from dinghies with outboard motors to large cabin cruisers which are kept moored on the waterways for weekend and holiday use, but excluding speedboats.[20] Participation in this activity nationally has increased considerably since the last war: the number of comprehensive cruising and mooring licences issued by British Waterways Board almost doubled in the decade before 1963.[6] The Inland Waterways Association expects demand to increase at the rate of eight per cent per annum.[28] The number of pleasure boats counted on a peak day (3rd August, 1971) in England and Wales was 5340 on rivers, 1928 on reservoirs and 10 782 on canals.[48]

Cabin cruisers require large areas of water, or access to long stretches of navigable river or canal, or the sea. They generally require a minimum depth of water of just over 1 metre. The west Midlands survey of inland waters[2] found that canals were used rather more than rivers by pleasure craft but there is of course an excellent network of usable canals in that region. In the survey of sports facilities undertaken by the Greater London and South East Sports Council[9] it was found that the growing numbers of power boats and the related numbers of inexperienced helmsmen with little appreciation of other water users has led to a certain amount of conflict between power boats and other water sports in areas where power boats have access to the water. This pinpoints the need for persons engaged in pleasure cruising to be familiar with The Water Sports Code.[29] A West Midlands Sports Council report[30] also emphasises the need for good stretches of navigable, weed free water, with silt free banks for mooring. It also describes how increased use can generate greater demand for ancillary facilities of all kinds, such as moorings, boat-yards, inns and restaurants, car parks and road access, toilets and refuse disposal arrangements.

Sailing

The Trent Valley Study[20] describes sailing as the boom sport of the post-war era in Britain and as more schools introduce sailing into their curricula so future demand is likely to increase. The Eastern Sports Council[32] has described how sailing takes place at sea, on rivers, reservoirs and wet gravel pits. Sailing waters should have a minimum depth of 1.5 m with fairly open banks and a width of not less than 30 m. Access roads suitable for cars and trailers are also desirable. Derbyshire County Council[23] stresses that inland waters are now more urgently required for sailing than ever before, primarily to meet the needs of young people who—without these facilities—could not afford the cost of travelling to the coast at weekends. There has been an almost threefold increase in the number of clubs affiliated to the Royal Yachting Association between 1950 and 1968. Dower[34] gives a 1200 per cent increase in expenditure on sailing dinghies between 1952 and 1962, compared with a 600 per cent increase on cars and motor cycles, with half a million people in the country sailing regularly.

It may be useful to draw a distinction between sailing dinghies, which are small craft with a maximum length of about 6 m, and keel boats which are generally much larger. Dinghies are pulled ashore and are usually parked in small compounds or dinghy parks adjacent to the sailing club.[35] Keel boats require afloat moorings, deeper water and more extensive chandlery and repair facilities than dinghies.[9] There are also multi-hull craft like catamarans and trimarans.

Canoeing

Canoeing takes three main forms: touring, slalom and racing. Canoe touring is a river activity essentially requiring overnight stops at recognised camp sites, good access to the river and the right to navigate. Unrestricted passage is of more importance than the extent or condition of the water, and canoes can negotiate areas of very shallow water. Canoe slalom offers competition of a particularly exciting and adventurous kind and takes place on 'white water', that is water moving rapidly with various wave formations, providing a test of handling a canoe over an obstacle course. Suitable sources are fast young streams or the artificial conditions created by weirs on larger rivers. Whereas canoe racing requires straight lengths of water,[20] minimum dimensions needed are a width of 600 mm and a depth of 225 mm.[11] The Eastern Sports Council[32] has estimated an annual growth rate of ten to fifteen per cent. The Greater London and South East Sports Council[9] has expressed the view that the increased participation arises mainly through schools and youth groups. Interest has also been stimulated since the last war by the production of British made rigid and folding canoes, and subsequently by the development of construction kits enabling canoes to be built relatively cheaply in schools, youth clubs and private homes.[27]

Rowing

The Eastern Sports Council[32] has advocated calm inland water, wide and straight enough to take six lanes for racing, as the ideal provision for rowing. The South Western Sports Council[11] has suggested that the basic needs for competition rowing courses are fairly still or slow flowing stretches of water about 30 m wide and more than 800 m long, with the length increased to 2000 m for international courses as at Holme Pierrepont. Rowing is essentially a competitive sport and therefore the majority of participants belong to a club. The main growth seems to be associated with educational establishments and youth organisations.[27]

Water skiing

This sport is comparatively new to Great Britain, with most of the development taking place in the last decade. It owes its present boom to the production of comfortable and effective protective clothing and to modern improvements in outboard motors and small craft hull design.[2]

The British Water Ski Federation believes that there are between 60 000 and 70 000 water skiers in England and Wales, and the Northern Advisory Council for Sport and Recreation estimates that on the north-east coast the number of skiers is doubling every 5–6 years.[27] A survey of outdoor leisure activities in the northern region[33] revealed that none of the 3828 persons interviewed had ever undertaken water skiing but eleven per cent wished to do so.

Nevertheless, as emphasised by the Eastern Sports Council[32] there are major obstacles to the further development of water skiing on inland waters. The formation of a club necessitates considerable financial outlay and a prerequisite is a reasonable expectation of security of tenure of water facilities. The minimum requirement is an unobstructed stretch of water, 550–620 m long by 180 m in width, with a minimum depth of about 1.5 m. There is often opposition to the introduction of water skiing on the grounds of danger, noise and pollution, and some form of zoning of water by area or time is frequently necessary.

Powered Boat Racing

There are two main forms of powered boat used for racing on inland waters: runabouts with a minimum length of 2.1 m with outboard motors and 2.7 m with inboard motors; and hydroplanes which are the marine equivalent of the racing car, with high powered engines.[9] There has been a rapid growth in power boat activity since 1945, due particularly to the development of the outboard motor, and this has been especially the case with the small speed boat which is often kept at the owner's home and trailed to the water. It is not possible to estimate the total number of people who take part in all forms of power boating as many do not become affiliated to an organisation or join a club until they are interested in racing or regular cruising.

Hydroplaning and motor boat racing require a minimum area of 6 ha of unobstructed water and problems can arise through conflict with other users, noise, backwash damage to banks, and petrol and exhaust contamination of water. As with water skiing, spatial or temporal zoning of water facilities is essential.

Sub-Aqua Activities

In 1970 the British Sub-Aqua Club had 10 000 active members and had trained over 50 000 people to use underwater breathing equipment through its 360 branches located throughout the world. All who join a branch of the club are able to proceed through a full training course, comprising snorkelling, aqualung training in a swimming pool and finally lake or sea diving. With increasing experience, divers can turn to more specialised fields such as underwater photography, wreck exploration, fish observation, underwater archaeology, geology or marine biology. Fresh water sites are useful for training, often being safer than sea diving, and frequently presenting aspects of particular interest. The requirements of underwater swimming are quite different from those of other water sports, depth being by far the most important dimension,[2] and most sand and gravel workings are relatively shallow, being in the order of 3–6 m deep. It is, therefore, difficult to find sufficient inland sites with clear water to a depth of 15–45 m.

Angling

Statistics from many sources show the tremendous popularity and continued steady growth of angling. The number of angling licences issued by river authorities rose from 578 000 in 1953 to 1 274 000 in 1966.[36] A national survey of anglers in 1970[37] estimated that there were 2.8 million anglers in England and Wales at that time. A leisure survey in the northern region[33] found that of the 3828 persons interviewed, thirteen per cent had fished at some time, six per cent were currently fishing and a further four per cent would like to fish. The popularity of angling must be due partly to the facts that there is virtually no upper or lower age limit; equipment is moderately priced; and adequate facilities are generally available.[2]

A count of anglers in England and Wales in 1971 gave 13 237 on rivers, 1071 on reservoirs and 15 297 on canals, with the greatest concentration on the River Witham navigation at seventy-six anglers per kilometre.[48]

Angling clubs use rivers, canals, reservoirs, lakes and wet gravel pits. In general, anglers require a depth of about 1 m of unpolluted and comparatively weed free water. Multiple use of water does not preclude angling, and most anglers will concede that the passage of pleasure craft in reasonable numbers on canals is desirable in order to reduce silting and weed growth.[30] Fishing rights on rivers are largely in the hands of private landowners who also own the riparian rights to the river and therefore control access. The majority of fishing rights are leased from the landowners to amalgamations or angling clubs. Conservation of the fisheries is the responsibility of the river authority who under statutory powers carries out duties in relation to pollution control, restocking with fish, weed cutting and dredging. Revenue for this is partly obtained through rod licences which all anglers have to pay.[18] In many parts of the country wet gravel pits are rented, leased or even owned by angling bodies.

Walking and Rambling

Riverside paths and canal towpaths need to be clearly defined and well maintained to ensure optimum use. A west Midlands report indicated that in many cases existing paths are not used extensively by organised groups at present, although their potential is considerable.[30] A number of studies including that of *The Tyne* have shown how riverside walks in urban areas can make a positive contribution to recreational facilities.

Nature Study

The basic requirements for wild life conservation have been listed by the South Western Sports Council[11] as quiet, unpolluted and undisturbed waters with varied vegetation cover and varying depths of water for different species, preferably sited away from human settlements. Nature conservation is not of itself a sport, although many people are concerned in its practice and with natural history as a form of recreation. But more important, the scientific interest of an area, which is the concern of nature conservation, is itself a resource of exceptional value and sometimes of overriding national importance which may be affected by other competing forms of land and water use. Conservation of water habitats and their flora and fauna is desirable not only to preserve unique or rare species but also for research and education; for sport itself as in the form of wildfowling and fishing; for man's enjoyment of wild life for its own sake; and perhaps even to help preserve his mental stability in the growing tensions of an increasingly advanced technological environment.[32] Disused gravel workings at Attenborough near Nottingham have been retained as a nature reserve. The banks and islands have become naturally colonised by vegetation and a survey in 1968 revealed more than 2000 duck of various species.

Swimming

The American report on outdoor recreation in 1962[1] stressed that swimming was one of the most popular outdoor activities in the United States and was likely to be the most popular of all by the turn of the century. The Wolfenden Committee[43] and the Sports Council[44] believe that the majority of new swimming pools should be indoor. They appreciate the great attraction of an outdoor pool set in pleasant surroundings on a hot sunny day, but feel that because of the unreliability of the British climate heated indoor pools offer a better solution.

WATER BASED RECREATION IN GREATER NOTTINGHAM

Figure 8.1 shows the rivers, canals and gravel workings in and around Nottingham with the locations of the sailing, boating and rowing clubs and ancillary facilities such as public houses and caravan sites indicated. Postal questionnaires were sent to all the sailing, rowing, power boat, ski and angling clubs in the area, and the analysed results are given later in the chapter.

The East Midland Sports Council[38] has described how the River Trent supports most forms of water based recreation, and is an integral link in the waterways system which permits extensive cruising within the region and access to other parts of the country. The Trent Valley Study[20] refers to the large post-war increase in recreational activities particularly on the stretch between Long Eaton and Newark. Congestion occurs at certain parts of this section of the river and at access roads, on fine summer weekends. Dinghy sailing has developed into a highly competitive sport—eleven clubs on the same stretch of the River Trent have a membership of approximately 1600 and an average boat capacity of seventy-five boats per club.[38] To avoid the possibility of conflict between users of speed boats and anglers, the use of speed boats and water skiing is restricted to the lengths of river indicated on figure 8.1 and then only at agreed times, when relaxation of the normal speed limits is granted by the British Waterways Board. A stretch of the river in the vicinity of Trent Bridge is used extensively by four rowing clubs.

In addition, the River Trent is probably the best known coarse fishing water in the Midlands, despite the fact that it contains the waste water from a population of almost 4.5 million people and in consequence about forty per cent of its summer flow consists of sewage effluent.[39] Other rivers in the Greater Nottingham area include the Soar, which is an attractive river and is used extensively for recreational purposes, and the Erewash which carries a substantial amount of waste water and is largely devoid of fish. There are four canals traversing the area: Erewash canal, much of which passes through relatively unattractive countryside, is badly neglected and little used but has recreational potential. Nottingham canal, parts of which have been backfilled, has little recreational potential. Beeston canal could, with landscaping, become a valuable amenity feature. Grantham canal is mainly in poor condition, part of it is dry and a certain amount of elimination work has been carried out on bridges and locks—nevertheless, it possesses considerable recreational potential.

The Trent Valley has become nationally important as a centre for the large scale extraction of sand and gravel derived from flood plain terrace gravels of pleistocene age, which form a continuous belt with an average width of about 3 km along the river valley. Many of the gravel extraction areas overlap into 'washlands' which act as natural balancing reservoirs in times of flood, and which therefore necessitate flood protection work as part of the extraction process. The gravel beds vary from 2.75–5.50 m in depth.

In some cases pits are being filled with pulverised fly ash from power stations and other waste materials for restoration to agriculture, but in other instances water filled lagoons are being formed for recreational use. They have the advantages of water which is clear to considerable depths, and freedom from currents and dense tree cover, making for ideal sailing conditions. With adequate pre-planning of deposition of overburden even better recreational resources could be obtained, possibly at reduced cost.

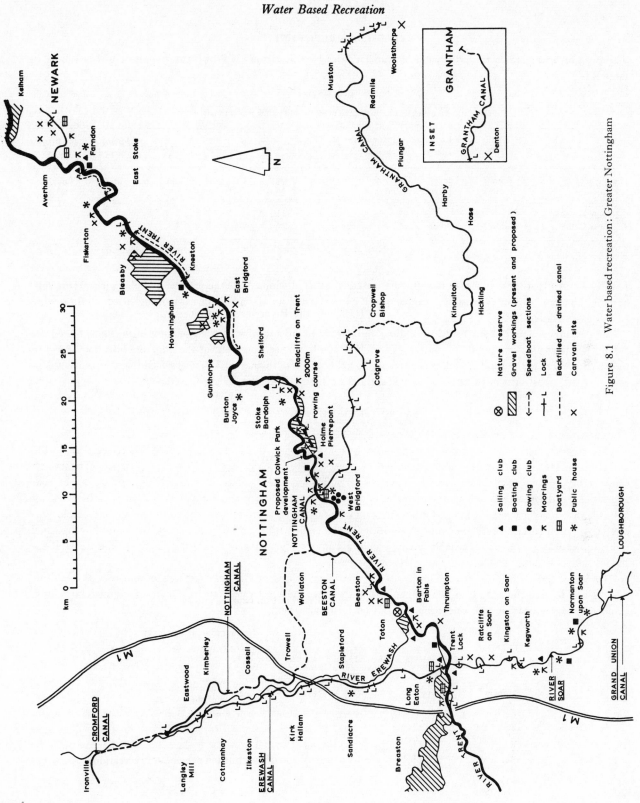

Figure 8.1 Water based recreation: Greater Nottingham

191

WATER SPORTS CLUB FACILITIES

The position in regard to the possession of club facilities by the various types of water sports clubs is shown in table 8.1.

TABLE 8.1

WATER SPORTS CLUB FACILITIES IN GREATER NOTTINGHAM

Type of clubs	Slipway	Changing rooms	Club room	Showers	Toilets	Bar	Restaurant	Facilities owned	Facilities leased
Sailing	84.5	100.0	92.4	15.4	92.4	53.9	23.1	30.8	69.2
Canoeing	20.0	100.0	60.0	—	20.0	—	—	40.0	60.0
Rowing	91.0	100.0	54.5	100.0	100.0	45.5	18.2	45.5	54.5
Power boating and skiing	100.0	66.6	—	—	—	—	—	—	100.0

Note: all figures are expressed as percentages

It will be noted that the majority of facilities are leased and that all clubs place the provision of changing rooms very high on their priority lists. The sailing, canoeing and power boat clubs all had ample car parking space but the rowing clubs possessed very little.

The average length of bank fished by angling clubs was 1400 m and ninety-three per cent of the clubs leased the fishing rights at an average annual rent of £75 in 1970. Only thirteen per cent of the angling clubs had access to toilets and access to the fishing bank was often across fields or along towpaths. The average car park capacity was in excess of fifty cars but car parks were on average 360 m distant from the fishing facilities.

CLUB MEMBERSHIP AND TRENDS

The average number of members per club varies widely between the different sports: canoeing—thirty-one; rowing—seventy-three; power boats and water skiing—ninety-six; angling—100; and sailing—108. There were also wide variations in the proportions of female members: rowing—0.4 per cent; angling—5.4 per cent; power boats and water skiing—6.9 per cent; canoeing—14.1 per cent; and sailing—23.2 per cent. The angling, sailing, power boat and water skiing clubs show substantial increases in numbers of members over the last 10 years, whereas the canoeing and rowing clubs have not maintained quite such a spectacular rate of growth. Of the sixty-one angling clubs completing questionnaires, twenty per cent have waiting lists whereas with the other water sports few clubs have reached their full capacity. As more schools include sailing and rowing instruction in their curricula the demand for membership of sailing and rowing clubs should increase.

Table 8.2 shows the date of establishment of water sports clubs in Greater Nottingham and reveals that some angling and rowing clubs are over 100 years old. It also shows the accelerated rate of growth of angling and sailing. Canoeing, power boating and water skiing are of fairly recent origin.

TABLE 8.2

DATE OF ESTABLISHMENT OF WATER SPORTS CLUBS IN GREATER NOTTINGHAM

Years	Angling	Canoeing	Rowing	Sailing	Power boating & water skiing
1860–1880	2	—	3	—	—
1881–1900	6	—	1	2	—
1901–1920	3	—	—	—	—
1921–1940	5	—	1	—	—
1941–1950	14	1	2	1	—
1951–1960	15	2	—	7	1
1960–1969	12	2	1	2	2

The Pilot National Recreation Survey[3] listed swimming as one of the most popular outdoor sports which fifty per cent of the respondents had experienced at one time or another. Six per cent of the adults interviewed would like to take it up seriously if they had the opportunity, compared with eight per cent in the northern region leisure survey.[33]

INTENSITY OF USE

The majority of angling clubs in Greater Nottingham are active for 7 or 8 months per annum. There is considerable activity on every day of the week with periods of maximum intensity on Saturday and Sunday mornings and afternoons when the amount of activity is about three times that during the remainder of the week. Canoeing is concentrated into afternoons and evenings with over thirty-three per cent of the activity taking place at weekends and with eighty per cent of the clubs operating throughout the year. The pattern of use with rowing clubs is rather similar, with forty per cent of the activity being pursued at weekends and all clubs operating throughout the year. With power boating and water skiing over half the total activity takes place at weekends, although in the fishing season these two activities are restricted to a 3.0 p.m. start; two of the three clubs in Greater Nottingham operate throughout the year. A considerable amount of sailing takes place on weekday afternoons and evenings but well over half of the total activity is at weekends. Fifty per cent of the sailing clubs in Greater Nottingham operate for about 9 months of the year (April to December) and the other half during the summer only. The Derbyshire County Council study of sailing clubs using reservoirs[23] found that the majority of these clubs sail for 8 or 9 months, mainly from March to October or November.

TRAVEL CHARACTERISTICS

Table 8.3 indicates the catchment areas of the various water sports.

TABLE 8.3

CATCHMENT AREAS OF WATER SPORTS

Activity	Average distance travelled by club members in Greater Nottingham	Travel characteristics for East Midlands[31]	Catchment areas of Gloucestershire clubs[11]
Angling	13.2 km	95 per cent not more than 8 km and remainder within 40 km	Mainly under 16 km
Sailing	13.6 km	50 per cent not more than 8 km and remainder within 40 km	County plus surrounding counties
Canoeing	6.8 km	85 per cent not more than 8 km and remainder within 40 km	County wide
Rowing	7.1 km	87 per cent not more than 8 km and remainder within 40 km	Under 16 km
Motor boat racing and water skiing	20 km	—	County plus surrounding counties

These catchment area statistics are interesting in that they represent three different methods of tabulation and also show considerable common ground in their findings. The relatively long distance travelled to angling facilities arises from the dispersed nature of the fishing sites, and the average distance would be much greater for persons from areas which are less well endowed with facilities.

With regard to lidos a higher proportion of visitors in the more remote locations travel by car (thirty-five to forty per cent), and a surprisingly large proportion (range of seventeen to fifty-seven per cent) travel by bus. The proportion that walk to lidos fluctuates considerably with a range of nine to forty-four per cent, while the proportion cycling is quite low and never exceeds nine per cent. By way of comparison the Government Social Survey[4] found that of the people interviewed twenty-nine per cent travelled to swimming pools in the summer on foot or by bicycle, forty-eight per cent went by private motorised transport and the remaining twenty-three per cent by public transport.

Between forty and fifty per cent of lido visitors go to the outdoor pools between two and five times per month, and about ten per cent visit as frequently as twenty or more times per month. At the Nottingham lidos, about twenty-five per cent of the respondents stayed for 1 to 2 hours at the pool, while just over fifty per cent stayed for half a day. Very few visited the pool for less than an hour and nearly twenty per cent stayed all day. Groups of people seem to favour a visiting period of 1–3 hours. There is a peak visiting period around 3 p.m. to 4 p.m., although there is frequently a drop in numbers around lunchtime when the morning visitors go home for lunch.

SOCIO-ECONOMIC CHARACTERISTICS

Tables 8.4 and 8.5 show the age and social composition of the members of the water sports clubs in Greater Nottingham that completed questionnaires.

TABLE 8.4

AGE COMPOSITION OF MEMBERS OF WATER SPORTS CLUBS IN GREATER NOTTINGHAM

Activity	Age composition							
	Under 20	20–24	25–29	30–34	35–44	45–54	55–64	65 and over
Angling	8.5	8.5	13.7	19.5	18.8	18.3	8.7	4.0
Sailing	39.9	9.2	8.9	10 3	15.2	13.4	2.7	0.4
Canoeing	66.2	18.8	6.0	3.8	3.8	0.8	0.6	—
Rowing	68.6	15.5	7.6	1.0	1.1	1.3	4.3	0.6
Power boating and water skiing	9.3	5.7	11.3	31.3	20.7	17.7	4.0	—

Note: all figures are expressed as percentages

Table 8.4 shows that canoeing and rowing are by far the most youthful sports with about sixty-six per cent of participants under 20 years of age. Sailing shows a good spread of ages with a predominance of under 20's resulting from the inclusion of university and school sailing clubs. Power boating and water skiing also show a good distribution over the various age groupings but with a predominance in the 30's. Angling shows the most uniform distribution of all with persons of all ages participating in the sport. The Greater Nottingham findings do not vary substantially from the national survey[37] which showed thirty-three per cent of anglers between the ages of 12 and 24; about seventeen per cent between each of the following age groups: 25–34, 35–44, and 45–54; and only about ten per cent over 54. It does not, however, support the view of the North Regional Planning Committee[33] that fishing is most popular among men aged 12–19, although it must be borne in mind that the Nottingham figures relate only to club membership. The northern region view is largely supported by the Government Social Survey[4] which showed that the following proportions of respondents participated in fishing at least once monthly: eighteen per cent of 15–18 age group; eleven per cent of 19–22 age group; nine per cent of 23–45 age group; and eight per cent of 46–60 age group.

Sixty per cent of Nottingham Lido visitors were children; the under-elevens accounted for about twenty-five per cent of all visitors and the proportion of teenagers ranged from just under fifty per cent up to seventy-five per cent of all visitors. The Government Social Survey[4] also showed a reduction in the numbers using swimming pools with increasing age.

TABLE 8.5

SOCIAL COMPOSITION OF MEMBERS OF WATER SPORTS CLUBS IN GREATER NOTTINGHAM

Activity	Social composition							
	Professional	Managerial	Skilled manual	Non-manual	Semi-skilled manual	Unskilled	Non-employed	Students
Angling	4.1	6.0	35.6	13.6	25.4	11.8	1.6	1.9
Sailing	12.4	15.0	7.8	18.0	1.3	1.5	3.3	40.7
Canoeing	5.0	3.6	11.8	8.6	6.8	3.4	0.8	60.0
Rowing	3.9	7.9	8.6	6.4	1.5	1.1	0.4	70.2
Power boating and water skiing	7.3	47.0	20.7	9.0	4.7	—	1.0	10.3

Note: all figures are expressed as percentages

Table 8.5 shows a high proportion of students in the sailing, rowing and canoe clubs, but very few in angling clubs. Practically seventy-five per cent of the anglers covered in the Greater Nottingham survey were skilled or semi-skilled manual workers or non-manual workers. Sailing shows a reasonable spread although nearly fifty per cent are in the professional, managerial or non-manual occupational classifications. With power boating and water skiing over fifty per cent are in the professional/managerial group and a further twenty per cent are skilled manual workers, doubtless stemming from the fact that expensive equipment is needed.

The national survey[37] also found that there was a larger than average number of anglers in the skilled and semi-skilled manual occupational groups, and this was confirmed by the Government Social Survey.[4]

The Pilot National Recreational Survey[3] described swimming as 'the most classless of sports', spanning every age range up to 45 years, every income and every educational and occupational level.

MAIN PROBLEMS AND NEEDS

Angling

One of the main complaints of anglers in Greater Nottingham has been the alleged disregard of their interests by boat users. They were especially critical of speed boats and water skiers and as stated by one angling club secretary—'speed limits have been imposed by the British Waterways Board but a single boat exceeding the speed limit can ruin the pleasure of hundreds of anglers'. Another club secretary described how the heavy wash from power boats or barges can scare away fish, discolour the water with dislodged sediment and cause anglers to lose their sport for quite long periods. Regard by all water users to the water sports code[29] will prevent these problems occurring.

A number of clubs made reference to the difficulty of securing access to local waters owing to the heavy demand and the high cost of transport to more distant waters. Some clubs complained of excessive rent increases in recent years and of insufficient finance to rent their own waters. A few clubs have suggested that all water should be taken over by river authorities and administered for the benefit of anglers; possibly a case could be made for river authorities taking over fishing rights. At national level anglers saw the main problems as harmful effects of other water users; overcrowding; competing interests; exclusion from private waters; and pollution.[37]

Sailing

Some of the sailing clubs in Greater Nottingham were subject to restrictions on the number of dinghies by the river authority or by the size of the dinghy compound. A number of clubs asserted that sailing activities were restricted by the narrow width of the river, heavy cruiser traffic and anglers, and stated that they would much prefer to lease reservoirs. Nevertheless, it is evident that the River Trent provides a good training ground for schools and youth clubs as an introduction to dinghy sailing.[31]

Canoeing

The major difficulty of canoeists around Nottingham, as in other parts of the country, is obtaining access to suitable waters. One club secretary described how they were unable to canoe on many rivers—particularly in Derbyshire and Yorkshire—owing to landowners refusing access, primarily because of fishing. There is also a need for toilet and refuse facilities at access points and camp sites at overnight stops, preferably near towns and other areas of interest. The North West Sports Council[40] has also drawn attention to the need for access to rivers and camping sites for the canoe camper and the competitive canoeist. The Eastern Sports Council[32] has described how a person planning a canoe expedition of 2 or 3 days' duration could be involved in approaching several hundred landowners for permission to pass along the river.

Rowing

Several of the Nottingham clubs described the restriction on activities stemming from insufficient accommodation to house the boats, lack of finance and the difficulty of finding sufficient coaches. All the clubs welcome the proposed 2000 m rowing course at Holme Pierrepont which is illustrated in figure 8.3.

Speed Boating and Water Skiing

There is a great demand for one or two areas of unobstructed water which can be used for these activities. Wet gravel pits would seem to be the ideal facility. In the absence of a separate facility, time or space zoning of a waterway is the only possible alternative.

Outdoor Swimming Pools

The main complaint about the Nottingham lidos in the summer of 1968 was the low temperature of the water, although it was equally evident that most lido visitors preferred outdoor to indoor pools and that they found their visit to be both exhilarating and enjoyable. Unfortunately, the vagaries of the British climate severely restrict the number of days per year when an unheated outdoor pool entices large numbers of visitors. To ensure continuous use

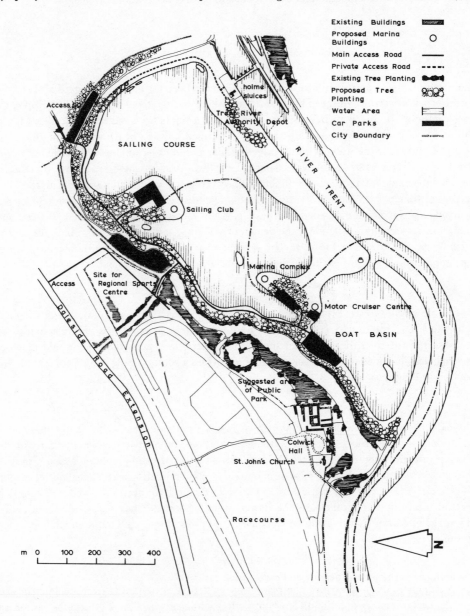

Figure 8.2   Colwick Park Proposals (Nottingham Corporation)

throughout the year and yet, at the same time provide for the peak use during very hot spells, lidos ideally need enclosing with sliding double glazed roofs and walls, so that under poor weather conditions they can be easily and quickly converted into enclosed pools. Provision also needs to be made for heating the water as and when required.

MAJOR NOTTINGHAM WATER RECREATION PROPOSALS

Colwick Park

The proposals are illustrated in figure 8.2 and comprise one lagoon of 12 ha primarily for motor cruisers with a 'cut' to the River Trent, and another lagoon of 32 ha principally for sailing and other non-power boat activities such as underwater swimming and canoeing. 'Sweetener' pipes are proposed from the river to the boat basin and between

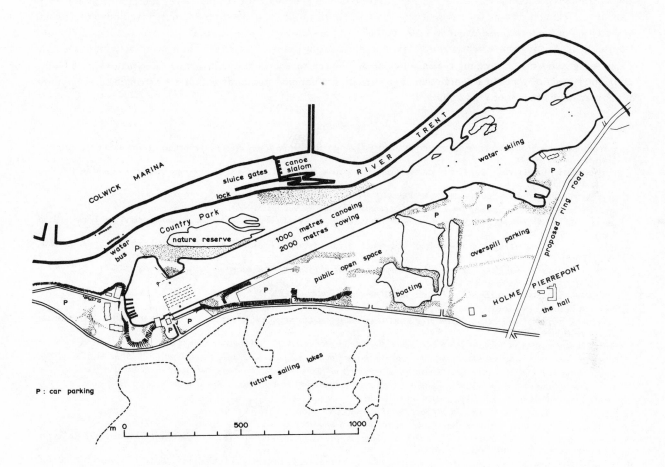

Figure 8.3   Holme Pierrepont: National Water Sports Centre Proposals (Nottinghamshire County Council)

the two lagoons. Three groups of buildings are proposed in the main marina area, motor cruiser centre and sailing club together with car parking facilities for 860 cars. Some earth mounding, formation of islands and landscaping is envisaged. Other proposals for the centre include a regional sports centre (4.4 ha) to cater for a range of sporting activities, comprising a large indoor games and training area; swimming pool; floodlit hard surfaced all-weather area; floodlit grassed area; residential accommodation; and a public park and amenity area.[41]

Holme Pierrepont

Nottinghamshire County Council's main proposals are for the linking and enlarging of the lagoons, resulting from gravel workings, to form a championship rowing, canoeing and water skiing course, as illustrated in figure 8.3. The area of the site is in excess of 80 ha and together with Colwick Park could occupy well over 240 ha; by 1980 it could be the largest water park in the country. The rowing course is 2200 m long, 140 m wide and 3.5 m deep with a water area of 40 ha. The water level is maintained by two existing streams, a sweetener pipe connected to the river and a weir at north end of the site. There are six rowing lanes, each 13.5 m wide. A new floodbank supports the building complex of 7405 m² floor area to accommodate competitors and spectators. The complex includes stand seating for 4000 people, restaurants and bars for 1000 people, changing rooms for over 1000 people and boathouses to accommodate the craft of 3200 people. Some of the new bank slopes are graded at 1 in 8 to provide picnicking banks and spectator viewing platforms with an excellent view of the course.[42] A number of national and at least one international event will also be held on the course and it is envisaged that as many as 130 clubs from outside Nottingham will use the course for practice purposes. Apart from the rowing activities extensive water skiing, canoeing and angling is also anticipated. The centre is a prototype involving three major sports bodies using one stretch of water to accommodate their activities to national standards within a constructional programme of 2.5 years and at a cost of £1.2 million.[51]

REFERENCES

1. OUTDOOR RECREATION RESOURCES REVIEW COMMISSION. *Outdoor Recreation for America :* Report to President and Congress of United States, (1962)

2. BIRMINGHAM UNIVERSITY, DEPARTMENT OF PHYSICAL EDUCATION. *Inland Waters and Recreation.* Central Council of Physical Recreation, (1964)

3. BRITISH TRAVEL ASSOCIATION/UNIVERSITY OF KEELE. *Pilot National Recreation Survey : Report No. 1,* (1967)

4. SILLITOE, K. K. (1969). *Planning for Leisure : Government Social Survey,* H.M.S.O.

5. DRUMMOND, I. *Recreation and River Authorities, Proceedings of Conference on recreation in the countryside, University of Loughborough,* (1969)

6. COPPOCK, J. T. The recreational use of land and water in rural Britain. *Tijdschrift voor Economische en Sociale Geographie,* **57.3,** (1966)

7. TANNER, M. *Recreational Use of Enclosed Waterways : The general problem. Proceedings of conference on recreation in the countryside, University of Loughborough,* (1969)

8. COUNTRYSIDE COMMISSION. *Digest of Countryside Recreation Statistics,* (1969)

9. GREATER LONDON AND SOUTH EAST SPORTS COUNCIL. *Sports Facilities : Initial appraisal. 2,* (1969)

10. NORTHERN REGIONAL PLANNING COMMITTEE/NORTHERN ADVISORY COUNCIL FOR SPORT AND RECREATION. *Water Sports in the Northern Region,* (1967)

11. SOUTH WESTERN SPORTS COUNCIL. *Outdoor Water Recreation : Report No. 3.—Gloucestershire,* (1968)

12. MINISTRY OF LAND AND NATURAL RESOURCES. *Leisure in the Countryside : England and Wales.* Cmnd. 2928, H.M.S.O., (1966)

13. DRUMMOND, I. *Water Recreation and Amenities. Proceedings of congress on the future of our rivers, London,* (1969)

14. HADFIELD, C. and STREAT, M. (1968). *Holiday Cruising on Inland Waterways,* David and Charles

15. ROLT, L. T. C. (1944). *Narrow Boat,* Allen and Unwin

16. BRITISH WATERWAYS BOARD. *The Facts about the Waterways,* London, (1965)

17. MINISTRY OF TRANSPORT. *British Waterways : recreation and amenity :* Cmnd. 3401, H.M.S.O., (1967)

18. COWLEY, G. (1966). *Bedfordshire River Valleys : A planning appraisal of outdoor recreation in the Great Ouse and Ivel Valleys in Bedfordshire,* Bedfordshire County Council

19. WOOLDRIDGE, S. W. and BEAVER, S. H. The working of sand and gravel in Britain: A problem in land use. *Geographical Journal,* **115,** (1950)

20. NOTTINGHAMSHIRE COUNTY COUNCIL, COUNTY PLANNING DEPARTMENT. *Trent Valley Study,* (1970)

21. GOODE, W. *The Nation's Water Resources. Proceedings of Annual Conference of Royal Institution of Chartered Surveyors,* (1966)

22. INSTITUTION OF WATER ENGINEERS. *Final Report of the Council on the Recreational Use of Waterworks,* (1963)

23. DERBYSHIRE COUNTY COUNCIL/PEAK PARK PLANNING BOARD. *Sailing on Reservoirs,* (1967)

24. MCLELLAN, A. G. *Recreational Use of Enclosed Waters : Derwent Reservoir. Proceedings of Conference on recreation in the countryside, University of Loughborough,* (1969)

25. GIBBERD, F. G. Derwent Reservoir. *Journal of Institute of Landscape Architects,* (August 1969)

26. SAXTON, K. J. H. *Grafham Water : A reservoir planned for recreational use. Proceedings of conference on recreation in the countryside, University of Loughborough,* (1969)

27. COUNTRYSIDE COMMISSION. *Special Study Report Vol. 1.—Coastal recreation and holidays,* H.M.S.O., (1969)

28. CHESHIRE COUNTY COUNCIL, PLANNING DEPARTMENT. *Cheshire Countryside : An interim report on recreation,* (1968)

29. CENTRAL COUNCIL OF PHYSICAL RECREATION. *The Water Sports Code*

30. WEST MIDLANDS SPORTS COUNCIL. *Recreational Use of Canals,* (1968)

31. EAST MIDLAND SPORTS COUNCIL. *The Recreational Use of the Wash and the Canals and Waterways of the East Midlands,* (1967)

32. EASTERN SPORTS COUNCIL. *The Use of Inland Waters for Recreation,* (1968)

33. NORTH REGIONAL PLANNING COMMITTEE. *Outdoor Leisure Activities in the Northern Region,* (1969)

34. DOWER, M. Fourth Wave: the challenge of leisure. *The Architects' Journal,* **141.3,** (1965)

35. SOUTH HAMPSHIRE PLAN ADVISORY COMMITTEE. *South Hampshire Plan: Study report No. 5—Recreation,* (1970)

36. MOLYNEUX, D. D. Working for recreation. *Journal of Royal Town Planning Institute,* **54.4,** (1968)

37. NATIONAL ENVIRONMENT RESEARCH COUNCIL. *National angling survey, 1970,* (1971)

38. EAST MIDLAND SPORTS COUNCIL. *Initial Appraisal of Major Facilities Used for Sport and Recreation,* (1967)

39. TRENT RIVER AUTHORITY. *The River Trent and its Tributaries*

40. NORTH WEST SPORTS COUNCIL, WATER RECREATION SUB-COMMITTEE. Working Party A. *Rivers: Interim report,* (1968)

41. CITY OF NOTTINGHAM PLANNING DEPARTMENT. *Colwick Park,* (1967)

42. NOTTINGHAMSHIRE COUNTY COUNCIL PLANNING DEPARTMENT. *Holme Pierrepont: A national water sports centre,* (1969)

43. CENTRAL COUNCIL OF PHYSICAL RECREATION. *Sport and the Community: Report of the Wolfenden Committee,* (1960)

44. SPORTS COUNCIL. (1968). *Planning for sport,* Central Council of Physical Recreation

45. DEPARTMENT OF THE ENVIRONMENT. *Circular 92/71,* (1971)

46. BRITISH WATERWAYS BOARD. *Memorandum on Government Proposals for Reorganisation of Water and Sewage Services,* (1971)

47. HARTLEY, C. Planning the recreational development of reservoirs: Derwent Reservoir. *Recreation News, Supplement 4,* Countryside Commission, (1971)

48. MOON, F. Angling and pleasure boating on inland waterways. *Recreation News, Supplement 6,* Countryside Commission, (1972)

49. BRITISH WATERWAYS BOARD. Reorganisation of Water and Sewage Services. Comments on Department of the Environment Consultation Paper: '*The Amenity Use of Water Space and the Reorganisation of the British Waterways Board*', (1972)

50. AKROYD, D. S. Empingham Reservoir. *Proceedings of Conference on Outdoor Recreation,* Department of Surveying, Trent Polytechnic, (1972)

51. SMART, C. W. W. Holme Pierrepont—*A National Water Sports Centre in a Country Park. Proceedings of Conference on Outdoor Recreation,* Department of Surveying, Trent Polytechnic, (1972)

9 OUTDOOR RECREATION PATTERNS, NEEDS, TRENDS AND OBJECTIVES

THIS CHAPTER DRAWS together and compares the main characteristics of the various outdoor recreational facilities which have been separately described and analysed in earlier chapters, and sets out to identify the main needs and desirable objectives.

METHOD OF PROVISION

Local authorities play an important rôle in the provision of many classes of outdoor recreational facility. Borough and urban district councils have been providing town parks since the latter part of the nineteenth century; in more recent times national park schemes have been implemented by public bodies; and both public authorities and private organisations can undertake country park schemes. Similarly with children's playgrounds the bulk of provision is made by local authorities as it is considered an essential public service. There are, however, a few cases where organisations other than local authorities—such as the National Coal Board at miners' welfare centres—provide children's playground equipment.

The pattern of provision of outdoor playing facilities is quite different from that of parks and playgrounds. Local authorities are the main providers of playing fields for team games, although employers and private organisations make a sizeable contribution. The public has also tended to look to local authorities for the provision of bowling greens and tennis courts, although a surprisingly large proportion of grass courts is provided by employers and private clubs. Local authorities provide about sixty-six per cent of athletics facilities in Greater Nottingham but less than ten per cent of archery facilities. In the case of golf courses there is a preponderence of private courses although future provision may be primarily in the public sector. The majority of outdoor swimming pools are provided by local authorities but there is some private provision such as at hotels and holidays camps. The majority of 'permanent' allotments are provided by local authorities under the Allotments Acts whilst many of the private allotment sites are on potential building land and constitute a transitional use.

PROBLEMS OF PROVISION

In practice, problems often arise in the provision of recreation facilities and they may be so demanding as to prevent an adequate level of supply from being established. Golf courses, for instance, require such large areas of land (40–60 ha for an 18-hole course) that it is often impossible to locate them close to urban residential districts. Children's playgrounds need to be sited in the midst of residential areas and yet the noise of children playing for long periods of time can cause considerable annoyance to neighbouring residents. Parks are frequently sited in rather out-of-the-way locations because land with suitable physical characteristics but in rather remote locations has come on to the land market, and there is an absence of suitable land close to heavily populated areas where parks are urgently needed. To construct playing fields on sloping sites must involve heavy expenditure in earthworks, which is better avoided wherever practicable.

Some facilities such as golf courses, bowling greens, lidos and athletics stadia have high initial capital costs and their provision may well be deferred in times of financial stringency. Some facilities are far less suited for multiple-use than others and this tends to make it more difficult to justify their provision.

Allotments should desirably be sited in close juxtaposition to residential areas, yet the unsightly appearance of many existing sites militates against this. With water sports, there is often a need to zone the resources by time and/or space to avoid possible conflict between participants in different activities.

Development Plan Provision

The development plans prepared by Nottingham Corporation and Nottinghamshire County Council for the built-up areas of Greater Nottingham in the early 1950's incorporated large areas of new open space much of it in rather remote locations on the washlands of the Trent. Although the total population has increased considerably in the last two decades, little of the additional open space allocations have been made available to the public.

There are a number of weaknesses in the Development Plan approach as far as open space provision is concerned:

(1) No real assessment of need is made and the National Playing Fields Association standard is rigidly applied in determining the probable shortfalls in playing fields and parks.

(2) Private open space is regarded as reasonably secure whereas in practice private facilities can be very insecure.

(3) In many cases the sites of new facilities are not specifically defined on the town map and are unlikely to materialise because of this indecisiveness.

(4) Some open space allocations seem to be prompted by motives of convenience rather than a soundly based and positively determined strategy.

(5) There is no effective machinery to ensure that the open space proposals are put into effect.

(6) There seems no satisfactory method of converting the vague Development Plan proposals into positive schemes aimed at meeting the needs of participants in a variety of recreational activities.

Effect of Changing Pattern of Urban Growth on Recreational Needs

As urban populations increase and towns and cities continue to spread, the greater will be the need for adequate provision of open spaces of all kinds. Furthermore, expansion of the open space area should proceed concurrently with the spread of cities and the sites should be acquired, or at very least be earmarked, well ahead of urban expansion while the land is still available and comparatively low priced.[41] In addition, as advocated by the Town and Country Planning Association,[42] the recreation potential of green belts needs to be thoroughly explored and more fully utilised so that—in addition to restraining urban sprawl—these protected areas may make a more positive contribution to the enjoyment of city dwellers. Better access for walkers, riders and naturalists is needed in green belts and it might be possible to site some country parks in these areas.

The changing pattern of land use in the central areas of cities may create different open space needs. Inner urban parks serving the needs of the residents of former town houses may no longer be entirely relevant, but in their place smaller open spaces—for sitting and resting and as settings to buildings or groups of buildings, connected by landscaped walkways—might be better suited to today's needs.

Some have argued that with the increasing prosperity, mobility and leisure time of urban populations, the need for additional open space in towns and cities declines as people are able to visit more frequently national and country parks, the coast and other more distant recreational resources. Yet sixty per cent of Nottingham residents, in common with those of many other cities, do not have access to cars; for them a journey to a distant resource would often be both difficult and costly and this adds weight to the need for an adequate urban open space network.

STANDARDS OF PROVISION

Standards of provision have been formulated for most outdoor recreational facilities by official or semi-official bodies. Nevertheless they can only constitute broad guidelines and will need to be varied to take account of local conditions. In the case of town parks opinions have varied widely as to desirable standards of provision ranging from 0.40 ha per 1000 population at the lower end,[1] to 0.70 ha per 1000 population at the higher end, increasing with size of town to 1.15 ha per 1000 population for the largest towns.[2] For children's playgrounds a commonly adopted standard is 0.20 ha per 1000 population[3] but this will also be influenced by the extent to which the playing of ball games is permitted on playgrounds. The National Playing Fields Association has recommended a provision of 2.40 ha per 1000 population for playing fields including school playing fields in regular use by the public outside school hours.[4] In practice a better method of assessment would probably be to base provision on the number of pitches rather than on area of land. The Ministry of Housing and Local Government advocated one tennis court per 2000 people and one bowling green per 7000 population.[5]

Athletics stadia are expensive features to construct and need to be sited in populous areas to ensure adequate use. It has been suggested that towns or areas with populations over 30 000 should have a stadium and that an additional stadium should be provided for every 200 000 population.[6] On golf course provision the Sports Council[7] believes that one 18-hole course is needed for every 20 000–30 000 population and this entails the very large land allocation of 1.6–2.4 ha per 1000 population. The position with regard to standards of provision for allotments has become increasingly confused in recent years. The National Allotments and Gardens Society[8] still advocates 0.8 ha per 1000 population whilst the Committee of Inquiry into Allotments[9] recommended a minimum provision of 0.2 ha per 1000 population of leisure gardens. The rate of provision in most parts of the country ranges between the two limits. It is even more difficult to prescribe standards of provision for lidos. In this connection the Sports Council[7] has suggested 0.93 m² per swimmer but in order to apply this standard it is necessary to know the number of swimmers, frequency of visits and the time they spend in the pool, as distinct from sunbathing. Little work seems to have been done on the formulation of standards for water sports and there are as yet no official recommendations.

CLUB FACILITIES

Investigations into club facility provision in Greater Nottingham showed wide disparities between different activities. Ranking team games in order of abundance of facilities they are: hockey, rugby, football and cricket. It is probably to be expected that hockey and rugby teams would have access to more facilities as a higher proportion of them have private club grounds, whereas the majority of football and cricket clubs hire municipally owned grounds. In general, tennis club facilities are superior to those enjoyed by bowling clubs, but here again a higher proportion of bowling clubs hire public greens. Investigations of other sporting activities revealed that golf clubs are well provided with facilities except for practise grounds and driving ranges; provision for athletics clubs is very good; archery about average; and that for cycling clubs is very poor. Club facilities for rowing and sailing clubs are very good but those for canoeing clubs are limited in scope and with angling clubs are virtually non-existent.

USE PATTERNS

The patterns of use of different outdoor recreational facilities vary considerably. With the larger Nottingham parks it was found that between thirty-three and fifty per cent of users visited the parks about once a month in the summer and the most usual time period for length of stay was 1–2 hours. Peak visiting periods occurred at weekends and the busiest time during the day was 3.0 p.m. to 4.0 p.m. The frequency of visits by children to playgrounds was surprisingly high, with over fifty per cent of 7–11 year olds visiting them over twenty times per month. The most popular length of stay periods were 1–2 hours for 11–14 year old children increasing to 2–3 hours for 5–11 year olds.

With team sports the period of maximum activity occurs on Saturday afternoons with a minimal level of use during the week, except on Wednesdays. On average, members play about 6 hours per week. The bulk of tennis is played on Saturday and Sunday afternoons whereas bowls playing extends over a considerably longer period with concentrations on Saturday afternoons and weekday evenings. Athletics activities occupy about 14 hours per week on average with Sunday mornings and one or two weekday evenings proving to be the most popular times. Archery occupies much the same overall time with periods of peak activity on Sundays and two evenings (Tuesdays and Wednesdays). Cycling is far less time consuming, the average club devoting about 5 hours per week to this activity with Monday evenings as the most popular time.

Peak golfing periods are at weekends, with maximum activity on Saturdays in the summer. It is thought that the average club member plays about twice a week in the summer and once a week in the winter. User patterns of outdoor swimming pools are largely conditioned by the weather. Extensive overcrowding occurs at weekends when ideal weather conditions prevail. About fifty per cent of the Nottingham lido users visit the outdoor pools about once a week and stay for approximately half a day, with a peak visiting time of 3.0 p.m. to 4.0 p.m., as for parks. Few visitors use lidos for training or competition purposes.

Sailing occurs for about 9 months of the year and over fifty per cent of the activity takes place at weekends, while about eighty per cent of canoeists participate in their sport throughout the year, with afternoons and evenings being the times of maximum activity. Over fifty per cent of rowing occurs at weekends. Angling is spread over 7–8 months in each year and some takes place almost every day throughout this period. Periods of maximum intensity are Saturdays and Sunday mornings and afternoons. Allotment gardening provides a departure from the more general pattern of use of facilities, as nearly sixty-six per cent of the Greater Nottingham plotholders visit their allotments over twenty times a month in summer and about twenty-five per cent visit just as frequently in winter. Activities are rarely restricted to weekends, especially in the summer; furthermore, this form of recreation continues throughout the whole year.

CHARACTERISTICS OF PARTICIPANTS

During school holidays half the weekday visitors to the larger Nottingham parks were children, but employees constituted forty per cent of all visitors at weekends. The majority of participants in team sports were under 30 years of age. About sixty-six per cent of those playing football and cricket were manual workers (skilled, semi-skilled or unskilled), whilst almost fifty per cent of hockey and rugby players were students. The majority of tennis players were under 40 years of age, whilst most bowls players were over 40. A high proportion of tennis players were either in the professional, managerial and non-manual categories or students, whilst the majority of bowls players were either manual workers or retired persons.

The majority of athletes were below 30 years of age and were either in the professional or managerial categories or were students. Those practising archery were predominantly in the 35–44 years age range and were mainly skilled manual and non-manual workers. The majority of members of cycling clubs were below 25 years of age and were either manual workers or students. Sixty-six per cent of the golfers were in the 35–54 years age range and were mainly in the professional, managerial and non-manual occupation categories.

Sixty per cent of the Nottingham lido visitors were children and there were very few visitors over 44 years of age. With sailing, forty per cent of participants were under 20 years of age, although in general they were well distributed both as regards age and occupation. Sixty-six per cent of canoeists were under 20 years of age and there were few over 44; sixty per cent of those in the Greater Nottingham canoe clubs were students. Rowing is another youthful sport with the majority under 24 years of age and seventy per cent of participants being students. Water skiing adherents showed a good age and occupational spread, although over half were in the 30–44 years age range and the same proportion was employed in a professional or managerial capacity. Anglers were predominantly between 25 and 55 years of age and were mainly manual workers. Over fifty per cent of allotment gardeners were also manual workers and this pursuit has followers with a pronounced elderly age structure—less than ten per cent were under 30 and seventy per cent were over 44 years of age.

CATCHMENT AREAS

Most visitors to small parks do not travel more than 1.5 km from homes to parks, but with the largest Nottingham park (Wollaton) forty per cent of the visitors travelled distances in excess of 10 km. With children's playgrounds over fifty per cent travelled less than 400 m and not more than twenty-five per cent exceeded 800 m, the majority of playgrounds being sited in the heart of residential districts. Seventy-five per cent of Nottingham lido visitors were resident within 6 km of the pools.

The only other outdoor recreational activities in Greater Nottingham where the average participant travelled a relatively short distance from his home to the facility were allotment gardening (1.5 km), bowls (3 km), and tennis (5 km). Persons engaging in certain water sports travelled the greatest distances to undertake these resource orientated activities, average distances travelled being: angling—13.2 km; sailing—13.6 km; and water skiing—20 km. Other outdoor recreational pursuits fell between these two extremes: athletics, golf and canoeing—6.5 km; team sports and rowing—7 km; cycling—7.5 km; and archery—9.5 km.

MAIN AREAS OF NEED

It seems essential to show the scale of demand if a convincing case is to be put forward for diverting resources to recreation—be they land, finance or whatever—from other socially desirable services such as education, health or housing, all of which face a shortage of resources. It has also been suggested that a periodical national household survey is needed at either 5 or 10 year intervals to show how people are spending their leisure time and what changes are occurring in their use of leisure.[15] The American recreation report[17] described how, as cities expand, the vacant land left behind 'is not effective open space, but often an agglomeration of bits and pieces, too small or too poorly sited to use well—a residue of expired choices'.

Consideration is now given to current needs of the principal urban recreational activities.

Parks

Urban dwellers need open space even if it cannot be justified on purely economic grounds. A city without its public parks, gardens and playing fields is unthinkable. Trees, shrubs, grass and flowers all serve to soften the harshness of the urban scene and to make the lives of urban dwellers more tolerable. In most towns and cities the provision of public open space occurred in a very piecemeal way. Dash[21] has described how 'the present day orthodox public park was often born in early Victorian times of the needs which stemmed from the nineteenth century Industrial Revolution and its inhuman march of commercial progress'.

Admittedly there are strong physical and practical difficulties inherent in a policy which aims at securing the maximum open space provision in the central area of a large regional city. One major obstacle is the high price of land in these locations and the absence of direct monetary return from the open space provision. The author suspects, however, that the concept of 'floating values' could well operate in situations such as these, whereby the addition in value arising from the difference between a particular building use and open space would merely be transferred to another site and the aggregate value of all central area land would remain much the same. The introduction of even relatively small areas of grass and trees into new shopping developments, between new office blocks and around new civic, educational and other public buildings, would have the most beneficial effects in humanising the urban scene and providing a pleasant contrast to the hard and artificial surfaces of buildings and paved areas.

Many urban parks are no longer conveniently sited in relation to the dwellings of the population which they are supposed to serve. The enclosing of these parks with formidable walls and fences and the excessive formality of their layouts are not conducive to their maximum use by visitors or of benefit to passers-by. The sharp distinction between parks and the surrounding townscape should be broken down by allowing landscaping to penetrate from the parks through neighbouring built-up areas to link up with other facilities. Law[22] has suggested that parks should turn their faces instead of their backs to the community, with social and cultural buildings, shops and other meeting points located on the fringes or even inside parks. Much thought obviously needs to be given to the problem of integrating parks with the urban structure.

Modernising of town parks on the lines suggested by the former London County Council[23] is vitally necessary. These suggestions were detailed in chapter 6 and included re-planning of park entrances on contemporary lines; transplanting of large trees from their 'serried ranks' into more informal groups; floodlighting of flower gardens; and the provision of a whole host of interesting facilities from ski-slopes and sailing lakes to restaurants and reading rooms, to help liven up our parks and provide many more facilities (some revenue producing) for old and young alike. The needs of elderly people in the winter months must not be overlooked and provision for those who merely wish to walk and sit are equally important. In order to incorporate all these desirable features some zoning of large existing parks and laying out of new parks will be necessary.

The Greater London Council[24] sees the need for a hierarchial structure of park provision based on small parks of at least 2 ha close to residential areas; intermediate parks of not less than 20 ha situated within about 1.5 km of every home; and larger parks of at least 60 ha for people travelling distances up to 8 km. This hierarchial distribution may prove far too rigid in practice but it serves a useful purpose by drawing attention to the need for rationalised provision and to the desirability of incorporating suitable landscaping through redeveloped sectors in the form of sheltered sitting places, children's play areas, pleasant views and precincts.

Neighbourhood Parks

It is desirable that there should be a sufficient number of neighbourhood parks conveniently sited to serve residential areas or districts, on the lines of the 'neighbourhood playgrounds', suggested by Butler[43] in America. They would each occupy an area of 1.5–3 ha and serve primarily the needs of children, but would also provide limited recreational opportunities for all people in the residential neighbourhood. They could advantageously be sited adjacent to a primary school and could usefully comprise children's playground equipment; open spaces for informal play; pitches and enclosures for a variety of games; shaded sitting areas; and shelter house. The neighbourhood park could possibly also form the local community centre with provision for indoor games, branch library, and so on. Emphasis should be on joint provision of facilities for educational and public use and on serving the needs of a wide range of ages and interests.

Children's Playgrounds

The majority of children's playgrounds in Greater Nottingham are located within local authority housing estates, and most other residential districts are woefully deficient in this type of facility. On occasions children's playgrounds could be incorporated into neighbourhood or district parks which could advantageously be provided near neighbourhood shopping centres.

The sites of additional facilities should be determined with the objective of ensuring that the majority of children would reside within 400 m of a playground and would not have to cross a main traffic route in order to reach it (the Nottingham surveys showed that the majority of children travel to playgrounds on foot). Facilities will still be needed in the present twilight areas to serve the children who will occupy the new dwellings that will be erected. Attention should be paid to residential densities and family structure when assessing the size of new playgrounds and amount of equipment to be provided.

Some of the main weaknesses of many existing playgrounds are: the failure to sub-divide them into separate sections catering for the needs of different age groups; the general absence of imaginative features; and a grave deficiency in kick-about areas. It is suggested that future playgrounds should comprise an enclosed area containing mainly orthodox equipment for young children not exceeding 7 years of age; another section planned on more imaginative lines for 7–14 year olds; and kick-about areas for teenagers generally in order to meet the majority preferences of the children interviewed. Pritchard[44] in his investigations of playing needs in New Towns has suggested that kick-about areas can quite well be sited on the perimeter of a housing area, and this suggestion is not without merit provided such provision is not overlooked as so often seems to be the case. It is vitally important to provide play spaces and sitting places in the landscaped areas around high density residential developments.

Playing Pitches

A strong case can be made for the public provision of playing pitches because of the uncertainties involved with those provided by employers. Many clubs would like to obtain their own grounds but problems of finance usually prevent it. The reduction in intensity of use of playing pitches in Nottingham over the last two decades indicates a need for extending playing time over a longer period away from the weekend peaks and possibly the introduction of some floodlit pitches. The provision of one or two combined sports centres in Nottingham with all-weather floodlit playing surfaces and greater dual use of school playing fields, as described in chapter 6, would assist in overcoming weekend congestion. The Wolfenden Committee[25] did not regard as improper in itself the participation in any form of games, sports or outdoor activities on Sundays but, at the same time, thought it reasonable to ask that there should be restraint in the organisation of sporting activities on Sundays. Thus local authorities were recommended to allow the use of playing pitches on Sundays, although this is still not universally applied, but organisers of games should avoid programming games during normal hours of worship and should prevent as far as possible causing Sunday work for other people. A number of Nottingham cricket clubs complained that no Sunday matches were permitted on the pitches which they used. Consideration must be given to changing trends and particularly changes of fashion; for instance, an extension of interest in rugby in secondary schools could generate a demand for more rugby pitches. There is also a need for increased social provision—in the form of changing rooms, toilets and clubhouses—on many existing public playing fields.

Tennis and Bowls

Both of these facilities need to be conveniently sited in relation to homes of the users. Interest in bowls and, to a lesser extent, in tennis has tended to decline over the last two decades, although fashions could conceivably change, particularly with regard to tennis through increased participation in schools. Under utilisation of resources in

Nottingham resulted in the conversion of several bowling greens into putting greens; there could be a case for converting some grass tennis courts into putting greens and hard courts into skating rinks, netball or basketball courts, or general all-weather playing surfaces in areas where there is a pronounced over provision of facilities. Seventy-five per cent of grass courts in Greater Nottingham are privately owned and they tend to become building sites when their use for tennis is badly depleted.

There is a strong case for joint provision of hard tennis courts at schools for use by persons other than pupils outside school hours. Some hard courts—preferably floodlit—could advantageously be incorporated in combined sports centres, to encourage greater use of facilities. Grouping of facilities for different activities would produce economies in provision of changing rooms, toilets, car parking space, among other amenities.

Other Sporting Activities

In our increasingly motorised society there is still a need to preserve the grassed footpaths and bridlepaths which exist in our towns and penetrate from the built-up areas into the surrounding countryside, as rambling and horse riding gain in popularity. Towpaths beside rivers and canals should be improved, landscaped and signposted, to improve the facilities available to the rambler. Disused railways often provide excellent routes for ramblers, cyclists and horse riders.

Golf

The increasing demand for golf facilities, evidenced by the congestion on public courses at weekends and waiting lists for private clubs, must result in saturation of the present resources within the next decade if the criteria listed in appendix 7 are accepted.

The provision of additional golf courses makes necessary the acquisition of extensive areas of suitable land. For this reason, and in the absence of any form of dual use, it is important that the most effective use should be made of resources, by the greater use of par-3 courses, 9-hole courses, driving ranges and pitch and putt courses, as well as spreading periods of use as widely as possible to eliminate or reduce the excessive demand at weekends. As indicated in chapter 3 it is also desirable to site golf courses and zone adjoining areas so that the maximum number of occupiers of dwellings obtain the benefit of the amenity value of these facilities; further, they must be integrated into a network of open spaces wherever practicable. It seems likely that more new golf courses will be provided out of public funds and this should increase the average intensity of use of courses.

Water Based Recreation

In inland areas of the country it is becoming increasingly necessary to utilise every available stretch of water for recreational purposes to satisfy the rising demand for water based recreation of all kinds. Resources are not restricted to rivers alone but encompass the whole gamut of canals, lakes, wet gravel pits and reservoirs. With wet gravel pits it is important that the form of recreational use is planned before the pits are excavated so that the over-burden from the excavations can be tipped in such a way that it will not interfere with future use. Similarly, reservoirs also need planning and constructing with the recreational use in mind, even to the extent of comparing differing scales of investment and probable monetary returns stemming from varying patterns of recreational provision. With canals, the economics of refilling, conversion to water channels, or complete restoration to navigable canals (cruiseways) have to be compared.

Years of neglect have made many canals more of an eyesore than an amenity but efforts are now being devoted to developing the silted canals for leisure use, including landscaping banks and building marinas and moorings for pleasure craft. Power boats assist in the maintenance of canals, arresting weed growth and—if water levels and locks are maintained—ensuring good facilities for anglers, other boaters and lovers of natural beauty. The urgent need for additional recreational water is indisputable; such a use for gravel workings should not be seen as one of expediency stemming from an inadequacy of filling material to reclaim the land for agricultural use but as a competing claim in its own right.

Some of the principal difficulties experienced by anglers have been listed by the South West Wales River Authority[26] and they are not confined to Welsh anglers. They include: too much private water in relation to club water; increasingly high rents; leases sold to highest bidder—often private individuals not connected with local interests; over fishing of better waters; some poaching; and lack of interest by various authorities. To remedy the situation the River Authority suggested the need for better relations with riparian owners; angling clubs to be run on businesslike lines with paid managers; fisheries maintained by local associations empowered to limit numbers fishing; grants available to clubs to buy their own fishing rights; more bailiffs; harsher treatment of poachers; and rationalisation of river use possibly through public ownership.

The Trent in the vicinity of Nottingham has considerable recreational potential which is recognised in the Trent Valley Study[27] but, in common with many English rivers, it is deficient in many essential facilities. There is an urgent need for more mooring places; riverside service areas; waste disposal facilities; public access areas; toilets; water points; improved riverside walks; and more riverside parks. Most water sports clubs need greater security of tenure and probably the best solution would be for local authorities to purchase water for recreational use wherever possible, particularly new water resources, with the intention of making leasehold arrangements with clubs. The right of non-club sportsmen to participate in water sports should be preserved, although casual users should be encouraged to become members of water sports clubs.[28]

Allotments

At the end of the Second World War there were about 1.5 million plots in England and Wales, and by 1970 this had dropped to about 600 000. Furthermore twenty per cent of the present day plots are vacant. Thorpe[29] has emphasised how the allotment movement has always been dragged down by its charitable origin, yet as shown in chapter 6 the prime motivating force at the present time is recreational rather than economic, although production of fresh produce was found to be a matter of considerable importance to Nottingham plotholders. Allotment holders in the Nottingham area are suffering from extensive vandalism, weeds from uncultivated plots, insecurity of tenure and general lack of communal facilities. These same deficiencies were highlighted in the Committee of Inquiry's report.[9]

The allotment holder's image is poor, mainly because of the untidy and unattractive appearance of many plots and of the buildings erected on them. Hence the Committee of Inquiry[9] saw the need to develop a system of better-class gardens termed leisure gardens, to be used primarily for recreational purposes and with the plots made attractive by the incorporation of flowers or flowering shrubs at strategic points.

There appears to be a hard core of present day allotment holders who would not be prepared to rent the new style gardens, although the concept has much to commend it. Improvements in the general form and pattern of allotments are badly required: in particular there is a need for small sites close to residential areas, with all basic services, landscaped approaches, children's play space and car park, with plots enclosed by suitable hedges or fences, individual sheds available on rent; and security of tenure.

TRENDS

The Keele Study[11] showed that on a national scale the greatest rate of increase in demand was associated with winter sports, archery, motor racing, salt water sailing and golf. Next in increasing popularity came inland sailing, fishing, skating, swimming, bowls, camping and hill walking. A moderate fall in interest had occurred in hiking and tennis and a large drop in team games, cycling and athletics. There would however, be regional and local variations on national trends and in some cases there can be potential demand which is not apparent owing to the insufficiency of facilities. Nevertheless, it is likely that many of the traditional recreations like cycling, athletics, football and cricket will continue to decline as greater personal wealth and increased mobility bring more sophisticated and often more expensive activities, such as skiing, sailing, golf, caravanning and motoring, within the reach of ever more people.[16]

In America the Outdoor Recreation Resources Review Commission[17] clearly established the principal factors relating to the future of recreation and leisure activity:

(1) Active use of leisure increases with rising income.

(2) Growing mobility increases the pressure on leisure resources.

(3) The better educated are more active in their leisure.

The Commission concluded that on the evidence of their enquiries the demand for recreation in the United States would treble by the year 2000, during which time the population would double. Yet it is also clear that the trebling of demand cannot be applied uniformly to all recreational pursuits and that each activity or group of activities has to be considered separately. A decline in interest in one activity will generally be accompanied by increased support for others and new forms of recreational activity may be introduced. It would also be unwise to assume stability of the historic relationship between recreation use and some set of socio-economic characteristics; changing tastes in recreation generate extra needs. Willmott[18] postulates that golf courses and marinas may soon be essentials.

Hence there are very real difficulties in predicting future demand for recreation. Present participation patterns associated with a particular social and economic structure of population may not be applicable to a population of the same type in the future. Changes such as fashion or the introduction of new forms of recreation could invalidate predictions. Some activities may be substituted for others and saturation levels may operate whereby increases in available leisure time will cease to be reflected in higher participation rates. Therefore it is not feasible to quantify exactly the future demand for each type of urban recreation activity.[19]

Burton and Wibberley[20] have suggested that emphasis upon recreation at the coast may slacken, largely because of physical limitations, and this could lead to an increased concentration upon inland water resources.

Rodgers[12] has clearly demonstrated the difficulties of trying to identify changes in recreational habits on a time-scale: possibly, within a decade the typical patterns of leisure associated with a working class life style may be closer to those associated with the middle class. Growth capacities of particular recreations can in general only be applied with any confidence to the short term; unfortunately, the short term trend may easily be disturbed by incidents such as credit squeezes. In the longer term of two or three decades, radical changes may overtake and even overturn conclusions derived from present trends. Rodgers postulates that the workshift may replace the workday in offices and factories. Universal late teenage marriage could eliminate or greatly modify what is presently the most active recreational phase, the period to which interest in competitive sports is largely confined. But teenage marriage in a second generation could produce couples unrestricted by children in their mid-30's with considerable financial and leisure capacity and might even change the period of maximum recreational activity from late adolescence to the 30's and 40's.

In greater Nottingham the number of cricket, football, rugby and hockey clubs has increased considerably since the last war, although club membership numbers have dropped appreciably in all team sports except hockey. Furthermore, playing pitches are in general being used far less intensively than they were 20 years ago. Nottingham tennis clubs have increased their membership over the last two decades but most of them still have spare capacity, whilst bowling clubs have been losing support fairly continuously. Cycling and athletics are losing popularity in Nottingham as well as on a national scale, whilst archery is gaining in strength. Golf club membership in Nottinghamshire increased at the rate of seven per cent per annum between 1961 and 1967.

The majority of water based recreational activities in the Nottingham area are on the increase. The angling, sailing, power boat and water skiing clubs have had substantial increases in numbers of members over the last decade. Canoeing and rowing clubs have not attained the same rate of growth but demand is likely to rise as more schools include rowing instruction in their curricula. The demand for allotment plots in Greater Nottingham has declined considerably since the last war and there is at present no evidence of the decrease in interest being halted.

MULTIPLE USE

With an increasing population and rising competition for land for a host of different uses, it is vital that resources allocated to recreation shall be utilised as effectively as possible. When laying out sports pitches on a playing field, the aim should be to accommodate as many as possible. With school playing facilities, maximum permissible outside use should be a prime objective. Regional sports councils have urged local education authorities to support and implement dual use of physical education and physical recreation facilities. Local education authorities could help by giving wider publicity to the opportunities that exist for the use of school facilities by sports organisations and by adopting a positive programme to ensure maximum use. In the last decade recreational use of reservoirs has been permitted in a number of cases but there are many more to which recreationalists do not have access. With only a small loss of timber production, forests can offer opportunities for many recreational pursuits, for walks, scenic drives, camping, skiing and observation of wild life.[13] Furthermore, as indicated by Colvin,[30] forests managed not only for timber but also for wild life and amenity would conserve better landscape types than extensive pure stands. We have only recently seen the start of the establishment of combined sports centres of the type provided at Bingham and Carlton (Nottinghamshire), and which are described in chapter 7. In this way a local education authority's resources are combined with those of one or more local authorities to provide a sports facility to serve both educational and community needs. Substantial advantages result from joint planning including the provision of better facilities at lower cost, and in some cases it may be the means of providing a valuable facility which would not otherwise be possible.

In local government in particular provision for recreation has developed as a side issue in a number of departments, each with different objectives and different criteria for decision making. This scatter of responsibility can easily lead to unimaginative and inefficient use of facilities and creates the need for a high degree of coordination which is difficult to achieve without the setting up of a special committee for this purpose. It is doubtful whether the regional sports council, acting in the rôle of an advisory body, can effectively perform the coordinating function.

It is also apparent that the present local government structure is poorly suited to serve the needs of recreationalists and the arrangements for local government reorganisation in 1974 offer little scope for improvement. The division of responsibilities in Greater Nottingham between the city, county and urban districts leads to varying standards of provision in different administrative areas and the lack of an overall coordinated policy. Nottingham city boundary is irrelevant to present day needs as more and more people live outside the city and problems of planning, roads, recreation, housing and education all need to be considered in a wider context—possibly in the context of a city region.

Another problem is the coordination of public and private investment in recreation. Industry can no longer be expected to provide in full for all the diverse and expanding recreational needs of its workers.[7] Conversely, many industrial based recreational facilities are badly under utilised and ought—through agreements with local authorities—to be more readily available to the community at large. It seems likely that public authorities will take an increasing part in recreation provision but commercial interests should be encouraged to participate and voluntary organisations should have a considerable interest. Local authorities, in addition to being major providers of facilities, also have an important rôle as coordinators, preferably administering larger and more viable areas than at present, with support from regional sports councils.

RECREATION MANAGEMENT

Recreation resources must be suitably located and properly managed if their full potential is to be realised. Full potential is closely linked to the carrying capacity of a resource or facility and, as indicated earlier, this must not rise above a level at which detrimental effects are experienced. In some circumstances it may be desirable to preserve a resource by restricting public access, as in the case of a nature reserve; in others, a resource may be preserved for public enjoyment by prohibiting alternative development, as with urban open space. The Huron-Clinton Authority at Detroit knows the capacity of each of its regional parks, element by element—beaches for example can take seventy persons per hectare, golf courses twenty-five and nature study areas eight.[14] Experience in this park system has shown that people are prepared to move on to an alternative when they know a park to be full.

As has been illustrated, the physical or temporal separation of users may be a useful way of increasing the carrying capacity of a facility. For instance, power boats could be excluded from one end of a reservoir during certain periods at weekends in order that more sailors and fishermen be accommodated. Valuable experience has been secured in certain forests in the Netherlands in the zoning of recreational activity. The 'gregarious' areas to which the majority of visitors will go are provided with car parks, refreshment facilities and a special attraction such as a paddling pool. For those visitors who prefer less gregarious activity, scenic drives and small clearings are provided in the forest. Lastly, there are the more vulnerable wild life sanctuaries, some away from main roads, to which there is access only by foot and where there are no facilities. To ensure success, the sympathetic interpretation by signs, leaflets and wardens is vital.[13]

Tanner[36] considered that the following management techniques were necessary to ensure the optimum recreational use of enclosed waters:

(1) Controlling the number of users.

(2) Reducing conflicts between recreational users by, for example, zoning and timetabling arrangements.

(3) Ensuring that management rules are respected, especially in relation to such matters as conservation, pollution and water safety.

(4) Determining the pricing policy to be adopted, and in particular whether the aim should be optimum use or maximisation of returns.

The South Western Sports Council[37] considered that making the best use of existing and developing potential water recreational facilities would entail: active cooperation between competing uses; positive education of young people in water activities; strict observance of the water sports code and possibly even more formal regulation by byelaws and bailiff services; and bringing together water providers and users to coordinate activities and resources on a rational basis. This latter recommendation indicates the need for a management committee to formulate an integrated strategy for a region or sub-region.

We must recognise that in Britain today there has been relatively little practical experience of the management of large scale recreational resources on multi-purpose lines, apart from areas managed by the Forestry Commission. We also know that not all urban facilities are managed so as to maximise their possible use by the community; school and college playing fields and gymnasia, in particular, may lie unused for large periods of the year. It is both desirable and feasible that these facilities should be made available for some use by clubs or the public. In similar manner private club facilities are often under used. There is scope for multi-purpose centres, catering for the diverse recreational needs of all the family at a single location and an urgent need for more combined sports centres on the lines of those provided at Carlton and Bingham. There is also a strong case for the making of access agreements in respect of attractive farmland around large cities.

An important object of management is to obtain a more even level of use of a resource throughout the day, week or year. With water resources, the South Western Sports Council[37] suggested that youth and educational organisations should be encouraged to use facilities in mid-week and other off-peak periods in order to spread use more effectively. The price mechanism can be used to smooth out the demand curve for facilities such as swimming pools and tennis courts. Clawson[38] has postulated how entrance fees can be used as a deliberate management tool in recreational areas and that the way in which fees or charges are levied may be as important as their amount. For instance, fees might be levied only on days or hours of heavy use; this would both reduce the costs of collection (which are sometimes high relative to the money collected) and provide an incentive for users to shift their use to times when the resource would otherwise have surplus capacity.

Recreation management includes such aspects as the design and maintenance of facilities, like picnic tables, litter receptacles, park benches, footpaths, fences and surfaces of various kinds. Hookway and Davidson[13] have shown how diversity exists in the design and cost of these facilities, developed as they are from local initiative. Bonsey[39] has described how carefully designed areas can be completely spoilt by thoughtless signing and has shown that there is a pattern of vandalism which seems linked to poor design and bad management. The most successful and most acceptable techniques of visitor management are invariably the most subtle, persuasive and informative. The greatest success in guiding people away from vulnerable areas has been achieved by the use of the less conspicuous barriers such as ditches and bollards, trees and shrubs and signs that explain the reasons for any restrictions.[13]

In recreation management we need to know what is wanted, where it can be provided, and how it can be provided.[39] As postulated by the Countryside Commission[40] management of recreation areas should aim to secure optimum use, protect recreational facilities from misuse and provide an effective information service. Finally, improved administrative machinery could help in achieving better management and more thought might beneficially be given to public ownership of recreational resources but using private agencies as concessionaires.

FINANCIAL IMPLICATIONS

There are two main financial aspects in the provision of recreational facilities—the expenditure incurred in supplying the facility and subsequently maintaining and operating it; and the charge, if any, to be made for its use. The rôle of local authorities and of central government in the financing of recreational facilities is a complicated one. Local education authorities are required by the Education Act, 1944, to provide adequate recreational facilities for recreation and social and physical training for primary, secondary and further education. Local authority capital expenditure on facilities is, however, largely dependent upon loan sanction from the Department of the Environment (formerly The Ministry of Housing and Local Government), and this is not always forthcoming. Under the general grant arrangements originating from the Local Government Act, 1958, recreation provision tends to be placed at the bottom of the list of priorities by local authorities, as being less vital than other services such as highways, housing and main drainage. Local voluntary associations receive financial help for capital projects from central government funds through the Physical Training and Recreation Act, 1937, and the same Act enables the Department of Education and Science to make grants to national voluntary associations for administration and coaching.

It is evident that the present system of financing publicly provided recreational facilities is unsatisfactory and is generally inadequate to meet the increasing needs. Consideration should be given to the proportion of national income which should be allocated to recreation. In times of national economic crisis the proportion of the cake would remain the same but the total cake would be reduced in amount, instead of the flow of funds reducing to a trickle as at present. The Central Council of Physical Recreation[25] as long ago as 1960 urged relaxation of capital restrictions on expenditure by local authorities and local education authorities on facilities for physical recreation. Dower[31] reported how in 1970 public expenditure on sport was less than in 1965. Local authorities who launched the regional sports councils with enthusiasm and helped to staff their initial surveys (which showed a clear need to double public expenditure on sport) are now very disgruntled to find scheme after scheme held up for want of loan sanction. It now appears likely that the 15 year programme for the Lea Valley scheme will be stretched to 30 years.

The Central Council of Physical Recreation[33] has reported that Britain spends less per person on its sporting amenities through central or local government than almost any other Western European country. The level of public expenditure on facilities will have to be substantially increased lest we are overwhelmed by inadequacies, and future generations are given an impossible task. In the Netherlands £3 million of public money was spent on outdoor recreation in 1965 and it is planned to increase this to £200 million per annum by 1980,[32] being equivalent to approximately £16 per head.

Dower[31] has described how patterns of land values and the growth of traditional cities with their concentric circles and pyramid of densities combine to prevent a properly integrated open space system. Urban renewal and roadworks often open up land which could with advantage stay open and be used for recreation; but the pattern of land values and subsidies compels rebuilding. In Birmingham, the outward thrust of housing demands and the straitjacket of the green belt force up the value of private open space and tempt or compel clubs to sell to building firms. To achieve a satisfactory and coordinated arrangement of open spaces within an existing city requires increased funds, a changed policy and more imaginative use of land and facilities.

There is ample scope for private enterprise to perform a greater rôle in the provision of outdoor recreational facilities. It is likely that it needs encouragement from local authorities and one approach might be for the local authorities to acquire the land and make it available at a reasonable price, to construct the roads, sewers and other essential services, and then to invite private enterprise to develop and manage specific facilities.

In the past there has been a general reluctance on the part of local authorities to charge for access to public parks and other recreational facilities, mainly using the argument that this could preclude the very people who would stand to benefit most from them. Difficulties of matching supply and demand through lack of finance, coupled with the increasing prosperity and mobility of the population, calls for a re-think on pricing policy. If entry charges produced a reasonable rate of return on capital, a local authority might then be able to provide more and better facilities and so ease the congestion problem. Charges could also operate as regulators of demand and the introduction of variable charges could assist in staggering the demand and in reducing weekend pressures. By failing to charge adequately for public facilities, local authorities are making it more difficult for private enterprise to operate in the recreation field. Eldon Griffiths, Minister of Sport, stated in 1970 that amateur sportsmen must expect to pay much more for facilities provided by the taxpayer and that the recreation explosion was putting a near insatiable pressure on our resources, both physical and economic.[34]

Sayers[35] believes that parks cost too much to maintain, and that more should pay for themselves by catering for intensive use. Adequate charges could be made for boating, fishing, water skiing, archery and other pursuits. Making parks pay for themselves would give greater incentive to develop new ventures, and by making one or two parks in a town economically viable would allow more money to be spent on parks of passive recreation. With large parks it should be possible to separate the park into two distinct sections: one containing a variety of facilities and attracting charges and the other catering for people who wish merely to sit and walk and on whom no charge should be levied.

FINAL CONCLUSIONS

The nature of recreational land use in Greater Nottingham is changing, but so far the changes have often been haphazard. Much of the nineteenth century pattern of recreation remains, but varied provision has been made for new uses—often without any really clear appreciation of the facilities which ought to be provided, where they should be located and at what cost. The author suspects that these criticisms will apply equally to recreational provision in the majority of cities in Great Britain. Morgan[45] has described how the laissez-faire methods and opportunism which sometimes characterised the past, must be replaced by researches, surveys, policies, planning and execution. Assessment of future demand is made extremely hazardous by rapidly shifting economic and social conditions coupled with changing fashions. Much more needs to be known about people's recreational and leisure habits and the motivating forces behind them, as well as people's patterns of expenditure. The measurement of the capacity of resources is assuming great importance and deserves more attention than appears to be devoted to it at present.

The author questions the validity of some of the generally accepted open space standards and is doubtful about the effectiveness of planning machinery in gaining its objectives in the recreational use of land. This is particularly serious as through planning the aim is to produce a new geography, a better distribution of activity and land use related to contemporary social and economic needs. It is also apparent that needs change more quickly than physical forms. Meyer and Brightbill[10] have expressed the need for recreational programmes which are better balanced and more carefully related to the physiological and psychological needs, interests and satisfactions of individuals and groups. The practical applications of such a programme would embrace such features as integrated open space systems; facelifts to town parks; increased provision of neighbourhood parks; imaginatively planned children's playgrounds and more kick-about areas; greater utilisation of water resources; conversion of allotments to other open space uses; and increased multiple use of larger recreational facilities.

The crux of recreational planning in an urban environment is land use allocation and re-allocation in the face of fierce competition from a variety of uses. The aim should be to secure an integrated open space system which is well fitted to meet the changing needs of a population which is increasing in size, prosperity, mobility and in the amount of leisure time available to it. We need to apply improved management techniques to our outdoor recreational facilities to ensure their more efficient use. Future needs are difficult to assess, influenced as they are by changes of fashion and the introduction of new activities. Current trends give a guide to future needs, but relatively small changes in present use patterns can have an appreciable effect on future projections. Hence there is considerable merit in aiming at maximum flexibility of use when planning recreational facilities for the future.

The financial aspects of the provision of outdoor recreation facilities are of vital importance. Large scale municipal provision of costly facilities offering little or no direct monetary return and consuming large tracts of land, which are often admirably suited for a whole range of other uses, cannot continue indefinitely. The majority of industrialists are no longer able or willing to donate recreational facilities to municipalities. Similarly, large landowners—subject to severe restraints of death duties and a high level of general taxation—cannot afford to donate or convey on advantageous terms valuable resources to public authorities. The age of benevolence has largely gone.

The majority of suitable sites for urban recreational facilities constitute potential building land and can accordingly command high prices on the land market. For public authorities to provide more facilities and to improve existing resources requires increased funds, and it seems highly probable that these can only be secured by making charges for entry to recreational sites or for the use of specific facilities on those sites. The author favours free entry into parks but recommends the levying of charges for car parking and/or use of specific facilities, with possibly the issue of inclusive all-in season tickets to cover ranges of activities, including under utilised ones.

It seems evident that concentration on investment in recreation in the countryside, whilst important, should at least be balanced by improved provision within or close to the urban fabric, particularly for those in the lower socio-economic groups whose income is unlikely to rise substantially, who do not own cars and yet whose demands are less space consuming. Immense value would be derived from an interlinked hierarchy of open spaces from small neighbourhood parks and playgrounds, through town parks, to regional open spaces on the urban fringe.[46]

REFERENCES

1. SOUTH HAMPSHIRE ADVISORY COMMITTEE. *South Hampshire Plan: Study Report No. 5: Recreation*, (1969)
2. LANCASHIRE COUNTY COUNCIL. *Preliminary Report: Survey of Existing Facilities for Sport and Physical Recreation*, (1967)
3. LIVERPOOL CORPORATION. *Report No. 15: Open Space*, (1964)
4. NATIONAL PLAYING FIELDS ASSOCIATION. *Planning for Recreation: Application of N.P.F.A. Standard*, (1967)
5. MINISTRY OF HOUSING AND LOCAL GOVERNMENT. *Method of Calculation of Minimum Acreage for Sports Grounds*, (1966)
6. NATIONAL PLAYING FIELDS ASSOCIATION. *Selection and Layout of Land for Playing Fields and Playgrounds*, (1963)
7. SPORTS COUNCIL. (1968). *Planning for Sport*, Central Council of Physical Recreation
8. NATIONAL ALLOTMENTS AND GARDENS SOCIETY LTD. *Annual report of the year 1968/69*, (1969)
9. DEPARTMENTAL COMMITTEE OF INQUIRY INTO ALLOTMENTS. *Report Cmnd. 4166*, H.M.S.O., (1969)
10. MEYER, H. D. and BRIGHTBILL, C. K. (1964). *Community Recreation: A Guide to Its Organisation*, Prentice-Hall
11. BRITISH TRAVEL ASSOCIATION/UNIVERSITY OF KEELE. *Pilot National Recreation Survey: Report No. 1*, (1967)
12. RODGERS, H. B. Leisure and recreation. *Urban Studies*, **6.3**, (1969)
13. HOOKWAY, R. J. S. and DAVIDSON, J. (1970). *Leisure: Problems and Prospects for the Environment*, Countryside Commission
14. DOWER, M. Leisure—its impact on man and the land. *Geography*, **55.3**, (1970)
15. COUNTRYSIDE COMMISSION. *The Demand for Outdoor Recreation in the Countryside*, (1970)
16. JAMES, J. N. C. *The Conservation of Urban Environment. Proceedings of Annual Conference of Royal Institution of Chartered Surveyors*, University of Warwick, (1970)
17. OUTDOOR RECREATION RESOURCES REVIEW COMMISSION. *Outdoor Recreation for America*, Washington D.C., (1962)
18. WILLMOTT, P. Some social trends. *Urban Studies*, **6.3**, (1969)
19. MALE, K. O. (1968). *Recreation in Cheshire: Provision for Urban Recreation*, Cheshire County Council
20. BURTON, T. L. and WIBBERLEY, G. P. (1965). *Outdoor Recreation in the British Countryside*, Wye College, University of London
21. DASH, E. W. Public park design. *Parks and Recreation*, **35.8**, (1970)
22. LAW, S. *Planning for Open Space in Greater London. Proceedings of Conference on Planning for Recreation, Institute of Advanced Architectural Studies*, University of York, (1967)
23. LONDON COUNTY COUNCIL. *Parks for Tomorrow*, (1964)
24. GREATER LONDON COUNCIL. *Surveys of the Use of Open Spaces, Vol. 1: Research Paper 2*, (1968)
25. WOLFENDEN COMMITTEE. (1960). *Sport and the Community*. Central Council of Physical Recreation
26. SPORTS COUNCIL FOR WALES. *The Recreational Use of Rivers*
27. NOTTINGHAMSHIRE COUNTY COUNCIL, PLANNING DEPARTMENT. *Trent Valley Study*, (1970)
28. SOUTH WESTERN SPORTS COUNCIL. *Major Recreational Survey, Gloucestershire: Outdoor Water Recreation*, (1968)
29. THORPE, H. *The Way Ahead. Proceedings of Annual Conference of National Allotments Society, Exmouth*, (1970)
30. COLVIN, B. Conservation of landscape. *Journal of Institute of Landscape Architects*, **89**, (1970)
31. DOWER, M. Sport and Planning. *Town and Country Planning*, **38.7**, (1970)
32. BOW GROUP. (1966). *A Better Country*. Conservative Political Centre
33. CENTRAL COUNCIL OF PHYSICAL RECREATION. *Annual Report*, (1970)
34. THE GUARDIAN. Price of sport going up, says Minister, (5 November 1970)
35. SAYERS, P. R. New towns from old: A plea for more active use of open space. *Park Administration*, **33.11**, (1968)
36. TANNER, M. *Recreational Use of Enclosed Waters. Proceedings of Conference on Recreation in the Countryside*, University of Loughborough, (1969)
37. SOUTH WESTERN SPORTS COUNCIL. *Outdoor Water Recreation in Bath and Somerset*, (1969)
38. CLAWSON, M. (1963). *Land and Water for Recreation*, Rand McNally, New York
39. BONSEY, C. C. *The Rising Tide of Outdoor Recreation. Proceedings of Annual Conference of Royal Institution of Chartered Surveyors*, University of Warwick, (1970)
40. COUNTRYSIDE COMMISSION. *Special Study Report Vol. 1: Coastal Recreation and Holidays*, H.M.S.O., (1969)
41. CLAWSON, M., HELD, R. B. and STODDARD, C. H. (1962). *Land for the Future*, John Hopkins Press, Baltimore
42. TOWN AND COUNTRY PLANNING ASSOCIATION. A policy for countryside recreation in England and Wales. *Town and Country Planning*, (December 1965)
43. BUTLER, G. D. (1960). *Playgrounds: Their Administration and Operation*, Ronald Press, New York
44. PRITCHARD, N. Planned social provision in New Towns. *Town Planning Review*, **38.1**, (1967)
45. MORGAN, L. E. Weekends in the parks. *Parks and Recreation*, **35.8**, (1970)
46. DEPARTMENT OF THE ENVIRONMENT/NORTH WEST SPORTS COUNCIL. *Leisure in the North West*, (1972)

PARKS SURVEY QUESTIONNAIRE

Please complete by placing a tick in the box or an entry in the space provided

---

1 How did you travel to the Park today?

	1	
Car/motor cycle		0
Bus		1
Coach		2
Scooter		3
Bicycle		4
Foot		5

Other means (please state)..6

2 If you came by car or motor cycle were you

	2	
Passenger		0
Driver		1

3 Have you come to the park straight from work

	3	
From work		0
From home		1

Location (please state) ....

4 Give approximate number of visits to this park *per month*

Summer	4			Winter	5	
0–1		0		0–1		0
2–5		1		2–5		1
6–10		2		6–10		2
11–20		3		11–20		3
Over 20		4		Over 20		4

5 Give approximate number of visits to all parks in the Nottingham area *per month*

Summer	6			Winter	7	
0–1		0		0–1		0
2–5		1		2–5		1
6–10		2		6–10		2
11–20		3		11–20		3
Over 20		4		Over 20		4

214

6 Show the activities in which you are taking part:

Strolling		8
Looking at trees, flowers, lake, etc.		9
Walking through to elsewhere		10
Exercising dog		11
Picnicking		12
Playing games		13
Sitting outside		14
Sitting inside car		15
Visiting hall		16
Using adventure playground		17
Using playground equipment		18

Other activities . . . .
(please state) 19

7 Give probable length of stay

20

Less than 1 hour		0
1–2 hours		1
Half a day		2
All day		3

8 Is there anything which prevents you making as many visits to the park as you would like? If so, please state causes.

. . . .

. . . . 21

9 What things would you like to see in the parks?

Floral/horticultural displays		22
More facilities (formal equipment)		23
For children's play (adventure type)		24
For children's play (with a ball)		25
Paddling pool		26
Games : Tennis		27
Bowls		28
Pitch and putt		29
Formal games (e.g. football, hockey)		30

Other games (please state). 31

Boating		32
More grass for playing		33
More places for sitting		34
Shelters		35
Cafés		36
Pets corner		37

Any other facilities. 38
(please state)

Please answer the following questions about yourself:

10 What is your occupation?

	39	
Employer		0
Self-employed		1
Manager		2
Foreman		3
Employee		4
Housewife		5
Student		6
Unemployed		7
Retired		8

Other 9
    (please state)

11 What is your age?

	40	
Under 11		0
11–14		1
15–19		2
20–24		3
25–29		4
30–34		5
35–44		6
45–54		7
55 and over		8

12 If employed please state the actual job that you do:

.... 41

13 Are you:

	42	
Male		0
Female		1

14 Are you

	43	
Married		0
Single		1

15 To show how far you travel to use this park, please give the address to which you are returning.

....road or street

.... town 44

16 Give approximate distance travelled (home to park)

	45	
Under 1 mile (under 1.5 km)		0
1–2 miles (1.5–3 km)		1
2–4 miles (3–6 km)		2
4–6 miles (6–10 km)		3
Over 6 miles (over 10 km)		4

17 If a child are you accompanied by parents?

	46	
Yes		0
No		1

18 Do you live in a

	47	
House		0
Flat		1
Caravan		2

Other accommodation (please state)........ 3

19 Have you a garden at your house?

	48	
Yes		0
No		1

20 Have you a car or the use of a car?

49

Always	0
Sometimes	1
Weekends only	2
No	3

21 Would you like to make any comments on (a) this park (including sources of annoyance, if any)

....

....

....

.... 50

22 (b) other parks in the Nottingham area

....

....

....

.... 51

Thank you.

CHILDREN'S PLAYGROUND SURVEY

Please complete by placing a tick in the box or an entry in the space provided

	5	6	7	8	9	10	11	12	13	14

1   Age

2   Boy [ ] 1   Girl [ ] 2

3   Home address (block letters please) ....
....

3a   School attended ....

4   Give name or location of playground that you visit the most.
....
....

5   Give the names or locations of any other playgrounds that you visit.

(1) ....

(2) ....

(3) ....

(4) ....

6   Give roughly the number of times that you visited the playground last summer.

0–5 [ ] 1   6–10 [ ] 2   11–20 [ ] 3   over 20 [ ] 4
(not more than once a month)   (1 or 2 visits per month)   (2–4 visits per month)   (at least once a week)

7   Give your normal length of stay

under 1 hour [ ] 1   1–2 hours [ ] 2   2–3 hours [ ] 3   over 3 hours [ ] 4

8   Is there anything which prevents you visiting a playground as much as you would like?
....
....

9   How do you travel to your usual playground?

Car [ ] 1   Cycle [ ] 2   Foot [ ] 3   Other 4
(please state)

10   Do you mostly go alone [ ] 1   Or are you mostly accompanied by an older person [ ] 2

11   Do you prefer playgrounds with a playleader?

Yes [ ] 0   No [ ] 1

12   Do you prefer adventure playgrounds to those with standard equipment (swings, seesaws, etc.)?

Yes [ ] 0   No [ ] 1

13   What is your favourite item of equipment?

(state) ....

14 What do you like best about your usual playground?

Playleaders	☐ 1	Equipment	☐ 2
Games	☐ 3	Nearest playground	☐ 4
Adventure activities	☐ 5	Sand play	☐ 6
Water play	☐ 7	Meet friends	☐ 8
Don't know	☐ 9	No feature in particular	☐ 10

Any other items (please state)

....

.... 11

15 Please give any things that you would like but which are not provided at your usual playground

(1) ....

(2) ....

(3) ....

Thank you very much for your help.

CHILDREN'S PLAYGROUNDS: RELATIVE POPULARITY OF DIFFERENT PLAY FACILITIES
(Items which children would like but which are not provided at their usual playgrounds)

Item of equipment	Number of children in each age group expressing interest		
	5–7 years	7–11 years	11–14 years
Swimming pool	31	58	59
Paddling pool	76	36	7
Aerial ropeway	39	164	46
Tubes and tunnels	7	46	13
Boating pool	21	39	11
Climbing frame	66	145	17
Ropes	18	78	32
Tree house	28	111	14
Trees for climbing	11	64	15
Grass for play	14	64	39
Ocean wave	1	5	4
Junk yard	7	12	14
Tennis courts	3	9	17
Goal posts	8	27	38
Netball facilities	—	20	12
Rocks for climbing	19	16	—
Old car or tractor	11	7	5
Sandpit	52	36	—
Slide	36	58	6
Seesaw	54	38	12
Plank swings	9	49	11
Rocking horse	14	8	
Merry-go-round	15	48	5
Trampoline	48	100	1
Miniature railway	9	18	3
Play house	9	—	
Crazy golf	—	2	4
Go-kart racing	—	21	4
Cycle track	—	31	—
Acrobatic bars	—	14	1
Indoor facilities	—	7	15
Maypole	—	20	4
Fishing facilities	—	21	4
Water play	—	21	3
Putting	—	5	—
Tyres on ropes	—	18	—
Refreshment facilities	—	—	8
Artificial ski slopes	—	—	5
Maze	—	—	7

ALLOTMENTS SURVEY QUESTIONNAIRE

Name and address of allotment holder ....

....

....

Site of allotment..

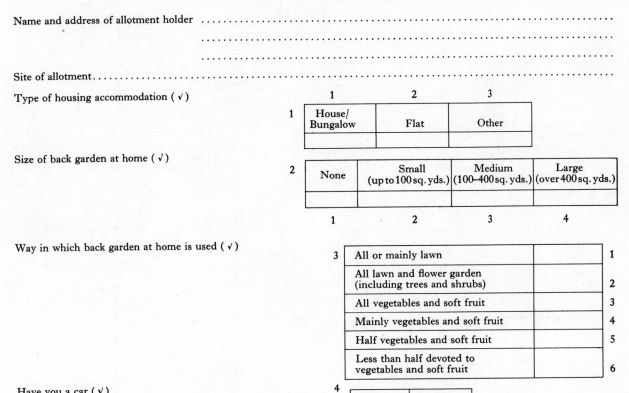

Type of housing accommodation (√)

	1	2	3
1	House/ Bungalow	Flat	Other

Size of back garden at home (√)

	None	Small (up to 100 sq. yds.)	Medium (100–400 sq. yds.)	Large (over 400 sq. yds.)
2				
	1	2	3	4

Way in which back garden at home is used (√)

3	All or mainly lawn		1
	All lawn and flower garden (including trees and shrubs)		2
	All vegetables and soft fruit		3
	Mainly vegetables and soft fruit		4
	Half vegetables and soft fruit		5
	Less than half devoted to vegetables and soft fruit		6

Have you a car (√)

4	Yes	No
	1	2

Do you take part in any of the leisure activities listed (√)

Football or Rugby	Cricket	Tennis	Bowls
5	6	7	8

Golf	Swimming	Angling	Boating
9	10	11	12

Type of occupation (√)

13	Professional		1
	Managerial		2
	Skilled manual		3
	Non-manual (including clerical)		4
	Semi-skilled manual		5
	Unskilled		6
	Non-employed		7

221

Age (√) 14

Under 20	20–24	25–29	30–34	35–44	45–54	55–64	65–74	75 and over
1	2	3	4	5	6	7	8	9

Main reasons for taking allotment (number in order of importance, 1 being most important)

Grow fresh produce		15
Physical exercise		16
Mental relaxation		17
Enjoy fresh air		18
Love of gardening		19
Family retreat		20

Maximum distance you are prepared to travel to allotment (√)   21

Up to ¼ mile	½ mile	¾ mile	1 mile	Over 1 mile
1	2	3	4	5

Do you have help on the allotment from (√)

Wife	Children	Relatives	Friends
22	23	24	25

Do you share your allotment with another person (√)   26

Yes	No
1	2

Period for which you have had an allotment in the Nottingham area (√)   27

Under 1 year	1–5 years	5–10 years	10–20 years	Over 20 years
1	2	3	4	5

Approximate number of visits per month (√)

	0–5	6–10	11–15	16–20	Over 20
28 Summer					
29 Winter					
	1	2	3	4	5

Average number of hours per working visit (√)   30

Under 1	1–2	2–3	3–4	4–5	Over 5

Did you take over your present allotment from a relative (√)   31

Yes	No
1	2

Do you belong to an allotments association (√)   32

Yes	No
1	2

222

Did you take over a previous allotment from a relative (√)

33

Yes	No
1	2

Have you on your allotment (√)

Water supply		34
Garden shed		35
Greenhouse		36
Cold frame		37
Summer house		38

Do you grow (√)

Soft fruit		39
Flowers		40

Please give also proportion of plot allocated to above uses
(if any)

Soft fruit	Flowers

Size of allotment plot .... sq. yds.

Annual rent paid £ ....

Approximate annual cost of seeds, fertilisers, manures, etc. £ ....

Approximate annual value of produce (based on shop prices) £ ....

Main needs:
Briefly outline your main needs and problems
(such as lack of facilities, drawbacks, any vandalism, etc.)

....
....
....
....
....
....

Thank you very much.

SURVEY OF RECREATIONAL FACILITIES IN GREATER NOTTINGHAM

Name and address of organisation: ....
(site of club facilities)

....

....

....

Type of sport and number of
playing units (pitches, courts, etc.) ....

....

Date of founding of club   ....

Names of leagues in which you
compete   ....

....

....

Have you any of the following facilities (√)

Pavilion	Changing rooms	Club room	Showers	Toilets

Licensed bar	Restaurant	Wives' club	Special spectator accommodation

Are the facilities (√)

Owned	Rented

Car parking capacity   Number of car spaces ....

Brief details of any future plans

....

....

....

....

	1969	1965	1960	1955	1950
Total number of members					
Numbers of female members (where applicable)					

Maximum number of members you can take   ....

Have you a waiting list (√)

Yes	No

If so, how many people are there on it   ....

224

Detail number of hours in each day in which the
facility is used
(take *average* week in your sporting season)

	Morning	Afternoon	Evening	Total
Monday				
Tuesday				
Wednesday				
Thursday				
Friday				
Saturday				
Sunday				

Please indicate the season during which your sporting
activity occurs (√)

Summer	Winter	All year round

During period of greatest activity, what is average
attendance by members?

Period	Number

Do you consider facilities adequate for shared use (√)

Yes	No	Don't know

Do you attract spectators, if so, please state number at
average event

. . . .

Membership fee per annum   £

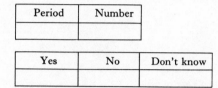

Adults	Juniors	Others

Age composition of members (If precise information
is not available, a broad assessment using percentages
or proportions would be appreciated)

Under 20	20–24	25–29	30–34

35–44	45–54	55–64	65 and over

Social composition of members (If precise information
is not available, a broad assessment using percentages
or proportions would be appreciated)

Professional	
Managerial	
Skilled manual	
Non-manual (including clerical)	
Semi-skilled manual	
Unskilled	
Non-employed	
Students	

Average distance travelled by members from home to
club activities

. . . .(miles)

225

A list of home addresses of members would be
helpful—if this is not available a broad assessment of
numbers of members in each residential district would
be appreciated, e.g.: Beeston 5, Bramcote 6

....
....
....
....
....
....
....
....
....
....

Details of restrictions on activities arising from any cause ....
....
....
....
....

Any other comments you may care to make ....
....
....

Thank you very much.

ENGLISH COUNTIES RANKED BY PROVISION OF GOLF COURSES IN 1965

Counties	Number of persons per 9 holes	Ranking
Surrey	7 900	1
Cumberland & Westmorland	11 300	2
Cornwall	11 600	3
Dorset	14 400	4
Hampshire	15 500	5
Cheshire	16 000	6
Worcestershire	16 000	7
Sussex	16 200	8
Hertfordshire	17 000	9
Kent	18 000	10
Northumberland	18 400	11
Shropshire & Herefordshire	19 000	12
Lincolnshire	19 400	13
Devon	19 500	14
Suffolk	19 500	15
Yorkshire	21 000	16
Essex	23 000	17
Norfolk	24 100	18
Berkshire, Buckinghamshire & Oxfordshire	25 800	19
Leicestershire & Rutland	26 400	20
Lancashire	27 000	21
Derbyshire	28 400	22
Wiltshire	29 000	23
Durham	30 000	24
Somerset	30 100	25
Northamptonshire	30 200	26
Nottinghamshire	33 800	27
Cambridgeshire	34 000	28
Bedfordshire	35 000	29
Gloucestershire	37 400	30
Staffordshire	42 700	31
Warwickshire	44 200	32

Source: Golf Development Council, *Preliminary report on playing facilities*

MAXIMUM DESIRABLE USE OF PUBLIC GOLF COURSES

1   *Weekend play* (average for whole year)
    Assuming 7 hours per day; continuous starting; all play by 4 balls; 8 matches starting per hour.
    Number of rounds per day, 224.
    Number of rounds per week, say   450

2   *Mid-week play* (average for whole year)
    To allow proper maintenance time, it is estimated that play will be at approximately half the
    rate experienced at weekends, say 100 rounds per day.
    Number of rounds per week   500
                                                                                                      950

3   *Estimated total rounds per week*
    Deduct for time lost by bad weather, by play other than 4 balls, etc., say 20 per cent.   190
    Estimated maximum number of rounds per week   760

4   *Estimated number of rounds per year above which course liable to be subjected to excessive use* 40 000

Source: Golf Development Council, *Preliminary report on playing facilities*

GROWTH OF MEMBERSHIP OF CLUBS PARTICIPATING IN WATER SPORTS: 1950–69

Sporting organisation	Club membership (number of affiliated clubs)				
	1950	1955	1960	1965	1969
Royal Yachting Association	501	738	1011	1332	1491 (1968)
National School Sailing Association		Founded in 1961		1500	2500
British Canoe Union			174 (1963)	272	300 (1967)
Amateur Rowing Association (approximate number of clubs)	380	420	450	460	470
British Water Ski Federation	—	5	30	60	80
British Sub Aqua Club	—	30	99	175	249 (1968)
National Federation of Anglers	80	98	108	112	140 (446 528 members)

INDEX